MERCHANDISING FOR TOMORROW

McGRAW-HILL SERIES IN MARKETING AND ADVERTISING

Steuart Henderson Britt, *Consulting Editor*

Baker—Advertising Layout and Art Direction
Baker—Visual Persuasion
Barton—Advertising Agency Operations and Management
Barton—Media in Advertising
Boyd, Fryburger, and Westfall—Cases in Advertising Management
Britt—The Spenders
Britt and Boyd—Marketing Management
    and Administrative Action
Crisp—Marketing Research
Crisp—Sales Planning and Control
Dunn—Advertising Copy and Communication
Haas—How to Develop Successful Salesmen
Hattwick—The New Psychology of Selling
Lazo and Corbin—Management in Marketing
Levitt—Innovation in Marketing
Lucas and Britt—Measuring Advertising Effectiveness
Martineau—Motivation in Advertising
Mauser—Modern Marketing Management
Messner—Industrial Advertising
Seehafer and Laemmar—Successful Television
    and Radio Advertising
Stanton—Fundamentals of Marketing
Stebbins—Copy Capsules
Turner—Sales Promotion That Gets Results
Weir—Truth in Advertising
Weir—On the Writing of Advertising
Weiss—Merchandising for Tomorrow
Wolff—What Makes Women Buy
Wright and Warner—Advertising
Wright and Warner—Speaking of Advertising
Yeck and Maguire—Planning and Creating Better Direct Mail

Merchandising for Tomorrow

E. B. WEISS

Vice-president, Director of
Special Merchandising Service
Doyle · Dane · Bernbach · Inc.

McGRAW-HILL BOOK COMPANY, INC.

New York   Toronto   London   1961

MERCHANDISING FOR TOMORROW

III

69070

To
Ned Doyle
Mac Dane
Bill Bernbach
and to all my other associates at D.D.B.,
with affection and respect

Preface

Peering ahead to the year 2000, or the year 1980, or the year 1975 is a rather popular pastime. But merchandising executives must focus sharply on next season, next year. And yet, as is true of all engaged in marketing, the merchandising man must take at least an occasional farther look ahead. Forty years ahead? Twenty years ahead? No—not even ten years ahead.

But perhaps five years ahead? Yes. Five years ahead would be sensible because the trends that will or should to some degree shape current merchandising decisions can be blueprinted with some accuracy for five years ahead.

Moreover, even though these trends may not operate with full dynamics for three, four, or five years, they must nonetheless be weighed in merchandising programs for next season and next year because they will be leaving their imprint more deeply, year after year, on the world of marketing.

So here is a run-down on some of the major trends in marketing that may help in developing near-term merchandising programs— an imaginative blueprint, if you will, for *creative near-term merchandising strategy.*

E. B. Weiss

Contents

Part 2.   500 Merchandising Ideas

PART 1

Blueprint of
Merchandising Strategy

CHAPTER 1

Revolt against Self-service

The shopper who feels that she has picked up several bargains at the supermarket might have second thoughts if she added up all the costs of those purchases."

That acid comment was made in a lecture at Cornell University by Dr. Helen G. Canoyer, dean of the New York State College of Home Economics. She suggested for consideration the *hidden costs* of a trip to the supermarket. And in that simple suggestion there may be the awesome potential of a coming revolt by the shopper—a revolt against self-service. There is no question that way back in the dim recesses of their minds, a number of shoppers here and there are asking, in effect: "Why in hell are we doing it?"

For example, some food super shoppers are just beginning to say to themselves:

> When I shop in the food super this is what I am now compelled to do:
>
> One: Take the car out of the garage; maybe bundle the children into it.
>
> Two: Drive to the food super—sometimes in bad weather and sometimes through heavy traffic.
>
> Three: Park the car in a huge parking lot—and the parking can be a neat trick. I also risk damage to the car while I'm inside shopping.

Four: Then I must walk from the car to the store.

Five: Next I must grab a gocart and start trundling it around the store (maybe with a child in the gocart and another hanging on to my one free hand).

Six: I parade up and down aisles, dodging other carts while looking for what I want. I bump into other carts; they bump into me. In front of some sections I can't get near enough to make a purchase because of crowds; I've got to come back minutes later when the shelf area may not be so crowded. I retrace and retrace my steps—trying to find some items requires the patience of a saint. And the stores are getting bigger and bigger.

Seven: I finally wind up at the check-out. The line is pretty long —it will be from five minutes to fifteen minutes before my turn comes.

Eight: I must help unload my purchases from the cart onto the check-out apron. This is a tough trick, especially reaching down to the lower level of the cart while the cart is alongside the check-out, and particularly when something heavy has to be picked up.

Nine: Then I wait while my purchases are tabulated. I wait while my purchases are put into bags that are guaranteed to tear. If I'm unlucky, I help with the bagging.

Ten: Then I lift those heavy bags into the cart.

Eleven: Next I trundle the cart out of the store—with the kids tagging along. Eventually, I reach my car—and this may be quite a hike with a loaded cart and kids.

Twelve: I lift up the lid of the trunk—haul out those heavy bags —dump them into the trunk (and, of course, a few bags are bound to break and strew the contents over the floor of the trunk, which is seldom immaculately clean). Sometimes I have a job crowding all of my purchases into the trunk; after all, a few other things are there. So I may have to shove a few packages into the car.

Thirteen: Then I wangle the car out of the parking lot—not always easy. And now I'm homeward bound—probably through heavy traffic.

Fourteen: When I get the car in the garage at home—I've got to drag those bags out of the car (including the contents of the broken bags) and tote the stuff upstairs to the kitchen. I may have to march up and down that flight of stairs a half dozen times to get all of my purchases up to the kitchen—and in the garage I bump into garden tools, etc., and sometimes tear a nylon as well as my guts.

Fifteen: All this I do—and more—*and for what?* For *what?*

This is not an exaggerated picture of so much modern-day shopping. And it applies to all other self-service stores—not merely the food super.

In so far as the modern food super is concerned, it takes *more time and physical effort* to shop for food than it did before the food super appeared on the scene. And since the food super now has a margin requirement of over 20 per cent on food—it is hardly offering food on a basis so much lower than was traditional in the service stores many years ago to justify the shopper's extra time and effort.

What is true of the food super is equally true of the variety chain and the drug chain. Have either of these outlets lowered their mark-ups since they went into self-service? Is the shopper *really* benefiting from the time and energy she is being called upon to expend—especially if car costs are included?

Therefore, it is logical to conclude that, in time, more and more shoppers will be asking themselves: "Why am I doing this—especially 'for cash'? For what?" Some day many shoppers will conclude: "I'll shop from my home—by telephone." Or by catalogue. Or from in-home sellers.

As a matter of fact, this is precisely what is happening. Total volume by telephone, by mail, and in the home is clearly on an upswing. And, as the shopper mounts this rebellion, new forms of retailing will emerge that will cater to the shopper who concludes that too much present-day shopping "is spinach—and to hell with it." These new forms of retailing will include low-cost warehouses—no retail store at all. The shopper will phone in her order, the order will be delivered, and she will be given credit. And the markup will be no more than most mass retailers presently take—it may be less.

Does this mean that the modern type of mass retailer will die on the vine? Not at all. The department stores are still with us! No one form of retailing ever takes over all retailing.

But a shopper revolt against high-cost self-service is definitely in the making. It will bring into being new forms of retailing that will affect all merchandisers precisely as did self-service.

CHAPTER 2

How Much Internal Competition?

It would be fascinating to learn how many merchandising ideas have been turned down because "we don't want to compete with ourselves." Yet usually, "We don't want to compete with ourselves" is a false premise for turning down a new number or a new line or discontinuing a formerly competitive line that has been absorbed through merger.

Analyze internal competition for a moment in fact, not in theory. When a manufacturer makes an item in more than one size, design, or price line he is, in fact, competing with himself. A large size of an item competes with a small size; different colors and shapes in a line are intracompetitive; varying price lines for an item are intracompetitive. They may help each other to a degree, but they very surely compete with each other as well.

The merchandising question really is not whether a manufacturer should foster internal-line competition—because it probably already exists. The basic issue really is: *How much* internal competition is economically sound?

In contemplating that situation for the near future, merchandising executives will probably find it wiser to lean toward broad reasoning rather than toward narrow examination. Internal merchandising rivalry is destined for substantial expansion. For example, when a manufacturer turns out private-label merchandise as well as his own nationally advertised label, the two lines are clearly competitive. This, of course, is common practice in some fields; perhaps the outstanding example involves the specification tires made by several of the great Akron tire producers for the great gasoline companies, for Sears, and for other chains.

Indeed, a substantial percentage of Sears's $4 billion volume is done on merchandise made under a Sears label by manufacturers who also make their own nationally advertised brands. Precisely the same is true of much of the controlled-brand merchandise promoted by the great soft-goods chains like Penney, by the variety chains, by the drug chains, by the food chains, and by the great hard-goods chains. (General Foods turns out Kroger's controlled brand of corn flakes. Quaker produces Kroger's controlled brand of oats, and Del Monte and Libby supply Kroger's controlled brand of canned fruits and vegetables.)

Then there is the fairly common practice of developing a premium operation for a branded line. A number of large manufacturers of nationally advertised brands have special-premium departments. These premium departments clearly compete with the regular sales department which sells through normal channels. (Sometimes the bitter rivalry between these two departments reaches the boiling point!)

Still more internal rivalry is to be found in decisions that involve competitive construction specifications in a line. For example, when the makers of wool rugs began to use synthetics, they had to decide to what extent it would be wise to encourage internal competition on constructions. Some of the woven-rug mills were loath to fan this sort of internal competition—today, practically all are strongly committed to programs that pit synthetic fiber combinations against all-wool. Some woven-rug producers are now also merchandising hard-surface floor coverings—this represents internal competition of a high order.

Another example exists in the field of fine china. The makers of fine china were faced with a mounting competition from such new materials as melamine. Eventually, two of the great china manufacturers decided to add melamine—and the roof has not fallen in. This is a particularly significant example of internal rivalry because for a fine china house to go into melamine might be considered to be something like Tiffany's going in for variety-chain jewelry. Similarly, some of the old-line makers of sterling flatware now merchandise stainless, an arch rival.

Hotpoint now competes somewhat more aggressively with its parent, General Electric. The two organizations will work closely on the manufacturing level; there will be an increasing exchange of components and parts between the two organizations to achieve operating economies. It is even possible that General Electric will take over some production for Hotpoint. But, in the total marketing process, there is to be more separation (which means more competition) between General Electric and its thirty-year-controlled Hotpoint Division.

A fascinating example of an extreme in internal rivalry is the fairly well-known case of Evinrude and Johnson outboards. The two brands are numbers one and two in the industry. They are controlled by the same parent organization. But even more interesting—the two motors have a complete interchangeability of parts. Except for stylistic differences in casing, they are virtually identical products. However, the two divisions—which have separate sales and dealer organizations—fight tooth and nail for industry leadership. In addition, the same parent organization also operates the Gale Division, which makes the Buccaneer outboard brand and builds private-label brands for Ward and other big outlets.

And, of course, the outstanding example of internal rivalry is General Motors in its automotive line.

What all this suggests, obviously, is that the question is not: *Should* we compete with ourselves? Rather, the basic query must be this: How, under existing market conditions and in line with future trends, can we compete with ourselves more profitably?

Over the next few years, internal competition will tend to be a planned program rather than a reluctant and hesitant approach. It will be pursued with competitive vigor rather than with dragging feet. This is inevitable for a number of reasons. As organizations become gigantic in size, internal competition automatically comes into existence. The full-line trend leads in the same direction. Sometimes mergers and absorptions stimulate internal competition. Competitive pressures lead manufacturers into programs that involve intraorganizational rivalries, whether deliberately planned as such or not. There is increasing recognition of the existence within an organization of internal competition, even though it may not be labeled as such.

But perhaps the major reason for the trend toward greater internal rivalry is the emerging conclusion among merchandisers that a manufacturer does not escape competition by not giving himself competition. The competition a manufacturer does not give himself will surely be provided by a competitor. Moreover, the competition a manufacturer gives himself is at least susceptible to a degree of control.

Many years ago, when manufacturers began to merchandise secondary and even tertiary brands, the term "fighting brand" was coined. It was a splendidly descriptive term because these secondary brands were deliberately (even if sometimes a bit unwillingly) planned to compete with the manufacturer's major brand. It represented a major step toward the concept of planned internal rivalry.

Then, as distribution broadened, it became necessary for many manufacturers to bring out competitive brands. For example, a manufacturer who had been selling through the drug outlet may have found it necessary to bring out a brand that would permit him to open up the food outlet without endangering his original distribution.

But perhaps more than any other single factor, the so-called "private brand" led manufacturers into an understanding of the realities of intraorganizational rivalry.

The upshot is that in a growing number of organizations merchandisers are endeavoring to apply rational planning to intraorganizational competition. This promises to become one of the big merchandising developments of the next few years; the development of a deliberately conceived and thoroughly planned program of intraorganizational competition set up in such a way as to provide true—not merely theoretical—competition.

CHAPTER 3

The Trend toward Giant Retailing

The end of the small independent—as an independent—is already a fact in the food field. Over 90 per cent of total food retail volume is now in the hands of corporate chains, voluntary chains, cooperative chains, and other groups. This is spreading into every major merchandising classification and into other types of retailing. Mass retailing in the major types of retail outlets will be controlled by corporate chains on the one hand and voluntary (or cooperative) chains on the other.

The largest retailer in dollar volume in 1960 was the A&P with an annual turnover of $5 billion. But we are coming into an era of $10 billion retailers! We will have more—many more—retailers in the over $1 billion category.

We are coming into an era in which no more than 50 giant retail organizations will account for one-half of this nation's total retail volume in most major merchandise categories, excluding automobiles. Naturally, this remarkable concentration of retail volume in a few powerful hands will have important repercussions on the merchandising plans of manufacturers. Today there is only a small handful of truly national chains and retail groups having broad coverage of the total population. (Even the A&P, with its immense $5 billion in annual volume, doesn't blanket the nation—yet.) But giant retailing is showing positive indications of spreading out geographically. "Nationalitis" among the retail giants means true national brands by the chains—brands that are *nationally advertised* and that have national standing. (Sears, Ward, Penney, Western Auto Supply, and other chains already have powerful national brands.)

Truly national chains and retail groups have been handicapped, to date, by physical limitations of communications and transportation. But with electronic communications making possible instantaneous inventory-taking on a national scale; with electronic calculators hooked up from headquarters to thousands of store cash registers; with the automation of warehouses; with vast new developments in speedier transportation—the physical obstacles in the path of national retail organizations of a size that will dwarf even our present giants are being removed rapidly.

In 1960, just 23 food chains accounted for 35 per cent of America's total grocery store business. By 1965, 15 food chains (corporate, voluntary, etc.,) may control 40 per cent of the total food business. And this same concentration will occur in the department store field, the drug field, the variety chain field, in hard and soft outlets.

We hear constantly about giant manufacturers—so much so that it is pretty common knowledge that 7 per cent of our corporations account for 72 per cent of sales, 87 per cent of taxes, 88 per cent of net income, and 92 per cent of dividends. We will now hear much more about giant retailers.

As for mergers—in numbers, mergers will probably be larger in total among retailers between 1960–1965 than among manufacturers.

This trend toward true giantism in retailing will result in—

1. National retail organizations that are, in fact, national advertisers, because their newspaper advertising will reach more of this nation's total population than can be said for 90 per cent of national advertisers. These giant retailers will be using national media—network TV, network radio, magazines. Thus giant retailing will create national retail users of national media.

2. Sizable manufacturing by giant retailers, either through owned factories or through factories in which financial control is exercised by retailers in a variety of ways.

3. A broad trend toward controlled-brand exploitation, particularly when giant retailing edges into manufacturing.

The larger the retailer grows, and the more concentrated total retail volume becomes in a few strong hands, the greater the development of retailer-controlled brands. This is the fundamental formula that will shape the strategy in the battle of the brands.

We will ultimately see efforts made by large retailers to put their brands *into outlets that are noncompetitive*—geographically or otherwise. This has been going on in a small way for years. This will put a new dimension on brand merchandising.

Moreover, before long, we will see several giant retailers (some of them with wholesale affiliations) sending out salesmen to call on other retailers and *to compete for brand distribution with brand manufacturers!* (In some instances, the retailer's salesmen will be selling a controlled brand actually made by a manufacturer with whose brands they will be fighting for distribution!)

It is significant for merchandisers in all fields to note what the General Foods Corporation had to say in an annual report: "Selling to the grocery trade through better service—making it more attractive to do business with GF—becomes increasingly important *as our customers diminish in number but grow in size.*" This will become increasingly true of other retail outlets for other merchandise categories. More and still more manufacturers will find that 5 per cent of their accounts provide 50 per cent of annual volume—10 per cent of accounts will provide up to 90 per cent of volume.

Traditionally, retailers were *customers* of manufacturers. Now, to a mounting degree, retailers will become both customers *and competitors* of their suppliers. And the very retailers who will account for the lion's share of the annual volume of so many manufacturers will also be the toughest competitors of these same suppliers!

The giant retailers will operate increasingly by formula. More and more, buying will be done by committees—and the members of these committees will seldom be available to manufacturers' salesmen. Buying will also be done increasingly by executives of the supplier and executives of the retailer.

The area for future growth of giant retailing is marked out by the situation in Canada. If Sears achieved the per capita volume in the United States that T. Eaton & Company has achieved in Canada, the Sears volume in our country would be just about $10 billion!

Through mergers, through holding companies, through other corporate forms, the giant retailer of 1960 will appear somewhat small by 1965. And these retail giants will grow more rapidly during this five-year period than will most of their suppliers! Moreover, they will be more powerful financially than at least 90 per cent of their suppliers.

They will turn to nonmerchandising for an increasing share of their net profit. Real estate and the management of money will become at least as important to them as the management of merchandising.

And by 1965, we will see retail organizations that will include under one corporate control a group of department stores, a food chain, a drug chain, a variety chain, and a miscellany of other types of outlets, including even gas stations.

Giant retailing will be the hallmark of mass retailing by 1965. Its imprint on all merchandising will be more dramatic than was self-service—and that was dramatic enough.

CHAPTER 4

Growth of Leased-department Operations

By 1965, the total volume done by various types of leased-department operations will show a 50 per cent increase over the 1960 total! Moreover, the number of merchandise classifications involved will broaden tremendously. It behooves manufacturers' merchandising executives to take a new look at the leased-department operator as a trade customer.

Why will the leased department spread so rapidly?

Basically, because the diversification of inventory by classification by all retailers has brought them into categories that they find, ultimately, they cannot merchandise profitably. In other words, the stronger the trend to one-stop store units, the stronger the trend to leased departments. And the one-stop store unit is the great trend in major retailing.

At one time the leased department was almost an exclusive with department stores. Today it is becoming common among variety chains and drug chains, among hard-goods chains and discount chains, among soft-goods chains, furniture chains, and others. And, of course, the rack jobber (a leased-department operator) does a gigantic volume on nonfoods in the food super.

According to a survey made by the Controllers' Congress of the National Retail Merchants Association in 203 reporting department stores and 21 specialty stores, the 10 most commonly leased departments, by percentage, are beauty salon, 55.2; better and lower-priced millinery, 46.3; photography studio, 44.3; shoe repair, 39.9; jewelry and watch repair, 36.9; sewing machines, 34.0; women's and children's shoes (main), 31.5; millinery (basement), 23.1; lending library, 22.2; and women's and children's shoes (basement), 18.2.

Leased departments comprise from 6.7 per cent of the total number of departments in a department store doing from $1 to $2 million to 15 per cent in the $10 to $20 million store, with a figure of 11 per cent for the over $20 million store and of 10 per cent for the under $1 million store. Rack merchandisers supply about two-thirds of food stores' nonfoods, according to a survey. Since nonfoods in the food supers will soon total over $2 billion annually, the leased-department operator is a giant factor in this area alone. The discount chains in most instances are deeply involved with leased departments. In some instances, up to 75 per cent of the total selling-floor area is leased and the discount chain may derive the major part of its net profit from lease rentals!

Why the variety chains are going into leased departments is well indicated by a single example. A Newberry variety chain store gave up the ghost on its ready-made slip-cover department and turned the operation over to a concessionaire. Sales had been so poor and the percentage of returns so great that, according to a Newberry spokesman, "we wouldn't have kept slip covers unless a concessionaire handled it." One of the major problems encountered was lack of inventory control. The many broken sets and incomplete pattern lines militated against large unit sales, or any sale. Customers wanted covers for three or four living-room pieces and could not find matching sets. Another problem was a high ratio of refunds to sales—because covers did not fit due to a poor cut or came apart due to insufficient stitching. When the concessionaire took over in this Newberry store he found "nothing but odds and ends in a $14,000 retail stock—nothing matched."

In some Newberry stores the sewing-machine department is leased. In other variety chains the phonograph record department is leased.

Phonograph records are complicated merchandise. There are 1,400 different labels on the market. Hit "singles" stay in demand only four to eight weeks, according to a West Coast rack merchandiser. Only a few tunes and artists have steady long-range appeal. The rack merchandiser's big job is to keep close track of these fast-changing sales trends and provide stores with the service needed to keep their record selections up to date.

Auto tires, fine jewelry, garden supplies—there is scarcely a category in which the leased department is not infiltrating strongly.

The head of a retail book outfit played host to a group of publishers, poured drinks for them, and served an elegant luncheon. He had arranged this luncheon because he had news for them, good news. He proposed to sell 15 per cent to 20 per cent more of their books during the current year. The host was Larry Hoyt. He is president of the Walden Book Company, which operates leased book departments in 62 department stores. Forty of these departments are located on the main floors of their respective stores. In his opinion, the best job is done in communities of about 100,000. The bigger the city, the tougher the job of competing with the book shops. Walden does about 2 per cent of all the book business in the United States, according to Mr. Hoyt.

The leased-department concept is leading to odd marriages. For example, while E. J. Korvette, Inc., promotional department store, does a bang-up job in merchandising such home-goods items as major appliances, housewares, radios, and television sets, it does not operate the furniture and floor-covering divisions. These are franchised, combining minimum—plus—percentage arrangements, to an outside firm for each type of goods. Yet simultaneously, Korvette operates leased departments in other stores.

Two Guys From Harrison, discount chain, leased space in all of its units for the operation of floor-covering departments to the management of Allen Carpet Shops, an 11-unit chain of local floor-covering specialty stores. Both hard- and soft-surface lines are being handled in the departments.

On the other side of the coin, White Front Stores, operator of several discount houses in the Los Angeles area, planned a giant discount house–drug store–supermarket combination in nearby Anaheim. It is understood that several local drug chains have been asked to operate the drug store on a lease basis.

Food chains are running food departments in discount chains. Discount chains are running hard-goods departments in food chains. Shoe chains are running shoe departments in discount chains. Drug chains are running departments in discount chains. This part of the leased-department trend is in its infancy. Even smaller chains are in on the act. Allen Carpet Shops, the promotional floor-covering chain in Long Island and Brooklyn referred to earlier, added leased departments of furniture and major appliances in its Mineola store. The furniture department, known as Allen Furniture City, is being operated by Michaels Furniture Company. The major appliance division is in the hands of Hardt & Reid, a three-store radio, television, and major appliance chain.

In the food outlet it has been found that the smaller the size of the company, the more control rack merchandisers are given over the choice of items. A survey asked the following question: "Where you use rack merchandisers, which one of the following statements best describes your relation to them?"

Statement	1–3 Stores	4–10 Stores	11–25 Stores	26 or More Stores	All Stores
They control selection of items completely	43.7%	13.1%	10.0%	....	7.5%
Their choice of items is reviewed by us periodically ...	31.2	71.7	38.8	37.4	44.4
They must have approval from us for each new item they place on our shelves	25.1	15.2	51.2	62.6	48.1

NOTE: Percentage of stores by size of company.

In conclusion, the following basic facts may be accepted:

1. More large retailers will soon turn to the leased-department concept in more departments.

2. Large retailers will analyze their present leased-department operations to determine how they may be made more beneficial to all concerned—including, of course, the shopper.

3. New areas of service by leased-department operators will be explored jointly by large retailers and these outside operators.

4. More willingness to experiment with and to test new forms of leased departments will be shown by big-store management.

5. Finally, the whole leased-department concept is achieving a new dignity. The businessmen in this field have their own associations. They are developing codes of practice. If some of them have been in the shadow, they are now coming out of the shadow.

6. The leased-department operator will develop his own controlled brands. This is already a fact in several merchandise categories. He will also become involved in manufacturing.

7. National "chains" of leased departments will come into being.

8. The mix-match marriages of various chains through leased-department arrangements will multiply. This will become one of the great trends of the next few years.

9. Big independent stores with a prestige background will increasingly go into franchise operations which are, actually, leased departments. This, too, will develop into a sizable trend.

10. The leased-department operator—whether it be a separate company, a chain, a wholesaler, a rack jobber, a franchise operator—will become the most important single customer classification to a growing number of manufacturers. Some manufacturers will find it advisable to set up special departments to service the concessionaires and this, in turn, may mean special numbers for this type of account —special prices, special packs, special terms, and discounts.

In the field of small housewares, the leased-department operator had emerged as a giant factor before some manufacturers were even aware of his existence as the dominant factor in merchandising housewares through the food super. In much the same manner, manufacturers in other merchandise categories will awaken, along about 1965, to discover that the concessionaire has become a dominant trade customer.

Keep a close eye on the leased department—and a wary eye, too. It promises to become one of the major and one of the most "headache-y" merchandising developments of the near future.

CHAPTER 5

Brand Marketing Becomes International

Manufacturers of hundreds of strongly presold brands have, of course, been selling in the export market for years. But over the next five years, merchandisers will find that—

• Much more of the manufacturing of domestic brands for foreign sale will be done abroad rather than in the United States. This will be a powerful trend.

• In these foreign markets, the American brands will be much more strongly advertised and merchandised—and these programs will be much more directly under the control and supervision of domestic-marketing executives rather than under the wing of a foreign-sales agent.

In Europe particularly, and especially in those nations brought together in the two great common markets, business may expand at a more dynamic pace than at home. These nations will become a new merchandising battleground for a multiplying number of American brands. (Interesting evidence of this is furnished by the step-up in activities abroad of American advertising agencies.)

All of these developments will be participated in, not only by domestic manufacturers who either have ignored foreign markets but, even more significantly, by a rapidly increasing number of domestic manufacturers who have either ignored foreign markets entirely or have merely touched lightly in them. More manufacturers of known brands—who had never operated abroad at all before—announced plans for brand exploitation in foreign countries in 1960 than in any previous two-year period. This trend is still in its infancy. (Even domestic manufacturers of women's garments are going abroad for volume—a move that only a short time back would have been characterized as carrying coals to Newcastle!)

The world is becoming Americanized. Coca-Cola and Wrigley pioneered the trend—now the rush is on. Hamburger stands actually operate in Paris and Rome! And in consequence, the merchandising executive must learn to look abroad, as well as at home, for volume —he must think now in terms of international, as well as national, brands.

It is interesting to note that this turn to foreign markets also affects the developing battle at home between manufacturers' known brands and retailers' known brands. It comes about because giant retailers are turning to *foreign suppliers* as sources for private-label merchandise. The classifications involved run the gamut from hard goods to soft goods, as well as other categories. As an example, it is reported that J. C. Penney is importing a growing volume of Japanese and European merchandise to be sold under one or the other of the Penney brand names. Penney is our second-largest retailer of general merchandise, concentrating on its own brands about as much as does Sears, the number-one retailer of general merchandise. Sears is moving in the same direction.

All by itself, over the next few years this may pose a considerable marketing problem for those responsible for marketing nationally advertised brands. The essence of the problem is that foreign sources of supply for retailer-controlled brands may enable large retailers to outsell manufacturers' brands at home, on both quality and price, to an even greater extent than is now the case.

Perhaps the strongest appeal to the shopper of the store-controlled brand is that it offers a better value than competing manufacturer brands. This tends to be the case—not always, but frequently enough —even when the same manufacturer turns out on the same production line both his own brand and the store-controlled brand (which is common practice). But when the retailer turns to foreign sources of supply, he may be able to land these goods, under his own labels, on his store shelves at less cost to himself than if he purchased them from his domestic suppliers—even with the special prices he gets.

And the intrinsic quality of the imports is apt to be at least comparable, and at times superior, to that of the domestic supplies.

Under certain circumstances, the shopper will not be aware that the controlled-label item was made abroad—unless some exceedingly fine print is read. Under other circumstances, the store may merchandise its foreign source—after all, that word "import" still carries a certain magic with the shopper.

There is another aspect of this situation that should be weighed. Our giant retailers are expanding abroad. They are doing this through their own foreign subsidiaries, by merger, or by other affiliation with established retailers in other countries.

Beyond question, this trend among our giant retailers to seek more retail volume abroad will pick up momentum. The explanation is simple: The domestic market for large retailing is becoming exceedingly crowded—even desirable store sites are increasingly difficult to find. Moreover, retail margins may in certain cases be more liberal abroad than they are here. Still more important is the fact, mentioned earlier, that some foreign countries are at this very moment in a true growth stage. They are especially ready for our mass-retailing concepts—aided and abetted by what is now correctly being called "the Americanization of much of the free world."

As our giant retailers move into retailing abroad, they will obviously come into closer association with foreign sources of supply. They will also gain a practical experience with the retailing of innumerable items made abroad. As a matter of fact, it is probably an awareness of this marketing drift that has been one of the factors that led a number of our giant manufacturers to establish production facilities abroad. In other words, these manufacturers are to some extent following—or leading—their domestic retailers into foreign lands. (The Sears brands are now international.)

This, in turn, means that brand marketing more and more will become international rather than merely national. We will be hearing more about *international brands,* perhaps a bit less about national brands!

A fascinating potential, this, for the merchandising executive—the coming era of the international brand.

CHAPTER 6

The Changing Nature of Mass Retailing

The department store is the "senior citizen" among mass retailers. It has survived one new form of retail competition after another, sometimes to its own astonishment. But the department store, especially the independent, has done little better than survive, with, of course, some notable exceptions.

By 1965, the following trends will be firmly established among department stores:

1. The day of the independent department store (particularly the family-owned store) will be clearly ended. The independent will be taken over by the large department store chains or by other types of mass retailers, and some will come together in mergers.

2. Thus department store volume will be concentrated still more strongly in a handful of powerful organizations.

3. The present department store chains will expand remarkably. Over the next five years they may grow as rapidly as they did in the entire decade 1950–1960. In brief, the department store field is ripe for consolidation.

4. The trend toward shopping center ownership and operation by department stores will pick up strength.

5. By 1965, the downtown-store unit will in fewer and fewer instances be regarded by store management as the "flagship" of the operation. Stark statistics will compel a long-overdue reappraisal of

the status of the downtown store. Already department stores like R. H. Macy & Company find that just about half of their total volume comes from branches. A few other department stores report a larger volume from branches than from the downtown store; there will be more in this position by 1965. The department store will thus emerge as a new type of chain—a trend that others have tended to recognize before some department stores did themselves!

6. Department store organizational charts will have to be completely revised for operation as a chain. Reorganization will be in full swing by 1965. Among other changes, the buying function of department stores will be drastically reorganized. Buyers at headquarters will concentrate more on buying; they will no longer be Jacks-of-all-trades. The branch-store manager will be given vastly increased responsibilities. The buying decision—and the promotional decision, too—will be made more and more at the branch. Incidentally, the size of the branch-store unit will continue to increase—otherwise, the branch may be smaller than some of its variety chain competitors in the same shopping center!

7. New systems of allocating expenses to branch stores will be developed. Current systems tend to make the branches look a bit too good.

8. As their empires become more far-flung, department stores will need more lead time to prepare for major promotions. At least eight weeks will be required adequately to prepare and schedule a specific promotion. Manufacturers will have to plan farther ahead.

9. More autonomy for the branch store means that manufacturers' salesmen will be compelled to make more calls on the branches.

10. Since one reason for more autonomy for the branches is that each branch-store operation has its own peculiarities, merchandising executives for manufacturers will find it advisable to compile more complete dossiers on each branch store. Also, merchandising executives will have to develop new broad-scale merchandising concepts for an entire department store chain—modified to suit the requirements of each of the branches.

11. More suppliers will be expected to ship directly to each of the branches. There will also be a demand for new types of warehousing services by manufacturers that will better serve the branches.

12. Several department store chains now have a central buying office. More department stores will turn to this concept—but the

relationship between the central buying office and the branches will be very much like that between the traditional chain-store buying office (variety, food, and drug) and their store units. The department store central buying office will seldom have the authority to buy exclusively for the branch stores. The needs of each branch will weigh strongly in the buying decision.

13. The branch stores will have broader, deeper merchandise selections. This has been one of the weaknesses of many branches. In some shopping centers, other chains have some departments with broader, deeper assortments than do the older department store branches!

14. By 1965, a number of department stores will have closed out their downtown-store units. This was true in 1960 in a few cities; it will be true in more cities by 1965.

15. The department store will go into still higher price lines. As the variety chains step up their price lines, to cite one example, department stores must move up still higher.

16. The department store will do a better job with hard goods— its weakest area.

17. More department stores will be selling food.

18. Department stores will go into such lines as boats, swimming pools, prefabricated houses—maybe even small cars.

But, despite all the changes through which department stores go, by 1965 they will (with a few notable exceptions) seldom do better than maintain their competitive status.

The food super is clearly trending toward the *super supermarket.* This will combine some of the features of the department store, of the variety chain, the drug chain, the discount chain. The Grand-Way stores, which offer 30,000 nonfood items, epitomize this trend. Since this is so, take a closer look at this division of the Grand Union food chain:

1. Some of the newer departments in the giant Grand-Way stores include cameras, shoes, automobile supplies, and complete stereo sections.

2. Grand-Way stores are competitive with department stores and discount operations in the areas in which the markets are located. Naturally, prices will vary with location and area.

3. Markup policy is to have merchandise as low as anything on

the market and to be competitive with department stores and discount houses in the same area. As an example, in pricing a dress which wholesales for $8.75, Grand-Way will retail the garment for approximately $10.97, again depending on store and area. A department store might sell the same dress at $13.95 or $14.95.

4. Grand-Way is trading up. Example: It started out with a line of $3 dresses and was soon selling styles up to $14.95 because customers asked for them.

5. Grand-Way provides dressing rooms and an attendant for them in several of the units. There are also separate check-outs for dress sales so that the merchandise need not come into direct contact with food and other items in the shopping cart.

6. What is the highest-ticket item sold? In excess of $500, although on occasion the chain will go well above this. As an example, it sold electric organs at Christmas in some of the stores at something around the $1,000 mark.

7. The three leading categories of items are soft goods, hard goods, and apparel. Soft goods comprise the largest segment because their potential is the greatest.

8. Grand-Ways range from 40,000 to 100,000 square feet. Sales areas given over to general merchandise range from a low of 40 per cent to a high of 75 per cent. As the stores become larger, the percentage of nonfood areas increases.

Fewer and fewer store units will control a growing percentage of the total food and nonfood volume done through the food outlet; and fewer and fewer chains will control these store units. By 1965, a national distribution of a type may be obtained for some manufacturers by distribution through no more than 50 food chains; in some instances, 25 food chains will provide adequate distribution.

The food chains will combine with other chains and with department stores. This mix-match trend will affect the food chain more than any other single outlet. Food chains will operate the food department in some discount chains. One food chain has bought out a small variety chain. Another food chain has bought into a drug chain.

The food chain will be selling on credit in a growing number of instances by 1965. Where the food chain goes into a type of department store, the big-ticket items compel credit—$1,000 organs are seldom sold for cash. It will not for long be able to sell nonfoods on credit and deny credit facilities on food.

By 1965, there will also be a trend to return the food outlet to telephone order-taking and to home delivery. This, in turn, may lead to a type of food outlet that will not be a retail store in the traditional sense. It will be a warehouse with no floor traffic at all; the shopper will telephone to this warehouse which will then deliver and bill later.

The trend toward bantam store units will be firmly established by 1965. In other words, the food outlet will combine a trend toward giant store units with a trend toward tiny store units. Some of these tiny stores will be in high-income areas and will offer gourmet foods and other luxury items.

The food super will, by 1965, be feeling keenly the competition on food of giant nonfood outlets. This will compel the food super to turn still more strongly to nonfoods. The upshot will be that, by 1965, the food-super concept of the early 1930s will have disappeared almost totally.

The food super will turn strongly to its own brands on food, and on many nonfoods. This will be a powerful trend by 1965. In this connection, it may be safely predicted that within a few years—

1. The food outlet will account for a rapidly growing percentage of its total food volume on its own controlled brands.

2. The variety of food classifications to be penetrated by these controlled brands will also mount rapidly.

3. The food outlet will do over 50 per cent of its total volume in more and more food classifications on its own brands.

4. These brands will offer the consumer excellent values.

5. These will be strongly presold brands with as much consumer demand, consumer preference, consumer acceptance as all but a very few manufacturers' brands.

6. These controlled brands will be advertised more and more heavily.

7. These controlled brands will get choice in-store display—the great salesmaker in the food outlet.

8. These controlled brands will be able to stand up under strict merchandising accounting against all but the most powerfully presold brands of manufacturers.

In general, the food super of 1965 will bear as little resemblance to the food super of 1950 as the variety chain of 1965 will bear to the prototype of this outlet, circa 1950.

Almost word for word, what has been said about the food super may be stated with equal appropriateness with respect to the variety chain.

One of the large variety chains left the variety chain association because it concluded—correctly—that it was no longer a variety chain at all. W. T. Grant Company now considers its operation to bear more resemblance to Sears, Ward, and Penney than to most other variety chains. As a matter of fact, the Limited Price Variety Store Association changed its name to the Variety Stores Association in order to have a name more correctly descriptive.

The variety chains will become department stores of a new type more quickly than any other chain. By 1965, the variety chains will be operating department stores with more departments, with larger assortments, with higher-price lines than most department stores— excepting only the 100 leading department stores.

And their volume will be gigantic. By 1965, Woolworth should have an annual volume reaching up to $1¼ billion. The 12 great variety chains will thus be challenging all but the biggest department store chains as volume outlets of a department store type.

Their merchandise classifications will break through all restrictions. They will sell big-ticket items in all categories—furniture, home furnishings, TV and radios, major appliances (on which they may do a better job than department stores), and rugs (including even wall-to-wall carpeting). Their price lines will move up with extraordinary rapidity. They will become major factors in fashion lines. And they will have become important factors in food retailing by 1965.

Some other variety-chain developments that will be clearly in evidence by 1965 include the following:

1. The variety chains will become major advertisers. They will represent the fastest-growing users of newspaper space among chains. Woolworth will be buying at least $10 million in newspaper space at this rate by 1965 (in 1960 Woolworth bought some $7 million of space in about 500 newspapers). Some of this advertising will endeavor to create a "fashion image."

2. The variety chain will turn more importantly to warehouses— as did the food chains. This will affect the merchandising programs of many manufacturers.

3. Credit facilities will be extended. The variety chains will be as

deeply in credit by 1965 as the department stores. At Christmas time, some variety chains find that credit sales exceed 50 per cent of total dollar gross!

4. The variety chain will increase its mail selling—catalogues will become larger and will be mailed more frequently. This outlet will also turn to telephone selling—because the department store is turning quite vigorously to telephone selling, among other reasons.

5. Variety chains will also turn to in-home selling—again because of department store competition. The department stores are doing a big job in home furnishings and a few other classifications through in-home selling.

6. In England, Woolworth has a mobile store set-up—stores on wheels. The idea may be imported for use here in the States.

7. The variety chains will open some discount-type units.

8. They will open many more small specialty store units—stores selling garden supplies, for example. This separate-store program will be quite important by 1965.

The discount chain will have made remarkable progress by 1965. That progress may be summarized this way.

1. The discount house is rapidly acquiring the trappings of legitimacy and permanency. It has come of age. Even traditional retailers no longer try to eliminate the discount house with adjectives.

2. The discount chains will be in an era of growth by merger, by affiliation, by absorption.

3. The discount house will broaden its inventory by classification. It began primarily with major appliances. Then it added traffic appliances. Then it added housewares. Then it went into furniture, rugs, home furnishings. Then it added beauty and health aids. Now it is moving into the broad soft-goods classification—from men's, women's, and children's ready-to-wear to linens, domestics, etc.

4. It expects to take a better gross margin on soft goods than on hard goods—an average perhaps of 20 per cent on soft, as compared with 10 to 15 per cent on hard. (Note that this 20 per cent on soft items will be considerably less than the food super takes on its soft items and about equal to the margin the food super takes on food!)

5. The discount house will wind up with its own controlled brands in many categories.

6. The discount house is going into credit. Bear in mind that credit

was not in the original scheme of things at Sears and the variety chains. Most mass retailers have gone into credit operations of one type or another. The discount house is heading in precisely the same direction.

7. There has been a good deal of nonsense spread about "no service" at the discount house. The discount houses have always given certain services; in certain instances, these services have been at a higher level than similar services offered by traditional retailers. The discount houses are now adding to their services.

8. The discount house is moving out to the suburbs. This is a positive trend. The discount house is also moving out to the regional shopping center areas—and where it cannot get into the regional shopping center itself, it is locating right near the regional shopping center.

9. The discount house is also moving into the smaller cities and even into towns of moderate size. This too is an emphatic trend.

10. Several discount chains will become *national* chains by 1965. Modell's has aspirations of this sort. So has Korvette's. So has Two Guys From Harrison, whose president has announced that a nationwide organization is its ultimate objective. Clearly, the discount chain has already begun to burst through the boundaries of a single metropolitan area; several discount chains are already multistate operations. There is every reason, therefore, to expect that they will aim toward national stature.

11. What is more, they are also aiming toward diversifying their techniques for reaching out to the shopper. In other words, they are moving from strictly retail store operation to a mail-order operation. Masters' mail-order venture in Washington, D.C., is a big business done on a national basis. Several house-to-house operations are tied up with discount store operation—and, of course, many house-to-house vendors are themselves discounters.

12. Since food is the greatest traffic producer of all retail promotional functions and since the vital ingredient in successful discount house functioning is traffic, more traffic, and still more traffic—it is only logical that the discount house should go into food. It will be strongly in food by 1965.

13. Discount houses will also tend to trade up. This process of trading will be quite strong among the major discount houses by 1965.

14. Korvette's thinking for its future stores is based upon the complete one-stop shopping center concept. It wants to control a food store as well as the promotional department store. The kind of center it envisages would be in the neighborhood of 200,000 square feet. This will typify the discount store unit of 1965.

15. Closed-door discounters or membership houses are currently spreading in many cities. Unlike other types of operations, customers are charged a fee and membership is restricted and enforced.

Government Employees Together (GET), the oldest and strongest closed-door discount operation in the San Francisco area, has increased its floor space five times, and probably has increased its volume at a similar rate since its opening in 1954. Its volume by 1965 will be in the $20 to $25 million area. This type of discount store will grow with extraordinary strength by 1965.

Home Furnishings Daily had this to say on the membership discount house:

> Closed-door discount or membership houses, the first cousins of the supermarket discount house, have successfully "dug into" the fertile soil of the national retail scene and are currently spreading their roots in many cities.
>
> Expansion is the word that immediately comes to mind when thinking about these operations. The opening of new stores and planned sites for others are daily items in the papers.
>
> Just what is the closed-door discount house and how does it function? The idea in each operation is basically the same, but there is variation on the theme in many cases.
>
> The closed-door discount house differs from the open discount operation in that a fee is charged and membership is restricted and enforced. Associate memberships are also available at various stores. The fee for members varies, but is usually not less than $2.
>
> Qualification for membership is in itself a unique feature of the closed-door discounter. Now a consumer has to pay to be able to shop in the store. Qualifications themselves vary from operation to operation. For the most part membership is restricted to Government employees, workers, veterans and State employees.
>
> According to a Fairchild News Service check, the closed-door discounter thus far has been concentrated in the Western part of the country with a particularly saturated area being San Diego with five separate membership houses. By 1965 the closed-door dis-

counters will have moved into the Eastern half of the country, which is the stronghold of the open discount house.

16. Another type of discount store is the so-called "mill" store. These stores started in abandoned mills in New England. They are multiplying like rabbits all over the country.

The best guesses are that almost five hundred of these soft-and-hard-goods "supermarkets" were in operation by 1960. From their spawning ground in New England mills, they are reaching out into the South, Southwest, and Midwest.

The outlets are becoming larger in size. Discount "supermarkets" of 100,000 square feet or more are becoming more common.

Many of the newer outlets are opening up in specially built and designed buildings as much as they are in the abandoned mills, factories, and warehouses where they had their beginnings.

They are seeking well-trafficked locations—on highways, on Main Street, in Suburbia—and they are finding them.

Their formula of low markup, self-service, first-quality merchandise, ample parking facilities, six- or even seven-night openings, and strong price appeal is finding wide consumer acceptance, especially among industrial workers and their families.

In many areas, this new arm of distribution is cutting into sales of the traditional retail stores.

The growth of the mill store is still in the surface-scratching stage. Prospects are that it will continue apace in the foreseeable future.

17. The discount house is becoming an advertiser. Whether it is spending any more of its own money for its advertising than do most of our established mass retailers is a moot point. But whereas established retailers were wont to point out that the discount house doesn't advertise locally, we now have a situation in which several discount houses have become strong local advertisers.

Finally, there is the drug chain. This chain has departed so far from drugs that one big chain has taken the word "drug" from its name. Its inventory is now described: "Everything for Health, Beauty and Home."

Actually, the position of the drug chain by 1965 will involve a combination of the plans of the food super, the variety chain, and the discount chain—plus a few department store overtones. This means that the drug chain will open still larger store units, will still further broaden its inventory by classification, will go into still higher price lines, will go into big-ticket items, will add credit facilities, will stress self-service still more, will hook up with food and other chains. In brief, the drug chain too will become a department store of a new type.

In turn, that means that by 1965 most mass retailers will be department stores of one type or another. They may be called "one-stop outlets," or "junior department stores"—but they will be multidepartment outlets and they will all bear a striking resemblance to each other.

And that also, in turn, suggests that by 1965 we will be seeing some new retail concepts that will not imitate, but will strike off into new formats. We will have more to say about some of these new retailing concepts in another section.

CHAPTER **7**

Distribution Patterns Go Topsy-turvy

For decades, our major retailers did not "change their spots." All major retail outlets remained essentially what they had been for generations—food, drug, hard- or soft-goods outlets.

Then after World War II came the trend toward diversification of retail inventory by merchandise classification. The drug outlet really led the parade—it was the first to diversify its inventory and it did so many years ago. Then the food outlet went into nonfoods. Then the variety chains broadened their inventories by category. The hard-goods chains went into new merchandise classifications. The soft-goods chains followed suit.

By 1960, our major retailers—inventorywise— were "taking in each other's wash." Lines of demarcation between our major retailers had just about completely broken down; traditional terms, such as "drug outlet" and "food outlet," no longer had real meaning.

But until 1960 the retailer himself continued to think within the framework of his original label. That is to say, the food outlet continued to think primarily of food, the drug outlet primarily of drugs, and so on. By 1965 this habit of thought among major retailers will change. There will develop a complete breakdown of traditional thinking with respect to retail types *among the retailers themselves.* And this trend will, in turn, make a total mockery of the traditional distribution patterns of many, if not most, manufacturers. That, in turn, will obviously deeply influence the merchandising practices of these manufacturers.

What is emerging right now in mass retailing is a mix-match pattern. Food chains and drug chains are merging. Ditto for variety chains and food chains. Department store chains are buying up food chains. Food chains are buying up department stores. There exist holding companies that control just about every type of retail establishment. This is a trend within a trend—the holding company era of retailing in which a giant holding company holds a huge umbrella over a vast and completely diversified retail empire.

Manufacturers are diversifying; retailing is diversifying. But between 1960–1965 retailers will diversify more extensively, more rapidly, than will manufacturers.

Distribution is to become topsy-turvy. Even tradition-bound industries like furniture will find that their traditional outlets have become factors of secondary importance. In furniture, for example, the department store and the traditional furniture specialty store will be ousted from first place as outlets for some manufacturers. Their place will be taken by a combination of outlets, such as the variety chain, the discount chain, and the hard-goods chain. In other words, the great difference in the retail inventory diversification pattern of the next five years as compared with the pattern of the last ten years, is this: Between 1960–1965 retail inventory diversification will take such giant strides as to turn established distribution patterns of countless manufacturers topsy-turvy. The newer outlets for established lines will not be secondary and tertiary outlets; they will become the *major* outlets for any number of manufacturers. And they will provide, in some instances, the best potential for dynamic growth for some manufacturers.

A classic example is emerging in food. And if it can happen in food, it can happen anywhere. So take a good look at the new distribution pattern that is emerging for food. Bankers Securities Corporation (the huge holding company with investments in department stores, variety chains, and others) acquired a substantial block of stock in Big Apple, Inc., Atlanta supermarket chain. The reason? The board chairman of Bankers Securities explains that the organization is exploring the potentials inherent in a combination of food and nonfood operations, especially in its nonfood outlets and most particularly for the department stores it controls. The conclusion was that control of a successful food supermarket chain would bring the Bankers Securities' affiliated nonfood-store groups a knowledge of food operations that would be difficult to acquire in any other way. Developing this point, the board chairman stated that merchandising experts of Big Apple are working closely with the nonfoods buying offices of Bankers Securities affiliates—and nonfood merchandising experts with Bankers Securities affiliates are observing the food chain's operations!

The entry of the food super into nonfoods on a big scale was bound to force their nonfood competitors into food. But the threat to the food super is now greater than their threat to the nonfood outlets had been. The explanation is simple.

• The food super aims to earn a handsome profit on its nonfoods. It does not put in nonfoods as a means of getting traffic; its food produces the traffic.

• But the new major outlets putting in food look upon food first as a traffic producer and second as profit producer. They may even take a loss on food in order to win traffic!

• Since the food super's net profit on the food operation has plummeted almost to the vanishing point, it cannot match cut for cut on food with these new competitors.

• But these new competitors *can* merchandise price rings around the food super on most nonfoods! If the food super tries to meet these competitors in a nonfoods price battle, the food super will wind up with figures dangerously close to the red-ink line.

Most of our giant nonfood retailers will move still more emphatically into food. Even Woolworth's executive head made it very clear that this huge chain will soon be involved in food on a much larger scale than is presently. (In England, Woolworth is very active in food.)

Variety chains, drug chains, discount chains, and department store chains (the last prodded by the Bankers Securities move, since Bankers Securities controls many department stores)—*all* will expand their food programs. These nonfood chains have a gigantic daily traffic. If they simply exposed food to their present traffic total, especially at attractive prices, they would move an enormous food total. But they will use food to produce *more* traffic. And food will produce still more traffic for their stores because they will offer food as bait. Then some of the newest forms of discount retailing will turn to food. The remarkably successful mill stores will turn to food. (These new types of discount chains will be turning in a $1 billion annual volume in a very few years, primarily on soft goods.) The older discount chains are, of course, already heavily involved in food.

In brief, the food super is to encounter powerful competition on food. Soon the food processors will find it advisable to reevaluate their distribution systems. They will plan their merchandising so as to give increasing attention to nonfood outlets—in particular to the great chains in the various nonfood categories. The era may not be far away when from 20 to 35 per cent of food volume at retail (varying by classification) will be done by nonfood outlets! That would be quite a revolution for food marketing. Some food processors will sell exclusively through nonfood outlets; some will account for over 50 per cent of their total volume through nonfood outlets.

If these percentage estimates prove to be reasonably correct, then it would appear that the food processors will be forced to come to two fundamental conclusions:

• Over the next few years, the area for dynamic increases in food volume at retail will come from nonfood outlets, *not* from the food outlet.

• The food super, and particularly the food super chains, will show only small increases in food volume over the next few years— increases of a size that may not quite match the increase in population.

What may happen with food is even more likely to happen in many other categories merchandised through other outlets.

The wise merchandising executive in most, but not all, lines will, in time, tend to function from the basic premise that distribution is where one finds it. That fundamental decision will be hastened, not only by the big trend among giant retailers toward giant one-stop outlets, but even more by the remarkable mix-match trend in corporate maneuvers among the large chains. As mentioned earlier in this chapter, we are coming into the era of true giant retailing—and this means an era in which most, if not all, lines of demarcation between the various types of chains will have lost practically all significance.

Yes, distribution will become topsy-turvy within the 1960–1965 era to a degree that will make the broadening distribution pattern of the postwar era appear to be just a tiny step. And merchandising executives will therefore be compelled to think in terms of retail outlets in general, not by type. When a large variety chain leaves the variety chain association because it concludes—correctly—that it is really no longer a variety chain in the historic sense of the name, then the handwriting is on the wall for the manufacturing merchandising executive to read.

CHAPTER 8

Nonmerchandising Income
for Giant Retailers

Traditionally, retailing has looked to the merchandising function for its net profit. Indeed, retailing historically concentrated on *merchandise movement* not merely as the primary, but really almost the exclusive source of its net profit.

Now the giant retailer does less and less to move brands off the floor of his store other than to give them shelf space (usually at a price!). Not only that—he is also beginning to find that other sources of income can become exceedingly attractive. This could conceivably lead to a still less dynamic floor merchandising job than now typifies many giant retailers—and, in their "law-library" store layouts, this is currently at a pretty low level. Never did retailers controlling the lion's share of total retail volume do so little to increase turnover velocity through merchandising as today! Manufacturers perform more—much more—of the total retail merchandising function in the giant outlets of giant retailers than these retailers themselves. Yet the trade margin tends to be at an all-time high!

Now, as the giant retailer turns increasingly to nonmerchandising sources for his net profit, the burden of retail merchandising will tend to be shouldered still more by the *manufacturer*. (Will the end result be a trend by manufacturers into control of retail outlets?)

What does this signify? It signifies that the era of retail turnover of inventory, as the basic source of retail net profit, is drawing to a close! And this will jolt the world of merchandising right down to its toes! Will nonmerchandising some day account for 50 per cent of total net profit for some large retail organizations? Yes it will—and by 1965.

The great banks in New York separate their security profits and their operating profits. It would be fascinating if our giant retailers were to separate their merchandising profits and their nonmerchandising profits! As it is, annual statements, Harvard figures, and many studies create the impression that merchandising alone produces the net profit for giant retailing. This is less and less the case. Ultimately, the *nonmerchandising functions* will contribute a *larger percentage* of the total net profit of an increasing number of giant retailers than will the merchandising functions.

Since giant retailers account for the lion's share of the total volume of most advertised brands—and since this concentration of retail volume in fewer hands will accelerate—this new retail revolution is of deepest significance to national advertisers.

It will leave an imprint on marketing at least equal to that left by self-service and self-selection, by shopping centers, by highway retailing, by giant retailing, by the store-controlled brand—each of which compelled fundamental shifts in the merchandising strategy and tactics of manufacturers of advertised brands.

As an example, since manufacturers really "sell" retail net profit via merchandising in their brand presentations to the trade, it is clear that, the more important the nonmerchandising function becomes to giant retailing, the more incumbent will it be upon manufacturers to reevaluate their fundamental marketing strategy.

There may not only be greater net profit for the large retailer as a real estate promoter than as a merchant—there may also be less risk. Mass retailing's net-profit percentage from inventory turnover tends to be microscopic; moreover, it simply cannot be dramatically increased. But a successful real estate promotion can throw off a handsome net on the invested dollar. Right here is the genesis of the retail move toward nonmerchandising income. Inventory turnover no longer offers dynamic net-profit growth; but nonmerchandising functions are fully capable of juicy net-profit growth. Giantism in any field ultimately leads to a mounting emphasis on real estate, on securities, on corporate maneuvers, on tax factors. This has been true of manufacturers. It is now becoming true of retailers.

Indeed, it is entirely probable that, more and more, the top heads of these giant retail organizations will be selected more for their knowledge (as lawyers and otherwise) of real estate procedures, taxes, and corporate securities than for their knowledge of retail merchandising! There is every reason to expect that the investment banker, the real estate consultant, transportation and warehouse experts, the financial consultant, as well as assorted security market specialists, will play increasingly important roles in the policies of giant retailers.

This development will hardly increase the importance of the merchandising functions in these organizations. The management of finances is becoming more important to some retail giants than the management of merchandising. The promotion of real estate is becoming more important than the promotion of merchandise. The acquisition of other companies for corporate profit is becoming more important than the acquisition of merchandise for resale. Naturally, the executives responsible for these nonmerchandising functions move up on the retail organizational chart.

Of course, our retail giants have been getting a growing percentage of total net profit from a spreading variety of allowances. It could be claimed that these allowances are a part of the retail merchandising process. But retail merchandising is presumed to embrace the *selling* function; allowances represent the *buying* function. And it is obvious that at least some large retailers earn a larger net profit from allowances than from floor merchandising—they are really landlords and not merchandisers, buyers and not sellers.

But allowances are by no means the largest single source of nonmerchandising income for giant retailers. In addition to real estate, other and newer sources of nonmerchandising income are beginning to assume respectable totals in the net-profit figures of some big retailers. For example, there is the growing practice among some large retailers of buying up other organizations (not necessarily retail) with an attractive tax-loss position.

Another example involves the growing practice by some large retailers of setting up subsidiary organizations to service other retailers. In the food field, for example, several food chains have set up subsidiaries to centralize the nonfood function. In a few instances, these nonfood subsidiaries are actually servicing other food retailers as well as their own stores; they are becoming a new form of service jobber. Clearly this will, in time, provide a new source of income that is not what tradition would define as a retail merchandising source of income. Certainly this income does not come from the movement of merchandise on the floor of the stores of the parent retailer.

The development of the holding company concept in mass retailing—which is a strong trend—involves corporate maneuvers that can throw off extraordinarily large net profit, primarily through the exchange of pieces of paper. This is a nonmerchandising function.

The leased department represents nonmerchandising income. It is currently enjoying a substantial boom in most major chains. It is nonmerchandising income for the retail landlord because the merchandising is done by an outsider.

Retailers are going into manufacturing. This promises to become a powerful trend, particularly as giant retailers concentrate on their own brands. Profits from the manufacturing operation are not retail merchandising profits. So here is another source of nonmerchandising income for a retail organization.

The wholesale-warehousing function performed by many retailers is not a retail merchandising operation, strictly speaking. It is only indirectly related to the movement of merchandise on the retail floor. In some instances, this function is lodged in a subsidiary organization which means it receives its own accounting analysis. So this too is a source of nonmerchandising income.

Credit retailing involves financial aspects that are not strictly retail merchandising. Here again, the trend is for retailers to form a credit-financing subsidiary. Since all mass retailing is turning to credit, the astute management of the financial aspects of the retail credit function is expected to throw off a net profit *apart* from the merchandising operation. (Department stores were recently urged by a store controller to separate income-from-credit operations from other income because it has become a major source of income in some departments, yet it has never been separately accounted.)

When Alden's arranged with Wieboldt International to do all its buying abroad, it was taking a major nonmerchandising step toward cost-cutting and a larger net profit.

This growing interest among giant retailers in nonmerchandising sources of income will reach a high pitch by 1965. It means that manufacturers will be compelled to take over still more of the total retail function. It may mean, too, that some manufacturers will be experimenting with their own retail stores by 1965, arguing that "since we are now performing most of the retailer function and still giving traditional margins, why not 'take over'—especially since the retailer is becoming a manufacturer, a promoter of his own brands, etc.?"

CHAPTER 9

The Decline of Giveaway Merchandising

It was being said early in 1960 that "the best known brand today is *10 Cents Off.*" How true! After 50 years of brand advertising, some merchandise classifications are so completely controlled by consumer deals that brand loyalty scarcely exists—the shopper's only favorite brand in these classifications is the one featuring 10 cents off.

In the dentrifice classification, some large chains have reported that from one-third to one-half of their total volume is accounted for by consumer-deal inventory, most of it "cents-off" deals. At certain times of the year, the deal figure will rise to as high as 75 per cent of dentrifice turnover. In other merchandise classifications, the deal-inventory situation similarly is fearfully unbalanced. This would be true of tea and coffee, of soap and detergents. It is also true in many soft-goods categories in the shape of trade deals. And ranging far off into hard goods, trade-deal inventory rules the roost in small and major appliances and in many of the nonelectric household lines.

There is every reason to believe that in 1960 more deals—both consumer and trade deals—were offered by suppliers than ever before in this era of presumably modern merchandising. Moreover, in 1961 the deal total once again established a new high-water mark.

Indeed, one of the few developments that could act as a brake on deals in some lines is the fact that there simply is no more room for substantial deal expansion in these lines. For example, when manufacturers account for up to 70 per cent of their annual volume on deals (and this is no longer extraordinary) how much more potential for deal growth exists?

The consumer deal, in particular, has reached the point of stalemate—and worse—in some classifications. Of course, Neilsen has been pointing out for years that most consumer deals fail to provide a lasting sales increase. Now the economics of this merchandising procedure become ever more disturbing. While there are exceptions, of course, as a general observation it may be stated with respect to consumer deals that—

1. Competitive consumer deals are tending to balance each other out. There are times, in some major outlets, when as many as five or six competitive deals will be concurrently displayed in a single classification.

2. Consumer deals are so numerous in some stores that the shopper is left in something of a daze. This state of shopper confusion is not alleviated by the fact that it is not unusual to find a brand simultaneously displayed both at regular and at deal price! Occasionally, the same brand will display two different deals simultaneously in the same outlet.

3. Consumer deals no longer serve as effective sampling procedures (one of the original objectives) for at least two reasons:

A. The shopper has become so thoroughly conditioned to expect price concessions that her brand loyalty is too weak to overcome the thrift appeal of the competing deals.

B. There is so little difference in consumer importance between many competing brands that there is small reason for the shopper to refrain from picking whichever brand is currently the "best bargain."

4. Consumer deals thus tend to increase brand disloyalty.

5. Consumer deals work at cross purposes to the great objective of modern advertising—the creation of a brand X "image." In the very merchandise classifications where there exists the much-talked-about brand image, there exist the most consumer deals. *What brand image is created by a 5-cents-off deal?*

6. Consumer deals tend to follow a formula. Not only is competing merchandise much the same, consumer deals also tend to be very much alike. The consumer deal at its best hardly represents creative

merchandising. When it is, for example, simply another cents-off deal, it is as uncreative as merchandising can become.

7. A blasé shopping public must be offered more—ever more. The sales reaction becomes less—ever less. Between the two, deal costs rise astronomically. There is no doubt that many, if not most, consumer deals no longer represent sound marketing economics. They can be justified solely, if at all, as competitive necessities.

8. There is little reason to believe that consumer deals of the traditional types any longer play a real role in inducing many shoppers to make an *unplanned* purchase. Thus, the shopper who does not have on a shopping list, or in mind, the purchase of a dentrifice is now seldom induced to make such a purchase impulsively because of a deal offer. Why should she? She knows that whenever she wants to buy a dentrifice there will always be a deal on an acceptable brand. The consumer deal is unquestionably losing its ability to create substantial impulse volume. Moreover, when five or six competing brands simultaneously offer a consumer deal, then the deal tends also to lose its ability to influence brand preference.

Clearly the demands of competitive necessity cannot be ignored. But even in a competitive society it is not impossible to plan along such lines as the following (and increasing examples of this kind of planning will be evident by 1965):

• To try to develop a persuasive point of superiority or difference in the item, its packaging, its pricing. This is part of merchandising. When competitive merchandise is identical—in fact or in shopper opinion—reliance on the deal is almost inevitable.

• Beg, borrow, or steal funds from deals, from allowance, from all of the other drains on the ad budget—and accumulate the largest feasible budget for advertising.

• Spend that ad budget primarily, if not exclusively, not for deal advertising but for true creative advertising that will persuasively present that persuasive point of superiority or difference.

• Apply to the deals that competition makes necessary creative thinking on a par with the creative advertising. There is too little creative advertising. There is even less creative merchandising. Most competitive advertising is dismayingly similar. Most competitive merchandising, especially with respect to deals, is dismayingly identical.

Modern merchandising's greatest need is for creative advertising.

"Me-too" advertising compels frenzied merchandising. Given creative advertising—then merchandising can be, should be, *must be* equally creative. The creative function has every bit as much opportunity to perform in merchandising as in advertising. The entire marketing program must be brilliantly creative. First and foremost in a sound merchandising creed comes *creative advertising*. Then comes *creative merchandising*—and, not infrequently, these two creative processes march hand in hand.

But creative both must be! And we will see more and more examples of creative merchandising by 1965 rather than "me-too" merchandising—because the economics of dreary deals will ultimately compel new merchandising thinking. The era of merchandising by giveaway must—and will—peak out and start a decline by 1965.

CHAPTER 10

The Diminishing Role of the Salesman

On balance, for the last fifty years, the role of the manufacturer's salesman—*as a salesman*—has been waning.

The trend started when the first few manufacturers established a brand with a degree of preselling. Ever since, the strictly traditional selling role of the salesman, as a salesman, has declined in such presold categories as food, health aids, and certain hard and soft classifications. By 1965, the traditional selling role of the salesman will shrivel in still more categories. More and more reliance will be put on advertising and on merchandising to do larger parts of the selling job.

Moreover, in the coming years the waning function of personal selling by manufacturers' salesmen will diminish for an additional reason, to wit: Other occupations will prove more attractive both financially and as a pattern of living.

Now, before moving further into this analysis, let us anticipate the "opposition." We will be charged with predicting the death of the salesman—everywhere, and for all time, and for all purposes.

Obviously, that is not our position at all. Our position is simply that on balance, the role of the salesman—as selling has been traditionally defined—has been waning. When one strikes a balance, one is weighing both plusses and minuses. Thus, when it is remarked that the role of the salesman has been declining "on balance," it follows that in some fields he is definitely more important than ever. But viewing the situation *as a whole,* no other conclusion is possible than that the role has declined broadly in our total economy. And this trend still has a long way to go.

This is not to say that the salesman may not have new—in some instances even more important—nonselling roles to play. But these new roles tend not to be selling as the selling function is *traditionally* viewed.

And right here is the crux of this situation. There continues a tendency to think of the salesman as performing the traditional selling functions even in fields where these traditional selling functions have obviously faded—in varying degree—in importance. To express it differently, there is a tendency for sales management to overstay tradition with respect to the role of personal selling.

This is exactly what happened in mass retailing. Originally, the retail salesperson was a *salesperson.* But with self-service and self-selection, floor personnel became *attendants,* not salespeople. Their functions changed but the semantics didn't—they are still called "salespeople" and managed as such.

Similarly, in too many instances, the manufacturer's representative who calls on the trade—wholesale or retail—continues to be called a salesman, even though his functions may bear only a remote resemblance to creative selling. And he is often hired, trained, compensated, routed, and managed as a salesman—but his present-day function may range from little more than that of a trade attendant to that of territorial advertising-merchandising representative.

Our giant retailers are all turning to a committee system of buying. The individual buyer has been shorn of much of his original authority —and this process continues. A manufacturer's salesman rarely can get into a buying-committee meeting—and surely filling out the printed form he is given under these circumstances could hardly be called selling. As giant retailers take over mass retailing and buy increasingly through committee, an impenetrable wall is set up between its deliberations and the manufacturer's salesman.

What is true of giant retailing is equally true of giant wholesaling —step by step and point by point. Even in industry, more and more buying is being done by executives seldom contacted by the industrial salesman. Thus, in a special report, the Research Institute of America (RIA) makes the point that in industry, top management's role in purchasing is growing. The following is quoted from an excellent RIA study:

> These facts aren't changed by the realization that all of the orders you receive are signed by the buyer or purchasing agent—that the bulk of your salesmen's calls are made at that level—and that the purchasing man, as a specialist, is and should be a key man in the transaction.
>
> The real problem is posed by a gradual but significant shift in buying procedures; one which can endanger your chances of holding your most important customers or gaining new ones if it is not recognized and met.
>
> The signs all point one way—toward increasing management participation in buying decisions even among large companies.
>
> You've probably run into some evidence of the change already. Your advertising and sales promotion may be just right, your salesman working as hard as ever. Yet, suddenly, the purchasing agent of a major account may tell him, somewhat embarrassedly, that he's switching part of the business to a competitor. Your salesman may not even be told; the orders merely begin to decline.
>
> Chances are the suggestion or order to switch the business came from "upstairs" and the salesman, by himself, is almost powerless to overcome the competitor's edge.

This same management participation in buying is, of course, equally true with respect to our giant retailers. Or maybe top-level-executive participation would be a better description with respect to some of our giant retailers.

As in *all* committees, the executive who sits at the head of the table tends either to make, or strongly to influence, the ultimate buying decision. (Some tape recordings of the proceedings of food super buying-committee meetings tend to bear this out.) He may be a management executive or a top-level executive—but the point is that this executive is seldom contacted by the manufacturer's salesman either before, during, or after the buying-committee meeting.

It might also be pointed out that a mounting percentage of what could really be called "selling" to giant retailers is done these days by meetings between executives—an executive of the supplier and an executive of the giant retailer (or giant wholesaler).

As an example of how the original meaning of the word "salesman" can mislead, consider a release issued by an association of wholesale distributors which pointed out that its salesmen spend some sixty-eight minutes each day with retailers and have to average close to $1,000 in sales to pay their way. But these salesmen will make from 20 to 30 and more calls per day—so, actually, they may be with a retailer for no more than several minutes per call. How much true selling can be done in from two to three minutes?

This is not to say that the role of these men is not important. Their role definitely *is* important. But it is not a selling role as selling is traditionally defined.

Of course, in the food and drug fields—some others, too—a number of long-established national advertisers years ago recognized the downgrading of the traditional personal-selling function. These manufacturers reorganized their sales organizations accordingly.

But many more manufacturers who have begun to presell their brands in more recent years have too often failed to apply rational reorganization planning to the personal-selling function. Their sales organizations have not been brought into conformance with the new buying setup of our giant retailers nor into conformance with the specific personal-selling requirements of the presold brand. Obviously, this is hardly likely to be the same kind of personal selling required when brands were not presold.

Moreover, these salesmen are being poorly trained to perform their new functions. How could it be otherwise when their new functions have so seldom been clearly delineated?

Finally, the merchandising function cannot be properly planned to help compensate for the decline in personal selling when this situation has not been clearly evaluated. By 1965 there will be a clearer awareness of the new role of the salesman for the presold brand—and of the resulting slack that must be taken up, in part, by merchandising.

CHAPTER **11**

The Shrinking Number of
Chain Store Units

It has been fairly customary for some years for manufacturers to evaluate their distribution within a chain on the basis of the number of stores within a chain that stock the item or line. Thus, if a chain operates 100 stores and a manufacturer is adequately inventoried in 75 of those stores then—presumably—he has a good 75 per cent coverage in that chain. But that may be presuming too much. Much too much.

Back in the days when the various store units in a chain were all within a narrow size range, this rough appraisal of distribution within a chain may have been reasonably accurate. But today, in most chain organizations—food, drug, variety, hard and soft goods—the size variation between the larger units in the chain and the smaller store units will be enormous. Giant store units of chains may be as much as ten times larger than the old bantam units.

One consequence is that practically all chains account for a growing percentage of their total volume in a declining percentage of their total store units. Example: A food super chain operates a total of 543 stores. Of that total, 346 account for no less than 92 per cent of the chain's total sales! Expressed another way, 197 of the stores in this chain account for only 8 per cent of its sales total! Clearly, a manufacturer whose item or line is stocked primarily in the 197 small stores of this chain is being given mighty poor exposure to this chain's total shopping traffic.

The situation dramatized by the figures cited is not at all extraordinary. In the majority of chains in most fields, some 50 per cent of the store units will account for from 70 to 90 per cent of total chain-wide volume. Moreover, this concentration of volume into fewer and fewer store units of the various chains promises to accelerate over the next few years as all chains concentrate on giant one-stop store units. By 1965, it is entirely probable that many chains will have a smaller total number of stores than in 1960—but with a larger over-all total volume. In this connection, many merchandisers have forgotten that in 1930 the A&P food chain had over twice the number of store units it has today—although its total volume has obviously multiplied many times. Much the same will happen among many chains in all retail fields by 1965—for the first time in over-all chain store history.

This concentration by the chains on giant store units deeply affects merchandising by manufacturers. Even these figures, however, do not show the distribution picture in its true light, and for this reason: The section in which a manufacturer's line is stocked may be puny in the small store unit. In the giant store unit, this section may be large, with full assortments, with dramatic display, and, of course, with vastly more traffic milling in front of it. Thus, 20 large store units may give as much volume in certain lines as 100 small store units.

Of course, some manufacturers have for years classified their distribution within a chain by the chain's own classification system—A store units, B store units, etc. But in most instances, these classification systems do a poor job of analyzing the current store setup of the chain—store setups have changed more dramatically than is usually made evident by these outmoded classification systems.

It would be appropriate, therefore, for many manufacturers selling through the various types of chains to reexamine their distribution store by store within each chain to determine whether their store-by-store inventory and promotion are in step with this broad trend by the chains toward accounting for *expanding percentages* of total volume in a *shrinking number* of store units. As already stated, within three to five years the chains in most fields will be accounting for a larger-than-ever volume in a smaller-than-ever store-unit total.

By 1965 in many chains, 75 per cent of the total volume will be done in a total number of store units equal to only 25 per cent of the total stores operated by the chain in 1955.

If that formula is reasonably correct—then some manufacturers are already losing distribution exposure in their chain outlets because they have not won stronger representation in the new giant outlets.

By 1965, the 100,000-square-foot chain store unit will be common —the 200,000-square-foot store will be coming along. Chain store units with an annual turnover of $5 million will also be common— some chain store units will top $10 million and even $25 million annually.

The chains will have become department stores of new types— and their volume, in total, will dwarf that of the traditional department stores. Merchandising men—take notice.

CHAPTER 12

Development of the Mass Recreational Center

The modern bowling establishment (we now have chains controlling up to 20 bowling centers and, within a few years, these bowling-alley chains may be operating up to 100 units each) is poised on the verge of a dynamic expansion. It has grown fantastically in number, size of establishment, and facilities over the last five years. But its rate of expansion over the next five years will probably double that of the last half decade.

However, merchandising men will be more interested in the possibility—and even more in the probability—that the remarkable growth of the modern bowling establishment presages the ultimate development of a new form of *mass recreational center* that will have an impact on merchandising in many merchandise classifications that are far, far removed from bowling pins.

This new type of mass recreational center will provide—

• Facilities for bowling
• Facilities for other old and some new games of mass enjoyment
• A giant year-round swimming pool
• Ice skating and/or roller skating
• Miniature golf, putting greens
• Tennis—indoors and out

This isn't a complete list of the future recreational facilities of the coming type of recreational center—but it gives a pretty good idea of a new type of leisure-activity center that will be, in effect, a shopping center for recreation—all under one roof and perhaps all under one ownership (with some departments leased out to concessionaires).

Our total leisure time is piling up. It is inevitable that the business of catering to our leisure time through recreation or leisure centers will capitalize on this vast jump in leisure time. And the modern bowling establishment seems likely to be the spearhead of this fascinating development.

However, there is another aspect of this development that is considerably more significant to many more merchandising men than the appeal to leisure time—this is the fact that wherever people gather in sufficient numbers, they constitute "traffic" in the retail sense—*and they will ultimately be catered to by retailers.*

That means that the recreational center will eventually become the focal point for new types of retailing. Even now, the modern bowling alley is going into food-service facilities ranging from stand-up bars to restaurants. Also, they have counters offering novelties, souvenirs, cigarettes, candy, beer, and soft drinks. But this is merely the beginning. They will sell bowling apparel, shoes for bowling—and, of course, apparel and footwear for swimming, tennis, and other sports. In time, they will sell health and beauty aids, sporting equipment of many kinds, take-home convenience foods. Small specialty food stores (the new type of midget food outlet) will open up alongside or inside these recreational centers. Several automatic laundries have opened in these bowling centers. And so, step by step, people seeking recreation will be tempted with a mounting variety of merchandise and, in this impulse-buying age, they will buy a mounting variety of merchandise before having, or after having had, a good time.

This will make an interesting full turn of the wheel of merchandising. Decades ago, shopping itself was a form of recreation. Then it became a chore. Now apparently it is once again to become tied in with recreation.

In this connection, bear in mind that in farmers' markets, in auction-type retail establishments, in the amusement devices for children, installed in many retail stores, in some of the newer services offered by retailers, including broadcast music—we have had the beginnings of a return of the entertainment factor in retail merchandising. And whatever looms up large in retailing must ultimately loom up large in the merchandising programs of manufacturers.

Perhaps our people will soon tend to seek more of their recreation nearer home; maybe tourism will peak out as it loses some of its novelty appeal. But the desire to get out of the home—neither radio, TV, nor any other new development kept people home for long— plus more leisure time, better incomes, the herd instinct—in our modern suburbs, across-the-street neighbors no longer meet!—all will combine to shove the recreation center into high speed.

And that, in turn, will bring about a new form of retailing—a new form that will be in full flower by 1965.

CHAPTER **13**

The Era of Presold Store Brands

Originally the battle between presold brands was waged primarily between manufacturers of nationally advertised lines. But the great brand battle of the next few years—fully mounted right now—is the battle between the manufacturer's presold brand and the giant retailer's or wholesaler's presold brand.

There really *is* such a thing as the private brand. It has existed for many years, and it will continue to exist for many more years. But the merchandising furor of the coming years does not involve the private (by which is meant "unknown") brand at all!

The great brand-merchandising trend revolves around the *distributor-controlled and advertised brand*—and, more particularly, the controlled brand distributed and advertised by our giant retailers. Indeed, the true private (meaning unknown, not presold) brand is being squeezed between the manufacturer's known brand and the giant retailer's known brand!

This confusion will be at least partly cleared up by firmly fixing in mind the three basic types of brands. These are—

• The manufacturer's *advertised brand.*

• The distributor's *controlled and advertised brand*—the distributor may be a wholesaler, a giant chain, a voluntary, or a cooperative group.

• The *true private brand,* having little or no consumer recognition or standing—it may be sponsored by a manufacturer, by a whole-saler, or by a retailer.

What will increasingly be referred to—and quite correctly—as "the battle of the brands," will really involve two principal antago-nists:

• The large *manufacturer* promoting advertised brands.

• The *giant retailer* and *giant retail groups* (including some whole-salers) promoting their own controlled and advertised brands. (In this connection, bear in mind that food super chains alone have spent over $2 billion in advertising over the last ten years. Their store *names* are presold and, since their brand names are usually based on the store name, their *brands* are presold.)

The trend toward retailer-controlled brands goes back many years. The FTC found—way back in 1922—that 3.6 per cent of the grocery volume of the reporting food chains was in own-brands; in 1928 it was 8.8 per cent; and in 1930 it was 10.1 per cent. With fluctuations typical of any marketing trend line, that uptrend in the development of controlled brands by giant retailers has continued to date—and by no means only in the food field. Sears alone does close to $4 billion in its own brands of nonfoods. The shoe chain brands outsell manu-facturer brands.

(Incidentally, the figures showing the per cent of *total* retail done on controlled brands in a specific chain can be highly misleading. If you are merchandising canned goods, and if one of your big chain outlets does 50 per cent on its own brand in that category, it does you no good to lean on the fact that only 5 or 10 per cent of that customer's total store-wide volume is in its own brands.)

When contemplating the store-controlled brand, one must project his imagination a few years ahead to get an idea (1) of how huge these large retailers and retail groups are destined to become, and (2) of what this vast expansion in retail giantism portends in the battle between manufacturers' advertised brands and retailers' ad-vertised brands. (This subject of giant retailing is covered in detail in Chapter 3.)

We are coming into an age of giant retailers and giant retail groups, some with an annual volume of $10 billion! There will be as many billion-and-over retailers (and wholesalers) as billion-and-over man-ufacturers of consumer goods.

It is in this age of giant retailing that the retailer's own advertised brands will really come into their own. Today, there is only a small handful of truly national chains and retail groups—that is, with broad coverage of the total population. Even the A&P, with its immense $5 billion in annual volume, doesn't blanket the nation—yet. But giant retailing is showing positive indications of spreading out geographically. And national chains mean true national brands by the chains—brands that are nationally advertised and that have national standing. Sears, Ward, Penney, Western Auto Supply, and other chains already have powerful national brands. Some Sears brands are more powerfully entrenched than any manufacturer brands. (Incidentally, let us bear in mind that few manufacturer brands have true *national* distribution.)

The giant retailer firmly intends to shorten the distance from factory to retail store. This was and is the fundamental Sears policy. It is to become the basic policy of most giant chains in most fields. As part of this strategic goal, the giant retailer plans to concentrate increasingly on his own advertised brands. The larger the retailer grows, and the more concentrated total retail volume becomes in a few strong hands, the greater the development of retailer-controlled brands. This is the fundamental formula of the giant retailer.

We will ultimately see efforts made by large retailers to put their brands into outlets that are noncompetitive—geographically or otherwise. This has been going on in a smallish way for years. This will give a new dimension to brand merchandising by giant retailers.

Moreover, before long we will see several giant retailers—some of them with wholesale affiliations—sending out salesmen who will call on other retailers and who will compete for brand distribution with brand manufacturers! In some instances, the *retailer's* salesmen will be selling to other outlets a controlled brand actually made by a manufacturer with whose own brands they will be fighting for distribution!

General Foods announced that it had increased its advertising budget in order to compete with store brands. At a stockholders' meeting of General Foods, that corporation's chief executive officer remarked: "Competitively, private brands are an important and disturbing factor to General Foods—and they are likely to continue to be a troublesome factor." If a General Foods finds private-brand competition "troublesome"—what about the smaller food processors and what about manufacturers whose brands are not presold as powerfully as the General Foods brands?

The president of Libby, McNeil & Libby, in a talk to the New York Society of Security Analysts, declared that there had been "a rapid increase in private brands sponsored by chain stores and voluntary groups. This has obviously increased the pressure on our brands, necessitating larger expenditures for advertising to hold for our brands their share of the consumer's business."

Richard G. Zimmerman, editor of *Super Market Merchandising*, in a public address remarked:

> I had been asked to give a talk before the top marketing and sales executives of a nationally-known food manufacturing concern. My subject was the same as today's.
>
> However, what made this particular appearance unique was that the policy makers of this big corporation were at that very moment contemplating a rather far-reaching decision.
>
> You would recognize this company as possessing one of the best known brand names in America. In addition, like so many of our other large grocery manufacturers, it also produces its product under the private label of numerous grocery chains across the country.
>
> The decision which these men were pondering was this: *Should the company continue to vigorously promote and advertise its brand?* Or should it instead cut down this effort sharply in favor of greater production and sales promotion of the product under the private brand names of individual Super Markets and grocery chains?
>
> I doubt that such deliberations are any longer unique. Assuredly, there are other major grocery suppliers now weighing the pros and cons of a similar decision. But that the possibility *even exists* that manufacturers could contemplate such a significant move should give us pause.
>
> In any event, there is little question that *the most important single issue* facing the food manufacturer at this time is: "How will private labels affect my business, and how can my company cope with the problem?"

For food, one may substitute innumerable nonfood classifications. If anything, Sears, Ward, Penney, some of the variety chains, Rexall, the discount chains, the auto accessory chains, and the shoe chains have gone farther with their own brands than have the food chains. Therefore, over the next few years the merchandising executive is to be faced with this fundamental problem: What program will develop for our presold brands the *strongest competitive posture* with relation to store-controlled presold brands?

Merchandising men need not be told that there is no single marketing plan equally appropriate for all industry—or even for all manufacturers within a single classification. But it is possible to sketch, in very broad outline, some of the considerations that merchandising men in *any* industry will be weighing in hand-tailoring a program that involves competing with the giant retailer's presold brands.

As a starting point, manufacturers of presold brands who, as basic policy, are not now making controlled brands for retailers will be regularly reviewing this policy in the light of the enormous growth of the controlled brand in most classifications and in the light of the near- and long-term plans of our giant retailers.

It is no deep secret that a substantial percentage of the total volume of merchandise involved in distributor-controlled brands is produced by the very manufacturers who are also merchandising their own nationally advertised brands. There may be, very roughly, some 800 manufacturers in this country whose advertising budgets are sufficiently large to permit advertising programs capable of really preselling their brands to the major part of the great national market. Of these 800 manufacturers, probably at least half turn out special labels for distributors.

Interestingly enough, among these very roughly 400 manufacturers of presold brands who supply distributor-controlled labels, we find that—

1. In some instances as much as 40 per cent—and occasionally even more—of their total production in branded merchandise is for distributor-controlled brands.

2. The total volume in distributor-controlled brands produced by these manufacturers is clearly on the rise.

3. The gross volume done by some of these manufacturers in distributor-controlled brands is, in some instances, increasing more dynamically than their volume on their own presold brands.

4. The net profit for the manufacturer on distributor-controlled-brand volume tends to be quite satisfactory—and may even be more predictable than on their own presold brands.

5. In some instances, if it were not for the factory production economies gained through distributor-controlled volume, plus the net

profit earned from this volume, it might not be possible for certain manufacturers to provide the required advertising budget for their own presold brands.

In brief, the time is not far distant—if it is not already here—when the greatest share of distributor-controlled brands will be produced by manufacturers who are marketing their own presold brands simultaneously. This is a marketing fact of life.

The controlled label will exist whether the manufacturer sees it or not. It's there. It can't be blinked or wished away.

Then there are such facts as the following that will be pondered when debating the production of controlled brands:

• The competitor who takes in controlled-brand business may be able to achieve manufacturing and other economies that will benefit his own advertised brands and thus win a competitive edge.

• The competitor who supplies a controlled brand to a giant retailer has a "good position" with that retailer; this could benefit that competitor's own brands in that outlet.

It would hardly be wise to contend that *all* manufacturers of presold brands should go out after distributor-controlled-brand volume. But it is reasonable to suggest that—

• More manufacturers will check into controlled-brand business— and will do so with a more open mind.

•Manufacturers now producing controlled brands for distributors will study their organizational blueprints involving this end of the business—and raise its organizational status. Maybe the vice president in charge of marketing controlled labels will be placed on a par on the organizational chart with the vice president in charge of marketing the manufacturer's own labels!

• More manufacturers will deliberately establish a greater degree of rivalry between these two divisions of the business. When the controlled-label division of the business and the manufacturer's-label division slug it out under healthy competitive conditions, not only the whole organization, but the manufacturer's own brands may benefit.

Manufacturers who have been producing distributor-controlled brands will be reappraising both their strategy and tactics. The total marketing situation with respect to the distributor-controlled brand has changed drastically—and will change even more drastically in the near-term future. Manufacturer programs for marketing distributor-controlled brands have tended *not* to keep step with the rapidly expanding problems and opportunities of this great marketing development. It has been considered almost exclusively a *manufacturing* situation. Today, controlled-brand production is also in need of *merchandising.*

All costs involved in manufacturers' own brands will tend to be rechecked. The manufacturer's own brand cannot continue indefinitely to bear a considerably higher price tag than the identical item made under a distributor-controlled label. In particular, the spread between the two on the retail shelf must be lessened. This is destined to be one of the great merchandising problems of the 1960–1965 era. The manufacturer's own brand labors under a distinct handicap when its pricing ranges considerably higher than that of the competing store-controlled brand. If the price cannot be brought down, then more may be done either to *give* better value in the manufacturer's own brand or to *create the impression* of better value. This is a critical point.

Manufacturers may be compelled to bring out new products and product improvements for their own brands on a larger scale—their merchandise must be more competitive with the lines made under distributor-controlled brands. This may mean finding new pricing points, new package sizes, new case sizes. The similarity between competing lines has been permitted to go too far.

Allowances to distributors will be rechecked. Too often these allowances wind up as an advertising budget for the controlled brand. This is especially true of the cooperative advertising allowance. Payments for shelf location and position may become more common. In-store display in a self-service, self-selection age is an advertising medium of great power. (This control over in-store display is the giant retailer's great secret weapon in the battle of the brands.)

Manufacturers' merchandising for their own brands will be compelled to trend away from excessive reliance on gimmicks, deals, contests, premiums—especially where these hypodermics do not really help to create a still-stronger brand image, do not create lasting customers, do not strengthen the presold status of the brand. It will become even less wise to sell a premium rather than the brand —to lean on the appeal of the premium rather than on the appeal of the *line* and the virtue of the *brand.*

Anything that takes away from brand-image building cuts into one's ability to compete against the distributor-controlled brands. The manufacturer's brand will have to be still more strongly presold. The manufacturer's brands must be presold so strongly that even a shift to a less desirable shelf position will not cut volume drastically —and this calls for creative brand-selling merchandising, not gimmick-y merchandising or merchandising via hypos! Too much merchandising contributes too little to long-term brand building. And too much merchandising is identical with that of the competing merchandise.

The trade franchise will wane in importance—the only sturdy support left to the manufacturer will be the consumer franchise inherent in a presold brand. In other words, as the trade franchise dwindles, the consumer franchise assumes larger stature. Merchandising must be conceived to this end.

The real story of the net-profit contribution to the retailer of the manufacturer's brand—where there is one!—will be spelled out for the trade and told time and time again. This is rarely done.

The disadvantages to the trade of the distributor-controlled label will be determined—and again, spelled out. For example, on their controlled brands, the trade has heavy financing, may have to carry large inventories, may have high advertising costs, may not achieve the turnover rate obtainable with manufacturers' presold brands, and so on.

The distributor-controlled brand is not all milk and honey—to the trade! But the trade tends to think so.

CHAPTER **14**

Cooperation and Joint Merchandising

In order more nearly to match size with size, it is entirely probable that we will be seeing more and more examples, in the near-term future, of joint merchandising by noncompetitive and even competitive manufacturers.

Example: Gulistan carpets and Ethan Allen furniture ran joint ads in the shelter magazines and cooperated promotionally. They are noncompetitive.

Another example: Three furniture manufacturers down South actually pooled their output into a combined sales and merchandising organization. Results included a more diversified grouping of furniture to show and sell. These three manufacturers had been competitive to a degree.

In Grand Rapids, two furniture manufacturers arranged for a "no-merger merger." The two companies are the well-known Imperial Furniture Company and the Grand Rapids Upholstering Company. Under the announced plan, these two manufacturers formed a business association designed to correlate sales and design functions. The national sales organization of Imperial will also represent the Grand Rapids Upholstering Company. And designing activities of the two companies will be correlated. However—and this is what makes this a no-merger merger—the two companies will retain their corporate identities and their new affiliation will not include any change in stock interest or ownership.

Such cooperation is not infrequent. Youngstown Kitchens and Tappan Stoves developed a joint arrangement of the same sort. Wagner Manufacturing Company and Glamur Products joined forces to introduce a wall-cleaning applicator. Glamur furnished the cleanser, Wagner the device. Out on the West Coast, Crown Zellerbach and Wilco Company joined forces in the merchandising, promotion, and advertising of Zee towels and Wilco window spray. And Vick's and DeVilbiss have cooperated on a sprayed medicament for colds. Bond Bread and Gerber baby products have joined in bringing out a bread for youngsters. These two are, of course, not exactly small companies, but if industrial giants join in merchandising then there is still more reason for medium-sized and smaller firms to do the same.

Actually, joint merchandising goes back many years. In the food field it has, of course, been quite common in a very simple form involving related-product promotions. But for the near-term future it is destined for more complicated corporate involvements and for considerable expansion in many nonfood classifications because it may offer a technique that will enable medium-sized manufacturers to obtain some of the benefits of large size and thus be better able to compete with giant manufacturers. It will also permit smaller manufacturers to achieve longer and more diversified lines—which is what is happening with the three furniture manufacturers mentioned earlier.

There is reason to believe that the day of the independent in all parts of our economy is waning—not disappearing, be it noted, but waning. More and more independents—manufacturers, wholesalers, retailers—will have to give up slices of their independence. This is obviously what happened to the independent merchant when he joined a voluntary chain or a cooperative. The voluntary or cooperative is spreading into drugstores, hard-goods stores, and many others and is destined to cover most independent retailers in most fields. Similarly, independent manufacturers and wholesalers may have to give up some of their independence by merging with competitors or noncompetitors in what are really no-merger mergers.

The grave problem of the medium-sized and smaller manufacturer —as was true of retailers in the same size bracket—is to develop a technique that will enable him to achieve the benefits of large size and still retain some of the basics of his independence. When he is absorbed by a giant corporation his independence exists only in theory, not in fact. Therefore, it is likely that independent manufacturers may develop what will really be their own form of voluntary chain and even their own form of cooperative, thus adapting the procedures used by independent retailers to their own requirements. As independent retailers accumulate strength through voluntary chains and similar procedures, giant wholesalers emerge, giant retailers become supercolossal, and giant manufacturing corporations sprawl all over the merchandise front—it becomes increasingly necessary for independent manufacturers to team up with one another in various forms of joint merchandising and in even broader areas of cooperation.

New forms of cooperation among independent merchants will come about, especially in retail fields where such cooperation has not been common. A decidedly interesting example of what some of the newer techniques of the independent retailer may involve is furnished by a suburban operation sponsored by three of Manhattan's famous specialty stores. The three stores are DePinna, high-fashion specialty operation; Georg Jensen, Inc., specializing in silver, china, crystal, furniture; F. A. O. Schwarz, billed as the world's largest toy store. These three merchants combined their forces when they ventured into suburban Westchester, New York. And they combined their forces in a highly unusual way. The three stores are housed in Eastchester, New York, in a 64,000-square-foot two-level building. Within the structure, the three merchants operate very much as might three families in a single dwelling. While each store has a separate entrance from the outside—on the interior they are interconnected. There are no interior doors or gates separating them! This is a real innovation.

Moreover, all customer facilities, and all receiving and other merchandising-handling facilities are used jointly by the three stores. This is another innovation. There is even a central switchboard serving the three stores! Within the building, each of the three maintains its distinct identity. There is no loss of character. Yet the merchandise groupings of the three stores have been subtly coordinated so as to complement one another. This, obviously, is still another innovation.

Basically, as already mentioned, the independent retailer has survived by giving up various degrees of his independence. He may not like to face up to this reality—but surely it cannot be denied that in a retail voluntary group, for example, the cooperating members have exchanged some degree of total independence for the security that comes from associated effort. This process, by which the independent gives up aspects of his independence, will continue. Certainly, if just a few years ago anyone had had the temerity to suggest that three staunch individual operations such as DePinna, Jensen, and Schwarz would ever merchandise in a single building in the manner I have sketched, he would have been termed a lunatic. Yet today these smart merchants have found a way to combine their investments and their merchandising without sacrificing an iota of their distinctive characteristics.

And this same process will apply to manufacturers and wholesalers as well as to retailers, especially in the area of joint merchandising.

CHAPTER **15**

Cooperative Advertising Reevaluated

Cooperative advertising is currently undergoing its first broad-scale reappraisal. It is being reevaluated by some manufacturers; it is being reevaluated by some wholesalers and other distributors; it is being reevaluated by a few retailers—particularly by a few giant retailers.

The reappraisal by several large retailers is particularly significant —for the very persuasive reason that, in some major industries, as much as 80 per cent of the cooperative advertising dollar paid out by manufacturers is credited to a small group of giant retailers. And it is these large retailers who tend either not to use the co-op dollar for advertising at all, or who take markups sometimes exceeding 100 per cent on the local rates they pay, or who use cooperative advertising in ads that are almost completely devoid of value to the manufacturer who foots the bill.

More of the co-op dollar allotted to large retailers goes into the cash-income till than of the co-op dollar allotted to the smaller retailers. Manufacturers are not eager to strengthen the treasury of giant retailers for a number of reasons, including the important reason that large retailers are tending strongly to the store-controlled brand—and a substantial part of the financing of private-brand promotion by retailers comes from the co-op allowance. Thus, manufacturers offering co-op to giant retailers are, in effect, underwriting their newest and most serious brand competitor.

This is a self-service, self-selection age. This setup demands a still greater degree of presell for manufacturers' brands. When co-op ad dollars are frittered way, the ad budget cannot achieve the required degree of presell. The demand for presell compels a restudy of *all* the innumerable nonadvertising charges that abound in the ad budget. This frequently includes co-op, since so often this allowance does not wind up as advertising.

We have more advertisers, more advertising in total, more media, higher advertising costs. More competition for the public's mind via advertising compels more effective employment of each advertising dollar. More often than otherwise, the co-op dollar is *not* effectively employed. When it is spent for advertising, the advertising tends to be not even third-rate. In some fields—food, for example—the major part of the co-op ad dollar never winds up as advertising; it is simply additional trade margin. And when it does wind up in omnibus price-list ads its degree of brand sell is almost nil.

As big retail accounts become bigger, the manufacturer's ad manager wants less and less to do with co-op decisions. He doesn't want to be responsible for losing a major account! The sales manager makes these major co-op decisions—one of the few cases in which one department makes a decision chargeable to another department. This is compelling the accounting department of some manufacturers to take a new look at co-op.

Manufacturers know that the co-op budget has become a fantastic catchall. If a list were compiled of all the charges that wind up in the co-op budget, it would be a yard long—and would be amusing if it were not so tragic. In brief, the co-op funds are used for all kinds of activities, few of which can be classified intelligently as advertising. Merchandise rebates, price reductions, tie-in deals, incentives to push slow-moving merchandise, free merchandise, gifts to buyers, and many other items unrelated to advertising are all charged to the co-op fund.

Manufacturers find that too much of the time of their salesmen; their sales, marketing, and merchandising executives; their sales department, home office, and branch staffs is taken up with co-op. The selling cost, the administration cost, the policing cost, the adjudication cost, the miscellaneous costs involved in co-op (entirely apart from the allowance itself) are staggering. If these costs were properly evaluated, it could very well be that our national co-op bill is not in the order of $2 billion as generally estimated—but maybe nearer $4 billion!

The percentage of the total ad budget snared by co-op has reached a point in a number of industries where it simply cannot go higher without endangering the entire brand-selling program. For example, in auto tires fully 40 per cent of the total ad budget goes for co-op. In shoes, the figure is probably around 32 per cent—ditto for major appliances. Since the percentage figure cannot go much higher but retail pressure to send it higher is relentless, manufacturers are compelled to turn elsewhere to achieve more effective selling and more satisfactory trade relations.

Theoretically, cooperative advertising is simply loaded down with benefits to the manufacturer. In actual practice, cooperative advertising seldom returns to the manufacturer, dollar for dollar, anything remotely resembling what the manufacturer's advertising dollar can buy when it is spent completely under his control.

In considering theory versus practice in cooperative advertising, it is vitally necessary to bear in mind that, with the majority of manufacturers, from 10 to 20 per cent of their retail customers account for from 80 to 90 per cent of the cooperative advertising dollar. This is a fundamental of enormous importance because the cooperative advertising dollar may be a sound investment when it goes to rank-and-file dealers—although even here it is seldom as well invested as the advertising dollar fully controlled by the manufacturer. However, when the cooperative advertising dollar lines up with the giant retailer—and this, of course, is where by far the lion's share of the cooperative advertising dollar winds up—its effective employment is at an all-time low and is constantly making new lows.

Therefore, viewing cooperative advertising theory and cooperative advertising practice primarily from the standpoint of what happens when manufacturers extend the cooperative advertising allowance to the *giant* retailer, here is what we discover:

1. Cooperative advertising *presumably* offers the manufacturer lower-cost advertising. Originally this was one of its great theoretical advantages. With respect to newspaper advertising in particular, the manufacturer ostensibly would buy newspaper linage at a local rate not available to the national manufacturer. So far as the giant retailer is concerned, this advantage is rarely obtained today. As matters now exist in more cases than otherwise, local newspaper linage

bought cooperatively with the giant retailer has a total cost that is *higher* than the national rate. This is equally true with respect to radio and television time.

This was true when the retailer simply took a markup on the local rate—and, of course, it is rare that giant retailers do not take this markup, which has been known to exceed 100 per cent of the giant retailer's actual local rate. It has become increasingly true since the giant retailer has added production costs and other charges. Indeed, right here is the reason that so many giant retailers find that their advertising department is their most profitable single department. Certainly the argument that co-op doubles the manufacturer's ad dollar has no basis at all with respect to giant retailers.

2. In theory, cooperative advertising provides an automatic control of expenditures—with the retailer's 50 per cent involvement functioning as a sort of automatic governor. It was also reasoned that, since the cooperative advertising allowance is usually premised on a fixed percentage of purchases, the cooperative advertising budget would follow the actual sales curve more closely than would be the case with any other type of advertising program.

In practice—and with particular respect to the giant retailer about whom we are talking—that 50 per cent stake tends to be pure myth. By and large, it is entirely correct to say that the giant retailer has no stake whatsoever in the space he buys for cooperative advertising. Indeed, since the giant retailer more often than not makes *a rather handsome net profit* on cooperative advertising, instead of there being an automatic safety valve on the amount spent, there is actually a *strong incentive* for him to ignore many, if not most, sane limitations in cooperative advertising expenditures! The theoretical advantage of automatic control of expenditures simply doesn't exist where the giant retailer is involved. If anything, the co-op allowance automatically results in a discouraging loss of control of expenditures.

3. Theoretically, the cooperative advertising allowance wins an extra degree of cooperation from the retailer. This extra degree of cooperation presumably stems from the fact that the dealer's interest in a brand bears some relationship to his advertising investment in it. He presumably gives the line sponsored by cooperative advertising extra sales attention, extra merchandising cooperation, extra promotional push—because he has made an investment of his own money.

It has even been said that the co-op advertising allowance almost obligates the retailer to cooperate—and there have even been assertions that it wins extra cooperation from salespeople.

Surely, it is obvious that *not one* of these theoretical advantages exists in fact where the giant retailer is concerned. Some of these theoretical advantages might exist if the giant retailer were *really* matching advertising dollars with the manufacturer. But where the giant retailer has little or no actual share in the cooperative advertising cost—and we have already made it plain that this is the typical situation—clearly the co-op allowance does not stimulate the giant retailer's interest in the manufacturer's brand or merchandising or promotional cooperation.

4. In theory, the co-op allowance brings about a closer relationship between the retailer and the manufacturer. This should reduce dealer turnover, make the retailer a partner in the success of the manufacturer, help keep competition out of the store. In practice—again thinking primarily of the giant retailer—these theoretical advantages rarely exist in day-to-day practice. As a matter of fact, it may be stated categorically that, so far as the giant retailer is concerned, good-will relations with manufacturers play an insignificant role.

Moreover, all of these specific presumed advantages of the co-op ad allowance are really premised on the rather naïve assumption that the manufacturer who offers co-op is offering something that his competition does *not* extend to the same giant retailers. This, of course, is entirely nonsensical—there are precious few, if any, fields in which only one manufacturer is offering a cooperative advertising allowance.

5. Theoretically, cooperative advertising allowances win local advertising that enjoys a high readership. In practice, of course, where the cooperative advertising dollar winds up in the purchase of space or time, the advertising itself tends to be of an exceedingly low caliber, having practically no relationship to modern professional advertising concepts and standards. This is almost totally true of cooperative advertising run by giant retailers, which is largely omnibus advertising featuring prices.

6. Again in theory, it is reasoned that the co-op ad dollar will result in copy better suited and better timed to fit local conditions,

and that it will have all of the presumed virtues of retail advertising. In connection with the last point, the retailer likes to say that national advertising merely develops interest, but that retail advertising *sells*. Again referring to the retail advertising of our giant retailers, it can hardly be debated that there is no form of advertising that does a *poorer* job of selling than the current advertising of by far the majority of our giant retailers.

7. Once more in theory, it is claimed that the investment of the co-op ad dollar is more closely in tune with product distribution. Inasmuch as most large manufacturers have broad distribution these days, and inasmuch as the giant retailer tends to invest the co-op dollar where he chooses, this is another theory that seldom exists in actual practice.

8. Then there is the theory that under a cooperative advertising plan a manufacturer gets a better media selection. If this theory ever had any validity, it certainly has no validity today, in so far as the giant retailer is concerned. Media selection by the giant retailer is done on a basis that will benefit the retailer—not the manufacturer —and, as a consequence, the co-op dollar too often winds up in a media program that the manufacturer himself would never buy.

There are a number of other theoretical advantages with respect to the co-op advertising allowance. But when each and every one is related to existing circumstances in the market place—and with particular reference to the giant retailer—they simply have no basis in workaday fact.

There are other reasons for concluding that cooperative advertising requires reappraisal. They include the following:

• Proper controls are often lacking. This includes checking of bills.

• Maintaining legal impartiality is extremely difficult.

• The cooperative advertising budget tends to skyrocket under pressure.

• Control of copy and insertion dates is a headache.

• Proof of performance is more and more difficult to obtain.

• A vast amount of correspondence, much of it touchy, is necessary to secure tear sheets and correct invoice.

• It requires too much time by both home office and field organization.

• Good trade relationships are often disrupted. Ill will is engendered between manufacturer and nonadvertising dealers.

- Establishing a program equitable to large and small dealers is difficult.
- Dealers are encouraged to shop around for the best deal.
- Even when used by dealers, cooperative advertising lacks consistency of amount and application. Coordination of program is practically impossible.
- Coordination with factory's national advertising is seldom feasible. There is no consistency in the co-op program run by giant retailers.
- Manufacturers' salesmen sell advertising allowance instead of brand.
- It is looked upon as an extra rebate rather than as advertising. It becomes part of the price. It tends to break down the price structure.
- Government regulations and restrictions on cooperative advertising are cumbersome and complex. Dealers tend to try to obtain exceptions which cannot be allowed.
- It is not adapted to building prestige for line. Brand names are lost in omnibus co-op ads and in other co-op ads too.
- Many stores do not use the cooperative allowance, which unbalances the budget.
- It makes for lack of uniform coverage.
- It is combined with other products in dealer's advertising in a hurtful way.
- It does more for the store than it does for the product.
- The co-op allowance is likely to be destructive to the maintenance of a sound price policy.
- Factory-suggested copy is seldom used by giant retailers.
- Co-op ads lack campaign continuity.
- Copy is seldom up to national advertising standards. Moreover, the manufacturer receives disproportional identification in space used; the dealer's name is likely to dominate.

These, then, are the major differences between theory and fact with respect to cooperative advertising. And facts such as these are forming the basis of the reappraisal that will take place over the next few years. It is especially interesting to note that cooperative advertising has been outlawed by several associations of manufacturers in the vast garment trades, where co-op has been an unmitigated evil. If co-op can be halted here, there is reason to believe that it will be curtailed or eliminated by more and more food processors, producers of drugs and cosmetics, appliance makers, and other manufacturers.

Other allowances may take its place. But it is possible that these other allowances will not come out of the manufacturers' advertising budget and will make a more discernible contribution to increased sales at a profit.

CHAPTER 16

Diminishing Returns from Open Display

A shopper recently reported looking for a certain cosmetic brand in a modern self-service-type drug chain outlet. She knew the fixture in which this cosmetic brand is displayed. Yet she had to walk around the cosmetic counter *twice* before she could spot it!

Remember—she was looking for this brand; she had a clear mental picture of the specific fixture. Yet she walked right by it her first trip around. The reason? The fixture was so hidden by other merchandise that it was almost buried from sight.

We have a good deal of jungle merchandising. In some food supers the shopper is greeted with a "bedlam" of merchandise on open display. The eye is constantly distracted; the mind is bewildered. There is neither a visual resting point nor an interrupting note—it is one grand shout. In some department stores, brands are so numerous in some classifications and assortments so gigantic that the shopper gets into a hopeless, bewildered frame of mind. Nor is this condition helped by salespeople who know too little about the respective merits of the various brands and models on sale.

It used to be said, back in the days of glass-counter fixturing, that the competent salesperson never showed more than *three* models or price lines at one time. This was almost a universal rule of floor selling—and it was a sound rule. (It still is.) It focused the shopper's attention on a maximum of three buying potentialities—which avoids shopper confusion due to being shown too much at one time. But in modern self-service and self-selection open display the shopper is being shown four, six, sometimes a dozen or more price lines or models. Is this too much of a good thing? Can *too much* merchandise, especially with respect to brand duplication and model multiplicity, be shown—to the point where the shopper finds it increasingly difficult to make up her mind?

Is some open display of merchandise showing so much variety that the shopper is given, not a variety of reasons for *buying*, but a variety of reasons for *delaying* a buying decision?

And are these questions especially pertinent when we consider the absence or paucity of salespeople in self-service and self-selection retailing as well as the continuing decline in the selling abilities of present-day floor personnel?

Consider these additional questions with respect to the fundamentals of modern shopping.

• The shopper is faced with open displays of brands that tend to be quite similar—for competing merchandise is becoming increasingly similar. It would be difficult to make a decision if there were major and obvious differences in merchandise. But doesn't it stand to reason that enormous displays of *similar* merchandise simply pile confusion on top of confusion?

• The shopper is compelled, for a variety of reasons, to shop faster, ever faster. Can she shop faster when faced with gigantic open displays of duplicated merchandise—duplicated models, sizes, price lines?

• The shopper shops more impulsively for an ever-growing list of merchandise classifications. But isn't the impulsiveness of the shopper watered down when too much merchandise on display makes it difficult for her to make a buying decision?

• The shopper tends to buy one known brand or another in many merchandise classifications. When one brand was truly dominant, its display alongside competing brands didn't confuse her particularly. But now that so many merchandise classifications are populated with three, five, and more strong brands—none with striking points of superiority—isn't the shopping fluidity that should come with willingness to take one known brand or another dammed up by the open display of too many known brands?

The open display of merchandise—in addition to new fixtures that make it possible to show as much as 40 per cent more merchandise—has unquestionably worked selling magic. But this procedure—like any business procedure—has an optimum point, a point of maximum return, *a point of diminishing returns.* That point has been passed by some mass outlets and is being rapidly approached by many others.

This is not to argue for a return to glass showcases, for a return to merchandise displays involving a slash of from 25 to 40 per cent on the merchandise openly displayed. Not at all. But the logic of the situation suggests that by 1965 the moment will have arrived when many mass retailers will want to reassess their utilization of the basic concept of open display of merchandise.

In doing this, it would appear to be important for retail executives not to consult their own preferences and prejudices, not to make decisions based on opinion, but rather *to study the shopper.*

Some manufacturers also may want to conduct these shopper studies. In studying the shopper, it would be highly advisable to avoid asking for her opinions. Her opinions are apt to be no more reliable than the opinions of store personnel.

A modern study is called for—a study of what the shopper does or does not do—*right in the store,* right in front of the huge merchandise displays. It calls for controlled observation by trained research personnel.

How many customers walk up to certain merchandise displays—look—and then walk away without even picking up a single item? How many customers walk up to certain merchandise displays, pick up one item, put it down—and walk away without making a purchase? How many pick up two items, three items, four items—and walk away without making a purchase? Most mass retailers are very much concerned with "walk-outs," the customer who comes in and then walks out without having made a single purchase. But considerably more important to most mass retailers (and to manufacturers) is the shopper who might be called the "walk-away" customer. She walks away from too many merchandise displays, in front of which she has momentarily or even longer, planted herself. She represents a huge loss in potential volume; she is responsible for the failure of the average sales ticket to keep pace with the increase in inventory by merchandise category. And she lessens the return on the manufacturer's brand promotion.

It has been said in retailing for years that in *some* stores only half the customers who enter make a purchase—and of these, only half buy nearly as much as they either set out to buy or are prepared to buy. Presumably, the open display of merchandise has tended to make these figures more palatable to mass retailers—and, indeed, this is unquestionably so.

But now, here and there, it is not unlikely that excessive display of duplicated merchandise brands, models, and price lines is bringing back the very condition that open display sought to eliminate. And these perplexing, confusing displays of enormous varieties of merchandise may even be resulting in more harm to the average sale than was true of the old-fashioned glass showchase.

Even in an age of leisurely shopping, merchandise displays made ponderous by excessive duplications would deter the shopper. In this age of breakneck shopping, this type of merchandise display works contrary to the inclinations, habits, preferences, requirements of the shopper. Too much duplicated merchandise out on open display can be at least as destructive of volume as too little.

The misery of choice offered shoppers by a jungle of merchandise is at least one cause of miserable average tickets and miserable sales per square foot. Retailers and manufacturers will study this situation by 1965 and come up with figures that might win better inventories, better display, better merchandising and promotion.

CHAPTER 17

Factory Financing of Dealer Inventory

Financial authorities appear to agree that so long as our economy moves to higher levels, or even so long as it remains on a high plateau, we will be faced with tight-money conditions more often than otherwise.

As a consequence, it appears likely that a spreading variety of industries will turn to various forms of factory financing of the dealer's inventory. This could turn out to be a merchandising development of great importance for the very simple reason that the manufacturer best able to finance his dealers will enjoy a distinct competitive edge. At the moment, factory financing is considered to be a big-ticket program, but tight money may encourage its spread into merchandise lines that are far removed from the big-ticket classification.

In any event, it would be well for merchandise executives in many classifications to study carefully what is happening in TV appliances. It might also be noted that what has developed in TV appliances was unquestionably stimulated by related credit developments in automobiles, where each of the Big Three now have financing subsidiaries.

In TV appliances, the program is generally called "floor-plan credit." However, it is not limited to dealer floor stock; it includes total dealer inventory. Under this factory-financing program, the general procedure is somewhat as follows:

1. When a dealer orders from a distributor, the dealer makes a 10 per cent down payment.

2. As the inventory is sold, piece by piece, the dealer must pay for it.

3. Within ninety days, sold or not, full payment must be made by the dealer.

4. The dealer really does not own the inventory. He does not own it until he both sells and pays for it. (And the law makes it a felony if the dealer makes a sale and does not remit promptly.)

5. The usual interest charge is 1½ per cent for the ninety-day term.

6. Factory, distributor, and dealer each pay ½ per cent. Frequently the distributor assumes the dealer's contribution—thus the distributor offers "free" financing to the dealer.

7. If in ninety days the inventory is not moved, the dealer renegotiates the loan, usually by making another 10 per cent payment and paying ½ per cent on the outstanding balance.

8. Under this plan, a dealer usually can obtain two to three times the credit that would be available from a distributor on open account. (Therefore, a dealer buying three lines may be able to acquire six times and even nine times the inventory available on open account.)

9. When a dealer places a larger order he may obtain a larger discount.

10. The plan may also tie a dealer closer to a distributor.

11. The distributor's salesman checks the dealer's inventory to determine whether all sold merchandise has been reported. (This may be a weak link because salesmen notoriously hate to report any delinquency by their accounts.)

12. If the dealer fails with merchandise bought on account, the distributor becomes simply another creditor. But under this plan, the distributor simply replevins the inventory.

13. It tends to discourage the dealer from selling merchandise bought on open account and using that money to pay another distributor.

In TV appliances, the major corporations now have financing subsidiaries. This includes RCA-Victor, RCA-Whirlpool, Frigidaire, General Electric, Westinghouse, Admiral, Philco, Kelvinator, Norge. It is obvious that when one manufacturer adopts a program of this kind, competitors are compelled to follow suit.

It should be pointed out that with so many manufacturers developing gigantic lines, thoroughly diversified, this type of financing program could be a potent factor in turning dealers into *one-line dealers*. It should also be pointed out that this financing plan brings manufacturers still closer to *taking over* the total retail function. And that may ultimately encourage still more manufacturers to go into retailing themselves, or to make still closer affiliations which will bring both distributors or wholesalers and retailers under one corporate roof!

It is possible that the expansion of this concept will continue to take place primarily in big-ticket merchandise—perhaps it will be adapted to the requirements of classifications such as furniture and rugs. But by 1965, factory financing of the inventory distributors and of dealers will spread to many other classifications for the reasons already listed plus one more—the enormous spread of credit retailing. Practically all retailers are offering credit—and this means they will have a growing need for factory financing.

It is significant to note that the president of a large discount chain suggested that small- or medium-sized manufacturers may come together to set up a credit-factoring service for their retail accounts. He said that this would mean much more to the dealers than deals or cooperative advertising allowances!

CHAPTER 18

Sophisticated Shoppers
and the Discretionary Dollar

It would be idiotic to take the position that *all* shoppers—or even a simple majority of all shoppers—are now highly sophisticated. But it would be equally wrong to deny that (1) a *substantial* and rapidly growing *percentage* of shoppers is composed of much more sophisticated shoppers than many in merchandising suspect; and (2) it is these very shoppers who control the *major part* of this nation's total *discretionary dollar*. This is the very dollar for which most merchandisers are competing.

Merchandisers have been misled by the false doctrine that the shopper has a twelve-year-old mind. This was and is a false doctrine. The shopper with the bulk of the discretionary dollars shapes up as above average in intelligence and therefore in sophistication. After all, sophistication is really a compound of native intelligence, education, observation, and experience.

If more manufacturers were keenly cognizant of the firm control on the discretionary dollar by sophisticated shoppers, surely we would not have so many advertising programs keyed to low-intelligence levels. Neither would we have so many merchandising programs obviously aimed *down* to even lower levels of intelligence. For example, most consumer contests are keyed to the lowest intellectual levels. How many sophisticated shoppers will enter a contest asking for 25 words on the subject: "I like Blank's because"? How many sophisticated shoppers will enter *any* kind of contest? Do you? Do members of your family? Isn't it time consumer contests were devised to appeal to a level of intelligence, not to say of sophistication, somewhat above that of a moron?

Or consider the premium promotion. For how long do merchandisers believe they can play fast and loose with their premium programs—without ultimately losing many of their more desirable shoppers? Example: A study covering 50 premium offers disclosed that the declared value of the 50 premiums was, *in every instance,* in excess of the price at which the item could actually be bought at retail! (Who is fooling whom?) A number of the premiums were of poor value, many of questionable value. The net finding in this study is that the self-liquidating premium may be self-liquidating for the promoter—but for the shopper, as a retail value, it is by no means self-liquidating. It may, however, tend to liquidate the good will of the brand with intelligent shoppers. Obviously, it hardly enhances the brand image.

Consumer contests and premium promotions are plumbing an intellectual *low.* The shopper is reaching new *heights* of shopping sophistication.

Many, if not most, premium programs and contest programs wind up with their primary appeal (if not their exclusive appeal) to that part of our population with the lowest income, the lowest educational standards, and the lowest brand loyalty. Maybe this suits the strategy of these merchandisers. But if their market is dominated by, or importantly influenced by, the sophisticated shopper—then who is fooling whom?

This applies equally well to consumer deals. Some deals involving "3 for 00 cents" and "5 for 00 cents" do not represent extra value at all—or they represent such a tiny extra value as to be misleading. Maybe the shopper is not too good at rapid arithmetic—but this is hardly something to bank on where the sophisticated shopper is concerned. Deals should be reevaluated with respect to their appeal to a more sophisticated shopper. (In this connection it should be noted that for years Nielsen has pointed out that deals seldom create new consumers—they simply switch customers temporarily.)

We have a whole new type of shopper—the customer who shops

for deals. The deal *shopper* tends to be smarter, more sophisticated, than some deal *planners*. It's high time that merchandisers begin to catch up.

It was sophisticated shoppers who concluded that the trade-in—excluding perhaps the auto trade-in—was strictly for the birds. So we have seen a sharp drift away from the trade-in in a number of merchandise classifications. Even in autos, there are shoppers who are now aware that they may do better if they sell the old car themselves (or keep it as a second car) and then bargain with the new-car dealer on the basis of a "no-trade" deal.

There is little reason to question that brand loyalty is at an all-time low. Is this due to shopper *ignorance*—or to shopper *sophistication?*

Clearly, the sophisticated shopper recognizes that there is too little difference of importance between competing brands in too many merchandise classifications. So—since she is smart enough to comprehend this, she moves quite freely from one brand to another. Ignorant shoppers buy "chop" marks. Informed shoppers buy value.

Is this true only of staples, only of food? Not at all. Look into any home with three radios, two TV sets, two or more room air conditioners. Note the different brands that are represented in each home in these duplicated items. When merchandising programs are premised on the assumption that the shopper can be persuaded to strong brand loyalty by minor or even nonexistent features—who is fooling whom?

Anyone in doubt about the mounting degree of shopper sophistication would do well to get a Sears catalogue of 1951 and one of 1961. Compare the two—and note the enormous change in the degree of sophisticated appeal that has occurred over the short span of a single decade! Here is a remarkable living record of brilliant recognition by a great merchandising organization of the growing sophistication of the shopper in intelligence, in taste, in culture—in all of those factors that total up to sophistication.

This is not to say that Barnum's famous dictum no longer has any application whatsoever. We are by no means a nation of sophisticates. We still have millions who are suckers as Barnum defined a sucker. But a sucker is no longer born every minute. And a sucker no longer comes into shopping adulthood every minute. Maybe the rate is now a sucker every two minutes—or better still, every three minutes. Even the lower rate, statistically, in a nation of 175 million, represents a gigantic change in shopper sophistication.

But the important point for merchandising men is that shopper sophistication is, today, not merely marching ahead—it is leaping ahead. It is leaping ahead both qualitatively and quantitatively. It is in a stage of explosive growth.

Merchandising men will be hard pressed to match shopper sophistication with *sophisticated merchandising programs*—even if they are fully aware of this remarkable change in our society. Where this awareness does not exist, merchandising sophistication will fall further and further behind shopper sophistication—and that has been, is currently, and will be damaging to volume and profit.

We have larger and larger numbers of our "shopulation" with higher education. We have larger and larger numbers who continue to improve their minds. (A large book publisher recently decided he might appeal to this self-improvement trend by reprinting a series of self-help volumes that achieved enormous popularity in the 1920s. After reviewing them, he decided that today's market would consider these tomes childish!)

Talk to magazine editors—they are doing a vastly better job of reflecting changing social mores than are the TV networks. The magazine editors know that their audiences are more sophisticated —in the broader sense of the word—than were their audiences of even ten years ago. And they look ahead to still more rapid advances in culture by still more of our people in the near-term future.

Do not miss the significance of the editorial changes in *Life*. The reception *Life* has won for its magnificent presentations of art and for its serious discussions of vital subjects—both total departures from its original editorial policy of pictures almost exclusively (sex, blood, and news)—reflect the smart awareness of its editors of vast changes in the degree of sophistication among its millions of readers. Some of *Life's* recent editorial features would have been considered highbrow by *Harper's* years ago!

Even Papa has become a pretty good shopper in his own right. The food super no longer considers him to be quite the sucker he was once found to be. In the big-ticket lines, he is at least as shrewd a buyer as his spouse—and, perhaps more often than otherwise, a shrewder shopper. And his resistance to style change in his apparel is clearly waning.

Great segments of our "shopulation" for generations lagged behind the better living offered by scientific advances. Today great segments of the public accept the newest scientific advances *as fast as they come out of the laboratory*. Tomorrow scientific horizons may not expand as rapidly as the willingness of the sophisticated shopper to accept the bounties of science!

Part of the great move toward more sophisticated living is the now-emerging trend toward ownership of two homes. A two-car nation is now determined to become a two-home nation. We will have 2 million two-home families faster than we acquired 2 million two-car families. How many merchandisers of everything that goes into the home are specifically planning right now for the sophisticated two-home family?

It is difficult to realize that less than twenty years ago the two-bathroom home was pretty rare. Today it is commonplace. Tomorrow the three-bathroom home will be commonplace. Even more fascinating is the probability that the *two-kitchen home* is about to emerge! It will be an outgrowth of the home bar, of the recreation room and family room, and of cook-outs. Currently, the refrigerator manufacturers have discovered that a remarkable number of owners of old refrigerators do not want to trade them in—these old refrigerators are kept as the nucleus of what is really a second kitchen. Would a two-kitchen home exist in a society that was not sufficiently sophisticated to accept such a concept?

The indoor swimming pool is undoubtedly the next great development in swimming pools. Several developers of moderately priced homes are already installing indoor swimming pools. (The Romans had them several thousand years ago—with heated water, too. Were those Romans an unsophisticated people?)

Take food. When instant coffee was introduced, our psychological experts predicted it would meet with great housewife resistance. Why? Because the housewife who did not brew coffee by traditional techniques would have a guilt complex!

But the guilt complex varies in accordance with the sophistication of a people! The kitchen techniques that might have left the housewife circa 1920 thoroughly shaken with guilt—all these will bounce harmlessly off the conscious and the subconscious of the more sophisticated housewife of 1960–1965.

Surely the remarkable growth of the convenience foods, which followed the introduction of instant coffee, proves this point. The convenience foods clearly would have sent the guilt-ridden housewife of the first decades of this century into a psychological tailspin. But, because she has achieved a remarkable new degree of sophistication, she accepted the convenience foods during the single decade 1950–1960 at a pace that was completely fantastic.

The remarkable expansion of the gourmet food market is another case in point. Among an unsophisticated people, there is a fearful resistance to any change in what is always, in these nations, an extremely limited national diet. The more sophisticated a people, the more they welcome dietary changes.

Our kaleidoscopic changes in food over the last decade clearly mirror a more mature and a more sophisticated society. And the food industry had better prepare for an even faster pace of change in food tastes and habits over the next few years.

In drugs and health aids we have many examples of products that actually could not be marketed at all in the first two or three decades of the century, but which are now mass-marketed. These range from sanitary napkins to drugs involving the menstrual and menopause functions. (Tranquilizer pills achieved a gigantic volume in one-tenth the time required to develop a great market for aspirin!)

The hearing aid could not be profitably exploited over radio twenty years ago. Today these devices are featured in radio commercials. A sophisticated people drops taboos—it is a mark of sophistication.

In proprietary medicines it has been said for generations that "people buy cures, not preventives." That was true of an unsophisticated people. But sophisticates buy many medical preventives today. They have been educated to visit the doctor and the dentist for preventive check-ups. (We brought our cars in for check-ups before we brought ourselves in for check-ups.) Sophistication is the answer.

It was traditional for the public to resist new drugs, as the old-time doctors will testify. But today the proudest boast of a patient is: "My doctor said this is the first prescription he has made out for this drug —it is the very latest thing." In cosmetics it took years and years to put over rouge and lipstick with masses of women. But eye make-up —which traditionally was strictly for "bold" women and actresses— has been put over in just a couple of years.

Yes—a sophisticated public is more open to buy new concepts, new products, new styles. Remember when Lucky Strike finally dared to advertise: "Blow some my way"? Now the liquor industry is moving toward women in its advertising. Sophistication!

Status symbols will not only become more sophisticated—but they will change more rapidly. Even business tycoons may eventually become sufficiently sophisticated to give up their black Cadillacs!

The blue-collar worker is superseding the blue-denim worker. Common labor is disappearing. This is the age of automation—of electronic data processing—of instantaneous communication—of space travel. A society of scientists and technicians, as Russia is now finding out, is a sophisticated society with wants that cannot for long be suppressed. New levels of high education for more people will demand from merchandisers more competition by *innovation*—less competition by *imitation!*

The whole *quality* of American life is to be remarkably *upgraded* over the next very few years. This means not only a spreading market for higher price lines (as evidenced by the great trend toward upping price lines by department stores, variety chains, drug chains, even by the food chains), but it means an upgrading in *taste* that will demand from manufacturers still greater degrees of good taste in design. It means also a stronger demand on manufacturers for better quality, better quality control. An intelligent, sophisticated people is less easily misled—and quicker to react when it has been misled.

An unsophisticated people stayed close to the home hearth. People stayed close to the *same* home hearth for decades. Now our people are fantastically mobile—and their mobility will accelerate. Everybody moves about; everybody travels. The big market for new homes even now is tending to be among those who already own a home—a totally new phenomenon in the home real estate market.

It has been postulated that the "high mobiles" are the pace setters in the acceptance of new products, new services, new ideas, new habits, new status symbols. The "high mobile" is another term for the sophisticated discretionary shopper who is the most mobile of our total population.

Even our leisure habits are becoming more adult, more responsible, more sober; they reflect a higher degree of sophistication. Spending for leisure and for recreation involves a huge list of sober items, as well as the nonsensical—and the proportion of the nonsensical is clearly dropping.

New types of recreational centers will open up—and will leave an impact on merchandising. The marina has already done that; it is a big new outlet for innumerable new items. The modern bowling establishment is newer and is growing at a fantastic pace. It, too, will become a big new type of retail outlet. (Decades ago "nice" women would not be seen in a bowling alley. Today, the magnificent new bowling establishments with their fascinating services are an accurate reflection of the requirements of a more sophisticated people.)

The market basket of the sophisticated discretionary shopper is totally different from the one measured by the Census Bureau and it has not been measured by anybody. Yet it is this market basket that represents the target for merchandisers of all but the most prosaic staples. (Even staples are being merchandised in attractive gift set-ups to appeal to the sophisticated gift buyer.) It happens to be the market offering the greatest growth potentials, the greatest net-profit potentials.

Here is the great market for the near-term as well as for the long-term future. Take good aim at it!

CHAPTER 19

Giant Wholesaling to Match
Giant Retailing

The food wholesaler has gone through a total revolution. This includes the unique cost-plus food wholesaler, the cash-and-carry food wholesaler, the wholesaler operating a voluntary group of retailers, and the wholesaler tied up with a cooperative retail group. What has happened with the food wholesaler, step by step, will happen with the drug wholesaler, with the hardware wholesaler, and with other wholesalers and so-called "distributors" of many types.

Giant retailing must be matched by giant wholesaling—the one must produce the other. As this happens, the merchandising plans of manufacturers must reflect the mounting control over wholesaling of a very small group of giant wholesalers—just as giant retailing has compelled merchandising adjustments by manufacturers.

The giant wholesaler in nonfood fields will not only go into manufacturing, he will also develop his own advertised brands, as the IGA (Independent Grocers' Association) has done in food. He will, therefore, be both an outlet for and a competitor of the manufacturer. Giant retailers will also use the wholesaler in various ways—there is a definite trend in this direction.

The rack jobber is, of course, a wholesaler. The leased-department operator is really also a wholesaler. Both the rack jobber and the leased-department operator will continue to move into new merchandise classifications.

The wholesaler has proved his ability to survive—time and again. In one field after another, the bell has been tolled for him, but he just hasn't heard it. He has survived, of course, solely because he performs a function that few manufacturers or retailers are able *completely* to duplicate on a sound cost basis. Moreover, the wholesaler has been able to change his spots—to conform to new requirements.

An interesting example of new wholesaling concepts comes out of the housewares and hardware fields and is illustrative of what will happen to still other types of wholesalers. This example concerns Liberty Distributors, a housewares and hardware promotional organization. Founded by William George Steltz, Sr., late president of Supplee-Biddle-Steltz Company, the organization originally comprised 6 wholesalers. It now takes in some 25 wholesalers covering the nation and achieved a $300 million turnover in 1960. This figure may hit $400 million by 1965. There are an estimated 34,000 hardware stores throughout the nation, and Liberty Distributors sell some 20,000 of them, in addition to lumber and building-supply houses, variety stores, and auto accessory chains. In addition to cooperative buying, Liberty Distributors draws up merchandising and promotional programs from headquarters. Three nationally promoted private brands have been developed by Liberty: Dainty Maid for electrics and certain other housewares; Trustworthy for hand and power tools and lawn and garden equipment; Sportmaster for athletic equipment. Another fast-growing wholesaler in comparable fields is Ace Hardware Corporation.

Part of the booming growth of these wholesalers can be accredited to the fact that, as wholesalers, they act as superorganizers. They supply a constant flow of products and massive dissemination of industry news which succeeds in giving the retailer a firm foothold in an ever-shifting field. In return for allegiance, he not only receives goods at a cost he could not otherwise swing unless he were a chain store, he also receives a selling plan impregnated with merchandising know-how. The little hardware-housewares dealer is not so little any more. He is becoming somewhat of a force in the retail world, thanks to the profitable and expanding influence of his champions, the wholesale buying groups.

Originally conceived to give the relatively small dealer a chance to meet the catalogue chains on a competitive basis, the wholesalers now also serve to assist him in meeting competition from discount operations as well as the omnipresent department stores.

That the wholesale buying groups continue to grow is due to the simple fact that it is increasingly difficult for an independent hardware dealer to operate at a profit. The vast product coverage required by a hardware-store operation plus the need for a sharp pricing system are primary problems. However, a retailer member of a purchasing group receives savings from bulk buying and thus can fight fire with fire.

The remarkable changes that have been made by the tobacco jobbers offer one more illustration of the wholesaler's ability, not merely to survive, but to grow. The tobacco and candy jobber is gradually moving toward full-line distribution in many areas, and is becoming increasingly important in the home-goods fields.

Typical of the phenomenal growth experienced by these former cigar-cigarette wholesalers is Mutual Merchandising Cooperative, Inc. (MMC). This cooperative buying and merchandising organization had 111 members whose combined volume exceeded $600 million in 1960. It may reach $750 million by 1965.

In 1960, MMC was doing a $10 million volume (at suppliers' selling price) in such "nonsmoking" items as clocks, radios, dinnerware and silverware sets, lamps, plastic accessories, and some furniture. Housewares accounted for approximately 24 per cent of the larger-ticket, general-line goods sold through Mutual wholesalers. Some $42 million of Mutual members' annual volume was accounted for by general-line merchandise in 1960. These wholesalers, in 1960, were servicing some 250,000 retailers of all types throughout the nation. Included among Mutual retailers are drug and grocery chains, stationery and tobacco shops, supermarkets, variety and general stores.

The dominant role being played by tobacco jobbers in the home-furnishings field is no accident. Surveys disclosed that only one of four tobacco jobbers was showing a profit. Caught in the cost-and-profit squeeze, they were forced to seek additional lines. Mutual's New York resident buying office has expanded into furniture, including occasional pieces, lawn and nursery items, and unpainted furniture. Lamps and similar accessories also account for a substantial share of over-all volume.

Although Mutual members for the most part concentrate upon name brands, they also are able to offer dealers specially packed private labels in sunglasses, men's socks, playing cards, and hosiery. Usually, these carry MMC's Harmony brand label.

Merchandise handled by Mutual wholesalers is selected by a committee which meets four or five times each year. Members inspect, evaluate, and select the items to be carried, after they have been recommended by the group's buying office. Items are chosen on the basis of popular price levels, packaging, potential for rapid turnover, minimum requirement for counter space, and impulse-buying appeal. Shipments are made by manufacturers direct to Mutual members' warehouses, since all are full-service wholesalers. Mutual, however, provides for its members complete merchandising and promotional services.

This "heads-up" attitude on the part of the wholesaler has put him very prominently back into the distributor picture. As a result, thousands of multiunit retailers are buying a major share of their merchandise, not directly from the manufacturer, but from the low-cost wholesaler. Lower prices aren't the only reason. There are store-planning and financing services, preprint order-buying, coordinated promotion and advertising, store accounting facilities and store supervision, and training programs for personnel.

The very retail giants who were apparently destined to choke the wholesaler out of existence are now feeding his growth. Take the development of nonfoods in big supermarket chains. It would hardly have got off the ground without the rack jobber. Take the development of catalogue selling by non-mail-order chains. In many cases the catalogue list is serviced by local wholesalers. And in recent years, any number of smaller chains have contracted to wholesalers to service their merchandise requirements.

The truth is that the wholesaler's *function* has never ceased to exist. It is just that chains believed they could perform the function more economically than the wholesaler. In the case of high-tonnage shipments that may be so. But in many categories, the wholesaler can *outperform* the largest of the giants. And the more precise a chain's cost analysis, the more often the value in wholesaler services may be evident.

The drug wholesaler has changed almost as drastically as the food wholesaler. Indeed, the former has tended to adopt and adapt the strategy and tactics of the latter—step by step. Even the voluntary-chain concept is spreading in drug distribution. The rack jobber is also operating in the drug outlet—independent as well as chain.

Then there are giant drug wholesalers such as McKesson & Robbins, which serves perhaps 50 per cent of all independent retail drug stores. The wholesalers' services, too, have multiplied and improved. So have their facilities. For example, in 1960 one large wholesale drug house had revolutionized its customer shipments. Orders are filled and shipped in less than an hour, *complete with invoice.* Discounts and price changes are calculated by this wholesaler, freeing the customer from this chore. Up-to-the-minute weekly statements are automatically prepared with *no manual handling.* Result? Customer payments have accelerated, *reducing outstanding receivables by $100,000.* In addition, this flexible IBM punched-card system provides this wholesaler management with *weekly* sales analyses by product, customer, and salesman.

Several types of wholesalers are doing a rapidly mounting percentage of their total volume over the telephone. This is, of course, outstandingly true of the wholesale druggist. A considerable number of wholesale druggists find today that over half of their units shipped are ordered by their retail customers by telephone. In dollars, total telephone volume will run from one-third to 50 per cent and more of total gross among perhaps the majority of better drug wholesalers today. The same trend is discernible with respect to the food wholesaler, and among other wholesalers as well, with particular reference to those whose major volume is done in small-ticket with rapid turnover.

As a consequence, it is becoming something of a question whether the wholesaler's telephone-order girl may not be destined to become somewhat more important, as a sales factor, than the wholesaler's salesmen! Among at least a few drug wholesalers, this rather radical change has already occurred. But whether or not the wholesaler's telephone-order girl is to achieve a sales position of greater importance than the wholesale salesman, it appears that manufacturers err when they continue to focus on the wholesale salesman and totally neglect the telephone-order girl.

Basically, the independent retailer has survived by giving up various degrees of his independence. He may not like to face up to this reality—but surely it cannot be denied that in a voluntary group, for example, the cooperating members have exchanged some degree of total independence for the security that comes from associated effort. This trend will continue—the original meaning of the term "independent" will tend to exist more in tradition than in fact. The survival road of the independent is in cooperative activity with other independents—and this inevitably involves giving up more and more of the independent's original total freedom of action. It also means close affiliation with a modern type of wholesale service. This trend will pick up speed.

Nor will the wholesaler serve only the independent. Some giant chains also will turn to the wholesaler for some merchandise classifications, for some of their store units, for some parts of the country. And, of course, as the big chains turn to the rack jobber and to the leased-department operator, they automatically are turning also to what is really a wholesaler.

As a matter of fact, if the various chains serviced to some degree by one type or another of wholesaler were totted up, the resulting tabulation would take in a blue-ribbon list of our greatest chains. And by 1965, this utilization of the wholesaler in his various manifestations by big, medium-sized, and small chains will have increased.

The wholesaler has survived, as previously stated, because he has smartly adjusted to modern-day requirements. He will do an even better job of adjusting between 1960–1965. And, as he improves and extends his services, he will come to occupy a position more dominant than the one he occupied several decades ago when wholesaling had apparently reached its peak.

Some of the newer services that wholesalers will offer which various types of retailers will find attractive include smaller inventory investment, faster turnover, store accounting services, reduction of accounts payable, more efficient warehousing operation, liberal credit, floorstock protection, advertising assistance, presold controlled labels, quick service on new products at a minimum risk, training of retail personnel, regular promotions, store-engineering services, low-cost supplies, financial aid in construction of new stores, financing of equipment and fixtures.

CHAPTER 20

Scientific Merchandising
through Electronics

Every activity involved in accelerating the movement of merchandise into consumption involves communications. Advertising. Selling. Merchandising. Promotion. *All* involve communications. And, within the next five years, the science of electronic communications will revolute—not merely evolute. No one in any way even remotely connected with stimulating the consumption of merchandise will be isolated or cushioned from the impact of the communications revolution.

As a small sample of the revolution in marketing that lies ahead, consider this brief revelation of just some of the marketing tasks planned by a major appliance producer for its data-processing "brains":

> We are completing a *long-range sales forecasting* job which will correlate such existing but inadequately used data as the birth rate and new family formations; disposable income and the level of employment; our models and prices compared with competitors' models and prices and the availability of electricity in new areas and the number of new homes wired for electricity.
>
> Our integrated system, when completed, will provide a *dynamic distribution analysis;* it will take information from sales records and

projections and provide for management an up-to-the-minute picture of the retail trade and a photo-flash picture of our company's distribution pipelines to all areas of the country. Coupled with budget applications and the production-control application, this should give management the opportunity to adjust selling effort and factory effort to make maximum use of the production facilities at its disposal. Properly handled, it should help us to make the right appliance and deliver it to the right place at the right time. This could have an immeasurable effect in producing more profitable operations.

Ahead lies *scientific* merchandising!

We may accept as foregone conclusions that—

• The speed of communications in every aspect of merchandising is to be accelerated to a degree that is truly breath-taking.

• The ability to *store* merchandising information will go through a complete transformation.

• The ability to *recapture* stored merchandising information instantaneously will be achieved.

• The art of decision making in merchandising will be drastically altered as a result of electronic "brains."

Electronic data processing is giving merchandising executives at the manufacturing level a startling degree of inventory control plus statistics essential for sound merchandising decisions. The cost of the necessary equipment is coming down, the sophistication of the equipment is moving up. The net result is that, over the coming five years, merchandising will take giant steps in innumerable manufacturing establishments toward a greater degree of scientific decision making based on electronic data processing. This is fairly well accepted as applied to manufacturers.

But not so well comprehended is the application of electronic data processing to wholesaler and retailer operation. Clearly, any major changes in wholesale and retail inventory techniques stemming from electronic controls will exert a profound effect on manufacturers. And this is clearly on the way. Typically, for one large wholesale house the following results have been accomplished by electronic data processing:

1. Centralized invoicing, billing, and customer's accounting, with resulting improved management and other controls as opposed to the disadvantages of duplication at multiple branches.

2. Automatic costing, pricing, extending, discounting, and totaling of invoices as an instantaneous by-product of invoice typing.

3. Centralized inventory control, branch by branch—another automatic by-product of invoice typing.

4. Weekly inventory-status-and-movement reports by item—branch by branch.

5. Frequent reports of over-all inventory status and movement (all active and inactive items)—branch by branch.

6. Sales analysis of each item class in dollars and quantities.

7. Merchandise-item cost and sales analysis by dollars and quantities.

8. Direct shipment analysis by dollars and quantities.

The end result has been improved merchandise management possibilities facilitating elimination of inactive unprofitable items; less working capital tied up in inventory; and, through placement of consolidated purchase orders, lower merchandise costs. Naturally, the resulting changes in inventory practices are reflected in this wholesaler's purchases from its suppliers.

For retailing, the long-term goal of electronic experts is a *complete electronic data-processing system for stores.* Such systems would begin at the point of sale or point of receipt of merchandise and ultimately provide *complete information instantaneously* on every step of the total transaction in report form for use by store management. Here is where the greatest of all retail revolutions will occur. Its marketing impact will be felt by *all* manufacturers.

Early in 1960, a group of retail electronic data-processing experts concluded that the use of electronic character-recognition equipment in retailers' accounts receivable operations is theoretically feasible. This was the consensus reached at the conclusion of a two-day meeting of the electronics committee, Retail Research Institute, National Retail Merchants Association. The committee met with various manufacturers of character-recognition equipment.

The group explored the merits of magnetic sensing, a method being used by the American Bankers Association, with those of optical sensing. Magnetic sensing involves use of magnetic ink, while optical sensing is a photoelectric process that picks up light and dark spots. These conclusions were reached:

• The rigid requirements of magnetic sensing limits its use in retailing at present, but optical sensing can be adapted economically, especially in accounts receivable operations.

• Optical-sensing equipment can be used together with paper or punched sales checks, in lieu of more expensive point-of-sale equipment.

The possibility of developing a merchandise ticket that could be optically scanned was discussed. In this regard it was emphasized that standardization of ticket coding was desirable. Tickets prepared by manufacturers would have to use a common language in order to be widely utilized by retailers.

Other retail developments reported in 1960 included the following:

1. Macy's New York installed a $1 million electronic data-processing system—initially in its accounts receivable operation—a development regarded as a milestone in the use of electronics in the department store field. The system, developed by the National Cash Register Company, is slated to go into operation in 1961.

2. J. C. Penney Company announced that it was pioneering a new electronic accounting system to control a tidal wave of paper work flooding its 420-store Eastern region. These electronic bookkeepers formerly have been used only in banking.

Five machines that actually read, write, and remember as they automatically perform dozens of routine repetitive bookkeeping operations have been installed at Penney's New York office. The equipment is expected to nearly double the speed of processing accounts in several bookkeeping operations, a spokesman for the firm reported.

3. An electronic device which can read printed characters directly from cash-register tapes was scheduled to be installed in 1960 by Boots Pure Drug Company, Ltd., at its head office in Nottingham, England. The installation is part of the drug chain's retail sales-accounting project, which is designed to obtain centrally processed information on individual salespersons' sales totals; gross sales totals, with differentiation for discounts to staff, doctors, and nurses; agreement between the amount processed and the total of each cash register's detail tape.

The company has more than 1,300 retail branches and in excess of 7,000 cash-register positions in all stores. Each year, the company makes some 380 million unit sales.

An integrated electronic data-processing system which starts at the point of sale to the customer and goes right back into distribution, buying, and production is regarded by Boots as an ultimate goal. Immediate plans, however, visualize integration in two distinct areas which are ultimately capable of being linked together. Application of electronics to the first area—retail sales accounting and statistics —is in full development. The second area—merchandise accounting —is the subject of a separate project. For this purpose, Boots has elected to use a system which will convert handwritten coded store orders directly to punched tape which, in turn, will be fed into a computer to produce picking orders, invoices, "outs" lists, minimum stock reports, theoretical stock reports, and error reports.

4. In New Orleans, Maison Blanche's electronic data-processing center was to be completed by 1961, according to I. Newman, president. The electronic processing center will be built around an IBM 650-tape system, with a substantial number of conventional IBM machines supporting it.

In addition, besides the usual key-punching section, there will be a clerical section. It will concentrate on sales audit, accounts receivable, billing, unit and classification control, and new approaches to merchandise control, along with promotional control.

5. Gray Drug, Liggett, Sun Ray, Katz, have installed electronic brains with enough know-how to track a rocket to the moon. This elaborate hardware, leased in some cases at close to $100,000 a year, is proving itself a valuable and practical tool in today's complex drug-chain operations.

6. Certified Grocers of California has announced a new service for its members. It prepares purchase analyses from its Datatron electronic computer. Called Member Purchase Analysis, this new program gives a complete summary of all groceries and nonfoods purchased by any individual member. It shows him just how many cases of each item he has bought for a given period. Members can also get reports that project the exact profit from sale of merchandise on a particular invoice.

The computer is a very efficient way of billing invoices as well as Certified reports. Now even frozen foods and delicatessen billing go on the computer, which will enable these products to be purchase-analyzed. This would have been impossible at one time because frozen items and delicatessen involve perishable foods. Through these reports, Certified members can find out which items are selling well, which they should discontinue or order low, how they can allocate the right amount of shelf space, how to plan new store layouts—aside from being valuable purchasing aids.

7. Burdine's, Miami, is well on its way through a five-year plan toward complete, electronically automated merchandising processing for the main store and branches. Clary electronic transactors are used on the selling floor to print sales checks and produce punched tape which collects complete transaction data. Tapes then go to the photoelectric reader machine feeding the Royal McBee LGP–30 computer at the main store, which does all accounting. Among the advantages of this system, Burdine's reports quick transaction time, freedom to intersell, with identification by clerk code on any department machine.

Within four hours after closing each day, Burdine's reports, complete sales-audit and merchandise-classification reports can be available, detailed by totals for the day, departmental totals, total sales by classification, by individual clerk, and, among other data, total sales by type, regular charge, c.o.d., term, and cash.

8. An up-to-the-minute inventory of 6,700 different types of merchandise is maintained by a random access computer at Montgomery Ward's new Allen Park, Michigan, warehouse and distribution center. The computer, and the inventory control and order-processing system which it makes possible, will be duplicated in each of 11 additional distribution centers to be opened by Ward's across the nation by 1965.

Incidentally, until the early 1960s, computers were able to accept information only in specially prepared form—usually from cards or tapes. Some of the new character-sensing check sorters mark the first step in simplifying computer input.

The next big development, already well started by a firm called Intelligent Machines Research Corporation (a division of Farrington Manufacturing Company), is to build devices that can read ordinary typed or printed characters. First National City Bank of New York is now using devices built by Intelligent Machines to read travelers checks directly into an electronic computer. A number of oil companies (Socony Mobil, Shell Oil, Tidewater) read credit cards directly into computers. Before long, machines will be built that can read off names, addresses, and other key information from such stand-ard documents as insurance policies, contracts, and automobile registration forms.

As part of the great trend toward electronic data processing, a companion trend involving so-called "automatic reorder systems" will accelerate. While this automatic reorder trend is most emphatic in the variety chains, there is every reason to believe it will spread to other outlets, especially since the food chains, the drug chains, and the discount chains are taking on so many typical variety-chain merchandise classifications.

Automatic ordering systems can't apply to short-season goods. These seasonal lines are only ordered once. Big-ticket items may not need an automatic ordering system because they're usually bulky and salesgirls can easily take a visual on-hand. Besides, turnover is generally too slow to warrant it. Automatic reordering may not apply to rapidly changing lines like barrettes and jewelry.

Yet a top executive at one variety chain remarked in 1960:

> In time, we may put our entire warehouse operation on an auto-matic reordering system. By working with punch cards, stores will automatically order their needs from the warehouse and the ware-house will automatically reorder goods from the manufacturer. This way, central management will remain in control of basic stock plans and be in a position to mastermind the entire operation.

What *is* automatic reordering?

The system simply is this. The supplier imprints reorder informa-tion (number, color, size, etc.) on a detachable stub. When mer-chandise is taken from understock to counter, stubs are detached and thus furnish an automatic record of refill needs.

A leading thread company went one step further. Its sewing- and art-goods stock boxes contain electronic control punch cards. As a box is taken from understock to the thread displayer, the control card is removed and placed in a special rack. At the week's end, cards are mailed to the supplier's warehouse for automatic replacements. A special new advantage is that the cards have perforated stubs, which the store retains as order copies.

With "auto" reorder, the store substitutes a ticket or card count for actual merchandise count, with each ticket representing a unit of merchandise.

Most chains began automatic stock-replenishment programs with basic small wares, i.e., notions, toiletries, stationery, housewares, and hardware. One chain has practically all lines covered with a combination of company- and supplier-operated systems. Another uses automatic reordering in basic apparel such as dresses, skirts, slacks, shoes, slips, and work pants. With minor variations, systems are similar.

Suppliers seed or patch merchandise with tickets or cards for merchandise shipped to the warehouse. From twice weekly to once a month, stores collect split tickets and cards and mail them to the warehouse or main office, where they are machine processed.

Most of the problems of automatic reorder in the variety chain are largely the result of the change-over in ordering procedure to a totally new system, managers indicate.

"The most important thing a manager has to do is work out a well-balanced basic stock at the start. It took us about four months to get rid of excess stock and since then the system has been working perfectly."

Although a purely mechanical problem, the danger of lost tickets is causing worry. Here's how one manager met the problem:

> Lost tickets are a serious problem. There's no way of knowing merchandise is missing when tickets get lost except through complete physical on-hands, which we don't do often enough. Putting the tickets on a spindle at the counter is very dangerous. We tried a file box and that worked better, but this year I'm going to attach a tax-type box to every register and I think that will be most effective in reminding the girls to put the tickets in a safe place as soon as merchandise is moved from stock room to counter. I'm also stepping up physical on-hands to once a month at least. You can get awful edgy after an experience I had, finding a box of fifty tickets about to be swept out with the rubbish during the Christmas rush.

Automatic ordering presents other problems to the retailer. For example:

1. With the new system, stores carry less inventory than before, since they are ordering from two to four times a month. This makes fast deliveries a vital factor in merchandising. When goods are shipped from distant points or by freight, deliveries are frequently unreliable.

2. One of the major disadvantages lies in the fact that there is

no control over seasonal shifts in merchandise requirements. Stores tend to ignore lines that are on an automatic reordering system and don't pay any attention to advance ordering for peak seasons. For example, white zippers or strapless bras peak sharply in the late spring, and even with more frequent ordering, stores may run out of merchandise unless stocks are increased in advance of the buying rush.

3. The fact that dollar control is taken out of the hands of central management can work to the disadvantage of an entire chain's operation. Before automatic reordering, store orders were validated by the home or district office and stocks were kept in line with over-all dollar investments. Now there is no check on how much a store is spending, and managers frequently overextend their investments in these lines so that other departments suffer from a lack of spending dollars.

Stores may, with impunity, carry styles they have no business stocking because of extremely slow turnover. One chain reports that it had cases of stores receiving inventory cards which were supposed to be put in old stock and instead they sent them back immediately to the manufacturer and received new supplies, which obviously overloaded inventories.

4. The automatic systems can lull a merchant into a false sense of security. Unless buying is closely supervised, the system can ruin instead of run a department. Stores have to watch out for excess investment and unbalanced assortments. Managers must not ignore departments that go on automatic reordering schedules.

5. On lines that are not prepaid, the stores run heavy additional expense by ordering six and seven times a month instead of the usual one, and paying that much more in repetition of shipping charges.

6. In order to work efficiently, automatic reordering systems must rely on many more people than were required for the old on-hand method. Before, one girl was responsible for checking and ordering merchandise; now every shift girl is responsible for tearing off box tops or putting cards in containers. With store hours expanding every day, this becomes a problem with additional help.

7. Even the most staple lines nowadays are affected by seasonal and fashion changes. Any system that works exclusively on the basis of past sales can't keep up with shifts in demand. Even pots and pans are affected by sharp changes in seasonal preferences.

8. In electrical lines, new items and changes in design are added

so fast that you have to constantly replace old items with new ones. If you keep ordering on the basis of what you sold before, you'll be out of the running with competition in no time. Lamps and shades are another good example. Style changes come so fast you couldn't operate on an automatic reorder basis.

9. Automatic reordering won't work on promotional lines. Whenever you have a department that depends for most of its volume on such items, you can't order automatically.

However, every new merchandising development has encountered problems, objections, "stand pat-ism." Retailers are finding that most of the problems involved in automatic reordering can be lessened. Examples:

• In one chain, the main office will take care of seasonal increases by sending the stores special assignments that cannot be reordered by the receiving store.

• When special promotions require additional stock, stores can order the merchandise separately, but they must be sure to destroy the inventory cards immediately so that the additional inventory will not become a part of basic stock.

• The system itself takes care of most seasonal or fashion peaks because when goods begin to accelerate in sales, the store will automatically increase orders. If sales warrant still greater inventory in certain items, additional handwritten orders can be sent to the manufacturer along with regular cards or box tops. In the case of seasonal needs, stores would then mark additional stock in some manner so that this merchandise is not reordered.

• On all fashion lines, it will be necessary for store managers to check their entire stock three times a year to readjust inventories in line with future seasonal and fashion requirements.

• Personnel today are spending more and more time in selling big-ticket merchandise and ignoring small wares. The new system simply takes care of merchandising lines that are getting lost in the shuffle anyway. In lines like notions, there's a real problem in getting personnel interested because the department hasn't as much glamour as costly lines.

• Inventories were low and lumpy. The primary effect of automatic reordering has been to level off the imbalances and bring stock up to a proper level for normal turnover. In test stores, investments were rarely increased but became properly proportioned.

• One variety chain reported: "In our chain, we found test stores with as much as 100 per cent increases as a result of controlling out-of-stocks on basic items."

• By bringing manufacturers and retailers closer together, auto-matic reorder systems have helped improve merchandise and merchandising.

Electronic merchandising—automatic reorder systems—this is the great near-term "control" trend in merchandising. Its rate of growth by 1965 will be fantastic.

CHAPTER 21

A Roundup of Secondary
Merchandising Trends

All business is in a constant state of flux. Naturally, merchandising is also being buffeted by constant change. Some of these changes involve major trends. A number of these major trends have been analyzed in these pages.

But, in addition, there are secondary trends that will be in clear focus by 1965. Let's examine some of the more emphatic of these secondary trends.

1. The second home promises to become an important new marketing phenomenon on the American scene. Someone in real estate has said that "second homes are the hottest thing since soda pop." Over 100,000 second homes were bought in 1960. Builders believe that by 1965, a minimum of 200,000 second homes (sometimes called "leisure homes") will be built annually. This will not only profoundly affect the building industry—it will boom the prefabricated home—it will also have an enormous impact on the market for just about everything that goes into the second home.

2. The process of trading up will accelerate. The public's income makes this feasible. And mass retailers are eager for it. Even the discount chains are trading up their price lines. As a matter of fact, most manufacturers have tended to lag behind the potentials for

higher price lines. By 1965 we will be in a superluxurious age—and merchandisers who properly plan for traded-up price lines will win a competitive advantage, as well as a better profit ratio.

3. There will be more truly new products put on the market each year during the coming five years than ever before. These will not be products involving simple refinements—but products either totally new or with improvements of a major nature.

4. The everyday-gift market will expand enormously. Merchandisers of almost every conceivable product, from bread-and-butter staples to novelties, will exploit the everyday-gift market.

5. The grandparent market will come into its own. This refers not to purchases by senior citizens for themselves, but to the purchases they either make or pay for (and thus influence) for children and grandchildren.

6. Because of the huge population total, and because this gigantic population is spreading out over the entire nation, merchandisers will tend more often to plan programs aimed for sections of the country or for segments of the total market. The magic of the *national concept* will tend to wane. The *segmented approach* to merchandising will assume considerable importance.

7. There will be a mounting trend among manufacturers to relieve stores of their warehousing function. This made an appearance, for example, in home furnishings early in the 1960s. As part of this trend there will be more plans under which the manufacturer drop ships to the shopper on order from the retailer.

8. Because so many women at work (men too) want to shop during the noon lunch hour, more retailers will develop special programs to enable the noon-hour shopper to buy more in less time. This will apply particularly to downtown stores—but it will be only somewhat less active in the outlying shopping centers. Manufacturers will help retailers stage special noon-hour events.

9. Many manufacturers will operate simultaneously two contrary marketing plans. One plan will involve unlimited distribution. The second plan will involve limited and even franchised distribution. The second plan may also involve special numbers (and sometimes special labels) available only to selected stores. The trend in big-ticket lines will be away from totally uncontrolled distribution—and toward an *increasing degree of control* over distribution. More manufacturers will tend to cut down their outlets, first by total number and second by variety.

10. Originally, the shopping center competed with downtown—now the shopping centers compete with each other. Moreover, each new shopping center will compete with any one of from two to five existing shopping centers. The grave problem, therefore, for the shopping center and especially for the great regional shopping centers is traffic—shopping traffic. The giant shopping center must get giant traffic counts.

As a consequence, the newer and larger shopping centers are almost frantically searching for great merchandising and promotional events that will benefit all of the stores in the entire center by producing peak traffic counts. Very oddly, few manufacturers, either individually or collectively, have endeavored to give the new large shopping center new and large traffic-producing merchandising-promotional events. Groups of competitive and noncompetitive manufacturers will some day get together and stage shopping center events that will rival Ziegfeld. They will have traveling troupes and will stage elaborate shows—ice carnivals and what-have-you.

11. Practically all giant retailers now offer credit facilities. These retailers will all be offering a variety of credit facilities in the near future. If nothing else, this means that the statement mailing can be effectively used by manufacturers in new outlets. It also means, however, specific merchandising and promotional programs that will hook on to the requirements of credit retailing.

12. As the authority of the chain-store manager broadens, especially in the giant one-stop store units of the various chains and in the giant branches of the department stores, manufacturers will find it increasingly advisable by 1965 to replan their personnel selling activities so that their salesmen not only spend more time in actual store calls—but also so that their salesmen will be equipped with better merchandising-promotional programs for individual stores. Moreover, calls will have to be made on assistant store managers and on other personnel in individual stores because buying authority for a multiplying number of lines will tend to percolate downward from the store manager. Few trends are more important to the merchandising executive than the decentralization trend of the chains and the department stores. The man to watch is the store manager and others on his staff.

This trend is particularly emphatic in the food outlet—and, as usual, this trend will spread strongly into other types of giant outlets. In this connection, *Progressive Grocer* cites a Kroger food chain executive as listing in the following way some of the new responsibilities the food store manager didn't have in 1950 but which he had been given by 1960:

A. *The manager is the boss.* He is the full, complete manager. He gets professional assistance . . . from division headquarters and fellow store managers—but he alone is responsible for the performance of his store.

B. *The manager must grow as a retailer.* He is expected to get around, keep his eyes open—and translate his observations into better merchandising. He is encouraged to read trade publications, to know his customers well, to work at broadening the capabilities of his staff.

C. *The manager supervises ordering.* While he orders most of the items handled in the warehouse—he is always free to drop slow items. He also is free to request new items or products that his store (or the warehouse) does not handle.

D. *The manager uses outside assistance.* The Kroger manager is no longer urged to beware of outside help. Salesmen, brokers, and merchandisers with good ideas are welcome. (Those without ideas never will be.)

E. *The manager develops his special-display program.* He is fully responsible for the most effective use of the display facilities in his store. Store-initiated ideas are encouraged. He is, of course, interested in featuring items that move fast and produce good profit.

F. *The manager must communicate.* His observations and views are important to headquarters—especially in the area of customer relations, merchandising, and selling. Store managers meet weekly to exchange ideas.

G. *The manager controls stock arrangement and facings.* He and his staff must make many of the decisions on location of product categories, the shelf positions and facings of each product and brand . . . to deliver maximum sales and profit at a minimum of shelf stocking and labor expense.

H. *The manager is fully informed on sales and profits.* Every four weeks he receives a complete operating statement on his store —which includes dollar and unit sales, gross and net profit. Manager bonuses are paid on the basis of net profit.

13. There will be a strong pick-up in new techniques for shipping

merchandise to the retailer so as to lessen his labor costs. This will include cases that are still easier to open; shipping cases which, when opened, may be placed right on the store shelf (the tray-pack concept); new sizes of shipping containers.

14. The multiunit package will become still more popular—and still larger. The twin-six in beer, for example, may outsell the single-six by 1965. As the multipack becomes larger and the shipping case tends to become smaller, the "twain" may meet by 1965. This will result in more case promotions by retailers.

15. The payola problem among large retailers will have led to Federal Trade Commission action by 1965—and maybe to new Federal legislation.

16. There will be a small return to salespeople in some departments of some big chains by 1965. The food super, for example, was using salespeople for exotic foods in 1960—and both the drug and the variety chains found they had to beat a bit of a retreat from full self-service in some departments. Even self-service can be overdone. This doesn't mean an end to self-service; it merely means that the stampede to self-service that was so evident in 1960 will be tempered to some extent by 1965.

17. There will, simultaneously, come into evidence by 1965 some of the first examples of truly automatic or robot retailing—using both mechanical and electronic techniques. This refers to floor functions; that is, the shopper will operate mechanical-electronic devices (other than vending machines) to get wanted merchandise. These will be fumbling efforts, but so was the early food super in the 1930s. These developments *must* come because, to date, our traditional department and chain stores have been totally unable, even with self-service, to bring down their costs. And their costs *must* come down.

18. While credit retailing will continue to expand, there will also be a reverse trend—a trend back to cash. Some of the newer chains in 1960 were, of course, strictly cash operations. As the shopping public becomes more aware of the cost of credit—aided by explanations in the public print by bankers and perhaps aided also by Federal legislation compelling labeling of credit costs—a very slow-growing segment of the public will display a willingness to buy more often for cash. Alert retailers will cater to this trend.

19. While reference has been made elsewhere to telephone shopping, in-home shopping, and mail-order shopping, these three related

trends are important enough to warrant second coverage. In 1960, telephone and mail-order shopping really leaped ahead. In-home shopping also showed a substantial increase in 1960. By 1965, these three shopping procedures will be vastly more common than in 1960. They will directly affect the merchandising programs of innumerable manufacturers.

20. Dining out will have assumed fantastic proportions. The restaurant end of the food industry grew ten times as rapidly as did food stores in 1958, 1959, and 1960. This will continue. It means somewhat smaller purchases of food for home consumption.

21. The market for the subteen will become almost as important as the teen market.

22. There will be a demand by the public for new status symbols. The auto will have lost most of its appeal as a status symbol by 1965. So will boats. So will the mink and the trip to Europe. The two-home concept will be one of the new status symbols of 1965. There will be others.

23. Mail by facsimile will revolutionize merchandising and promotions. So will the coming speed-up in mail due to electronic handling techniques.

24. And, finally, as befits a "soft" nation, our dog population will be reared more luxuriously than were most children at the turn of the century. There will be dog "wardrobes," including lined garments for winter, unlined garments for warmer weather, and even rainwear for dogs. The air-conditioned doghouse will outmode the original meaning of that famous phrase "in the doghouse." And the whole pet market will zoom ahead—reflecting a luxury-laden people.

So will the birth rate of our people continue to move up—because prosperity will continue to hit new heights through to 1965, and prosperity brings a higher birth rate along with it just as surely as it encourages mink collars for dogs.

CHAPTER 22

*A Grab Bag of Predictions
about Retailing in 1965*

As retailing goes—so goes merchandising by manufacturers. Manufacturers seldom inaugurate innovations in retailing. Most often, manufacturers react, with more or less promptness and emphasis, to new developments in retailing.

For example, manufacturers did not have anything to do with self-service retailing—other than to make it possible by creating the presold brand. And, as self-service spread to one form of retailing after another, to one merchandise category after another, manufacturers tended to lag behind the requirements of retail self-service as it affected their lines. Even by 1960, manufacturers of many soft-goods classifications had still not planned adequately, in packaging and fixturing, for the self-service trend in the retailing of soft goods. In that year, some rug companies were still unaware that the variety chains and other chains were selling even 9 by 12 rugs through self-service—newcomers tended to be the suppliers of the required packaged rugs.

But there is no doubt that the manufacturer who reacts promptly and intelligently and creatively to new retailing developments can pick up a competitive lap—sometimes two. For the merchandising executive in manufacturing organizations who wisely wants to keep ahead, not merely abreast, of forthcoming innovations in retailing—here are some predictions about retailing in 1965, in addition to those spotted elsewhere in this discussion.

1. The helicopter or other vertical-rise planes will emerge as a new form of mass transit. This will push retailing out farther and farther, geographically speaking, not only from the city but also from the suburbs, because it will enable our people to live farther and farther out. The entire technique of short-haul transportation will be revolutionized—and, just as the auto revolutionized retailing, so will these new techniques of short-haul transportation change the face of retailing.

2. The air transport of merchandise will have assumed proportions that can scarcely be conceived today. This will bring about great changes in inventory practices.

3. Some stores of the future may revolve—with the customer sitting in front of merchandise that is conveyed in front of the shopper for push-button recording of purchases.

4. The moving sidewalk will bring vast changes. It will bring shoppers from parking lots to the stores. It will be used inside the store as moving aisles. (Stores are already so big that shopper fatigue is becoming a problem.) It will make every floor, including basements, a main floor.

5. Certain categories of merchandise will arrive at the retail store on their own shelves or fixtures. Merchandise will be price-marked with electronic devices—the cost of price marking will be slashed.

6. Closed-circuit television will be used to instruct store managers, floor personnel, and warehouse personnel. Headquarters will be able to "see" every step of the retail process through electronic eyes.

7. Store-window displays will be "installed" by the use of screens on which setups are flashed from a central closed-circuit TV control room.

8. Some shopping will be done electronically from the car—the car will pull up to a huge electronic bulletin board on which merchandise will be featured; remote controls in the car will permit the shopper to record her purchases. This will be electronic drive-in shopping.

9. Electronic store directories will help shoppers find their way around the huge stores of the future.

10. The electronic recording of telephone orders will surely be

common by 1965—and telephone ordering on a twenty-four-hour basis will be commonplace.

11. Store hours will have been shortened—perhaps to fifty store-open hours a week. Morning openings will be rather rare. Over half of total retail volume will be done in most categories at night. And the new types of vending machines will make twenty-four-hour retailing a practicality in certain classifications.

12. Electronic systems will make it more practical for more stores to develop practical mail-order systems.

13. Selling in the home will have become a much more important factor—and will be controlled from headquarters by electronic communications.

14. Shopping expeditions will be less frequent; this trend is very much in evidence.

15. Prepricing, preticketing, prepackaging will be much more common.

16. Trips to market may be revolutionized. In some classifications, the retail buyer may be able to "go to market" via the television screen (in color). This may revolutionize trade shows, etc.

17. The obsolescence rate, not only of the retail store itself, but also of all of the retail office and warehouse will have been greatly accelerated. This will affect the whole basic concept of retail accounting practice.

18. The peak periods of retailing each week will become still more peaked.

19. The store-in-the-round will be quite common. Several food stores in-the-round were operating in 1960. A rug store found decided economies in a round store. The store-in-the-round will call for new concepts in fixturing, in store posters—perhaps even packages may have to be redesigned for the somewhat different slant from which they will be viewed by the shopper.

20. The vending machine will be in a period of explosive growth by 1965. By that time, the vending machine will be capable of accepting paper bills and making unlimited change. It will also protect merchandise from heat and cold. It will be able to handle much larger units—physically and in price. As a consequence, the vending machine will become, by itself, a new form of retailing. It will take the form of retail stores entirely equipped with vending machines. It will be found in new locations—even in the basements of large

apartment houses. It will appear more frequently in various stores; and in front of various stores. It will sell merchandise twenty-four hours a day, seven days a week. It will call for new concepts in pricing, in package sizes, in package design, in promotion.

21. Retailing really started out as an outdoor "outer-space" procedure. The oriental bazaar was the prototype; it was followed by the village-square form of retailing. Then came the open fair, and so on. In the early 1900s, one of its manifestations was jamming the sidewalks with merchandise to the point where local ordinances had to be passed to give the pedestrian walking space. Currently, retailing is again going "outer space." However, it isn't only the vending machine that is returning retailing to its original starting point of outdoor merchandising. Other forces are pushing retailing in the same direction.

A. The telephone companies are proving that telephone sales (a retail function, by the way) can be stimulated by the installation of outdoor booths in a truly amazing variety of locations.

B. Coca-Cola is proving that soft-drink sales can be boosted by making Coke available out on the golf course, in front of gas stations, and in other unlikely places.

C. Innumerable retailers are putting merchandise out on the parking lot.

D. The drive-in type of retail structure tends to be an outdoor operation—not always and not completely, but still at least in between outdoor and indoor.

E. Hundreds of food stores, especially in the South, make it possible for the shopper to shop right from her car. An attendant comes out to take her order and then returns to the car with the order; the shopper can inhale the great outdoors through her car window while waiting for the merchandise.

F. The auction type of retailing, even though it may be held under a tent, is essentially a form of outdoor retailing. It has made substantial strides.

G. Retailers—including some of our retail giants—are again putting merchandise out in front of their stores. (The store-front vending-machine installation is simply the mechanical application of this age-old concept.)

22. Then there is the new type of shopping center where the entire

area is really under one roof. This may lead to stores that have no fronts, perhaps no sides—a return to the medieval bazaar!

23. Temperature-controlled malls will be standard installations in shopping centers of the future. This will develop into a keen-edged merchandising tool. (Of some 312 possible shopping days in the year, about half are affected by adverse weather—rain, snow, excessive heat. The covered temperature-controlled mall neutralizes the weather and permits the shopper to attend to all her diverse needs in comfort. An amusing sight in one such center in the North is the fashion show for beach items in January while snow falls outside.)

The mall concept offers a major merchandising advantage when it comes to center promotions such as fashion shows, boat and auto shows, and other special events. Whereas these programs are usually held in parking lots of typical shopping centers, and the problem of converting spectators to shoppers is ever present, the air-conditioned court draws the spectators to the very doorsteps of the stores.

24. The marginal retail location will regain some favor. Not only are some of our fastest-growing young merchants eagerly seeking out marginal retail locations, but even some of our established large retailers are beginning to eye this type of location with some interest. For example, the Neisner Brothers variety chain blueprinted a low-cost-construction type of variety outlet—in itself a reverse-the-field technique, since the modern variety store unit is quite a retail palace. Simultaneously plans were made to put these low-cost buildings into marginal locations. Several extremely fast-growing discount chains take only marginal locations.

25. There is an interesting trend toward retailing from *trucks*. One manufacturer is now planning trucks that represent a compromise between the requirements of a *shipping* truck and a *shopping* truck. Somehow, selling from a truck carries the connotation of special values.

26. Shopping centers will tend to specialize. The first shopping center devoted almost exclusively to fashion merchandise was opened in California in 1960.

There is no supermarket in Fashion Square, as the new shopping center is called—and this is really historic. There is no variety-chain outlet. Instead, the stores stock, basically, ready-to-wear, shoes, jewelry, furniture, and decorative home furnishings. The major emphasis is on women's ready-to-wear; perhaps 75 per cent of the total square footage in the center offers merchandise that could—broadly —be classed as women's fashion merchandise.

Actually, throughout the country, there have been for some years rather highly specialized shopping centers. For example, a number of shopping centers specialize in furniture, rugs, home furnishings. But Fashion Square differs from these pioneers in the following respects:

A. It is a large shopping center—some 550,000 square feet of store area is involved. (Of course, there are larger shopping centers, but Fashion Square is quite a bit above the median in size.)

B. It is probably the first sizable shopping center with the main emphasis on fashion merchandise.

C. The bellwether store—Bullock's—involved some 340,000 square feet. That is larger than at least 80 per cent of the downtown units of all the department stores in the country.

D. The other fashion outlets include some of the topflight fashion names on the Coast. This development is of unusual significance because it seems to cut away the basic prop on which a good deal of downtown's hope rests—namely, large assortments of fashion lines.

27. Prestige department stores will turn to warehouse promotions. Carson, Pirie Scott & Co. operates a warehouse store in which the emphasis has been switched from hard to soft goods. Selling space in the one-story building was increased from 30,000 to 40,000 square feet. New fluorescent lighting, flooring, and air conditioning were installed. Wall areas were refinished, pegboarded, and shelved. New metal and wood self-service-type fixtures were installed. Completing the conversion was the installation of six check-out counters. Self-service is applied to 25,000 of the total 40,000 square feet of selling area, with lines such as carpeting, major appliances, and furniture operated as conventional clerk-service departments. This is really a new version of the bargain basement.

28. There will be many chains operating stores with price limits —as did the early five and dimes. These will be stores limited to items priced at 88 cents. A big chain sells nothing over $3.

Like similar chains (for example, John's Bargain Stores in the East), 88¢ Stores operate simply. One such chain has stores that measure between 2,100 and 3,600 square feet and carry about 30,000 items with inventory ranging from $30,000 to $50,000. Stock turns are eight times a year. Store managers do their own buying. Since every item or package of items sells for 88 cents, price-marking overhead is at a minimum. Signs carry the price message. Fixturing resembles that of variety stores and nonfood departments of supermarkets.

29. The gas station is destined to become a major retailer of nonautomotive lines. This will be a major trend by 1965, when some 50,000 gas stations will be offering many manufacturers of nonautomotive lines a sizable new outlet. The remaining 500,000 gas stations will also be selling vastly more nonautomotive lines.

30. Retailing in solo and strip locations on highways will be in full swing. And, like every major change in retailing, the highway location will leave a deep imprint on the total marketing programs of manufacturers in every merchandise category.

31. Sunday will emerge as an important shopping day, particularly in certain areas of the country. Incidentally, in those areas where Sunday retailing is now quite strong out on the highways, it is developing into something like a circus; highway merchants are putting fun for the family into their Sunday retailing techniques and this may mark the first reversal in the broad trend which has changed shopping from a pleasurable excursion into a chore! Sunday is a *family* shopping day—a point of major importance to merchandisers.

32. Closed-circuit TV will enable chain headquarters actually to "look in" on the floor of any store unit—to see what is going on. It will also enable headquarters to look in on various internal departments of each store unit. Some, if not most, of the present-day field forces will be done away with—headquarters control will be via the electronic eye.

33. Also, through closed circuit TV it will be possible to flash promotions from headquarters not merely to each store—but actually to set up these promotions within each store automatically and instantaneously. Sound impossible? It's being done at this very moment. It is entirely probable that there will also be small screens placed within the various shelving areas that will sell—with sight, sound, and color—as the shopper's hand is reaching out for merchandise.

34. Nocturnal retailing will continue to move ahead. In 1960, at least 50 per cent of total retail volume was done after 4:30 p.m. By

1965, the figure will be nearer 65 per cent. Nighttime shopping also tends to be family shopping—in particular "Pop" does more shopping at night and on Sunday than any other time.

35. Independent retailers will band together in new fields. The voluntary and cooperative concept will spread even more strongly into drug retailing and hardware retailing. Also, small groups of retailers will band together in a large variety of ways.

36. The various chains will experiment with many types of new stores. Thus, some of the variety and department store chains will experiment with discount stores. They will experiment with specialty stores of various types.

37. Strong retailers will franchise other retailers. This trend was quite strong by 1960—it will be still stronger by 1965, especially as chains develop their own controlled brands.

38. The peak hours of retailing will become still fewer—and therefore still more peaked. By 1965, over 50 per cent of all retail volume will be done in about twelve to fifteen hours during the week!

In conclusion, it may be said that, between 1960–1965, more experiments of a bold nature will be made in retailing than during any previous full decade. This will be compulsory because retail costs are too high and the net profit percentage is too low; and the "Ike-and-Mike" similarity of most stores will compel a search for the new and different. Several of these bold experiments will become the great retailing patterns of the future—and the merchandising man who first spots them and who then rides them most intelligently will have scored a competitive scoop.

CHAPTER **23**

Fifty Areas for Manufacturer Cooperation
with Retailers

Programs and ideas on which retailers are working mark out areas within which manufacturers may find opportunity for merchandising cooperation. Here are 50 such areas:

1. *Complaint Handling Needs Rechecking*

Complaint-handling standards have deteriorated—generally speaking. They never recovered, really, from the lows they hit during the wartime shortage era. One store recently arranged to call, five days later, all customers who had registered a complaint. It found an astonishing percentage of unsatisfied customers. Not only are some complaint-handling systems inefficient—but the procedure tends to be cold, formal, devoid of niceties. Customers still cost money to get —and poor complaint procedures lose more customers than any other single store malfunction. This doesn't mean leaning over backwards to cater to the lunatic fringe of shoppers—but it does mean offering desirable customers a more courteous, more intelligent, faster complaint service.

2. *Saying "Thank You" to Regular Customers*

The regular customer is so seldom followed up by retailers with anything other than a sales pitch! Of course, there may be a card at

Christmas—too often, however, it lacks totally in warmth. Or there may be a calendar. But why not try an actual gift—even if it is a very small one? For example, a huge hard-goods outlet sent each customer who had bought a dishwasher during a three-year period a gift of a pretty dress-up apron. With the gift, there went a letter which remarked: "We realize that you were among the first to discover the convenience of a dishwasher; we are sure, too, that you've helped introduce this appliance to your friends. To show you our appreciation, we're sending you a pretty little dress-up apron as a symbol of enjoyment in the kitchen." That little gift and that short letter—tied up with a clever newspaper ad inviting any who failed to get the letter but who had bought a dishwasher to come in for the gift—paid for itself many times over.

3. *How to Stimulate Better Housekeeping*

Self-service, self-selection shopping plays hob with store displays of merchandise. So do other factors—sometimes including the failings of part-time help. A mass retailer developed the following program to encourage better housekeeping:

A. A date was fixed for "Operation Clean-up."

B. This date was circled on all calendars in the store.

C. It was announced that, on that date, top management from the store would visit all sections of the store and rate each section.

D. Each section was to be rated by two different executives and the scores of the two would be averaged.

E. All sections receiving a score of 90 per cent or more would get a "Sales Appeal Award"—framed.

F. Special awards would be made to each member of each winning section.

G. It was announced that, in the scoring, cleanliness would be rated 30 per cent; arrangement of merchandise 30 per cent; departmental displays 15 per cent; stock in drawers or cases 15 per cent; adjacent stockroom appearance 10 per cent.

H. There were 12 inspection teams composed of the 24 members of top management, ranging from the store president to divisional merchandise managers.

4. *Highway Retailing—Next Big Trend?*

Retail locations out on major highways promise to become the next great locational trend. This trend will be spurred by the gigantic

Federal road-building program. These highway locations will differ from shopping centers in that they will—more often than otherwise —be occupied by just one store, or merely a few stores, operating entirely independently. Also, they will be right on the highway rather than off the highway, as is typical of most shopping centers. Also, they will tend to be farther away from established centers of population. These highway locations will call for new concepts in store architecture. The *round* store, for example, seems to fit in well at these locations. New concepts in store fixturing will be developed to encourage so-called "drive-in" shopping. There will be new merchandising and promotional concepts, new store hours. Just as retailers found that the shopping center location called for a break with previous tradition and experience, so will the highway location call for a break with much shopping center tradition and experience.

5. Can Retail-employee Turnover Be Reduced?

Employee turnover is costly—from every standpoint. Can it be reduced? Yes—it can be reduced, with such techniques as the following:

A. Better programs for interviewing and testing.
B. Better programs for selling retailing as a career to youngsters.
C. Better programs for acquainting educational authorities with the opportunities in retailing.
D. Smarter use of classified and display space in the local newspapers—this is much too neglected.
E. Appeals to customers.
F. Appeals to present employees.
G. Better supervision.
H. Regular special-incentive programs.
I. Provision for young employees to continue special studies.

Retailing may or may not have as much to "sell" to prospective employees as other endeavors—but, to date, retailing has unquestionably planned less than other endeavors to develop and then to sell itself to prospective employees.

6. Are Assortments Growing Too Big for Self-service?

Retailers are finding that, under self-service and self-selection, there is a maximum size beyond which it is uneconomical to expand a department. Their experience proves that departments with assortments that are too large confuse the shopper. This point is being overlooked—and is consequently slowing turnover, upping costs. Departments that are even larger under self-selection than they were in the days of competent clerk service are apt to show poor results. One merchant who made a stop-watch study found that customers were taking too long to make up their mind—and, as a consequence, his average sale was declining almost as rapidly as he enlarged his assortments. There's a point of diminishing returns in assortments under self-service and self-selection—make a particular point of finding it, classification by classification.

7. *Store-fixture Leasing May Soon Be a Trend*

The tax situation plus problems of capital entailed by the competitive need to expand combine to suggest the wisdom of applying the leasing concept to new fields. Thus, truck leasing is moving ahead rapidly—and now car leasing is making big gains also. One of the newer fields for leasing—store fixtures. Several companies now specialize in this field. More will probably operate in this field before long. Some stores have arranged to sell their fixtures and then lease them back on a purchase–lease-back plan. (One company in this field claims to have leases totaling almost $100 million.) It remains to be seen whether we will ever reach the point where the tax load and other factors may compel retailers to own little, if anything, in the way of plant. But there is little doubt that the leasing concept is destined for still broader applications in retailing—we understand that even bookkeeping and billing equipment is leased by some retailers. Check into store-fixture leasing—it may simplify your expansion problems and also simplify problems stemming from new credit services offered to customers.

8. *Good Humor—the Best Way to Control Waste*

There's a strange quirk in our nature that makes many employees actually resentful when they are asked to save money for their employer. There's no use railing against it, particularly since there's a way to get around it. The solution—make waste control fun. A crude poster showing a character with a gigantic waistline—and a bit of copy about holding the waste line can accomplish more than a serious lecture. An award of a silver dollar can bring in more good waste-control ideas than a stern warning. A few lines of lyrics on waste, sung to a popular tune, will be hummed all day by some employees—and is bound to penetrate. In brief—while waste is no joke, you'll find that good-natured satire will eliminate more waste than the heavy hand. A little idea like a Tomahawk Club, with tiny tomahawks awarded to the best waste-cutters, worked wonders.

9. *Picking Up Lost Sales during Peak Hours*

From a number of retailers we have heard ideas on how they have successfully cut down walk-outs during peak hours. These ideas include the following:

A. Getting everybody—from the porter to buyers—out on the selling floor during the peak hours.

B. Adding more part-time help—and checking their cost against sales; part-time help is plentiful and includes men and women who work part-time in a second job.

C. Doing an extra good job of helping shoppers locate wanted items; this is doubly time-consuming when the store is crowded.

D. Making sure that floor stocks are ample before rush hours begin.

10. *Our Mobile Population*

In 1958, no less than 21 per cent of our total population—some 35 million people—will change their residence. Of that total, about 23 million will move within the same county; 7 million will move to a different county within the same state; 5 million will move to a different state. Perhaps 90 per cent and more will make new retail contacts when they move. Thus, over 30 million people, representing close to 9 million families, will be picking new retailers this coming year. While several services are available to retailers to welcome these newcomers, it seems clear that too little is done to capture their business—and too much of what is done is done in a humdrum way.

In addition, at least another 21 per cent of our population will change one or more retail contacts for one reason or another. Thus, at least a 40 per cent turnover in customers can be expected by many retailers each year. Figures such as these should make more retailers more fully aware of their basic problem of attracting new customers on a substantial scale.

11. *Customers More Willing to Pay for Services*

Discount houses are adding services—but charging for them. Department stores are charging for more and more services formerly offered at no fee. Various types of chain stores are offering a few services at a charge. All this means that the customer is being conditioned to expect service even in low-margin outlets and that the customer is being conditioned to expect to pay for services. As a matter of fact, the customer is also being conditioned to expect to pay extra for extra features in merchandise. The auto industry, for example, charges for scores of extras. In new homes today, there will be a difference of as much as 25 per cent in the "basic" price of a home and the "complete" price.

All this suggests that many retailers would do well to reevaluate their policies involving charges for services to determine whether certain "free" services can now be charged for. The public may be more willing to accept service charges than some retailers believe to be the case.

12. *Giant Models as Attention Winners*

Put on display a real giant chair—a real monster of a chair—and note how much attention it attracts. (Note, too, how the small fry will insist on clambering over it!) A 9-foot replica of a baseball or football or basketball hero will draw eyes from all over the store— and exclamations too. There's something about outsize models that catches and holds the eye. Even giant-sized packages will stop in-store traffic.

13. *Cutting Marking-receiving Room Costs*

Interested in a program that increased production in the marking and receiving rooms by 15 per cent above norm?—that permitted a one-third cut in employees for these two operations?—that reduced payroll cost despite higher wage rates?—that cut employee turnover in these two functions? Here's the program.

A. A group incentive—not individual bonuses.
B. Incentive payments start when group achieves 75 per cent of standard or normal output.
C. For performance above 75 per cent incentive is an additional 1 per cent for each multiple of 5 percentage points. If any individual performs under 75 per cent, his operation is reviewed and corrections made if indicated.
D. Mechanical improvements were made—and are still being made.
E. Time studies have been made of each of 46 functions.

F. Basic costs have been established.

That's the program. There are further benefits:

A. Employees have enjoyed a bonus every pay period.

B. Shipments move faster than ever before.

C. Overtime has not been necessary.

D. While this store—a fine specialty store with a national reputation—is not unionized, it is understood that the program will not encounter union opposition.

14. "We Advertised It in Today's Paper"

It is always discouraging to walk into a retail store that has a sizable ad in the local newspaper and find nary a sign of that ad inside the store or in the window. No reprint on display. No mention of the ad or the items by the salespeople. Nothing on the counter where the featured merchandise is stocked to say, in one way or another: "As Advertised in Today's Paper." Advertising pays off still better when it is merchandised in the store—that's elementary. Yet only a small percentage of retailers remind the shopper in the store of what they have told her in their newspaper advertising.

15. Check Ordering Procedure on Fast Movers

A national research organization which checks retail inventories in a substantial number of stores made a study recently of the ordering procedure of certain retailers for 22 fast-moving items. This research organization reports that "the percent of sub-normal orders on these 22 fast movers ranged from 23% to 66%." The study goes on to report that "the average fast-moving brand is regularly or generally ordered in sub-normal quantities by at least 17% of these retailers." Clearly, subnormal buying means understocks or out-of-stocks, increases handling costs, cuts down on display, and in general tends to reduce volume on these fast-moving lines. When proper orders for these fast movers are placed, the advantages include lower buying and stock-handling costs; earning additional discounts; better display, which means better volume; a curtailment of understocks and out-of-stocks; better customer satisfaction; larger average sales.

16. Is the Bottom Shelf for Slow Movers Only?

One retailer reports that he stocks some of his fastest-moving items on bottom shelves—and his figures prove they move as well as at eye level. However, his basic aim is to take typical bottom-shelf lines and make them move faster. He does this by displaying bottom-shelf merchandise cleverly, so that it wins added eye appeal. For example, packages are placed to show their greatest surface—thus they can be easily seen from a standing position and hit the shopper with the greatest possible impact. Another trick is smart shelf planning. In this store, the lowest shelf may be 22 inches deep and 12 inches high, with the next shelf up being 14 inches deep and 10 inches high. Each shelf thereafter decreases by 2 inches in depth but remains 10 inches high. In general, bottom shelves can be made to do a better job by giving them special fixturing and display attention. A woman who bends constantly in housework, gardening, and other domestic routines will bend for a bottom shelf—if the proper appeal is made. As for the increasing droves of men shoppers—they have little, if any, objection to bending.

17. *Bringing Dead Space to Life*

One highly successful retail merchant walks through his big store once a week looking for just one thing—dead space that can be turned into a sales producer. A typical example is a television department housed alongside the "wall" of an escalator. Another is using unused space on certain doors by fixing pegboard panels on them and displaying such items as belts. One more example: Swing frames swing out from previously dead wall areas. Keep a list of dead space that you bring to life—publicize this list to executives, and to rank-and-filers, too. Run a contest among all employees for ideas on utilizing dead space. Every square foot picked up is worth money—and there is dead space in every store.

18. *A Manual for New Store Openings*

In too many instances, each new store that is opened gets an expensive "hand-tailored" opening plan. This may be necessary up to a point—after all, each new store unit presents individual problems and opportunities. But several retailers have found that each store opening also involves certain basic items that can be charted in advance. Consequently, one retailer's director of store openings has compiled a special manual—a so-called "preopening manual." It maps out every situation involved in opening a new store—starting some ninety days before O-day. New-store opening costs have reached staggering figures. One way to cut these costs is by achieving a greater degree of step-by-step standardization of each detail. A loose-leaf manual that is constantly kept up to date and adjusted to the specific requirements of each new store unit can prove an effective way to keep new-store opening costs down to a point that will enable new store units to operate in the black more quickly.

19. How to Keep Customers Coming Back

A major problem with most mass retailers is to induce shoppers to come back regularly. This is premised on the correct assumption that the best prospect for any retailer is the present customer. A smart idea for persuading shoppers to come back time and again works this way: A photographer takes license number pictures in the store's parking lot. These are posted regularly inside the store. A customer who spots her license number up on display is entitled to a worthwhile prize. Newspaper advertising is run showing the license-number display inside the store and showing the photographer taking pictures in the parking lot. Winners are also listed in the newspaper ads. A good idea—try it.

20. Make the Parking Lot Work 24 Hours Daily

The parking lot can make bigger returns on the investment when it is kept busier more of the time. Here are some of the things that are being done. More and more merchandise is being sold in the parking lot. More promotions that are being staged inside the store are promoted with signs and banners in the parking lot. When the store is closed, the parking lot is being used for square dancing and for civic and charitable events. One retailer stages a shuffleboard competition on his parking lot when the store is closed.

Nothing should interfere with the basic purpose of the parking lot—to enable the shopper to park conveniently. But in off hours and when the store is closed, the parking lot can continue to bring back a return on the investment. And, even when it is open, many feet of ground space, wall space, and air space can be put to work without in any way cramping the parking facilities.

21. Demonstrations in the Window

Simple demonstrations of skilled workmanship always pull window traffic and hold that traffic for unusually long periods. For ex-

ample, showing how a chair is upholstered attracts amazing attention when demonstrated in the window. And sidewalk tests (of
rugs, for instance) continue to move merchandise. (Incidentally,
a definite trend back toward selling displays *outside* the store has
set in—garden displays in the parking lot started this trend; now it
has spread to other categories. The vending machine outside the
store is part of this trend.)

22. *How to Identify Departments and Sections*

The novel touch in departmental identification can give a store
that all-important interrupting note. A gigantic watch identifies the
watch and clock section. Caricatures of storks identify the infant
section. A humorous rendition of a mop and pail identifies the clean-
up shop. And in preparing all store signs, bear in mind that women
who wear glasses seldom wear them when shopping—an amazing
number of shoppers shop almost "blind." Be sure your signs can be
read by the astigmatic and the nearsighted.

23. *Employee Incentives Gain in Retailing*

In one field, the chains report that 65 per cent had profit-sharing
plans for employees in 1956 as compared with 38 per cent in 1950.
Some 45 per cent had stock-purchase plans (although usually for
executives rather than rank-and-file employees). Even the percentage
of these chains running employee contests had jumped, over the
six-year interval, by almost 50 per cent. In another field, the chains
reported large increases in the number offering employees noncon-
tributory group life insurance, hospitalization and accident-sickness
insurance, retirement plans, etc. Where part-time employees of teen
age are employed, plans are being developed under which a stipulated number of these teen-age employees are offered college scholar-
ships. (Incidentally, these special plans for teen-age employees are
designed to provide a source of future retail executives.) In retailing,
there is a wide opportunity and a desperate need for brilliant thinking with respect to employee incentives. It is questionable whether
merely duplicating what industry offers in so-called "fringe benefits" will be enough. This doesn't mean that retailing will have to be
more lavish in its fringe benefits—but it will certainly have to be
more astute; retailing will have to develop more ingenious plans,
like the scholarship plan for teen-agers.

24. Better Display for Higher-price Lines

There is reason to believe that, in many merchandise categories, the shopper is willing to buy higher-price lines in larger volume. But space and position in too many stores continue to be assigned to price lines as though there had been no change in customer buying habits for years. Every retailer who gives special display to larger sizes reports that larger sizes move well. Why not give extra display to higher-price lines? Give them more shelf frontage, better position, and, above all, "talking" signs that will sell higher-price lines. Retail profit comes from dollars, not from percentages. The more high-price lines you move, the more dollars you take in. The cost per sale for a low-price line is every bit as high as for a high-price line. Public income has gone up faster than retail-price lining. So has public taste. So has public sophistication. So has public desire to own better merchandise in order to achieve social status. Give higher priority to your higher-price lines. Interestingly, one store reports featuring stainless steel flatware at both 97 cents and $1.69 per place setting for $5.00 worth of register receipts. Over a fourteen-week period, with a total of $70,000 done on both price lines, the higher-price line outsold the cheaper by three to one!

25. Slow Down Traffic—and Jump Average Sale

In some modern stores, traffic moves too fast. This is one reason shoppers are seen doubling back in their tracks—they've moved so fast they raced right by some needed purchases. And this is one reason why so many shoppers buy only half as much on each shopping trip as they had intended. Slow down traffic (within reason, of course) and you'll add to your average sale. How to slow down traffic? There are many ways. You may deliberately arrange for several partial "road blocks." Or put some merchandise in bins or dump baskets on the floor or close to it. Plan for interrupting notes in aisle displays—it is excessive regularity that speeds traffic right past a sale. Put better selling copy on signs; "talking" signs can "talk" shoppers into stopping—and then into buying. Break up those mile-long bowling-alley aisles. Finally, use a variety of fixtures—different styles, heights, and shapes. It's so easy to keep right on walking past several hundred linear feet of completely uniform displays.

26. *Selling in the Window*

As a promotional unit, the window is on the decline. But as a *selling* unit, it is in a positive uptrend. This new trend takes the form of putting vending machines in the window. Hundreds are now in operation; soon the total will be in the thousands. These window vendors work twenty-four hours daily and on Sunday, too. Interestingly, they sell more during store-open hours than when the store is closed. What is being vended this way? Cigarettes, candy, and some health aids are some of the categories. One of the country's largest builders of shopping centers is planning to install window vendors in the majority of the stores in his centers. These vendors will even be refrigerated and will sell certain foods, including butter and milk. Techniques have been developed for putting these vendors into the plate glass. Tests are being made of the items that move best through the window vendor—locality by locality and store type by store type. This is all part of the broad trend toward more sidewalk retailing and toward selling twenty-four hours daily seven days of the week.

27. *Fewer Shopping Trips*

There seems little doubt that a broad trend is developing among shoppers to make *fewer* shopping trips each week. This trend can be bucked, the shopper *should* be induced to shop more often. But since this is a fundamental fact of retail life, it is necessary for the retailer to develop techniques that will encourage the shopper to buy more on each shopping trip and enable the shopper to buy more in less time because time is of the essence.

28. *More Gaiety in Retailing*

Americans are a fun-loving people—bear in mind that our most popular TV entertainers are usually comedians. Retailing needs more gaiety, less formality. That's one reason many retailers are turning to the circus. But whether it's a circus-y concept or something more simple like some witticisms on the back bar of a fountain, be gay. The shopper who chuckles will be more apt to make the retailer "checkle."

29. *Next: Invisible Fixtures*

Good fixturing should be neither seen nor "heard." In other words, the invisible fixture has many merits. It is merchandise—not the fixture—that sells merchandise. Glass shelves are being used in some fixtures to achieve a degree of invisibility. Plastic shelves may be employed for the same purpose. Studies are now being made of invisible fixturing; keep in touch with the leading fixture houses and store architects on this trend.

30. *Getting Customers to Visit More Departments*

The larger stores become and the more varied the number of categories stocked, the more difficult it becomes to induce the shopper to visit more and more departments. Some suggestions to achieve that goal are given here. Install a really dramatic store directory; soup it up! In addition, other directories may be installed at many points throughout the store—this is seldom done. Use humorous and attention-getting section markers. Phones may be put in so that shoppers may inquire about the location of a wanted section. Drill your salespeople so they won't send shoppers off on wild-goose chases —and check them with your own shoppers. Put up miniature directories of nearby sections at many spots, especially directories covering related merchandise. Most important, have your executives shop the store periodically to determine *their* problems in locating merchandise—what *they* experience difficulty in locating, the shopper simply will never find!

31. *Keeping Youngsters Happy while Parents Shop*

A Kiddyville or Kiddy Corner or Kiddie Korral, designed to keep the youngsters content while Mom or Pop, or both, shop can have a number of benefits. If coin-operated machines are installed, for example, the revenue may pay for the space used. In addition, parents shop longer and buy more when not distracted by the children. Housekeeping costs in the store are cut by such innovations, for one youngster on the loose can play havoc! The nearby display of toys and other children's merchandise will usually encourage the parent to make a purchase either when leaving the child to shop or when returning to pick up the child. Mothers—and fathers—who otherwise might not want to shop at all are more apt to come into the store when they know the children will not be a headache. Finally, adults with no children will be less annoyed when youngsters aren't under foot.

32. *Window Shopping by Motorists*

Although window shopping is definitely declining, some of the lack of interest of the pedestrian in store windows may be made up by planning windows for passing motorists. Try driving by your store windows—it's time to look upon them as *selling fixtures* rather than as display units. Vending machines are going into and in front of windows for tweny-four-hour selling. Merchandise is again being stacked on the ground in front of windows. Floor fixtures are being put up against window interiors. The window area, inside and out, should be considered a *sales* area—and planned as such. Try it— and add from 5 to 15 per cent to your main-floor selling area.

33. *The "Oldest-model" Promotion*

There are certain promotions that continue to pull year after year —and one of these good old standbys is the "oldest-model" concept. It's been used for china and for appliances, for wedding gowns and for shoes, for furniture and for lamps. Even a rainy day failed to discourage over 800 shoppers from thronging a store for an Oldest China Contest. Nine extra showcases were required to house the collection. The prizes need not be big, the total cost is small—and, if properly planned, this can be a direct salesmaker. Why even an old-pan drive has had a unique success—it brought in utensils up to fifty years old.

34. *Encouraging the Whole Family to Shop*

A number of retailers are developing plans to encourage the whole family to shop simultaneously. Shopping decisions are more and more family affairs, and because so many couples both work, because baby sitters are expensive, and because families are closer together— family shopping is on the increase. When whole families shop, the average ticket is higher. Decisions are made faster and tend to stick —returns are fewer. How to encourage families to shop? Stores can remain open evenings, offer small refreshments, take care of babies, have special premiums for youngsters and teen-agers—in addition to running advertisements urging the whole family to shop.

35. *Don't Sail into the Wind*

Some retailers are debating the wisdom of trying to build up volume on Monday, Tuesday, and Wednesday, and early in the morning. The consensus now is that this is like sailing into the wind. More and more merchants are concluding that the time to sell the shopper the largest volume at the lowest cost is when the shopper wants to shop—not when the retailer wants her to shop. The problem here is to enable the shopper to buy faster during the peak hours. It's been said in retailing that only half the customers in a store buy, and only half of those who buy purchase all they intended to buy. During peak hours, walk-outs and half walk-outs are even higher than these figures indicate. The great opportunity to increase volume at lowest cost is by developing plans that will enable the shopper to complete more buying transactions during the peak hours. Focus on that fundamental objective—don't spend big money trying to entice the shopper to shop when it isn't convenient for her to shop. It's costly to try to change basic shopping habits—it's wiser to change your procedures to conform with new shopping habits.

36. *A "Thank You" to the Big Customer*

A customer buys a big order in furniture. Or in major appliances. Or in rugs. How seldom that customer gets a thank-you letter. One retailer reports highly successful use of a thank-you letter that goes out about a month after the big-ticket sale has been delivered. The letter expresses the hope that the customer is happy—and a stamped return envelope is enclosed for the customer's convenience in replying. Over 85 per cent of the customers do reply—the majority with enthusiasm. The few complaints that come in are welcome—the customer who has a complaint and doesn't voice it may never be a customer again.

37. *The Snack—the Break—as a Traffic Builder*

For those stores in which shopping is a bit more leisurely, the coffee break and the Coke break are becoming remarkably common. In fact, the coffee break has been used to encourage morning shopping in food supers—where shopping is not exactly leisurely. This nation has developed an amazing addiction to the coffee break in factories and offices—it is just becoming established in retailing for the shopper. But these breaks will not for long be limited to coffee or Coke. The snack break is on the way. It's being used right now in some appliance stores as part of range demonstrations; it's long been popular in food demonstrations in food supers—and, actually, the fountain in the drug store is part of the snack-break tradition, with the difference that here the shopper pays for the snack. In any event, both to bring in traffic and to hold traffic longer, food and drink are coming up as promotional devices. Call in the chef—or the automatic coffee maker!

38. *Working with Clubs*

Women's clubs, church clubs—all of the multitude of organizations to which women belong—offer retailing constant opportunities for mutually interesting tie-ups. Special price offers are, of course, common. But it isn't always necessary to cut margins. Some stores, for example, simply offer a flat sum (25 to 50 cents) for every club member who shows up on a specific day. This may be done every month. It brings in traffic—and that traffic feels an urge to buy. The coffee break—referred to earlier—is sometimes made a part of this idea, with the club chairwoman as the hostess.

39. *"Talking" Elevators—"Talking" Escalators?*

Elevators that "talk" are now a reality—in office buildings. And one such installation has been made in an exclusive women's specialty store—with others to follow. These are the new electronic devices that say "Going up," and "Going down," and with regional accents, too! These electronic voices can, of course, do much more than simply give elevator orders and lessons in elevator etiquette. They can also deliver a selling message—and there's no doubt that they will soon be used for this purpose. Once the elevator does robot electronic selling—will the same or similar devices be used for similar purposes on escalators? We think so. And the electronic voice will be used in other ways, too, throughout various stores. Maybe it will be employed to admonish a group of chatting salespeople to "break it up."

40. *Action—Action—Action!*

There are fewer action displays in all types of stores than for years. Why? One reason—stores have become too sedate, too uniform. Retailing needs the *interrupting* note; action displays can provide it. A second reason for the trend away from action displays —mechanical trouble. But today these troubles are fewer than ever before. A hard-goods store reports excellent results from a carousel showing small appliances; a food store has used the same device for special foods. Many of your suppliers offer excellent action displays; some of these displays use merely the heat from a lighted bulb to provide action. Try action displays—in your windows, inside the store. Action displays can give you *action!*

41. *Round-the-clock Promotions*

In the stimulation of volume for major appliances, round-the-clock promotions have been amazingly successful. Stores have been kept open twenty-four hours a day for three days and more. Just why the idea appeals to the shopper is a bit of a mystery, but its appeal can't be disputed. Why not adapt the same idea to other fields—to soft goods, home furnishings, and others? Give it a thought—and bear in mind that the warehouse sale, which started with major appliances, has now been successfully employed for furniture and home furnishings and even for soft goods. Of course, some food stores have remained open day and night for years; ditto for some drug stores. But these are *traditional* hours for these particular stores—what we are talking about is the generation of a huge excitement for an *unusual* store-hour schedule for a limited period.

42. *The Gambling Instinct*

Various techniques have been used by a number of stores for keeping shoppers on edge through prizes that are announced unexpectedly. For example, periodically during the day, a customer who is nearest a certain item at the moment gets it for free. In another store, the shopper who is getting a demonstration at the moment that an alarm clock rings gets a special trade-in value. The gambling instinct runs high and this is an effective technique for catering to it.

43. *Everybody Has a Peeping-Tom Instinct*

The sidewalk superintendent is really a kind of Peeping Tom. That's why some builders surround their construction jobs with fences equipped with peepholes. That, too, is why for many years a retailer has occasionally covered his windows with paper, leaving only a peephole. The well-known shadow box is really a form of peephole. In brief—appeal to the Peeping-Tom instinct which, in turn, is part of the curiosity streak in practically all humans. It may or may not be true that curiosity killed the cat—but it most certainly is true that whatever is partly hidden generates an almost irresistible impulse to get a good look. Just try walking down your street with a large picture carried upside down—and see what happens!

44. Needed: More One-stop Shoppers

As more retailers diversify their inventories by classification, we get more so-called "one-stop" or "one-half-stop" outlets, competing for the same shopper with much the same merchandise. Consequently, the number of one-stop shoppers is lagging seriously behind the number of one-stop outlets. As a further consequence, the turn-over rate in some of the new categories is not what it should be. You attract more one-stop shoppers by *actively following up the accounts on your books*. Planned telephone solicitation is becoming more popular in this connection. So is more direct-mail advertising—with post-cards personalized by the salesperson. Newspaper advertising specifically directed to customers—prospects will read it, too!—is a splendid idea. In most retail businesses, your best *prospect* is your present *customer*. Pin that up on your office wall—and read it aloud at least once each day!

45. Incentives for Multiple Sales

The trend toward merchandising multiple units is remarkably strong. It is best evidenced in the tote-home pack of soft drinks and beer, but is now winding up with canned goods and a host of other items. This, in turn, is encouraging various stores to develop incentives for salespeople to push multiple units. One merchant gives 20 cents to each salesperson who sells a box of hosiery—three to a box. Store shoppers are ordered to hand in reports on salespeople who do a good job of selling multiple units—and these salespeople are suitably rewarded. Training programs are being developed to show salespeople how to write up more multiple sales. A larger average sale is the royal road to a better retail net profit and the multiple-sales unit is the best approach to that royal road.

46. Convertibility—the Big Trend in Fixtures

Maximum quick-change flexibility is the great trend in floor fixtures. Convertibility is the key to present thinking. Indeed, some tricks of the theater are being studied to learn more about "quick change." Merchandising has been tailored too much to the floor fixture—now the fixture is being so designed that it becomes the servant, not the master, of merchandising. A face lifting and a new appearance can now be given overnight to a small department or to a whole floor—no shut-down, no loss of selling area, no loss of time or volume. Show-window flexibility is now being applied to store interiors—a splendid trend.

47. Is the "See-thru" Window Through?

Is the "see-thru" window about through? Well—that may be an exaggeration. But, since nothing in the world of retail merchandising is perfect—many retailers are having second thoughts about windows which give a broad view of the store interior. And as a consequence, a new look is coming. The reasons? So many stores now have see-thru windows that they all look alike. In addition, they fail to show the back-of-the-store sections and they reflect light. If the store is rather empty, shoppers may be discouraged from coming in; if the store is rather crowded, shoppers may also be discouraged from coming in when a quick look through the open window gives them an easy view of the whole store.

The new technique? Half-back window displays are given over in particular to back-of-the-store merchandise. Slanted glass cuts down reflection and enables street traffic to get a better view of merchandise shown at a low level in the window. Big posters featuring specials are being used, with the posters mounted so that they will not blank out the store interior. Low-level platforms are being used for merchandise display.

48. Weddings Become Store Events

A department store staged a wedding in its windows! Another large retailer celebrates its anniversaries with a special offer to wedded couples celebrating the same anniversary—thus on its twenty-fifth business anniversary, it staged a huge event for couples in the area married twenty-five years. An appliance dealer ran an ad asking couples about to celebrate their fiftieth anniversary to write. (This was a teaser ad.) They were promised an exciting gift and were told they would be guests of honor at a party. Wedding anniversaries have a lot of sentiment attached to them—and anything sentimental offers a good promotional opportunity.

49. *Incentive-compensation Plans for Salespeople*

In outlets selling big-ticket merchandise, especially where the salesperson has leeway in meeting price competition, incentive-compensation plans for salespeople are taking the following forms: a flat percentage on selling price plus a flat percentage on gross profit; a sliding commission rate based on selling price with the rate highest at list price and diminishing a percentage point at every 10 per cent of list; sliding-scale commission on total month's volume; a base commission plus sliding dollars on selling price; and various combinations of these basic procedures.

50. *Coming Fixture Changes*

Store fixtures seem to be on the way to a number of construction changes: Glass shelves may give way to clear plastic—the latter is unbreakable, easy to handle, cut, clean, and install. Moulded plastic drawers will take the place of wood drawers; ditto with respect to trays. The whole moulded concept will make big strides in fixtures. The process reduces weight and tends to cut costs. There's less problem with sticking. Even completely moulded tables (in color) are on the way. More metal will be used in fixtures—colored metals. These metals will include anodized aluminum and various alloys in stainless steel and nickel. One object will be to get away from the chromium look, which has had its day.

PART 2

500 Merchandising Ideas

Introduction

Approximately five hundred merchandising ideas, accumulated through painstaking research and study, appear in the pages that follow. Several thousand ideas were brought together from both large and medium-sized manufacturers in every conceivable industry. Those selected have a record of successful use and hold promise for equally successful adoption or adaptation by merchandisers in fields far removed from those of the original use.

Each idea is described briefly, in from 150 to 200 words. Moreover, the potential area of use for each idea is indicated. In other words, this is not merely a case of reporting ideas, but rather a case of interpreting and analyzing each idea so that wider areas of exploitation quickly become evident. Moreover, the ideas are classified by basic subjects so that, for reference use, ideas within specific subject classifications may be quickly located.

However, the principal value of this collection of five hundred tested merchandising ideas lies in its use as a mental prod. If it is correct to assume that one excellent way to develop ideas is by immersing oneself in them, these pages should be helpful in stimulating the imagination and providing merchandising concepts and tactics.

Business executives are primarily concerned and involved with the coming year, the coming season. This is as it should be, especially with respect to executives whose primary responsibility is the stimulation of merchandise movement. I am myself dubious about the forecasting ability when attempts are made to look ahead more than a very few years, and this work does not attempt long-term projections. Part 1 has dealt with fundamental trends, some now barely visible, that must be considered when planning merchandising for the near future. It has been intended to provide a framework for strategic concepts. Part 2 is a collection of some five hundred proven merchandising ideas, and it should provide happy hunting for the executive seeking specific suggestions for moving more merchandise more profitably.

CHAPTER 24

The Product

The "Limited-edition" Concept

From major appliances to soft goods (laundry combination units to swim suits) the "limited-edition" concept has been successfully exploited. And the stronger the snob appeal becomes in the acquisition of merchandise—and this is a powerful social trend—the more pulling power exerted by the limited-edition concept. This merchandising event calls for pulling out all of the snob stops. Example: For a ready-to-wear line, (1) the counter "poster" consisted of a gold-etched fabric; (2) the manikin was framed like an objet d'art, including a rhinestone-inlaid golden crown; (3) the event was featured in magnificent ads in the high-fashion publications and distribution was limited to a small group of top-prestige stores, which love this type of event. Do these events pay off for the manufacturer? Not always directly—but the indirect values are many: (1) The line is given additional prestige; (2) considerable special promotion is obtained from the cooperating stores; (3) the shopper tends, as a direct consequence, to give more attention to the higher-priced units in the line; (4) frequently considerable publicity is obtained. (If possible, adapt the design for the limited edition in regular price lines.)

New Products vs. New Uses?

New products get a vast amount of merchandising attention. Question: Should we bring out a new product—or find new *uses* (and thus new markets) for our present item or line? For the maker of what had been for years a completely prosaic item—a swab stick—the decision was to find and exploit new uses. Results have been quite remarkable. Reasoning that led to the decision included the following: (1) We've known of many uses other than the few familiar ones but we've never promoted them; (2) we know this item inside out—a new product and its markets will be new to *us,* too; (3) we have a stream of new uses coming in, proving that other new uses can be found; (4) we won't have to persuade the trade to make a substantially larger investment with us at a time when the trade is cutting inventory; (5) we won't have to dilute our own capital funds, our own promotional funds, our own sales-force time and ability, and our total costs will move up only slightly; (6) the gamble is smaller, the results more predictable. It is worth pondering whether merchandising strategy calls for a new *product,* or the merchandising of new uses for the established product. New-use merchandising has been too neglected.

The Small Size Recaptures the Spotlight

For some years, one of the great trends in packaging has been toward the larger size and toward multiple units. This, of course, has been a thoroughly sound and extremely effective merchandising development. While simultaneously there has been some exploitation of smaller sizes, this has been something of a side issue in most merchandising programs. But now a definite trend is emerging involving "the small size for small families." It received major emphasis from a top bottler of soft drinks, and was promptly followed with a special push by one of the great canned-food brands. The soft-drink development was especially significant since in this category the emphasis in recent years has been toward larger sizes. The breweries are giving renewed attention to smaller sizes. So are several other classifications. This renewed interest in smaller sizes is traceable to (1) public interest in and need for smaller sizes; (2) the end of the line had been reached in large sizes in some categories—the only way to go therefore, was back to smaller sizes; (3) the new concepts in multipacks lend themselves admirably to merchandising the smaller size in such a way as to avoid cutting the average unit of sale.

Increase the AREA of Use

New uses often have an ability to make a volume and profit contribution to an established item that could involve larger totals (with less risk) than the introduction of a new item. New uses may involve new *areas* of use, rather than a new form of application. Example: A highly successful health aid, originally introduced for chapped lips—is now being promoted for cold-weather use for the entire area from tip of nose to chin. Obviously, this could triple the total consumption, because the total area involved is at least three times that of the lips exclusively. Maybe lipsticks will some day be promoted for use on the face elsewhere other than the lips. Depilatories were originally planned almost exclusively for under-arm use—now they are applied to larger areas of the body. Actually, putting radios in many rooms in the home involves this same principle of new area of use. Now the same concept is being applied to the refrigerator, which is finding secondary uses in the recreation room. Explore this concept of wider *areas* of use—on the body, in the home, etc. The principle has potential application in many merchandise classifications.

Taking Net Profit on the Package

As a spreading variety of staple and semistaple or convenience-merchandise classifications turn to special packaging for special gift occasions (as well as for the year-round market), a trend will grow that involves *taking a net profit on the package*. The net profit on the package may, indeed, be larger than the net profit on the contents! Also, the price of the package may be *several* times that of the contents! These are all fairly new merchandising considerations in the classifications just described. Example: The manufacturer turns out an excellent line of packaged candies. The retail will be in the area of $2.50 per pound. For Christmas, some magnificent packages were developed, for instance, a cocktail ice bucket of insulated aluminum, an Italian import. Another package was a jewel box. A third package was a beautiful casserole and warmer. The retail value of each of these "packages" was at least equal to the retail of the enclosed candy—in the case of the casserole, the retail on this package was close to *three times* the retail of the candy. In each instance, the net profit on the package was close to, or exceeded, the net profit to the candy maker (and the retailer, too) of the candy itself. As packages for the gift market multiply—more merchandisers will take net profit on the package.

Sleepers in the Line

A large food advertiser, rechecking his line (which is done periodically), discovered that, for two years, an unadvertised item showed larger percentage increases (from a smaller base, of course) than his advertised items. Now, that sleeper is to be strongly advertised; it will also get a de luxe package and special promotion. In somewhat similar fashion, one of the great drug brand names was given recently to a ten-year-old item that had been merchandised with a 16-letter professional-type name. A new bottle was designed—and a large ad budget put behind this sleeper. Another example: The tank-type vacuum cleaner took the play away from the upright cleaner. But recently, several manufacturers noted revived interest in the upright vacuum cleaner—it is now being advertised-promoted heavily and may ultimately achieve larger volume than the tank-type. In many lines there are neglected items, ripe for modern exploitation. Actually, with Detroit now committed to the smaller or compact cars that were popular years ago, something of the same principle is at work here. New products can be old products reincarnated—or sleepers that are given the breath of new merchandising life.

Designers on the Retail Floor

Several manufacturers have arranged for their designers, stylists, fashionists to participate in specially planned clinics and shows staged for the public in retail stores. Two purposes are being realized: (1) The prestige and the knowledge of the designers add pull to this sort of store event; (2) the designers get out among the public, rub shoulders with the public rather than confining themselves so exclusively, as they tend to do, with fellow designers. The second benefit is probably the more important. Designers tend to insulate themselves from the ultimate customer. Too often, this results in designs that give the merchandising executive real headaches. In several department stores we spotted special promotions being staged with designer participation by a maker of lamps, a maker of shoes, a maker of rugs, and a maker of major appliances. (It's also interesting to note several demonstration-type store events with top executives of the supplier not merely attending—but participating. There's no better vantage point for sound merchandising planning than the retail floor!)

Let Retailers Sell That Booklet

When booklets made available by manufacturers for consumers distribution are sold rather than distributed at no charge, the general practice is to offer the booklet in the manufacturer's national advertising. But now a growing number of manufacturers are merchandising these booklets as though they constituted another number in the line. Several manufacturers have followed this plan for a few years—proof that it works. Example: A maker of drapery hardware has a splendid window-decorating booklet for the home. The booklet is made available to the retailer on a basis that permits him to sell it at a normal profit. Thus, the merchant has two reasons for promoting the booklet: (1) The profit on the booklet itself; and (2) the probability that the woman who buys the booklet will also buy the merchandise. There is evidence that more manufacturers are putting the consumer booklet into the line and having the retailer sell it at profit-making margins. Thus, booklets can be made partly or wholly self-liquidating—more effective distribution is obtained—and the booklet does a still better job of promoting the merchandise it features.

TV for New-model Trade Announcement

For a widely distributed line does a TV network program offer a sound technique for introducing a new model? A razor maker decided the answer was in the affirmative. TV commercials were prepared, therefore, on its regular national network hookup that would introduce its new model simultaneously both to the trade and to the public. What is more—these announcements began several weeks before the new model had reached the retailer! This may have marked the first time that a national TV hookup was used to announce a new model simultaneously to the trade and to the public in advance of the availability of the model. The trade was urged to order in advance—the public was urged to buy promptly. There is no doubt that this plan created considerable excitement in the trade—very likely up to 50 per cent of the trade saw at least one of the TV announcements—a higher percentage of trade attention than might be achieved by any other technique. This very likely was also as true of jobbers' salesmen as of retail salespeople. Store owners, owners of wholesale establishments, other distributor executives were also reached.

A New Size for the Item

New sizes for packages are common. But new sizes for the item itself are not nearly so common. Since the trade is beginning to rebel at the mounting total of new package sizes—new sizes for the item itself may help justify the resulting new package size in the eyes of the trade. Thus, a plastic bandage brings out an extra-wide bandage—larger than any on the market. There is a definite first-aid need for this extra-wide bandage. Thus, the resulting new size package has a logical reason for being stocked by the trade—it opens up a new market and will not cut into the sale of existing packages. Many items that have been on the market for years in a traditional size or sizes might be subjected to size study. For example, tablets of sugar might be ready for new-size testing. Maybe the loaf of bread is ripe for some new sizes—some successful work has been done on bread over recent years along this line but the end of the line has not been reached. Moving way over to floor coverings, maybe opportunities exist either for some new sizes—or for extra emphasis on one or more sizes that are sleepers. Maybe a toothpaste with a still wider ribbon is indicated. In brief—check historic sizes (not counts); the time may be ripe for a new size for the item itself.

De Luxe Line for a Staple

A maker of copper cooking utensils, primarily a staple line, brought out a de luxe group of numbers to retail at an average of 25 per cent higher than the regular line. The de luxe line was made differently— designed differently. It obviously "looked the value." The de luxe numbers were introduced initially through department stores—distribution to be broadened both as production increases and as public acceptance grows. Interesting merchandising points involved include the following: (1) A staple line can be given a dynamic sales lift by planning a de luxe group; (2) the de luxe group obviously will add glamour to the regular numbers; (3) in this instance, the regular line had begun to appear in food supers in price promotions—the de luxe line will counteract this situation (if department stores, for example, throw out the regular line because of food super cut-price competition, they may welcome the new de luxe line); (4) the manufacturer's sales force is given something excitingly new to sell—distributors are shaken out of the doldrums, too; (5)—finally, the rapidly growing market for higher-quality, better-designed merchandise is catered to. This is the germ of the thinking: Many staple lines were designed in an era different from the present era of one vast nation of middle-classers.

Place New Products inside the Family

One of the giant manufacturers of major appliances has a strong program involving putting new models and new products with the corporation family. This program starts at the top—with the company's management executives. It goes down through the sales force, factory employees, office employees, and even its distributors have similar programs involving their executives and rank-and-file personnel. This company reports that the plan achieves the following: (1) It reveals virtues as well as flaws of new models and products; these comments are encouraged; (2) it creates favorable conversation that spreads out; some 10,000 families are involved; (3) it enables the salesmen to talk about new items with authority—they use these items in their homes; (4) it brings in the wife as an enthusiastic booster. (Too often, manufacturers do a poor job of selling their own line *to and through* their own family —and especially to and through the salesman and his family. Ownership and use of the item is a straight road to this important goal.)

Great Artists Become Merchandising Gimmicks

Great artists won't approve our semantics—but they are clearly becoming a merchandising gimmick. And a productive one, too. Henri Matisse and Pablo Picasso have contributed designs for fabrics. Picasso's designs have also been used for men's ties. Other great artists will be making their contributions by way of design for a multitude of products. They will move in on the industrial designer, to some degree. They will also be making contributions to package design—and thus move in on the domain of the package designer. And their art will be increasingly employed in merchandising programs. For Christmas, 1959, a famous-brand liquor came in a special package that contained famous works of art. All this becomes completely logical when the merchandising man remembers that our people are becoming more sophisticated, their taste is improving. Then, too, the race for social status was never more intense; and possession of anything by great artists clearly confers social status on the owner. Finally, a well-heeled people can afford to indulge themselves in this way. So—think of our great artists as merchandising gimmicks. They'll shudder—but your sales charts may be made quite happy!

The Role of Gadgetry in Merchandising

Currently, some stereo-set makers are featuring three-channel stereo. According to technicians, three channels offer no true listening advantage over two channels. But the shopper is unquestionably influenced by numbers in this instance—precisely as shoppers were influenced by numbers in the early days of radio when a receiving set with a large number of tubes was generally accepted as being superior to a set with a small number of tubes. In much the same way, at least some of the automatic washers are of dubious advantage to the user—but apparently the more the panel board of a washer looks like the panel board of an atomic sub, the more shopper appeal it has. Merchandisers must be cynical—because, even if one doesn't approve of these tactics, competition usually compels one to follow suit, willy-nilly. An amazing variety of merchandise premises its merchandising concepts on the froth rather than on the substance, on the gadget or the gimmick rather than the basic product. Indeed, when a merchandiser plugs the package rather than its contents, he is following this same brand of thinking. Incidentally, as competing merchandise becomes increasingly similar in principal features, it follows that secondary and even tertiary features must be conceived and then promoted in order to achieve some point of difference.

The Built-in Greeting Card

There appears to be no limit to the annual increase in total volume done on greeting cards. The figures are simply fantastic—and the end is nowhere near in sight. As a consequence, a small number of manufacturers are now enclosing greeting cards in their merchandise packages—some top cigarette brands do this for Father's Day and for other gift occasions. The built-in greeting card fits in logically with the enormously expanding year-round gift market—as well as with the special-occasion gift market. It becomes a plus feature that lends itself to effective merchandising and promotion. Of course, if the built-in greeting card is strictly seasonal and if it cannot easily be removed from the package, then it becomes a merchandising hazard. These are, however, solvable problems. The built-in greeting card has a lot to recommend it —and there is little doubt that scores of merchandise lines will soon be using the idea.

New Sizes with New Merchandizing Appeal

Retailers tend to complain—and with justification—that far too many new sizes of a wide variety of merchandise involve little, if any, new merchandising considerations. The flood of new sizes with little merchandising merit has now got the retail fraternity up in arms. There is still plenty of room for new sizes, but they must be new sizes based on brilliant merchandising reasoning, not on playing copycat. Example: Fresh-roasted ground coffee is traditionally sold in 1- and 2-pound containers. Once the container is opened, the contents begin to lose flavor. And in by far the most homes, coffee is taken out of the pound container just a couple of spoonfuls at a time. Therefore, it becomes highly logical to bring out a 2-ounce tin for ground coffee. This comes more closely toward matching typical consumer use (2 ounces are adequate for six cups of coffee). And most homes have six-cup or eight-cup coffee makers. The 2-ounce containers are then put up in six-serve cartons to achieve the same total unit sale as with the traditional larger unit. New sizes in the sales unit should start with an analysis of what the user needs, with analysis of changing consumer requirements, not with the desire simply to imitate competition.

Ideas from Customer Complaints

A customer objection may turn out to be a merchandising opportunity. Example: Milk of magnesia. It has always tasted like a cotton ball, pretty awful. Now milk of magnesia is available mint-flavored. (And, of course, with such a development a staple item wins new selling and marketing excitement.) Another example: The pedestal electric fan has sadly lacked fine design in an age in which housewives take interior decoration quite seriously. Now pedestal fans have been given beautiful modern design. Another example: A disinfectant with a horrible odor is now available pine-scented. (The usual merchandising practice is to keep the old item on the market—permit the two to fight it out.) Manufacturers tend to be too well insulated these days against customer gripes. How long since you compiled and studied customers' complaints? One more example: Air conditioners are hardly decorative. One brand now features a handsome picture panel because women objected to its appearance.

Timely Limited-edition Packaging

The limited-edition concept is especially timely in the rapidly developing market for superluxuries. At one time, the limited edition was really looked upon as a showpiece; it was planned more for conversation than for sales volume. But now an increasingly sophisticated public (also a well-heeled public that can indulge its more sophisticated taste) has assumed large enough proportions to offer a large-volume market for the limited edition. This is true not only for gift selling—but also for "own use" purchase. Some interesting examples of limited-edition merchandising emerge in women's hosiery. These hosiery limited editions start with novel, beautiful hosiery construction; unique styling that is in perfect taste. Then, instead of packaging the traditional three in a box, only two are put in each magnificent box. The pricing is way-out-yonder high. Markups to the trade are also high. Distribution is also limited— to better outlets. [One mill offered special "push money" (P.M.) to salespeople on its limited-edition packages; it worked extremely well in better department store and specialty store accounts.] The limited edition is on the verge of a big expansion—it is one more step, and a big one, in the broad trend toward trading up.

Building "Parts" and "Satellite" Volume

In some merchandise lines, parts and accessories or "satellite" items eventually come to assume large sales volume. Example: A rug cleaner marketed by a rug mill which even has a separate sales manager (good idea) for these accessory items. Another example: The electric shaver. Here such accessory items as a preshave powder stick or lotion, after-shave lotions, special tune-up oil for the shaver, coil cords, cleaning brushes—all show spurts in volume as the basic product gets into broad use. In these instances, there is a tendency for the part and accessory line simply to expand haphazardly. (Moreover, in some cases, outside organizations get the gravy involved in the parts and accessory volume.)

A major electric razor house planned a complete parts and accessory line, coordinated packaging, gave a play to the line in its TV commercials, planned a special incentive for its salesmen, prepared a special floor fixture for the line, which was offered as part of a deal to the trade. Check the satellites that rim your product—they may offer interesting volume potentials.

Introducing a New Related Product

You have a new item ready to be launched—but it will not do well unless it is tied in with a related product because *in use* it is employed only with this related item. What to do? The solution, as developed by a drug item, was to develop a cooperative merchandising plan with the related item. This is the setup. The new drug item was a medication for use in a steam vaporizer—no other way of using the medication. And the producer of the medication did not want to go into the steam-vaporizer business. So the drug producer hooked up with one of the leading producers of steam vaporizers—both drug and vaporizer manufacturers were well-known names. A joint deal by the two companies offered a counter rack that displays both the medication and the vaporizer. The display also offered 2-ounce free samples of the medication. This joint use of a fixture by two noncompeting manufacturers will undoubtedly become more common because items are related, because retailers like related-item merchandising events, and because of the fierce competition for fixture space.

Line Standardization Can Be Carried Too Far

In several fields dealers are crying for more standardization in sizes and colors by all the manufacturers. They complain that lack of standardization results in (1) mismatching (especially of color) which aggravates the customer; (2) excess inventories; (3) complicated selling and even lost sales; more costly time added to the selling process; (4) enforced acceptance of excessive returns (especially when the housewife finds that colors clash). But in several industries, manufacturers have turned a deaf ear to these complaints. Why? Because they concluded their gains from line standardization would not balance out the loss stemming from the merchandising values inherent in distinctive sizes, colors, etc. (The trade complains particularly about lack of color standardization. But even white cannot be completely standardized.) Solution: Manufacturers faced with this problem report they are selling customers and the trade on the monotony of complete color uniformity, selling the idea of mix-match, selling the idea of color contrast. Too much merchandise looks too much alike to go along with this trade demand for standardization; the merchandising man must find ways around it.

New Items and Intrafamily Competition

When a major consumer contest is planned to boost a new item in a line, the net result may be that gains for the promoted item are at the expense of the remainder of the line. While the price paid may be warranted in terms of getting the new product off the ground, the side effects, particularly on the trade, deserve consideration. A food manufacturer therefore designed a giant consumer contest which would give impetus to the *entire line* and *still* give particular impetus to a *new* product. The contest asked customers to send in a label from any of the company's products. However, if the label was from the *new* addition to the line, the first prize would be $500 larger. Prizes all the way down the line were proportionately higher for entries using the new product label, yet they were not so much higher that movement of the other items in the line was discouraged. As lines get longer, intraline competition multiplies. A new product can take as much volume away from other members of the family as from competition. Merchandising concepts such as this sell the family as well as the new item.

Special Sizes in Price-cut Market

In a market overrun with price slashing to a point where, on a category that usually took a 30 to 40 per cent margin, dealers were averaging little better than a 9 to 12 per cent margin! A manufacturer found that department stores were playing down the line. They figured they lost money on each sale. The price battle could not be stopped. But the manufacturer reasoned that a *special* size, offered *exclusively* to the department store, would win stronger support from this major outlet— and that proved to be the case. The special size was priced so as to permit the department store to feature it as a special value—a very necessary ingredient in this case in view of the price slashing. The package text also smartly features special value. Yet the department store was able to take its full 40 per cent markup. A plan of this kind will, ultimately, lose some of its appeal when and if the new size is not closely policed. It is vital to control department stores themselves, because— like all retailers—when a department store is given the margin it screams for, it tends then to cut that margin by constant price promotions. In this instance, the special pricing of the special package, which permitted offering a special value, has helped keep the department store in line.

Creating Style and Design Obsolescence for a Staple

Every so often a staple is given an added touch that takes it out of the merchandising rut that characterized it for years. Example: Color in light bulbs—and now a totally new shape for these bulbs. Example: Bringing out the traditionally white nurses' uniforms in color. Nurses' uniforms in color promise to increase the total number of uniforms sold. Broaden the market; perhaps permit somewhat higher margins; accelerate obsolescence. There's reason to believe that, within a year or two, nurses' uniforms in color may equal and even surpass the volume done in traditional white. If such a staple of staples as nurses' uniforms can be given fashion significance, perhaps it's time to look at a few other traditional staples to determine whether they must continue to languish. Style and design can turn staples into dynamic specialties. (Note what has been done with that other staple of staples—dental floss. It's a classic example.)

A Special Line for Each Outlet Type

Now that some manufacturers are having second thoughts about the presumed advantages of broad unrestricted distribution, one of the solutions being applied is the development of a special line for each type of major outlet. Thus, one of the large TV manufacturers has a special brand-name line for the department stores. It also has a special brand-name line for the credit jewelers. So long as these special lines are kept confined to the retail type for which each is planned, this concept has merit. But once the line gets into the hands of the transshipper, the special brands eventually wind up in outlets far removed from the one for which each special brand was designed. The plan is fully capable of lessening jungle merchandising conditions. But it will achieve this end only if it is carefully policed. Moreover, another problem in enforcing this plan rises from the fact that it is so difficult these days to identify some dealers by type. The lines of demarcation between the food super and the variety chain, for example, are becoming vague; ditto for department stores and some of the new giant food supers. Moreover, as different types of chains are brought into one holding company, another confusing factor enters.

Merchandising Big Sizes

The initial appeal of the big economy size is tending to wear off. Simply displaying the large economy size alongside the smaller size or sizes is no longer sufficiently effective. Consequently, the shopper savings offered by the economy size must now be merchandised more strongly;

under self-service, the shopper cannot be expected to grasp, in a flash, the actual savings. For these reasons, a drug chain predesigned its economy-size package so that "Save 21 Cents" is splashed across the top front of the package—it can't be missed. (How effectively does your economy size-package get over to the shopper the actual savings?) Incidentally, this serves also as a reminder to salespeople—if any. But, more important, it spells out the savings for those who race as they read —and this typifies the modern shopper. (Incidentally, on this item the 89-cent retailer in some stores is outselling the 44-cent retailer, which shows what can be achieved when the economy size is smartly merchandised.)

De Luxe Lines to Excite Trade

After a once-new category has hit a sales plateau, the trade loses its initial flush of enthusiasm. Promotion by the trade slackens; price promotions tend to take over. Solution by a maker of electric blankets: (1) Bring out a new de luxe line under its own label; (2) sell it only to franchised dealers; (3) sell direct to the franchised retailer; (4) operate the new line under Fair Trade where permissible; (5) jump the price lining on the de luxe line; (6) allow the trade a larger margin; (7) develop a complete promotional program for the franchised stores; (8) intensify national advertising for the de luxe line; (9) continue regular promotion and advertising on the regular line. (A somewhat similar plan was developed by a maker of hard-floor coverings.) Nonfranchised dealers will complain—but the franchised dealers will probably provide the supplier with his major volume. Moreover, between a dealer's complaints and throwing out a strong brand there is a big gap.

Spotlighting New Items

The drug outlet now estimates that 40 per cent of its volume is done each year on items not yet five years old. The food outlet also does a mounting per cent of its total each year on new items. The consequence in these and other mass outlets is that there are so many new items on the shelves (new sizes, colors, counts, improvements, as well as strictly new items never before on the market) that ordinary emphasis on the new item is no longer enough. Too much of the total inventory consists of new items. Several manufacturers are, therefore, selfishly-unselfishly, encouraging dealers to feature a "new-product" section. Others are testing new shelf devices for attracting attention of a jaded public to new items. Example: A shelf pointer, measuring 3 by 5 inches, that clips onto the shelf-edge price molding. It reads: "New item," and is shaped like an arrow. Under self-service display, devices of this kind take a new item

out of the rut of innumerable items equally new. In all merchandising
of new items, bear in mind (1) the flood of new items; (2) the resultant
overwhelming of the shopper; (3) the consequent need for a dramatic
shelf device to win attention to the new product.

Special Models for Small Retailers

While for most manufacturers the giant retailers are the major outlet,
in some merchandise classifications smaller merchants represent, in total,
a desirable market. Moreover, the terms "giant retailer" and "small
retailer" are not precise—a small retailer can be somewhat larger than
the term might denote. A maker of traffic appliances, aware that smaller
dealers are usually unable (and unwilling) to compete pricewise with
big retailers, is merchandising so as to play both sides of the street.
The plan involves bringing out special models of traffic appliances exclusively for dealers that would not be classified as "large." (These
models, in other words, are not available to the big discount chains, other
hard-goods chains, big department stores, etc.) That gives the smaller
retailer a degree of freedom from low-margin competition. This is sound
merchandising—smaller retailers rarely cut prices to the extent typical
of large retailers. Moreover, their price lining tends to be somewhat
different from giant retailers. Special models for smaller retailers will
become more common where the volume of these dealers justifies the
move.

Exchange Privilege Pushes a New Item

A maker of a small appliance used primarily by men brought out a
special model for women. The women's model has a long way to go
before matching the volume done on the men's model. The manufacturer
wanted to clean up old retail inventory in preparation for the big
Christmas-gift season. He also wanted to get more of the women's model
into retail inventory. And, most important, he wanted the trade to have
adequate stocks of the specific numbers to be featured in national advertising during the Christmas drive. He therefore developed the following return policy: (1) Dealers could get full credit at original price for
each old unused model they wanted to return; (2) however, the dealer
had to order, on an exchange basis, one new man's model in a specified
line (the Christmas-featured number) *and* one of the women's models
(also a Christmas-featured number). Dealers don't go for exchange privileges that have too many strings. But where it can be pointed out that
the aim is to enable the trade to have a proper inventory for a top season
on numbers featured in powerful national advertising, resentment may
not run too high.

Getting the Trade to Promote Color

For a foundation-garment line (a category now developing color much the same as has been done in hosiery) one company offered two new colors free for one season—contingent on minimum orders in basic color assortments. The two new colors were not offered for sale on regular terms; they could not be purchased as separate items from the line. (Typical terms: Two dozen free of one color with the purchase of a total of some fifteen dozen of assorted colors and white.) The object: To pressure the trade to promote color and, of course, to offer the trade an attractive deal. In connection with color—when color invades a new category, it is seldom welcomed, in the early stages, by the trade. To the contrary, the trade tends to resist, if not fight, color early in the game—the trade worries about larger inventories, slower turnover, larger markdowns on slow-moving shades, etc. A deal of this kind is smartly calculated to lessen some of these trade worries.

Find a "New" Product in an Old One

Look for that "new" product in one of your old products. It can save huge sums and the percentage of successes may be higher than with totally new items. Example: It had been possible, for years, to predict almost within 1 per cent what the total market for dental floss would be annually. Then one of the major companies developed a brilliant new package with several attractive features including a much-needed cutting edge; it was made in several sizes; the price lining was made more attractive to the trade. Sales showed a splendid jump. While some manufacturers spend great fortunes looking for new products, it could be that what to all intents and purposes would be a new product (as was certainly true of the revitalized dental floss) may be found lurking in the Cinderellas of the line. Many line sleepers need only the magic touch of modern merchandising. (The amazing jump in volume in hassocks and floor pillows, stimulated by TV viewing, was due also to better styling, major new ideas, more exciting promotions.)

Related Item Plus Staple Equal Gift

Staple items are successfully catering to the enormously expanded gift market (special-occasion and year-round) by several techniques including, of course, special put-ups. Now the special put-up, which usually consists of de luxe versions of the staple in a handsome gift box, is developing into an interesting combination gift box. Example: Two packs of cigarettes are put into a handsome container—along with an automatic lighter. The lighter obviously sells for much more than the two cigarette packs but, in combination with the cigarettes, it makes a logical gift unit. Incidentally, the trade-mark of the cigarette was imprinted on the lighter, thus carrying the trade-mark into the home, or into a man's pocket. An exciting revolution is taking place in a growing list of staples as a result of new ideas for catering to the great gift market. Current thinking is that almost any staple can be made into a gift item with smart ideas.

Search Hospitals for New-product Ideas

Some years ago, several highly successful coffee-brewing devices were marketed that had their origin in technical equipment used in hospitals. The inventor specialized in studying hospital equipment and supplies for ideas for new consumer products. A current example of this interesting technique for uncovering ideas for new products is seen in the big campaigns that are being run to introduce the bed that can be raised or lowered into various positions. (One of these beds lays claim to 101 positions, all achieved through push-button control.) This bed is, of course, simply a variation of the traditional hospital bed. In the realm of relaxation, of relief from aches and pains that plague mankind, hospital equipment offers many suggestions for new and improved products for the consumer market. Indeed, the whole field of equipment used in exercising paraplegics will some day be adapted for use in the home as exercising equipment. From food to drugs, from soft goods to hard goods, hospitals offer product ideas for the consumer market. Even some of the ideas for décor and for lighting will find home-market adaptation.

Coattail Merchandising for New Items

Riding a new item to market on the coattail of a strong, established family member sometimes is smart merchandising. Example: The maker of one of the largest-selling drug items brought out another, somewhat related, drug item. Big brother is a pill; little brother is a spray. In some instances, the two items may be used somewhat simultaneously—but one in no way supplants the other. To get the new item off to a flying start, coattail merchandising was planned. The name used on the pill was also given to the spray—it's one of the great trade names. A special floor display was distributed—this merchandised the pill. However, a sign above the display featured the spray—mentioned that a carton top from the pill package, mailed in to the maker, would enable the shopper to get a full size of the spray for free by mail. The offer was good only on a package containing 100 pills—thus stepping up the sales unit on pills while simultaneously enabling sprays to ride on its coattail. For the deal period, the trade was also offered a 1-free-with-11 deal on the spray. Good merchandising.

Merchandising Art—"Make It a Gift"

Staples are constantly being brought into the *gift* classification. Example: Gold-initialed paper napkins in a gold box—a hostess gift at $2.50 retail! Another example: Housewares. Here styling, coloring, and functional developments have turned many everyday houseware items into highly acceptable gift merchandise. This serves two merchandising purposes: (1) It opens up the enormously expanded gift market, which outpaces in growth the expansion in mass income; (2) the item given gift appeal becomes that much more attractive to the shopper buying for herself or himself. Retailers tend to be receptive to gift promotions— especially, of course, during the big gift occasions of the year, and especially when the gift item is so merchandised as to give the retailer a larger unit sale and a better margin. Even the elastic stocking—a dreary staple for years (almost in the same class as medical bandages) has become something of a gift item now that it has been smartly styled, comes in colors, and is effectively packaged. Two danger points: (1) Don't sacrifice the staple demand for gift appeal; (2) don't package or design in a way that results in dead inventory at the end of a gift season.

Introducing New Item as Premium

One of the giant manufacturers of tapes recently entered a new market —scouring pads. With the idea of sampling the item in a new way, getting it into millions of homes quickly and in a way that tended to assure its actual use, this new scouring pad was included, *as a premium,* in one of the great brands of detergent. Thus the scouring pad won these benefits: (1) It received the tacit endorsement of the big detergent brand; (2) it won a degree of advertising that the item itself might not have been able to finance; (3) it got shelf space that it could not win by itself as a scouring pad; (4) it reached into millions of homes quickly; (5) since it accompanied a detergent it would be more likely to be used than if it came into the home by itself. (The sample was a full-sized pad— 25 cents retail value.) This plan had an extra value in this case because the scouring pad is entirely different from other pads and by distributing it as a premium, housewife reluctance to change long-entrenched habits was well punctured. (Large-size packages of the detergent carried as many as four free pads, thus encouraging use of the pad in a number of areas in the house.)

Forecasting Style Changes

When a fashion, style, or design trend can proceed no further in one direction—it *must* reverse itself. (Fashion never stands still.) Thus, when women's hosiery could not be made any more invisible, color hose was inevitable. When women's hair could no longer be cut shorter, it had to get longer. When the short appearance in women's shoes and the heavy appearance in men's shoes reached the end of the line—the pointed look came into women's shoes and the light look in men's shoes. When wall-to-wall carpeting had become too popular, area rugs simply had to come in. When painted-room interiors became dark as morgues—a trend toward lighter colors had to set in. When kitchens had become all metal, a trend toward wood was inevitable. When color in kitchen items ran riot, a change-about was inevitable. (Note the return of black in autos.) Moral: Watch for that point which marks a fashion, style, or design swing that either can go no further or has become so commonplace it no longer confers social status. When that point is reached, a reverse trend is overdue.

CHAPTER **25**

Packaging

The Assortment Package for De Luxe Merchandising

A few years ago, a breakfast cereal available in a half-dozen forms assembled its various types in an assortment package. It has become an established merchandising unit. This was not a de luxe number—but it started a number of manufacturers, both in food and nonfood, thinking in terms of an assortment package for de luxe merchandising. Thus, makers of spices put up special gift packs containing an assortment of spices in beautiful small cabinets. Moreover, it is becoming common for manufacturers to implement their own assortment packages with related items which they do not make themselves. This promises to develop into a merchandising trend of substantial proportions. Example: A cigarette company brings out a special assortment pack that also contains an automatic lighter. Example: A distillery brings out an assortment of liquors in a package that also contains mixing implements. The de luxe assortment package usually is conceived initially for Christmas promotion. But it is generally found that it appeals as well to the year-round gift market. Incidentally, one manufacturer tells us that he finds that exploitation of the year-round gift market with de luxe numbers tends to act as a sort of advance expedition for the promotion of much higher-priced numbers bought by the shoppers for their own use.

How Big for Big Economy Size?

A famous detergent scored a ten-strike with a huge-size carton. Seemingly it defied all logic: It would be too large for women to get it into their cars, into their homes, and even too large for them to pour from into a smaller container. But it has been a great success. Now a dog food is making available a 50-pound size. And a producer of instant coffee is merchandising a giant economy size that upsets tradition for this item. This trend toward true giant sizes is made more logical by (1) auto shopping; (2) more shopping and household work by men; (3) women are no longer considered the weaker sex—not even by women! (4) homes are larger; (5) shoppers are making fewer shopping trips; (6) the economy appeal. (This same trend is encouraging the merchandising of twin packs of beer six-packs; it is also encouraging the merchandising of case lots—sometimes in new case sizes). The "big" economy size now gives way to the "giant" economy size. The ability of the shopper to lug home big items is simply fantastic—that's one reason so many big-ticket items are being sold self-service today. Some merchandising has yet to catch up with the lug-it-home, keep-it-home, use-it-at-home abilities of our "shopulation."

Special Case Packs for Deals

The full potential for some deals cannot be achieved because the initial order is too often not followed up, during the deal's life, by reorders. This is especially true in big chains, where reorders come from the store manager. And the explanation, as discovered by a maker of household paper supplies, is that the case pack, while not too large on the initial order, may be too large for reorders. This manufacturer now has special case packs for deals so planned that initial orders remain as high as ever—but reorders are encouraged because the store manager feels he can move the reorder during the remainder of the life of the deal. Few items in the total merchandising program have been so hidebound by tradition as the size of the case pack; for some categories the case-pack size has not been altered for years, while the retailing of the category has gone through a revolution. This is one of the great causes of retail out-of-stocks. Too often the *purchasing agent* dictates case decisions; it should be a *merchandising* decision.

Thumbs Down on Demonstration Packages

A soft-goods maker of an infant's item decided that mothers would be more willing to make a purchase if they could self-demonstrate a new closure recently adopted for the item. The package was therefore designed so that—presumably without opening it—the shopper could demonstrate, without clerk assistance, the new closure. But it was soon found that damaged packages were the result. It is a fact that, under self-service and self-selection, retailing of many items of soft goods, of toys, and other small items, packages are getting a fearful battering. This is especially true at peak hours and during peak seasons such as Christmas and Easter. A maker of model sets finds that, during the Christmas season, his fixtures show beat-up packages to a dismaying extent. The small advantage of enabling the shopper to self-demonstrate, to feel, is more than balanced out by damaged packages that discourage buying. Smart text and illustration on packages will give 95 per cent of shoppers all the information they need—the risks involved in encouraging the shopper to open up the package, in whole or in part, are seldom justified, especially in this era when shoppers are so thoroughly conditioned to buy packaged merchandise.

Cutting Receiving-Marking Costs

The receiving and marking operations are getting considerable cost-cutting attention from both wholesaler and retailer. (This involves largely manual labor, and manual labor comes high.) One problem in the receiving and marking operation stems from costly peaks and valleys in these two departments. Several big retailers are checking into this; one has already instructed its buyers to avoid placing ship-when-ready orders because such orders usually cause a peak load in the receiving and marking rooms on the first of the month. Prepricing, where practical, is being favored by more retailers as part of the program for cutting down receiving and marking costs. So is the automatic reorder plan (going big in the variety chains). In general, every step of the merchandising process (the shipping case in particular) should be examined to see where a better contribution can be made to lower receiving and marking costs for the retailer.

Slant Up for Shopper's Eye

Most shelving in retail stores displays merchandise straight up and down—perpendicular. Now—picture yourself looking at bottles, packages, tins thus displayed. If the shelf is *below* your eye level (and by far most shelving is below eye level), you'll soon realize that looking down at an item displayed on the perpendicular does not offer best visibility. And the lower down the item thus displayed, the less visible it becomes. This shelf situation has been generally overlooked in package design, label design, bottle design. But now a food company has designed a bottle that *slants up*. Since the bottle slants up—the label is tilted up just at the right angle, when displayed from a perpendicular shelf, to catch the shopper's eye from a below-eye-level location. At eye level, the up-tilt is also effective. Above eye level it is no less effective. (Moreover, some retail shelves are now being tilted. A tilted package on a tilted shelf wins extra visibility. It has other advantages; its broad bottom permits sturdy displays; the slant creates the impression of a larger and taller bottle; it is more attractive on the table.)

More Prewraps for Gift Occasions

Gift wrapping as a whole is in the stage best described as "explosively dynamic." Wonderful designing, splendid fixtures, exciting merchandising programs are making gift wrapping in retail stores one of the great developments of the last decade. In turn, this is prodding a number of manufacturers into gift prewraps—from liquor to food to cigarettes and with soft goods and hard goods in between. The explosive growth of the gift market—a development that is still rather vague to some merchandisers—has encouraged gift wraps. And, to suggest the scope of the gift market—here are a few figures: 77 per cent of all women's watches; 46 per cent of all pen-and-pencil sets; 52 per cent of all jewelry; 77 per cent of all perfume; 46 per cent of all luggage; 87 per cent of all silverware are given as gifts. And between 40 and 60 per cent of all infants' supplies, such as blankets, clothing, and toys, are purchased as gifts. Then there is the great gift market in small appliances, cosmetics and toiletries, housewares, and boxed candy. (Think for a moment about the gift giving in your own home.) Give thought to gift prewraps—they are coming in fast.

The Shopper's Unit-buying Habits

It is amazing to note how few merchandising men have precise data on the typical unit purchases of their ultimate customers—that is, what percentage of typical shoppers buy just one of the item on each trip, how many buy two per shopping trip, etc. Moreover, where this information is available, it is too seldom determined whether the existing pattern exists solely because that is how the line is packaged, or whether that is how the shopper really prefers buying, or whether these unit-buying patterns can be changed. A study of this kind for men's underwear disclosed that purchases of just one shirt, or one pair of shorts were surprisingly low. The findings revealed that 95 per cent of the purchases involved units of two—yet the trade continues to merchandise on the basis of single-unit sales to the shopper. The brewers really just stumbled on the six-pack—and now they are stumbling into the twin six-pack and new case sizes. The distillers are discovering that an amazing number of shoppers buy even fifths, two and three at a time. But even where multipacks are in use, there is too little in the way of exact information concerning the shopper's unit-buying habits—and too little testing into how these unit-buying habits may be capitalized or changed.

Cutting Package Inventory

Inasmuch as the merchandising executive is very much concerned with package costs as well as package design, note this idea which lowered package inventory for a large manufacturer and thus reduced package costs. The idea also involved better design, so two objectives of the merchandising executive were achieved. The company makes bras. The numbers in the line required 60 different packages. That total was slashed to just *six*—by arranging to imprint on the package, *during the packaging operation,* all data relative to the item such as price, size, style, and color. Previously, these facts were preprinted on the package, thus necessitating a large package inventory. Because of this drastic cut in package inventory requirements, the manufacturer was able to switch from black and white on the packages to full-color illustrations and increase the size of the package—yet simultaneously achieve a savings of some 8 per cent in over-all packaging costs.

Outwitting the IBM

As the various chains turn to IBM and other forms of electronic and even automaton controls, manufacturers' merchandising executives must learn how to outwit the automaton. This becomes vitally necessary because automative inventory control, for example, inevitably leads to robot inventory decisions. Example: Food supers tend to reorder on the basis of rigidly fixed case-lot movements as recorded by IBM. To the robot, a case is a case. But a case, of course, can be one dozen of an item, or two dozen, or three dozen. Consequently, one company has cut its case size on one line to a dozen, instead of the former two dozen. Result: The IBM records now show twice the case movement! In one chain, where an order had been handed down to buyers not to reorder in a certain classification when movement dropped below a case per week per store, the smaller case size saved the day for the manufacturer. These robot controls will lead to more frequent ordering, to better inventory control, but will include a trend toward automatic buying decisions. Beating the automaton will be a new requirement for the merchandising executive.

The Case for Frequent Package Changes

Years ago, package changes were viewed with dread. Today there is a trend of thought that favors frequent package changes—not merely for the sake of change but in line with a specific objective. It started perhaps with the cereal packages, which change frequently to feature premium offers. Now a major producer of cake flour changes every sixty days or so the picture of the cake adorning its new package. On the old package, housewives always saw the same cake; now it is reasoned that a change of cake on the package will give the package renewed interest periodically. That packages can lose interest when they remain the same was interestingly proved by a packer of eggs. Eggs have been packed in conventional dull-looking containers for years. This egg packer switched to a six-color job on its egg cartons—and sales promptly jumped 38 per cent! Package changes can be achieved without losing easy identity, without causing shopper confusion, without interfering with trade-mark objectives. When a package has become a "landmark"— it may be due for a change.

Reuse Containers with Quantity Use

The reuse container as a rule, is a one-time shot. If, for example, a package can be put to use, after its contents have been consumed, as a small jewel chest—then most families will be satisfied with just one. Ditto when a package for a man's belt can be used as a cigarette humidor. This, of course, limits the appeal of the reuse container. Consequently, some merchandisers are looking for reuse-container ideas that invite quantity or multiple use. Example: A food item is packed in a plastic jug that can be used for a score of purposes in the kitchen, in the home shop, in the garden, in the garage, etc. Moreover, the food processor in this instance features the multiple uses of the plastic jug both on the jug itself and in store displays and in advertising. This broadens the appeal of the reuse or dual-use package. And this broadened appeal is important; when the secondary use of the package or container is of limited appeal, its merchandising significance is sharply shriveled.

Plan Package for Multidisplay

Products with wide distribution end up in retail outlets that employ an infinite variation of display techniques covering the broad spectrum between self-service, self-selection, and full service. Consequently, it frequently happens that a package which serves well in a fully self-service section may not be equally suitable in a service section. This has suggested to some merchandisers the advisability of designing the package for adaptability to any type of retail merchandising procedure. Example: Hardware stores today run the range from self-service to full service. A maker of shears therefore has designed a package that permits regular carton display on shelves—or the shears, wrapped in an informative sleeve, may be removed from the package and hung on a pegboard for self-selection merchandising. This dual-use concept for the package, to enable it to straddle the varied merchandising requirements of the retail outlets through which the line moves, has tended to be neglected. Have you checked your packages against the display requirements of your varied types of retail outlets?

The Home-décor Package

The package so neatly designed as to be acceptable for use right on the dining table at home—including better homes—is obviously destined for much broader use in the food field. Gourmet foods will increasingly be packaged this way. So will certain spices, additives, etc. But this principle will not be limited to food and to the dining table. It will be extended to nonfoods used both at the dining table and in other areas of the home. The cosmetic manufacturers have, of course, been using this packaging concept for years; many of their packages have been designed for use at the vanity table, for example. The liquor distillers really developed the same concept when they brought out their decanters. The new plastic containers for detergents are part of this same trend—the old packages looked horrible in the kitchen. The whole concept starts with the correct premise that the taste of our people is rising rapidly. They will not bring to the table, or otherwise display in the home, packages that offend their new levels of good taste. But they will put smartly designed packages out on open home display if the package can be considered part of the home décor. How does your package meet this requirement?

The Broken-case-lot Problem

The broken-case-lot problem continues to plague retailers—frequently the wholesaler, too. Whatever plagues the distributor inevitably plagues the manufacturer's merchandising executive. The high handling costs (and the inventory shrinkage) involved in handling broken cases are mounting. One solution, of course, is to change the size of the case. Multiple case sizes are fairly common in certain categories today. Another and perhaps more attractive solution is to arrange the case so that it can almost automatically be split into several units for reshipment by the wholesaler to the retailer, or by the retail warehouse to the store units. Thus, a large-selling razor is shipped in a shipping container that may be broken up for reshipment in half-dozen units. The smaller unit is taken out of the regular shipping container with a minimum of effort, and thus a minimum of cost. This approach to the broken-case problem has a good deal to recommend it. However, the concept needs refinement. Present problems include (1) still too much labor involved in splitting the case; packaging ingenuity could lessen this cost factor;

(2) the number of units remaining in the shipping case is not identified easily enough under typical warehouse conditions; (3) shelf condition of the half-empty shipping container in the warehouse is sometimes impaired.

Checker Errors on Deal Packages

In most self-service self-selection outlets, the check-out or the cash-wrap facilities do from 60 to 75 per cent of the week's work in from twelve to fifteen hours. The operator of the cash register consequently rings up the lion's share of the week's volume under high pressure. Most of these operators are teen-agers. Result: A huge total of errors. A frequent cause of these errors is the price marking on special consumer-deal packages. Example: When text on a package reads: "Buy this size and save 28¢," the checker may ring up the sale as being 28 cents. Even "15¢ off," if printed large enough, may be rung up as a 15-cent sale, under pressure at the register. Some packages will have a "2 for" offer printed on one side, a "saving" price on a second side, and another deal offer on a third side. Retailers are sometimes compelled to mark out conflicting pricing on such packages with crayon—a costly operation. One merchandising executive reports that all of the pricing on new packages for his long line is tested in a variety of outlets at the check-out, as well as at the warehouse and store back room. As a consequence, the salesmen for this line are able to tell the trade how their packages save the trade both on handling costs and on avoidance of costly errors at the check-out.

Identifying Price Lines Quickly

As manufacturers broaden their price lines (a fairly general trend) the retailer (wholesaler too) finds it increasingly difficult to identify price lines quickly when the packages in the various price lines are of the same size. This not only adds to retail labor costs, it also results in errors that sometimes cut the trade's net profit. It is becoming increasingly necessary to plan the package so that each price line is quickly and unmistakably identified by store personnel. Some manufacturers use a different color for the package for each price line. This tends to be only a small help. Another approach: A maker of hot-water bottles merchandises three price lines; the highest-priced line package has three windows, the middle-price line has two windows, the lowest-price line has one window. This also is a small help. Generally speaking, there is considerable confusion in retail stockrooms, reserve areas, on the shelves, and at the check-out with respect to the price lining of items that now come in multiple-price lines. How would your various price lines show up under such a study?

More Arty Packages

Life magazine has had a remarkably favorable reaction from its millions of readers to its continuing series of reproductions of famous paintings. The phonograph-record companies have also found an amazing upsurge in public interest in art—as a result of experiences with their record albums. (Indeed, the record pressers claim they give more work to competent artists than any other manufacturing business in the country.) Albums now show abstract paintings or the painstaking reproduction of an old master. RCA-Victor reports sales of 20,000 for a classical reproduction marketed with a prosaic cover. When it was given a highly artistic cover, sales jumped to over 200,000 copies. All this suggests that the true art touch may work well not merely for de luxe lines, but even for more staple merchandise. If an abstract painting on a jazz record album helps its sales—and it does—then maybe an abstract painting on the package for a food item might do equally well. Years ago, merchandisers were warned away from art for art's sake on packages. Maybe the time is ripe to disregard that axiom.

More Take-home Appeal for Bulky Items

The shopping public has displayed an astounding ability to "take-with" bulky items. Even major appliances are now lugged home, and large-size rugs now come in take-home packages. Take-home cases for portable air-conditioners are another example. Many furniture items in knock-down form are now packed for take-home. Even a smaller item like an electric clock is being packed so that the store-display package also can be used as a convenient take-home carton. Merchandisers, studying this subject of more take-home package appeal for bulky and not-so-bulky items, are thinking in terms of (1) packages and packing methods that lessen the burden of take-home; (2) adding attractive design to the take-home carton so that it serves both as a selling display piece in the store and as a take-home object as appealing as shopping bags have become; (3) arranging the pack so that it can be opened easily and so that the contents arrive at home in perfect condition; (4) improving factory-inspection facilities—too much prepacked merchandise is faulty.

Fractional Packaging—a Spreading Trend

The package so planned that it is divided into logical consumption units is gaining favor—and not only in food, which is where it started.

As a matter of fact, the tea bag was really one of the early fractional packages. Now special breads come in a package that holds seven slices in a special glassine envelope with four envelopes to the bread package. Hosiery is being packed in what could be called fractional packages. The object of the fractional package is to enable the shopper to take out a logical consumption unit as needed, without exposing the remainder of the contents of the package to damage. These fractional packages appeal to the "squirrel" instinct; they give the shopper the feeling that there will be no waste. New techniques make possible fractional packages at little more cost than ordinary packages. Nonfood examples are now found in health aids, in beauty aids, and in a few soft-goods items. In food, the fractional package is unquestionably destined for a much larger use. It can serve a particularly valuable purpose in encouraging the purchase of large or giant economy sizes.

What to Spend for Packages

What percentage of the manufacturer's selling price may be properly assigned to packaging cost? This is one of those merchandising questions that is regularly debated and is also a phase of merchandising in which perhaps too much thinking is frozen by policy and tradition. Actually, packaging costs vary from 3 per cent of the manufacturer's selling price to 80 per cent—and it is highly significant to note that the 80 per cent figure applies to aerosol toothpaste, not to cosmetics. This should surely throw out the cliché that "we're an ordinary staple line—we can't go above 3 per cent for our packaging." Anyhow, here are some typical figures of the percentage of manufacturer's selling price represented by packaging cost. Aerosol toothpaste, 80 per cent; baby food, 30 per cent; bar soap, 50 per cent; beer, 27 per cent; butter, 3 per cent; cakes, 14 per cent; cereals, 13 per cent; chewing gum, 13.8 per cent; cigarettes, 3.1 per cent; cleaning compounds, 52.6 per cent; crackers, 9 per cent; detergents, 18 per cent; lamp shades, 6 per cent; men's socks, 3 per cent; nylon hosiery, 10 per cent; potato chips, 17 per cent; silverware, 7.5 per cent; stationery, 7 per cent; vacuum-packed luncheon meats, 19 per cent; vitamins, 18 per cent; wax polishes, 21 per cent.

Shelf Space Hogs

In their fight for more shelf space, some manufacturers deliberately plan packages that take up additional shelf space. When the retailer is convinced that these shelf hogs do not earn their keep, he is doubly resentful. Thus one giant retailer reports that a bottle item retailing at 29 cents, which usually was given three facings in most food supers, had been redesigned so that one-third more shelf space was required for the same number of items. This large retailer cut down the number of facings for this item from three to one—resentment sometimes plays a role in retail decisions! Working on the opposite side of the fence, a popular food item has redesigned one of its packages so that it reads and stacks vertically instead of horizontally. The object: To help retailers display more packages in less space. With justification or not, every retailer—small as well as large—is totally convinced that he suffers from a shelf-space shortage. Consequently, he resents the shelf hog—and may go out of his way to cooperate with the shelf-space saver.

Front Panels vs. Off Facings

Frozen-food packers have found that many housewives do not stack frozen food packages in home freezers in the same way they are faced in the store freezer. Consequently, brand and item identification on the sides of the package are becoming common in this category, both for home display and store display reasons. A drug house has found that drugs are squeezed just as much on the pharmacist's shelves as is merchandise on the resale shelves, so side labeling as well as front-face identification is now used on these packages. Another drug house finds that drugs in the medicine cabinet are not positioned as is typical in stores, so, again, side labeling is being used. In stores, the pressure for shelf space (plus erratic stock filling by stock boys) leads to the side display of packages—again a reason for better side labeling. There are strong sales potentials in so-called "off facings." Every side (top and bottom, too) of the package can do a brand- and item-identification job in warehouse, reserve area, forward area, and in the home. In total, the off-facings may outweigh the front panel in sales-making power!

Retailer Shipping-case Blues

Check your shipping cases against these common trade complaints: (1) Case packs out of whack with shelf movement; (2) packing that compels retailers to spend two-thirds of total price-marking time in preparation of the cases, only one-third in actual price marking; (3) units packed in so tightly that it is impossible to slide out the contents; (4) failure to indicate on the outside where the case should be opened— knives thus cause merchandise damage; (5) failure to use inside slip-sheets that prevent cutting into the shelf packs; (6) failure to use easy-opening tear-strips; (7) failure to pack so that price-marking surfaces can be reached without dumping items out of the case (die-cut holes in case packs above blank price-marking spots solve this problem); (8)

failure to designate merchandise on all sides of the case. (One merchandising man prowls around retail receiving-marking rooms, follows his merchandise from there to forward areas and restocking areas on retail floor.) Retailers are clearly upset about handling costs, and whatever upsets the retailer spells opportunity for merchandising men.

Smaller Sizes Can Be Dangerous

A drug house brought out a package for a first-aid staple in a new package that was reduced, roughly, by one-third. (The package held exactly the same quality and content as the older and larger package.) To the trade it offered the advantage of less space needed, more profit per square inch, easier to handle. But whether the shopper will therefore readily recognize that the smaller size is the same value may be subject to question. Moreover, this merchandising maneuver presents a target for competitive sharpshooting. It is debatable whether the small advantages to the trade of the smaller size are balanced out by the merchandising promotional disadvantages; that is, for the short term. For the long term, this item will undoubtedly prove successful. One reason: Competition for space in the home medicine cabinet is hitting an all-time high, a point not adequately recognized by merchandisers whose items wind up in the medicine cabinet, as well as in the pantry, in kitchen cabinets, etc. (The home, as well as the retailer, has a shelf-space problem!)

New Merchandising for New Outlets

Retailers continue to complain that too many manufacturers fail to package and fixture established items properly for new types of retail outlets. (Right now the food super is making this complaint—and properly—about many of the soft-goods items it is adding.) An interesting example: A large maker of clocks decided that the food outlet would be a logical outlet for clocks in the lower price ranges—$1.98 and $2.98 retailers. It arranged to put its clocks in "cans"—a real departure in this category. (Hosiery and several other soft-goods items are now being put up in cans for the food super.) Its reasoning: (1) This would lower handling costs for the food outlet; (2) it would protect against breakage (common in this self-service outlet) and against deterioration; (3) it would add emphasis to its guarantee (one year); (4) it would win added attention on the shelf; (5) it would be easier for the shopper to pick up, put into the shopping cart, take out to her car, etc. (A maker of spooled thread selected his best sellers for the food super, developed an ingenious new carded concept for this outlet, plus a small trial assortment in a smart fixture.)

Packages That Divide

You've heard about bacteria that multiply by division; somewhat the same concept is now being used for packages. Example: A table-napkin package that divides into two table dispensers. The box separates at a center perforation. It's the same size as the old package. Thus the housewife can have one package in the kitchen; one in the dining room or recreation room. With so much packaged merchandise finding its way into several rooms in the home, packages that divide have a clear appeal. Also, packages that divide can help sell the large economy-size concept —some economy sizes are too bulky for convenient use. Then too, many items are used both in the home and in the car—diapers, facial tissues, etc. The divisible package would be practical here. For picnic home-use purposes, indoor and outdoor cooking, the divisible package may have uses. Certainly the two-bathroom and the three-bathroom home suggests a number of divisible package uses—and so does the home with several medicine cabinets.

Bridging Unit Packages and Case Lots

As multiunit packs become ever larger, the total count begins to approach that of the traditional case lot. Thus in beer, the traditional 24-can case is now only twice as large as the "twin sixes" that are being currently promoted. When the multiunit pack and the regular-case count begin to get close to each other—and this will happen with increasing frequency in a growing variety of merchandise classifications—more manufacturers will make changes in the case count, in the design of the case, and there will be more case promotions. In beer, one brewery has already brought out a 12-can case—it offers the shopper some savings over two six-packs, provides somewhat easier handling and storage. Merchandisers would do well to reexamine the traditional case from the standpoint of how it is being affected by the increase in size of the multiunit pack. There is no question that the remarkable expansion of the multiunit pack has brought it to the threshold of the case pack— and this clearly suggests a rapidly mounting merchandising importance for the case pack.

Tray-pack Stocking Trend

In self-service outlets—food, drug, variety, etc.—the cost of shelf stocking and restocking is mounting astronomically. This, of course, leads to the tear-strip cases; to new methods of stocking merchandise in cases, etc. But now some mass retailers are encouraging suppliers, whose lines move at a minimum rate of one case per week per store, to study what is called the "tray-pack case." This promises to develop into one of the great merchandising developments of 1959–1960. Under this concept, the case is cut by the stock boy so as to leave a shallow lip—and the remainder of the tray and its contents then go right up on the shelf. Shelf-stocking time can be cut over 30 per cent; price-changing time is also cut; breakage and damage are reduced; employee productivity increased substantially. This plan calls for packing two-tier cases head to head; sometimes it requires new pack arrangements; cartons must be made with tear tapes and two-tier cartons should have two tapes for making trays top and bottom. Check into tray-packs—they represent a potentially big development.

Visual Packages That Hide the Item

The mere fact that a package is made of transparent materials doesn't always mean that something the shopper may want to see may not still be hidden. Example: A line of sleeping garments was beautifully packaged in transparent film. But the shopper could not tell how the folded garment would look unfolded and *in use*. And it was not practical to put full-size illustrations on the package. The ingenious solution developed involved printing a pictorial insert to be slipped into each package. This insert appears between the transparent film and the merchandise; thus it is completely visible. It shows a full-length rendition of a model wearing the specific number in the package—so the shopper sees, at a glance, how the garment looks. There is no need to take it from the package. The insert also gives price, fabric information, washing instructions, and size. (The trade-mark appears on the polyethylene.) That insert also permits one package to be used interchangeably for many different items. But the big point involved here is that (especially in certain soft-goods lines) merely seeing the item through a transparent window is not always enough; a visual package can still hide its contents.

Put That Item on a Card

Years ago the variety chain pioneered the idea of putting merchandise on cards. For a long time only small, rather staple items were put on cards. Now every major outlet is merchandising carded merchandise— indeed, to avoid pilferage of small items in self-service outlets, large cards have been used that almost dwarf the item. But cards are also being used for items that, just a short time back, would never have been considered as logical for carding. Example: One of the great names in small cameras has put its $5.95 and $8.95 retailers on cards. And displayed this way, with effective selling text on the cards, this small camera is benefiting from impulse buying in a highly gratifying way. If carded cameras can be sold, it would be sensible to conclude that the merchandising use of the put-it-on-a-card concept in a self-service, self-selection age has been barely scratched. (Even paintbrushes are now merchandised on cards and also many small items of hardware.)

Merchandising to Shoppers in Case Lots

As shoppers tend increasingly toward fewer shopping trips, even the multiunit carry-home pack may prove to be an inadequate merchandising activity. Perhaps merchandising by the *case* may become more important. In toilet paper, case promotions have been fairly common, are becoming more so. There have been some case promotions for facial tissue. One of the liquor companies has been running a case promotion consistently. Some baby foods are being promoted by the case, even dog foods and other canned foods too. Larger families favor case promotions. So does the spread of credit selling into new merchandise categories and new outlets. Auto shopping creates a favorable situation for case-lot buying. So does the vast increase in home ownership—homes have more storage space than apartments. Moreover, homes are now getting larger—meaning still more storage space. There will be more case merchandising in more categories and this, plus other factors, will probably tend to bring about smaller case sizes. Also, the case will be prettied up, given reuse design.

That Matter of Shopper "Feel"

Many items still are not prepacked because, presumably, the shopper *insists* on "feeling" before buying. (Shoppers today really don't know what is determined by "feel.") In phonograph records, tradition has had it that the customer insists on seeing and playing the disks. But now some disk brands are coming out in sealed polyethylene-film envelopes. (Automatic vendors are also being developed for phonograph records.) The makers of small hardware items have found that even the artisan— as well as the less skilled do-it-yourself-er—will buy innumerable items prepacked that, formerly, simply had to be hefted. Tradition dies hard. The outstanding example of the decline of "feel" is women's nylon hosiery. Today, prepacked hose is taking over the field, especially in the newer outlets. A maker of bras has a complicated and expensive package designed to permit "feel"—yet more millions of bras are sold each year sans "feel." Merchandisers made wary by demands by old-line retailers for "feel" should see how food supers and drug and variety chains merchandise without "feel."

Restocking Shipping Cases

Generally, when the shipping case is designed for use as a floor display, the contents of the special shipping cases are usually the same, in quantity, as the regular shipping case. This gives the retailer a problem—when the stock in the floor display runs low, he must split a case from the reserve stock to refill. The only alternative is to permit the stock in the floor display to run out completely and then refill from a full reserve stock case. But that means out-of-stock and understock—and who wants to encourage that? Solution: A maker of household paper items designed his special-floor-display shipping case so that it holds *more* than a regular full case of each item stocked in the special display. As a consequence, the maker can correctly tell the retail trade: "It's a snap to keep stock because it holds more than a full case of each item. This means you can restock it with new cases before the display is empty." It is attention to merchandising details such as this that makes for successful merchandising programs.

Mr. Big—the Stock Boy

The stock boy in self-service outlets is the new "problem child" for the merchandiser. Reason: He places packages, bottles, cans on shelves in ways never contemplated by the designers. This is one reason for the trend toward all-around design for packages, labels, etc. A different solution is a flat-sided square glass bottle. Unlike a round bottle, which can wind up in almost any position on the shelf, the square bottle helps assure a face-forward display. A maker of detergents had hundreds of photos taken showing the amazing variety of positions in which its packages wound up on shelving. The photos were then blown up—and whenever a new container is planned, the designers first study those photos in order to remind themselves of the stock-boy problem. Another merchandiser offered "fun hats" to stock boys for a summer merchandising event—the object was to win their good will. (Rumors multiply about "special incentives" offered stock boys for an extra facing.) Color bars on a package to identify numbers in the line were put there to simplify shelf stocking by the stock boy.

Packaging for a Mobile "Shopulation"

Even babies are traveling these days—and that suggests changes in packaging certain baby items. A disposable diaper points the way, with a package containing a convenient handle. The same handle is, of course, a convenience when taking the package from one room to another in the home and from the inside of the home to the carriage out-

side. Too few packages have shown proper recognition of travel requirements, travel conveniences. A box of tissues for car use has yet to be
designed. Yet the "visor wallet" has been developed. A special work
glove for the car glove compartment is being merchandised. (There are
55 million neglected glove compartments.) Check the merchandise carried in millions of autos on tour—note the problems involved getting
these into the car, out of the car, into use while on tour. Aside from auto
and plane travel, there is also a need for the "tote-around" package;
tiny packages for pills are in this category, with the pillbox staging a
comeback. Ditto for some beauty aids. And when will someone develop
an "organizer" for the car trunk? Billions of dollars of merchandise are
carried home in messy car trunks.

Shelf Packs and Out-of-stock

Shelf packs of regular stock merchandise sometimes encourage out-of-
stock conditions. Example: A manufacturer found that in his major outlets (which are the outlets to be favored) the general pattern was one
of stocking the shelf with twelve of the item. The brand was shelf-
packed twelve to the pack. The consequence was that many store managers would not reorder until all twelve were sold; they didn't want
more than twelve on the shelf and they didn't want broken packs.
Solution: A shelf pack of six. The shelf pack calls for continuing study.
And that study should differentiate between various types and sizes of
outlets. Obviously, the major objective should be to plan the shelf packs
so they will win the best merchandising results from the 20 per cent of
accounts that these days give so many manufacturers 80 per cent of their
total volume. In general, manufacturers tend to blame retailers for out-of-
stock conditions. But out-of-stocks can be traced back to weaknesses in
the manufacturer's merchandising program at least as often as to the
retailer's shortcomings.

Cutting Factory Inventory of Packages

Here is an item made in a variety of sizes that necessitated five sizes
of folding cartons, plus an equal number of sizes of shipping containers.
The resulting inventory of cartons and containers was expensive. Then
inventive genius was applied and, as a result of a clever improvement,
it became possible to cut both carton and shipper inventory from five
sizes to two. This permitted savings exceeding 25 per cent. The improvement involved a scored partition that yields just enough to accept
the size variation of the item—in this case an electronic tube. Package
costs, including purchase price, inventory costs, handling costs, are leaping sky high. This trend is accelerated by the constant increase in

number of sizes, shapes, counts. And with every new size of item, there almost automatically comes another-size package. The concept of flexibility in the package may offer a method to many manufacturers of getting a single package that can accommodate a number of sizes, with resulting economies.

Packages That Challenge Shopper Test

A number of packages have been designed so as both to permit and encourage the shopper to test the item—something that presumably a package makes impossible without damage to the package. A recent example involves a floor mop that is bagged in polyethylene. It is almost instinctive for a woman to want to try the squeezing action of a floor mop. With this in mind, the mop is moistened at the factory before being enclosed in the polyethylene bag. Then, printed on the bag are the words "Try Magic Action Squeeze." Since the polyethylene bag retains the moisture in the mop, when the salesperson or shopper squeezes as directed, a very reasonable facsimile of the mop action is obtained. The item itself remains untouched and unsoiled. Thus, visibility and test are both achieved. Moreover, even dull salespeople are somehow fascinated by the ability to test the mop. Other packages that have a test feature have electrical items that can be plugged in. (These test-'em-yourself packages have a considerable appeal to men—and "Poppa" is becoming quite a shopper!)

Help Trade Cut Manual Labor

The retailer was never so conscious as at this very moment of his imperative need to cut his costs for manual labor. This is especially true of the managers of chain stores, who find labor to be their number-one problem. Therefore, ideas that promise a cut in manual-labor costs are increasingly welcome. Example: A food processor now uses a *single-tier* shipping carton. This elimination of the cumbersome double-decker carton has a big appeal to retailers. It lessens lost motion, wasted time. Price marking on a single layer of packages is obviously speeded up considerably. Moreover, the single-tier carton was so designed that it interlocks and stacks, which eliminates sliding and toppling during palletizing. As part of the great desire among retailers to cut manual-labor costs, there is a growing trade demand for revising the size of the pack so as to correspond more closely to store movement. Since every chain has stores with a huge variation in sizes, and thus a huge variation in merchandise movement, this means that manufacturers may find it advisable to increase the variety of packs in which they ship. All these developments are directly within the province of the manufacturer's merchandising executive.

CHAPTER **26**

Pricing

Vive la Différence

Keen merchandising occasionally involves breaking with an industry-wide tradition. Example: A maker of greeting cards decided to
go counter to industry practices—this company now prepays freight on
its greeting card line. It claims, "Ours is the only nationally-known line
offering this feature. Difference: 4 to 6 per cent extra profit for you—
retail prices stay the same; your cost remains the same." Retailers tend to
be amazingly conscious of shipping charges—and there is little doubt
that some merchants will be favorably impressed by the assertion that
"we pay the freight—you pocket up to 6 per cent more." In another
industry, a manufacturer who made a similar move put a special label
on his shipping cases, which reminds the retailer that the shipment has
come prepaid—a good idea because, after the first flurry of interest, the
allowance may be overlooked or casually accepted. There is a tendency
in too many fields, not only for merchandise and its pricing and packaging to be similar, but also for the merchandising program to be identical. Every part of the total marketing program can benefit by a departure
from the traditional—wisely thought out, wisely costed.

Price Promotion under Manufacturer Control

In various big-ticket lines in which price slashing by retailers had
become frenzied, several manufacturers have instituted *factory-controlled*
price-cutting programs. In these controlled programs, the retailer is per-

mitted to cut prices within prescribed brackets. (This plan has been common in health and beauty-aid items.) The retailer is also given discontinued models, special-price promotional models, special allowances based on volume, complete promotional programs featuring the cut prices. These factory-controlled programs tend to alleviate the situation, but they are more of a palliative than a cure. In one instance where the manufacturer slashed retail outlets by 20 per cent, cut his distributors by an almost equal amount, and made a determined effort to police the controlled price-cut program, the net result was a greater degree of equilibrium in the market. Even here, however, trade checks indicated that trade evasions were numerous. Transshipping could not be completely eliminated, which tended to upset the situation in certain areas. Where the manufacturer does not make a strong policing effort, the program has clearly bogged down. Of course, it's a fact that in some instances these programs are planned more to placate the trade for a time than for any long-term goal.

Pricing the Complete "Package"

Several big speculative home builders are now pricing their homes "complete." One luxury-home developer prices his homes not only with landscaping and decorating included—but will even include basic furnishings. A new Caribbean tourist development also prices the complete "package"—in other words, its rates cover not only rooms and meals, but also bar, sports, barber, etc., so "guest will know exactly what his entire stay will cost." Mobile homes have traditionally been priced on a complete basis—including appliances, floor coverings, drapes. Actually, the law-impelled price list that must now appear on all new autos in dealer showrooms is another instance of pricing the complete package. One reason for this trend—shoppers have become more sophisticated; they are less and less fooled by the so-called "basic price" of the "complete package." Since this is so—why not give them the full price? Airlines may come to complete pricing. Draperies tend now to be priced complete. It should come also in major appliances. In brief, as the shopping public becomes more sophisticated (and this is a constant process), merchandisers must match sophisticated merchandising with sophisticated shopping.

Progressive Incentives for Early Orders

Extra discounts offered the trade for advance-of-season or early orders are common. Usually, though, these incentives to stimulate advance buying by the trade offer a single percentage cut, varied only by size of order. Recently, several manufacturers of big-ticket lines of a highly seasonal nature have been developing advance-of-season buying incentives that are graduated by the calendar. The greatest incentive is offered to the earliest trade buyer. Thus, a manufacturer who offers a choice of merchandise prizes and expense-free vacations for early orders points out to the trade that "earliest orders pay off *nearly double!* Your choice of thousands of merchandise prizes and hundreds of expense-free vacations, even including a trip around the world. *The sooner you order, the bigger your winnings.*" This concept of progressive incentives for early orders has much to recommend it. However, it also raises problems such as placating the dealer who places an order just twenty-four hours after the passing of one of the deadlines. Of course, the big objective is the early order—and the minor headaches are probably worth accepting if the required advance-of-season volume is obtained.

Getting Dealers to Jump Price Lining

Retailers tend to be excessively timid about departing from traditional price lines. When they do move up to a higher-price line, the step-up is usually a small one. Can the trade be induced to make a *sharp* upward move in price lining? A maker of towels has had great success in getting dealers to make a leap upward with price lining, rather than a mincing step. This was accomplished with a complete program, which started with the design of beautiful and highly imaginative towel concepts. Packages carried out the super de luxe concept. Displays and advertising were in the same tempo. A fifteen-minute sales training film was prepared for salespeople. The manufacturer's showroom was given over to the top of the line—and visiting buyers were given thorough presentations. Letters were sent to store management as well as to merchandising executives explaining the volume and net-profit potentials in the higher-price lining. The line was made available on a limited-distribution basis. Case histories of results were compiled that made a convincing story for the trade. It was pointed out that even a price-promotional category like towels could be promoted at full markup by trading up *sharply.* Maybe some manufacturers are right now almost as timid as the trade about moving up price lines.

Larger Inventories for More Outlets

The supplier is becoming more and more the "banker" for the distributing trades. And as retailers go increasingly into credit, a trend for manufacturers to finance the trade will accelerate. A drug house (aspirin, toothpaste, hair tonic, etc.) extended its discount period from the traditional fifteen-day period to ninety days. The plan works this way: On all orders placed for delivery between a ninety-day period customers will receive special dating on credit discounts. These are one-third payable within thirty days, 2 per cent discount; one-third payable within sixty days, 2 per cent discount; balance within ninety days, 2 per cent discount. (One objective of this plan was to lessen the constant out-of-stock condition so common in drug and other outlets.) A major appliance producer tells the retailer he need pay only 10 per cent cash to fill his sales floor—no matter how large—with any variety of these major appliances he selects. Then he gets a ninety-day scot-free grace period before paying carrying charges. This usually means that a dealer can put in a whole floor of new models without having funds tied up in inventory for a considerable period. The appliances are paid for as sold during the ninety-day period.

Dangers in Changes to Trade Terms

A highly competitive era inevitably brings with it a trend toward more liberal terms for the trade. Example: A drug house announced that purchases made from the twenty-sixth through the last day of the month would be billed on the following month's statement and discounted at 2 per cent if paid by the tenth of the following month. These changes in traditional trade terms involve hazards. Once instituted, they are difficult to bring back to the original point. And how they will affect the trade's schedule of ordering (which, in turn, could affect the timing of salesmen's calls) is also difficult to predict. Historic trade terms perhaps are not exactly inviolate, but they should seldom be modified for reasons that may be temporary. Or put it this way: Don't turn to a change in trade terms for a hypodermic. Trade terms are, really, long-term merchandising instruments; they should not be too quickly changed for short-term objectives.

Shrinking Obese Trade Margins

One cause of price slashing is a trade margin established when the item required—and got—specialty selling. These margins tend to be out of line in a self-service, self-selection age of presold brands. The more luscious the margin, the greater the temptation to slash prices. That's why several industries are trending toward a shrinkage of their traditional trade margins. The electric razor is one example—pricing programs for the electric razor allowed discounts of up to 50 per cent (and more) to large outlets. That sort of discount may have been necessary when the electric razor had to be demonstrated. But today it's bought by self-service and self-selection. Consequently, this industry may now be going to a 30 per cent or 33⅓ discount basis (which still may be too high). Several of the watchmakers have also cut back on trade margins. Here margins ran between 50 and 100 per cent and a good deal more. Now some watch lines are being put out with margins limited to 35 per cent. In appliances, margins have been lowered slightly by several producers. Other industries will unquestionably follow suit.

Price Lists Multiply

A major soft-goods line has four price lists for dealers stocking its TV set: a *regular* price list, a *key* price list, a *master* price list, an *associated distributor* price list (the last was a designation coined for a few very large accounts, which included both a department store and a major chain in one area). There had been a fifth price list in this manufacturer's price-list repertoire—it had included a giant tire company that has a big chain of retail outlets. Another example: A major maker of small tools (hammers, screwdrivers, etc.) brought out a special set for women (gold-plated!). It found that the hardware section in a department store traditionally gets a different volume discount than the household-supplies section and the gift section. It, too, has individual price lists for each "trade." (Usually, to simplify the salesman's problem, these price lists are differently colored.) Merchandising men will find that price lists will continue to multiply. Still bigger retailers, for example, offering new types of warehousing services plus gigantic volume, will pressure to this end.

Odd-pricing above Even Figures

It is customary when odd-pricing to fix the odd price *under* a traditional even figure. Thus, $4.95 would be a fairly typical pricing point, right under the even $5.00 figure. However, some merchandisers report that the vast change-over in traditional pricing points, necessitated by the inflation of recent years, has presented an opportunity for odd-pricing at pricing points *above* the even figure. One manufacturer stumbled on this discovery. His retail for the East was the traditional $24.95. In the Far West, the retail was fixed at $26.95. The higher pricing point above the even $25 figure was found to be no obstacle—and now, quite gradually, the higher pricing point is being moved East! In odd-pricing *above* an even figure, experience suggests moving out of range of the traditional even figure—this manufacturer says that $26.95 is a better pricing point than $25.95. It also provides more attractive margins. If we are in a long-term price uptrend, odd-pricing *above* the even figure might be tested by more merchandisers.

When Price Lining Has Too Big a Spread

A maker of packaged curtains marked his line, at retail, to start at a $6.49 pricing point. Other numbers in the line ran up from that point— the next pricing point in its line was $7.98, then $9.98, etc. This was an advertised and branded line. Unbranded (and sometimes unpackaged) competition came out starting at a $4.98 pricing point. In time, trade analysis showed that the two most popular pricing points were $6.49 and $4.98. That gap of approximately $1.50 suggested that a new volume-price range might be opened up somewhere between those two figures. The final decision was to bring down the $6.49 retailer to a $5.98 retail pricing point. The $7.98 retailer was brought down to $6.49. The $5.98 pricing point obviously brought the branded, packaged line closer to the popular $4.98 pricing point of the unbranded competition. Whether competition would, in time, drop down to $4.48 remained to be seen. But, in the meanwhile, this sequence of price lining indicated that when one's big-volume pricing point on a branded line is too far above the big-volume pricing point of unbranded competition it is advisable to narrow the price-lining gap.

How Much Margin on Step-up Numbers?

Where step-up numbers (special low-priced models planned to step up the shopper to higher price lines) are common, it is fairly customary to cut the trade's usual margin on these numbers. Periodically, the trade fights for regular margins on step-ups. But experienced merchandisers resist these demands for these reasons: (1) The amount of stepping up done by the trade is constantly decreasing due to poor-caliber floor selling; (2) competition compels increasing emphasis on the step-up numbers; (3) the more liberal the margin on the step-up, the more likely the trade will be to neglect the higher-priced numbers. Actually, many manufacturers would be quite shocked were they to conduct shopping tours among their outlets and discover the small extent to which step-up numbers are being used to step up the sale. Such a study might lead at least some merchandisers to revise basic thinking regarding step-ups and to arrange for more effective robot presentations that will achieve a higher degree of step up. The step-up concept was founded on true specialty selling. That's a shaky foundation today. Too often the trade sells *down* to the step-up number.

Trade Incentives for Early Payment

In one industry, recent experience has shown that a discount plan offering 5 per cent in ten days, or 4 per cent in sixty days, has tempted too many merchants who pass the ten-day limit to wait out until the sixtieth day. These accounts figure that since they can get the 4 per cent discount any time from the eleventh day to the sixtieth day—why not use the money for operating capital until the very last moment? What's more, some dealers have discovered—when they need cash—that they can transship the merchandise, at cost, to other dealers on a cash basis. (In this way, they really borrow money at 4 per cent for up to seventy days.) Several manufacturers in this industry are now considering a revamped discount plan that will make it less attractive for dealers who pass the initial ten-day payment period to wait out the sixty-day payment period. This experience points up the close attention the trade pays to cash discounts and to the increasing shrewdness of the trade in manipulating cash-discount dates for capital advantages.

Optional Pricing under Fair Trade

Even the most ardent price-fixed retailer wants to do some price merchandising—to meet competition. Consequently, some fair-trade manufacturers will bring out a number (or a line) with an optional markup. This may—or may not—bear the family name. But it is clearly merchandised to the trade as a price-promotional number. It is usually marked at a wholesale figure that permits a retail down in the lower price range. Example: A fair-traded line of brushes, priced in the higher-price lines, brought out a line under another brand name to be optionally priced by the retailer. Its wholesale was way down at the low end. The parent company name was listed, inconspicuously, on the low-end number. Interestingly, it has become one of the big leaders in the line—significant because the retailers merchandising it presumably had been so pounded by price-cutting competition that they tended to favor this fair-traded line to escape price competition. Yet they promptly turned to a low-end, optionally priced number and promoted it strongly. Moral: What retailers say they want—and what they will promote—may be two different things.

The Case AGAINST Prepricing

Prepricing offers many advantages—to manufacturer, wholesaler, retailer. It is destined to be adapted more broadly. But its spread as a merchandising practice will be braked so long as some weighty problems continue to arise when certain categories are prepriced. One manufacturer who prepriced and then dropped the plan lists the problems this way. Shipping costs to various areas vary widely. State and local taxes are a problem—when retailer must stamp these taxes on the package, most of the laborsaving of prepricing is lost. Many retailers use differently colored inks so check-out operators can ring up sales by classifications; these colors cannot possibly be matched at the factory. Many retailers insist on retaining pricing initiative; they do not want to merchandise in a price-marking strait jacket. This is especially true of price-promotional outlets. Some retailers want to take a higher price than the prepriced figure. Some retailers object because they want the customer to believe that *everything* in the store is marked down. When the manufacturer changes the price, especially in an upward move, the retailer is compelled to move his inventory at the old and lower price, which he seldom likes to do!

Getting Advance-season Orders

An air-conditioner distributor, to get advance-of-season orders, told retailers that they would have full return privileges until June 15 on any conditioners bought by January 15. Also, purchases made before January 15 would be delivered free of transportation costs. Also, a dealer who ordered 12 units would be required to take only 3 by January 15 to be eligible for a 12-lot price. Also, when the twelfth unit was taken by the dealer, he got a bonus unit—entirely free. If he ordered 60 units and took out a dozen by January 15, he got carload price plus free delivery. And, if the complete order was taken by April 15, the dealer got special dating terms—one-third in May, one-third in June, and one-third in July. He got a bonus de luxe unit for each 12 units he took, and if he completed the 60-unit order by April, he got an additional bonus gift. List prices guaranteed through July 15. This is giving away a lot, but if costs are sufficiently reduced, the net may be satisfactory. However, any program of this kind must be accompanied by a strong plan for moving merchandise ahead of season.

How to Price a New Size

Problem: How to price a new size attractively without cutting into the volume on the old size? Solution: The old 98-cent retailer (a deodorant) was kept at that pricing point—but 50 per cent more of the deodorant lotion was added to it. The new size (two-thirds the size of the old) was priced at 73 cents retail. This not only worked out as a good shopper value, but it also enabled this merchandiser to anticipate trade objections to additional sizes. He could make out a strong case for reaching new markets, for attractive value for larger total goods, and net for trade. Quite frequently, a new size is deliberately planned so as not to disturb pricing and margins on existing sizes. This may result in a weak merchandising program. Where costs permit and where the total marketing situation so suggests, a new size may actually involve considerable revision in all or some other sizes. Sometimes that is indicated procedure in other cases—all sizes may have to be juggled either in price or in size of sales unit to keep the entire line competitive, both with respect to rivals and with respect to each number in the line.

Will Trade Keep Larger Margins?

When a maker of household electrics announced lowered wholesale prices, the statement to the trade declared that the move was made "to enable the retailers to make a margin of profit on today's discount selling prices comparable to that formerly made at fair trade prices." But it is the nature of retailing to slice margins to meet competition. This particular line offered the trade satisfactory margins before discount selling became prevalent; the trade really had to be bullied into hanging onto that margin. In a discount market, larger margins simply melt away. Moreover, too many lines are offering the trade margins that were originally established when these lines required—*and got*—specialty selling. When lines no longer require—or get—specialty selling (and this is certainly true of household electrics, which are correctly called "traffic items") then, in this self-service discount age, a larger margin can prove only a temporary stimulant. In due time that extra margin will be swallowed up by competitive necessity.

Trade Margins on Stylized Staples

When a staple item is given fashion or design appeal, the retailer tends to take a second look at traditional markups. Fashion appeal became important for a formerly staple soft-goods line. Retailers found that their markdown average had jumped from 2 or 3 per cent to 6 to 8 per cent—a jump of some 300 per cent. Unfortunately for manufacturers, markdowns are a retail preoccupation. And retailers continue to suffer from "percentage-itus." Total gross sales on this formerly staple line has zoomed as a direct result of design developments. But the manufacturer made little progress trying to persuade his accounts that increased dollar volume more than balances out increased markdowns. He felt compelled to change one price line in order to permit giving the trade an initial 41 per cent mark-on as compared with the traditional 37.7 per cent. Another price line was changed to provide a 42.5 mark-on instead of the usual 39 per cent. But the trade accelerated its price promotions, and markdowns are just as bad as before. Conclusion: Fight it out with merchandising statistics; don't tamper with margins.

Dangers in Lower Price Lines

Inevitably, a new line finds the trade reporting: "This is swell—but bring it out in a lower price line and we'll really go to town with it." The advice is not always bad. But one step down the price-line ladder usually brings a trade suggestion about the wonderful volume that will be done when still another step down is taken. Eventually, the retailer complains about too many price lines; about excessive inventory; that there's no profit in the low price lines that are moving (and on which he concentrates his promotions). His attention—and his buying dollar— turn elsewhere. A maker of upper-price-line summer furniture bearing a strong brand name has entered the "promotional-line" end of this price-promotion-plagued industry. The known name is *not* being used. This lessens the merchandising problem. But the fight to keep the trade focused on the advertised brand and the higher price lines must now be redoubled. Lower price lines tend to be temporary hypodermics.

Packaging for a Higher Margin

A maker of a small-unit item recently adapted for his line a new type of packaging—a "blister" pack. The item had been retailed for 29 cents. The blister pack added 3 cents to total costs. But because the new pack added so much appeal to the item, the retail price was marked up to 39 cents; a whopping jump. Margins were made more attractive to the food super (through which the item is moved). And, with the resulting support of this outlet, sales showed a dollar increase of several hundred per cent. When there is no other way to put over a price increase—an improved package can sometimes turn the trick. And if the new price permits the trade a higher margin, the trade may give it the additional push needed to compensate for shopper resistance. Where competitive conditions permit, new packaging and new pricing (plus better trade margins) may go hand in hand. This is common practice when staple items are specially packed de luxe for the gift market—it is not so commonly done as it might be for regular markets.

Trading Down Class Line for Volume Market

From electric vibrators to electronic organs, the marketing world has witnessed some interesting examples lately of trading down a class line for volume merchandising. Another example is supplied by the room divider. In the furniture department, the shopper could spend up in the three figures for elaborate room dividers. Now a manufacturer has brought out a line of room dividers traded down to a $9.98 retailer. This is mass-market pricing. In order to derive full advantage from the volume-market pricing, this line has been put into the housewares department which has more daily traffic than furniture. Accompanied by a strong promotion, the line was offered simultaneously to the housewares department of four department stores in one large city. All four took it, reported remarkable results. Interestingly—there was no price cutting.

One buyer commented: "Why kill a new item? It's selling in good volume at a 42½ per cent margin, it offers an excellent value to the customer, it's a good pricing point." Interestingly, the volume-pricing point brought in mail and telephone orders—a good test of success in appealing to the volume market.

Discounts on "Fighting" Brands

Where a secondary or "fighting" brand begins to assume both brand stature and volume—the time may come when it will be found advisable to take a second look at its discount schedule. This becomes particularly true as the private brand in general becomes stronger—which is a powerful trend—and as the manufacturer's private-brand lines thus compete more and more strongly with the maker's nationally advertised line. A maker of housewares, for example, recently found it advisable to hike the retail prices of its fighting brand—and, simultaneously, to reduce the distributor discount. The announced objective was "to equalize" the trade discount and trade pricing on the secondary brand as related to the nationally advertised brand. Many manufacturers will find it advisable to recheck discount and pricing schedules on private-brand lines, secondary-brand lines, etc. In many instances these schedules now put the nationally advertised brand in a weak competitive position.

Quantity Discounts on Deals

Where a trade deal involves a comparatively small unit purchase, a special price may be fixed when the retailer buys a quantity of the deal. For example, here is a deal that costs the retailer $6.24. If he buys three deals, the price becomes $5.92 each; for six deals, the price becomes $5.62 each. Another variation of this concept is to offer the single deal at a fixed price and the multiple-deal purchase at an extra discount. For example, on a deal billed singly at $7.20, one manufacturer offered twelve deals at $7.20 each, less 15 per cent. Quantity discounts on deals assume greater importance as deals are planned for large accounts as well as small accounts. Too many deals have more appeal for small accounts than for large accounts; yet the large accounts may move 80 to 90 per cent of a manufacturer's gross volume.

Price Reduction without Price

Must a price reduction *always* be featured in dollars and cents? Or could there be merchandising advantages, at times, in featuring a price reduction through some other symbol? A maker of instant coffee (a category overrun with such offers as 10 cents off) decided on a no-price

price reduction. It was done this way. A special "bonus jar" was created for the event. This was a different size and shape than the regular instant-coffee jar; it had an extra-large neck. This elongated neck was packed with enough extra coffee to make 10 extra cups. A foil neck label was then used. It read: "Free! 10 Extra Cups." When a category swings over to almost a single merchandising event—in this case one variation or another of the 10-cents-off event—there may be particular reason to develop a *whole new approach;* a whole new image that just as effectively shouts, "Price reduction," but that wins the benefits that come from being different.

Women Can't Multiply beyond Three

The food supers started multiple pricing with the "2-for" concept—offering two of an item at a special (sometimes *presumably* a special) price. (They did this so far in advance of manufacturers that they had to do the bundling themselves.) Then the count went to "3 for." One day, a smart food operator discovered that by far the majority of women, in the split second in which so much shopping is done, can't multiply beyond the order of three. This was an important merchandising discovery—because it meant that in a "4-for" or a "5-for" or a "6-for" merchandising event, it would not be necessary to make a *deep* slash in the pricing (especially if the total price were put at an odd figure). Indeed, it was soon found that at "5 for," for example, a *higher price per single unit* could be obtained than at "2 for"—whereas exactly the opposite should be the case! Thus, the merchant gained two advantages: a higher unit sale and larger margin on the higher unit sale. Merchandising really involves a race between the shopper's cupidity and the merchandiser's ingenuity. The merchandiser can win that race if he will bear in mind that women cannot multiply well (while shopping) beyond the order of three.

Quoting Lowest Possible Unit Price

In certain lines of merchandise—floor coverings are an example—techniques for quoting price are enormously important. Thus, tile flooring clearly benefited because it was quoted *by the tile,* which, of course, represented a unit price so low as to make a tile installation appear to involve a lower total cost than the shopper might have initially expected. Other types of floor covering began to quote square-foot prices, which, of course, involved much smaller figures than traditional square-yard pricing. So powerful did this pricing technique become that the woven rug industry felt compelled to initiate square-foot pricing (and encountered some dealer resistance to the idea which, in time, will be overcome). This same pricing concept has worked in such far-removed fields as life insurance and installment selling in hard goods and autos, where big figures were reduced to small figures by getting down to a per-day-payment basis. Here we have an old merchandising basic that is just as effective today as it was years ago—get your unit price down to the lowest possible basis and melt shopper price resistance.

Annual Rebates on Purchases

For hosiery, an annual rebate plan offers a 25-cent rebate on each dozen pairs—if the account shows a minimum 10 per cent increase. A 15 per cent increase brings a rebate of 50 cents. Another plan provides a 2 per cent annual rebate, provided purchases do not fall below the previous year—and provided the account gives the brand "adequate display" (which is meaningless), controls its inventory properly (which is also meaningless and unenforceable), provided the account runs a specified amount of co-op, and provided the account carries a minimum of five styles. A giant maker of major appliances tells his accounts that if they choose a 20 per cent higher quota they get an extra 5 per cent cash rebate at the end of the year, figured on a quarterly basis—to be renegotiated quarterly. Annual rebate plans are complicated, lead to endless bickering, lead to unwise buying and selling practices by the trade, encourage the trade to hatch out snide evasions, tend to wind up as extra allowances.

The Time Factor in Pricing

One of the great object lessons in time-factor pricing has been furnished by American Telephone—the special rates after 6 p.m. and on Sunday. (Now that Saturday is becoming a universal holiday, AT & T is considering extending its lower rates to Saturday.) Western Union has employed the same pricing device in its special night rates. The Florida State Turnpike Authority tested a bargain rate for night drivers. For years many retailers have featured special prices for limited hours. The seventy-two-hour marathons staged by many major appliance dealers are typical. (This concept was originally sponsored by one of the larger appliance manufacturers, which shows how a manufacturer can capitalize the time factor in merchandising.) Department stores have promoted opening-hour specials to get customers down earlier in the morning. (Results are only fair.) Six-hour sales have become popular. A few downtown stores are promoting noontime specials. Manufacturers have yet to exploit deeply the time factor in pricing as a merchandising stimulant.

Large-quantity Pricing on Small Orders

A maker of flooring tile developed a pricing system that has application in other categories. It works this way: The dealer may enter a qualifying order to start the season for any one or any combination of numbers in the line. This order will be billed at the applicable price as determined by the number of cartons ordered. Shipment of this qualifying order qualifies the dealer to make subsequent fill-in purchases of 20 cartons or more, of any combination of numbers in the line, *at the same prices as the qualifying order, for the remainder of the season.* (Dealers first qualify by ordering 45 cartons or more, or 99 cartons or more.) A dealer who has qualified for fill-in pricing in the 45- or 99-carton bracket may requalify for fill-in-bracket pricing in a higher category by upping the order; the pricing then becomes retroactive on purchases made for that season. The details of this pricing system are, of course, specifically worked out for the floor-tile industry. However, the basic idea could be adapted for other lines to induce the dealer to place a substantial advance-of-season order and then to get the dealer to fill in as required.

Split-pricing the Sales Unit

The auto makers have, of course, demonstrated for all to see the great merchandising advantages inherent in split pricing the sales unit. So have the big, speculative home builders where, as with cars, the complete home may cost from 25 to 50 per cent more than the base price. When TV sets and major appliances are priced sans installation and/or servicing, we have another example of split pricing. But can the same principle be successfully used in smaller-ticket items? Yes it can. Example: A new type of cookware, introduced originally in 1959, was priced at $5.95 for the saucepan and the handle. This was soon changed to a price list that priced the saucepan at $3.95 and the handle at $2.00 retail. The change in shopper willingness to buy was remarkable. Apparently the $3.95 price for the saucepan created such a strong desire for the saucepan that it was easier for the shopper to invest the required $2.00 in the handle than was the case when the two were merchandised for a combination price of $5.95. Moreover, shoppers began to buy several saucepans of different sizes. (The one handle fits all.) Thus we see that split pricing is feasible, not only for big-ticket merchandise, but also for small-ticket lines.

Coding to Lessen Retailer's Price Stamping

Where prepricing is not practicable and where the retailer's cost of hand-stamping price is high, merchandising men are now finding it necessary to develop techniques for cutting the retailer's price-stamping costs. Developments in the case pack have, of course, been designed to this end—the time factor involved in price-stamping merchandise in the case has been cut sharply in this way. But in some fast-moving merchandise categories this may not be enough; other ideas may be required to bring the cost of price-stamping down to a reasonable level. A large producer of canned-food products which enjoy an enormous turnover has developed a special coding system for this purpose. This coding system eliminates hand stamping of price by the retailer entirely. The code is put on each can by the producer. The food super then lists the code on its price list, maintained next to the checker's cash register. The checker need only consult the figure on her price list to determine the price. Naturally, this system could not be used by many manufacturers without becoming cumbersome—but it suggests new avenues of thinking.

Special Pricing for Influential Groups

The home economist is an influential factor in the ultimate sale of a wide range of merchandise. To win the support of this special group, a major maker of traffic appliances—and a stickler both for price maintenance and for strict adherence to distribution practices—has broken with policy on both fronts. At an annual meeting of home economists, this company featured at its booth special prices for its appliances "when used for home economics demonstration purposes." Example: A regular $49.94 mixer was offered to economists for $27.44—considerably less, be it noted, than this item could be bought at discount houses. Moreover, the manufacturer made the sale directly to the home economist, although its firm policy is to sell through authorized distributors only. Check into special groups that wield influence—particularly our educators at all levels. They have a world of bearing on what the youngsters of today do—and buy—tomorrow.

Unnecessary Seasonal Markdowns

Reports a soft-goods manufacturer: "We made considerable progress in 1959 in inducing variety chains to comprehend that summer doesn't end on the Fourth of July. We conducted tests in selected store units which included refraining from putting Fall and Winter lines out on the counters by July 10. In these selected stores our summer category was one of the few classifications in which a good selection was still available to the shopper after August 1. And the final figures showed convincingly that turnover on the summer merchandise was excellent into August—and that the Fall and Winter lines actually did better when they were put out later." Too much seasonal merchandising by retailers is based on tradition, but air conditioning, new living habits, new merchandise constructions, tourism, new vacation schedules are causing shoppers to change their seasonal buying habits. Retail tradition is difficult to break—and store tests may be needed to induce retailers to reevaluate their seasonal markdown dates, seasonal inventory practices, etc.

The Reverse Trend in Size of Sales Unit

Much sales-unit merchandising planning currently involves larger, and still larger sales units. But this should not blind merchandisers to the fact that there is also opportunity for volume in the reverse trend—in the development of smaller and still smaller sizes. Example: One of the great packing houses, as part of a determined effort to make turkey appear on home menus throughout the entire year rather than seasonally, is now merchandising frozen turkey roasts in quarter sections that average about 5 pounds each. This smaller sales unit, it is reasoned, will appeal to a vastly larger market than that available when turkeys of 10 pounds, 20 pounds, and more are the typical sales unit. Similarly, a headache pill has been put out in a two-pill pack—as a pick-up for people who get a headache while away from home. This smaller unit, about as tiny as a sales unit can get, thus fills a logical market niche. So, while exploring still larger sizes, check also into still smaller sales units. The one extreme may offer opportunities that equal the other extreme in sales-unit size.

Premium Pricing for Established Staple

When a long-established staple has achieved such a high percentage of total market as to make further sizable gains either unlikely or too expensive, which way should the merchandiser turn for a dynamic sales jump? One procedure: Check into a premium-priced number. This is the procedure followed by one of the leading makers of razor blades. Its share of market is substantial. In its regular pricing points, it cannot hope for large sales gains. Since its regular pricing points are not low-end, it might have gone down to cellar prices. But this would have meant more volume, little extra profit. Moreover, it would have cut into the existing price lines. So this blade maker turned in the other direction—up. It has brought out a "super" line of blades to be marketed at the top of the company's price line—a new pricing top for this brand. In line with the broad trend in all merchandising toward upping price lines (which, in turn, is soundly based on the public's expanding desire for, and ability to pay for, better quality) this will bring this established staple into a new market that will cut little into its existing markets. Premium pricing for an established staple has much to favor it today.

CHAPTER **27**

Distribution: Markets, Outlets, Salesmen, Distributors

Introduce New Lines Regionally

A merchandising executive for a nationally advertised and distributed line of housewares reports that a study brought out the following advantages of regional introduction for new lines: (1) Margins in this category are now too small to permit big errors—regional introduction lessens the risks; (2) greater flexibility is achieved; (3) "bugs" in the line and in the marketing program can be eliminated on a lower cost basis; (4) the manufacturer gets a quicker return on inventory investment; (5) the advertising investment is less; (6) each region can be more intensively developed—stronger financial power and man power can be concentrated region by region; (7) public reaction is more easily studied and charted regionally than nationally; (8) where local differences exist, they can be better exploited; (9) the total time involved will be little more than that required for a national effort—"tooling up" for the national effort in marketing as well as in production takes so long that the total time elapsed for the regional programs is seldom excessive. Even some giant manufacturers are finding that regional introduction has many advantages over chasing the mirage of immediate national distribution.

Will Manufacturers Open Retail Stores?

As retailers become manufacturers, as they produce and promote and distribute their own controlled brands, and as manufacturers perform 90 per cent of the total retail function—will manufacturers eventually open their own retail stores? Answer: Definitely "yes." Singer Sewing Machine has done rather well with its own retail stores for years. Some shoe manufacturers have done well with their own shoe chains. Midget food stores are spreading, several giant food processors might very well open up their own bantam stores. Now that giant manufacturers of appliances have enormously long lines—why not operate their own retail stores? Department stores are opening tiny "twig" branches—several giant soft-goods manufacturers could open similar types of chains. In brief, retailers are taking on more of the trappings of the manufacturer—even to the point of selling their own controlled brands through noncompetitive retail outlets. Manufacturers perform the major part of the retail function and underwrite a good part of the remainder through allowances—why not take the final step and jump into retail stores? When manufacturers answer this question in the affirmative, a great new merchandising revolution will begin.

Analyze Yearly Changes in Distribution

Usually it is only when the merchandising executive looks back over a period of years that the scope of retail-outlet changes becomes self-evident. Then it may be too late to do much, by way of either capitalizing on or discouraging the trend. Several merchandising executives report that they have developed comprehensive research study programs designed, not only to *measure properly* changes in distribution by outlets, but, much more important, to uncover the *reasons* for these changes and their ultimate scope. Retailing in every field promises to change at a faster pace over the next five years than over any previous full decade. (The major appliance makers are just now becoming keenly aware that, in some areas, the builder right now moves more appliances than regular dealers.) Overstaying declining traditional outlets (as some furniture manufacturers have done) or permitting a line to wind up primarily in discount chains (as several makers of electric shavers have done) can both create serious merchandising hazards. Market research should be employed more broadly to measure and to offer interpretations of yearly changes in distribution.

The Coming Era of Committee Buying

The food outlet's buying of new *propositions* (as differentiated from so-called "new *products*") is already controlled by committees. The buyer in the major food outlets has lost a substantial degree of his buying authority. Other major outlets are also turning to committee buying of new propositions. And the larger retail giants become, and the greater the slice of total retail volume they control, the larger will be the total buying of new propositions by committee. (One executive usually makes the actual decision; where he sits is the head of the table.) The manufacturer's salesman can rarely get in to the committee meeting. The great problem of the merchandising executive is how to reach the committee members and, in particular, the member who really decides. The buyer's presentation to the committee tends to be horrible. The forms filled out by the salesman are inadequate and frequently are not on the committee table. One solution: A special trade-advertising program specifically keyed to retail *executives*. These trade ads talk in terms of retail *management*—they talk in terms of grand strategy, not in terms of daily tactics. Manufacturers simply must open up communications with higher retail executives.

Exclusive Numbers—Selective Distribution

As one answer to the many problems inherent in enormously broadened distribution, merchandisers are developing a program involving exclusive numbers and selective distribution for these exclusives. (This plan is operated concurrently with the existing unlimited distribution.) Thus, a maker of small appliances brings out special numbers for department stores exclusively. In other words, instead of attempting to shrink distribution—which is seldom either practical or wise—the present concept is to hang on to practically all present outlets but to develop a "package" for selected outlets that these selected outlets will find attractive. When the package includes special numbers (models, patterns, price lines, packaging) the deal may prove attractive to important outlets, including the top independents. Its appeal is that the merchant knows the shopper cannot compare his prices with discount outlets because models will not be identical. Incidentally, one manufacturer is bringing out exclusive numbers for his small retailers who are least able to meet competition.

New-product Distribution by Mail

Years ago, a company that is today a leader in latex items experienced strong resistance when it sought department store distribution for one of its early—and new—items. That resistance was broken down by a national advertising program which included a coupon for this $1 retailer; the coupon to be mailed to the manufacturer. Coupon returns ran into the thousands. They were credited to selected retailers, although filled by the manufacturer. Then the coupon returns were spread before these retailers as evidence of consumer demand. More recently, a new cosmetic brand put together a handsome sample package, priced it a low $1 and offered it in fashion-magazine advertising as a mail-order proposition. The thousands of returns were then properly collated geographically and presented to the appropriate retailers. This technique for winning distribution for a new product—especially a new specialty item —has considerable merit. It achieves preselling while simultaneously providing the salesmen with powerful evidence for the trade of active demand.

Coming—Bazaar-type Stores

The next great development in the shopping center will be the completely roofed-in, year-round air-conditioned center. Several are now in existence. More are on the way. In these completely enclosed centers, there is little need for store windows. Consequently, store windows are disappearing in the newest shopping centers. The open front is now really open, very much as in the days of the medieval bazaar. Several merchandising executives have reported to us that they are studying closely the merchandising techniques of retailers in the several completely roofed-in, completely air-conditioned shopping centers now in existence. They have already found that merchandising tends to take a different course in these shopping centers. They have also discovered that special events are developed to capitalize on the weather-protection feature of the roofed-in center. They find that seasonal merchandise sells better out of season in these locations. Clearly, this is the coming type of shopping center—the time to prepare for the new merchandising and promotional concepts required in these centers is right now.

Two Basics in Market Broadening

Two basics in market broadening include new uses, and new outlets capable of merchandising those new uses. Current example of effective development of these two basics: Office furniture in general and typewriters in particular. Office furniture is now being promoted for home offices: millions of men take business work home—the home office is therefore logical—and it constitutes a brilliant new-use merchandising concept. But it won't be adequately developed so long as office furniture is retailed primarily through office-supply outlets—among other reasons, because women still buy most office furniture for the home and they don't shop that outlet. This broader market demands broadened distribution. And the portable typewriter is pointing the way. This line, formerly sold primarily by the office-supply outlet and some department stores, is now going into the food super, various types of chains, gift and furniture stores, appliance outlets, even music stores. In general, the portable typewriter is now being merchandised as another appliance—this even includes a number in "antique white."

Keep Step with the Year-round Gift Market

It is very likely that the shopper is more aware of her *year-round* gift needs than can be said for some manufacturers, who continue to think of the gift market as a special-occasion affair. It is interesting to note in this connection that more and more retailers are now putting in year-round gift sections or departments. Example: The variety chains are going strongly in the development of year-round gift departments. These year-round gift departments in this outlet get exceedingly flexible merchandising. The seasons are accurately matched by the merchandise assortments. Said one chain buyer: "There's a terrific volume and profit in year-round giftwares. People in big numbers need gifts every day of the year. And almost anything can be a gift—including many staples; and usually at a higher margin." Several chains now have home-office coordinated gift departments—previously much of this gift merchandising was done by the local store manager on his own initiative. The year-round gift market will soon (if it does not already) equal the gift-market total of the traditional gift occasions—particularly in many otherwise staple items. Watch these new year-round gift departments in major outlets for ideas.

Section Buyers More Receptive to Fringe Items

Departmental rigidities in departmentalized stores of all types—department stores, variety stores, food and drug outlets—have, of course, been becoming more elastic for some years. Now, with all major retailers committed to the concept of permitting nothing to stand in the way of impulse sales, section buyers are being given still more latitude with respect to so-called "foreign" items not usually carried in the section. Thus in hosiery we now find that the hosiery buyer is permitted to buy such accessories as slippers, ankle-novelty jewelry, carrying cases for hosiery, special hosiery soap. Moreover, hosiery buyers now show a considerable interest in these fringe items, especially since some hosiery departments now trace *20 per cent of dollar volume* to these accessories and fringe lines. As one checks inventory in many sections, it is obvious that some manufacturers have done an excellent job of getting their lines, or certain items, into new departments; others stick to the traditional department. For most manufacturers, the merchandising objective must be broader exposure in every store—and this usually includes a need for getting items into departments in which these items would be classed as "fringe" items.

Merchandising to Leased Departments

The leased department has returned to popularity. (Bear in mind that rack jobbers really constitute a leased-department operation.) Every type of mass retailer—department store to chain store—is today increasing its total of leased operations. And, as more departments evolve *services* as differentiated from *merchandise*—watch repair, optical, etc. —leased operations will multiply more rapidly because few stores can operate service departments efficiently. One leased operator offering a rug-cleaning service has over 4,000 stores and does a $10 million volume. One operator has built an amazing business selling tires in a leased operation in department stores. Variety chains have leased departments— will have more. Drug chains are heading this way. The food super, as it adds new nonfood categories as well as service departments, has become a huge user of leased departments. The leased-department operator is developing into a new type of middleman-retailer. Many manufacturers who, just a few years ago, did not have special departments for chain-store selling now have such departments. Special departments for merchandising to leased departments are now springing up.

Collect Buying-committee Forms

One merchandising executive for a big food processor claims to have the biggest collection of buying-committee forms used by the food-super committees. Moreover, he claims the file has enabled him (1) to plan presentations that furnish the information these committees believe they want; (2) has given him ideas on how to warm up these cold-fish presentations; (3) has enabled him to spot loopholes for squeezing in a bit more information than the committee may expect; (4) has been made the basis of a series of form paragraphs for his sales force to use when filling out these forms—which enable the salesmen to "say" much more in the small space provided; and (5) has become his "bible" when planning a merchandising event. The home office in too many instances has heard a great deal about the buying-committee data sheet—but has seen too few and studied even fewer. Here is the heart and soul of a whole new world of merchandising; a file of these forms, constantly referred to, is a must in many merchandising offices. (Bear in mind that the buying-committee concept is spreading to the drug chain and other major outlets.)

Strengthening Wholesaler Relations

For the manufacturer selling both direct and through wholesalers— a fairly typical distribution setup in many fields—a situation rises almost regularly in which the wholesaler charges he is neglected or worse. His pet peeve: The direct accounts get pampered treatment. To counteract this perpetual complaint, and to win more active cooperation from its wholesalers, a drug house has developed a series of merchandising events *exclusively* for its wholesalers. Even retailers who buy direct and who "want in" on these events must order through the wholesaler! (This is the key—here is persuasive evidence to the wholesaler that the manufacturer is not leaving him out in the cold.) Each event will be made exceptionally attractive to the wholesaler and his accounts. Moreover, merchandise purchased for each promotion by retailers will earn a 6 per cent extra discount—the manufacturer returns 6 per cent of the amount of the wholesaler's invoice to the retailer. There is a positive drift back to more dependence on the wholesaler in certain fields— which makes still more important the need for strengthening wholesaler relations.

Wholesale Deals That End Up as an Extra Discount

The trade deal that simply offers the wholesaler a price concession too seldom winds up as a price concession for the retailer. Many manufacturers have found that a deal of this kind stimulates heavier orders from the wholesaler. But then certain things happen. The merchandise goes into the wholesaler's warehouse; no price concession is offered to the retail trade; no special push is put behind it; succeeding orders from the wholesaler are delayed; total movement of merchandise is increased slightly, if at all. The only real result is that the wholesaler enjoys a larger margin temporarily, while the manufacturer takes a smaller margin. Obviously, the purpose of a deal offering a price concession to the wholesaler is not to enable him to build inventory at low prices, but to get him to offer these special prices to his retail accounts. Any deal offered through the wholesaler to the retailer must be examined from this vital viewpoint: Will it induce the wholesaler to put *extra selling drive* behind the deal merchandise, or will the deal merchandise wind up simply as regular wholesale inventory brought in at a special price?

Industrial Items for Consumer Market

One of the large carpet companies tested the in-home use of a commercial carpet which it has been selling exclusively through its contract sales department for commercial installation. This brings once again to the attention of the merchandising man the opportunities for *consumer* exploitation that may exist in items and lines traditionally sold to *industry*. Indeed, instead of depending so exclusively on the laboratory for entirely new products—new consumer-market items may be found right within the organization in the industrial-sales end of the business. As a matter of fact, certain of the currently popular tapes were introduced initially to the industrial market, or were looked upon originally as having greater potentials in the industrial end rather than in the consumer end. Indeed, it has been discovered in a few instances that factory workers take home items made for the industrial market and put them to ingenious use in the home. A "new-use contest" among factory employees offering rewards for the in-home use of industrial items might uncover some interesting new-product leads.

The Tent—a New Merchandising Vehicle

Now that the circus is departing, the tent is finding its way into retailing as a new merchandising concept. Fine prestige department stores have put up tents on their parking lots to sell home-furnishing items, appliances, furniture, outdoor equipment, etc. Shopping centers cotton to the idea. Even Sears has used tents in some of its parking lots. There is something enormously appealing about a tent; that undoubtedly was one of the reasons the circus was so successful. And, of course, kids love tents—and since children accompany parents on millions of shopping trips, this is an added reason for the use of tents. Most of these tent events play up the circus theme. Manufacturers, cooperatively or singly, will ultimately be developing special tent merchandising events—in some cases supplying the tent, putting it up, supplying the big-top excitement, maybe even a clown or two. And the tent will be moved from one parking lot to another. A few manufacturers have already tried the idea in a small way and talks have been held concerning joint tent events for noncompetitive products.

Is Your Line Sold in a "Starved" Department?

Years ago, the infants' department of department stores was a "starved" department. A newcomer supplying several items to this department launched a full-fledged program including business-paper advertising aimed at top store management; its object was to convince store management (hard to believe this was ever necessary!) that the infants' department rated a separate buyer, more space, large inventory allowance. (This was one time buyers and section managers did not object to a resource going over their heads!) A top brand in luggage has been communicating with store management to the same end for this classification. Another department is faced with this problem currently—the nurses' uniform department. Management tends still to think of uniforms as—uniform. Today uniforms are highly styled. It's now a fashion business, fast-moving, calling for larger stocks, constant watching by the buyer. But in many stores the uniform buyer's attention is spread over many categories; space for the department is miserly, budgets are tiny. A large maker of uniforms prepared factual messages addressed to store management through business-paper advertising, by direct mail. Also special presentations for salesmen to show to higher-ups were developed.

Checking Market Penetration

The manufacturer selling through wholesalers seldom has an accurate knowledge of his line's market penetration. He makes educated guesses —but it's still a case of guessing. A maker of a small hardware item solved the problem in this way: (1) A questionnaire and accompanying letter were sent to a competent cross section of the retail trade (names furnished by wholesalers); (2) accompanying the mailing was a free sample of a popular number in the line that was being introduced in a new packaging setup (thus bringing the new number to the trade's attention); (3) a return stamped envelope was used; (4) dealers were told they could take the free item home—or sell it. Returns were excellent—32 per cent. The manufacturer learned that only 60 per cent of the hardware stores were stocking the item—and that a small percentage did not even know the item existed. Other facts, rather than guess-estimates, concerning market penetration were obtained, including facts about competition. Obviously, merchandising programs based on market knowledge are more apt to bring back the proper returns.

How to Drop Exclusivity

Generally, exclusive arrangements—particularly those involving new lines—have a cancellation date. When the manufacturer decides to broaden distribution, what happens to the attitude of the originally franchised stores? (1) The original exclusive stores have gone through this experience hundreds of times. They know they are used as bell-wether stores; they don't object too violently—they simply want to be first. (2) But since their aim is *prestige* as well as volume, they tend to lessen their promotions when they lose their exclusivity. (3) If the line continues successful, they will eventually give it renewed promotional play. However, smart merchandisers plan *special* programs for the original stores that will encourage them to continue their early activities; this usually includes special co-op and the other allowances. One manufacturer says he buys his way into an exclusive arrangement and buys his way out of it. It's a good principle to remember.

Specialty Setups via Junior Departments

As merchandise classifications become broader, the retailer can some-times be sold on merchandising a part of the expanded inventory as a junior department. Usually, lamp departments present a veritable forest of lamps. A lamp manufacturer is therefore suggesting that retailers set aside as little as 200 square feet exclusively for displays of specialty-type lamps. Specific achievements of this specialization-segregation mer-chandising policy include (1) higher markup; (2) a large jump in average sale; (3) a big cut in returns; (4) increased turnover; (5) smaller markdowns; (6) higher conversion rate of lookers into customers. This is somewhat different from—yet related to—the typical junior-department concept. Examples of the latter: Drapery hardware is mer-chandised by one manufacturer as a separate junior department. A chintz resource does the same in the *fabric* department. This merchandising concept wins for certain numbers in a big line specialty display, specialty promotion, some specialty selling—all highly desirable.

Service Men as Accessory Salesmen

Point One: The public shows an increasing willingness to buy in the home.

Point Two: As more items placed in the home require installation and servicing (for appliances, etc.) more service men make more service calls on the home. Why not put one and two together—and come up with programs planned to encourage and equip service men to do more selling in the home? Several makers of major appliances have well-established programs of this kind—but, in general, the potentials of the service and installation man as a salesman have scarcely been tapped. Perhaps one of the best opportunities in utilizing the service and in-stallation man as a salesman is by giving him a particularly attractive accessory item to sell. Thus, a refrigerator manufacturer suggests that on every service call the service man should take along an ice-ejector-accessory package—this accessory lends itself to dramatic, quick, and simple demonstration. Of course, the service man also can function in ferreting out leads for major sales—but it is in the actual sale of small related and accessory items that his limited selling talents and time may be best utilized.

Small Outlets for Big-ticket Lines

In a few merchandise classifications, the small outlet continues to be the major outlet. Example: Cameras. While there are a very few large camera retailers and while variety chains, for instance, promise to become big outlets for cameras, currently the Mom-and-Pop outlet is the major outlet for one of the big camera makers. Since cameras can run into high tickets, this company found that its small outlets just couldn't afford to tie up the required money in the number of units needed for a balanced inventory. It also found that compelling these small merchants to repackage and ship cameras back to a middle western city for the repairs that are occasionally needed when a camera reaches the store caused trouble, because the merchant's capital was tied up for several weeks. It has therefore swung over entirely to warehouse-service facilities in seven locations throughout the country. It can thus render overnight inventory to most accounts. And time for repairs on dealer stock has been cut drastically.

Salesmen and Co-op

A manufacturer of foundation garments reports pressure from his sales force to change this company's traditional fifty-fifty plan to the 75 and 100 per cent offered by some competitors. An analysis of its figures showed that to go to the higher figures would cost another half-million dollars—but would produce just about the same linage it was now getting on the fifty-fifty basis. The figures also showed that, if the company continued to limit its co-op expenditures to 3 per cent of total sales, it would actually wind up with 11 per cent *less* advertising on a pay-all plan than it was now getting with its fifty-fifty plan. The sales force agreed the change would not make sense. Then the sales force insisted that the bulk of the co-op linage was coming from its smaller accounts—that department stores, the big outlet, were not using the co-op privilege because of the resource's strict policy. A check of the company's 100 top accounts (which give it 25 per cent of its total volume) showed that these accounts took up 26 per cent of its total co-op pay-outs. Of course, the salesmen will come up with new complaints concerning co-op, but their spines can usually be stiffened by sound statistics.

Separate Brands for Different Outlets

A number of merchandisers over the years have developed brand programs involving separate brands for different types of wholesale and retail outlets. This procedure really started in soft goods, and more particularly in fashion lines. Now it has spread way over into hard goods —a power-mower manufacturer, for example, has one brand for exclusive distribution through appliance, automotive, and sundry specialty fields. As manufacturers have broadened their distribution, both wholesale and retail, separate brands for different distribution channels have become more important. But one manufacturer reports that a recent check disclosed that, in practice, his plan was working less efficiently than it appeared to do in theory. The great problem today, he finds, is that wholesalers and retailers are tramping all over each others' lines *and* territories. The brands therefore wind up where they never were intended to be. Moreover, transshipping is encouraged by this merchandising program—wholesalers will supply each other with brands. Generally speaking, the diversified-inventory programs of wholesalers and retailers (plus retail mergers involving, under one corporate roof, various types of retail operations) have made a shambles of some of these brand programs.

Broadening Everyday-gift Markets

For many industries, Christmas unnecessarily remains the sole gift occasion of the year—so many items could be sold in larger gift volume for innumerable everyday-gift occasions. But in most industries, the creation of multiple-gift occasions throughout the twelve months is too big a job for any one manufacturer. It is not too big a job, however, for the industry to tackle on a united front. The electrical industry points the way with a national promotion of electrical gifts for Mother's Day, weddings, showers, graduation. The everyday-gift market—with certain exceptions—has been developed more by the shopping public than by industry. Yet the total volume of gifts bought for everyday occasions clearly runs up into the billions. There is every indication that more manufacturers are becoming keenly aware of the quickly expanding market for everyday gifts—probably the first to appreciate this market were the greeting card producers. Now the producers of gift-wrap materials are after the everyday-gift market. But the true potential of everyday gifts will not be adequately exploited in some fields initially except by industry-wide effort.

When It Pays to Turn to Small Outlets

In some merchandise categories, a market situation has developed under which even the medium-sized suppliers get short shrift from the giant retailers. These large outlets look upon smaller suppliers as legitimate bait; painful concessions are forced from the small supplier and if one of his promotions is used (after exorbitant payment), the line tends to be buried or dropped promptly after the promotion ends. Under these circumstances, it sometimes becomes advisable for the small or even medium-sized manufacturer to decide to cast his lot primarily with the smaller outlets. Such a program, to be attractive to the smaller outlets, usually calls for selective distribution, price maintenance to assure generous margin, and a promotional program geared to these small outlets. This marketing decision means selling through the short end of the distribution stick: It puts a ceiling on volume; it may increase selling costs. But it spreads the risk, avoids the "big stick," provides a greater degree of stability, and sometimes permits more generous margin for the manufacturer as well as for the trade. From major appliances, traffic appliances, floor coverings to writing instruments, medium-sized manufacturers are tending to embrace this policy.

Crashing Historic Departmental Barriers

There have never been more examples of the breakdown of departmental barriers than exist right now in every major outlet. Yet every breakthrough continues to require astute merchandising planning. Example: The china department in department stores had not been partial to plastic dinnerware. Ultimately, the china department added the higher-price lines in plastic dinnerware. When a low-priced plastic-dinnerware line tried to get into the china department, it met strong resistance. Solution: A special merchandising event was set up in the china department of one of the great bellwether department stores. "Liberal" arrangements were made for the test, including big-space co-op. A particularly attractive group of dinnerware sets were brought together —specially priced. Careful figures were kept; 1,600 sets were sold by this store in three days—a remarkable turnover. The results were then publicized to the trade. Case histories, based on the experience of bellwether stores, can break down trade resistance based on tradition!

Sample Rooms on Trains

Planes have been used as sample rooms and, of course, trailers are commonly employed for this purpose. But one manufacturer reports that the use of a special Pullman train has decided advantages. His experience is that the train can be more easily reached, in most instances, than an airfield and trailers have difficulty finding main-stem parking space. The train obviously affords much more room. A dining car can be attached—and the trade can be wined and dined. More of the line can be shown. Special displays can be erected. Arrival time can be quite definitely fixed. In general, open house on the road combined with sample-room selling is possible using a train, and in the present hungry state of the railroads they should be willing to make special concessions.

Drop Shipping Comes to the Fore

Drop shipping both to the trade and to the shopping public is clearly on the rise. A trade example is a merchandising plan developed by a big wholesale drug house. This wholesaler's accounts are permitted to buy a specified minimum quantity of over 30 selected sundries to be shipped direct to them from the manufacturer, with all charges prepaid. (One merchandising object: To enable the independent druggist to better compete on sundry promotions with the big chains.) Drop shipping to the public is more common than ever before—many of the special promotions of big-ticket merchandise by the food supers involve drop shipments by the manufacturer directly to the public. And, of course, a good deal of "sample" selling by department stores (of furniture, for example) really winds up as a direct shipment by the manufacturer to the shopper. The mail-order selling plans of several discount chains also involve direct shipments to the public by the producer. Getting back to direct shipments to the trade: While many manufacturers put a special charge on such shipments—a tool maker charges an extra 5 per cent to its distributors for direct shipments—competition can—and has—made their charges more theory than fact.

What Is a "Legitimate" Dealer?

Every so often, a merchandising executive will remark: "We won't sell such and such a type of dealer—they aren't legitimate." Question: What *is* a "legitimate" dealer? It is fascinating to note that every one of our present-day retailers was originally labeled "illegitimate." That was true of the department stores, the mail-order houses, the variety chains, the drug chains, even the food super back in the 1930s. Most recently it was true of the discount chain. Actually, *high-margin* retailers tend to label any *low-margin* retailer as illegitimate. But if the low-margin retailer performs a public service, the public labels him as being entirely legitimate, and the manufacturer eventually follows suit. Over the next few years, new types of low-margin retailers will emerge. The merchandiser who promptly labels them illegitmate may wind up as "Johnny come lately" in an important new outlet. Hundreds of manufacturers wooed the mail-order chains too late; ditto the variety chains, the drug chains, the food-super chains, the discount chains. It is costly to get into new outlets *after* competition is firmly entrenched. Keep an open eye and an open mind for new types of low-margin retailers—and be not the first, but neither the last, to merchandise through these new retail forms.

Paying Wholesalers to Handle Returns

Returns from the retailer always plague the manufacturer. Generally, manufacturer policies involving acceptance of returns tend to be crude. Consequence: Trade ill will, evasion, high costs. A large pharmaceutical house has applied modern merchandising thinking to its return-goods problems. As a consequence, the following program was developed: (1) Return goods from retailers will be accepted only when returned by the retailer to the wholesaler—no direct returns by the retailer to the factory will be accepted; (2) the wholesalers are paid a 15 per cent handling allowance for assuming this responsibility—a distinct merchandising innovation and one with considerable merit; (3) wholesalers are provided with special return-goods forms designed to simplify the paper work involved in returning merchandise—another excellent idea. Incidentally, a program of this kind not only lessens the ill will that so often accompanies returns—it also actually encourages the retailer to return merchandise that, for various reasons, should no longer be carried in his inventory.

Direct Selling

One of the largest manufacturers of small appliances, who markets through distributors, discovered that its power mowers and power tools were not getting into a sufficient number of giant outlets in which the major volume in these lines is done. The explanation was simple: These giant outlets insisted on buying power mowers and power tools direct from the manufacturer. And, if they could not buy these classifications direct, either they did not buy the brand at all—even though in this instance it was a major brand name—or they did not actively promote the brand. The decision was made, therefore, to open up these two new categories for direct sale to large prestige outlets. Naturally, such a decision is not calculated to make distributors of other categories in the line very complacent; they will naturally wonder whether and where the axe may fall again. But diversified lines plus diversified distribution compel the manufacturer to ride several horses simultaneously—and that, in turn, inevitably leads to merchandising decisions that will tend to solve one problem and simultaneously create another problem. The basic question is whether the problem solved is of larger dimension than the problem created. No dynamic policy is totally without headaches.

The Mobile-home Market

Merchandising men are paying increasing attention to the fast-growing mobile-home market (the former house trailer). It's expanding rapidly —in numbers, in size, in luxury of appointments. A large appliance company has formed a special Mobile Home Department—its purpose is to service the mobile-home industry. This manufacturer's design engineers have concocted new high-fidelity devices, etc. Service warranties are to be the same as those on regular numbers. Makers of floor coverings, kitchen equipment, furniture, cooking utensils, dishes, towels, lamps

—the list is endless—will find the mobile-home market worthy of special study. The market consists, not only of original equipment, but also of additional purchases and replacements. Some retailers will, before long, be setting up special departments of supplies for owners of mobile homes, and there will also be retail salesmen calling at mobile-home colonies.

Leased Departments by Manufacturers

The leased-department concept was never more widely employed than it is today. It is very much in evidence in discount chains; in farmers' markets; in department stores, where it has been traditional for decades; in food supers, where the rack jobber really operates a type of leased department; even in the variety and drug chains. As part of this trend some manufacturers are taking a second look at the merchandising possibilities inherent in the operation—by the manufacturer—of a leased department. When a cigarette company puts in a huge fixture for all brands and services that fixture completely, that is, of course, a leased-department operation. In cosmetics and in foundation garments, the sections operated by manufacturers are, really, leased departments. In major appliances—and especially with respect to the packaged kitchen —manufacturers are developing merchandising programs that involve one form or another of the leased department. The essence of the thinking here is that the manufacturer, step by step, has reached the point in innumerable lines where he performs or pays for most of the total retail function. Why not then formalize and properly organize this setup through a leased department?

Booming RX in Drug Outlets

The retail druggist—chain as well as independent—is returning pell-mell to the RX department. One reason: To nail down this "exclusive," as other outlets redouble their merchandising of health and beauty aids, as well as other categories formerly associated with the drug outlet. This year, the RX department in drug outlets will be given a more important position, will be importantly remodeled, will be expanded, will be given special lighting, will be made to dominate the entire store. All this means that the RX department is to become a new A location in the drug outlet. Since it is also being used to merchandise lines other than pharmaceuticals—cosmetics, books, toys, greeting cards sell extremely well adjacent to the RX department—it is clear that merchandising men will be developing special programs to get their brands close up to the RX department. This may mean special sizes of packages, special fixturing, special merchandising themes tying up with the somebody-is-sick symbol of the RX department—maybe special payments for this new choice location. (A toy manufacturer has a complete program for the prescription section.)

Winning Rack Jobber's Service Personnel

Several soft-goods merchandisers, now marketing through the food super, have developed special-incentive offers for rack-jobber personnel. As the whole concept of leased departments expands (and it is expanding rapidly) the service personnel involved becomes important to manufacturers—more important, in some instances, than jobber's salesmen. The leased-department operator and the rack jobber depend more and more on service personnel, who, incidentally, include women as well as men. This service man has been given considerably more latitude in his various functions. Frequently he performs more merchandising functions than does the regular jobber's salesman. This is an important development—particularly as these operators go into many nonfood classifications and as they spring up in outlets other than the food super. Merchandisers would do well to give new attention to the service personnel of these operators—how to reach these service people, how to stimulate them, how to get extra service from them. (Route men for local dairies are the object of loving attention from some merchandisers.)

Check Chain-store Order Forms

A variety-chain manager of a comparatively small store unit reports: "Because of my store's size, I can't order out certain items. These items are listed on a separate order sheet and the use of that order sheet is strictly limited to our large-volume stores. When I try to get special permission to handle some items on that special order sheet I run into red tape." As the size of the newest store units of the various chains dwarf the size of the older store units, special order forms for the exclusive use of the giant store units will become more common. This will freeze many manufacturers out of the somewhat smaller units. One large manufacturer in soft goods arranged a precise check of the order forms of each of the several types of chains through which he sells. He then set up high-level visits between his executives and chain-store executives; the purpose was to arrange for specific tests in the smaller store units. These tests have demonstrated the turnover potentials of his line in these smaller stores.

Merchandising to the Children's Market

When baby foods were introduced years ago they marked the first attempt to merchandise a line specially prepared for infants. In recent years, the cosmetic industry has cultivated the children's market—starting with special permanents for children and going on to entire cosmetic kits for children. A famous maker of hair shampoos has brought out a special shampoo for children under twelve that "will not sting the eyes"—a common complaint by children when their hair is being washed. Currently, a special bread for children is being marketed with the combined efforts of a famous baby-food company and an equally famous bread brand. Clearly, the whole concept of merchandising a specially developed line of items for children in merchandise classifications where children formerly used regular adult merchandise is breaking out of its narrow range and is destined for truly broad application. If we may assume that this children's market consists of youngsters from birth to perhaps twelve years of age—then it may be said that this market is now destined for the same expansion as the teen-age market has gone through in recent years.

Wholesalers and Exclusives

Wholesalers tend both to fight *for*—and shy away *from*—arrangements involving exclusive tie-ups with one manufacturer. The wholesaler likes, of course, to have a line exclusively in his territory—but he tends to have second thoughts when he is asked, in turn, not to handle any line that competes with his exclusive. The explanation: When a wholesaler cannot supply what a retail account wants—that retail account is apt to place an order for the wanted line with another wholesaler. Naturally, wholesaler number one doesn't want to send business to his competition. He may even buy from a wholesaler in another territory in order to make available to a customer a brand that wholesaler has agreed not to stock. A maker of small electrics concluded that the way out of a messy market situation would be via limited and exclusive distributor tie-ups. He found (1) distributors liked the limited-distribution concept; (2) but they didn't like being tied down to handling this brand exclusively; (3) even where they agreed to exclusivity, they developed methods of getting around it.

Reaching Managers of One-stop Outlets

Within a few years, every major chain—food, drug, variety, hard goods—will be accounting for the lion's share of its total volume in a limited number of its newest giant one-stop store units. At this very moment, some food chains get 60 per cent of their total volume from 20 per cent of their store units—and this is true of some variety and drug chains, too. This trend will accelerate—the time is not far distant when our great chains will be doing a larger volume than ever in a *smaller percentage* of their total store list than ever. The managers of these giant one-stop outlets constitute a new breed of store executive. Too few merchandising executives among manufacturers are thoroughly informed about these managers of stores with multimillion-dollar annual volume. One merchandising executive tells us he has begun to compile a dossier on the store managers of giant one-stop store units of the variety chains which constitute his prime outlet. He contends that, within five years, a small handful of these store managers will account for at least 55 per cent of his total volume from variety chains and that he must stop thinking in terms of the *thousands* of outlets in the variety-chain grouping.

Unselective Selective Distribution

Even when a manufacturer sells direct to the retail trade, a policy of selective distribution is difficult to enforce over the long term. In *indirect* marketing, selective distribution tends inevitably to become quite unselective. (Any merchandising policy that necessitates constant policing by the manufacturer will usually deteriorate.) The manufacturer's own sales organization will nibble away at it; the distributor will bite away at it. Example: A major appliance manufacturer insists that dealers display at least 10 pieces of equipment to get a franchise. Question: If a dealer will stock no more than 9 pieces—or 8 pieces—will the distributor turn him down? Similarly, culling distributors to lessen price battling (as small appliance makers are doing) accomplishes little if prices and discounts afford so large a margin as to encourage price slashing. New policies of selective distribution may start off in high gear, but usually they slip back into low gear, especially when the market turns soft.

When Is Distribution Not Distribution?

Retailers sometimes put in an inventory of a line for reasons that promise little benefit to the supplier. Example: A line will be taken on to keep it away from a competitor. Another reason: To impress customers that the store has the line, even though the inventory is tiny. Another reason: To be able to point out: "Look—we carry it and you can have it if you insist; but we don't recommend it." This is a pretty potent argument, too! This suggests that distribution is not always distribution. It also suggests that some new-account drives may not be as productive as the initial figures may indicate. Broader distribution is sound policy in many instances. But programs involving broader distribution must include merchandising thinking that will place the line in the new outlets in a way that will produce satisfactory volume. This may suggest minimum-order requirements, model or basic stocks, etc. Always bear in mind that an inventory of a brand may not prevent a retailer from actively "selling away" from that line—if the inventory is small.

Help Wholesale Salesmen Check Stock

The wholesale salesman has a time problem second to none. This is especially true of the wholesale drug salesman. And that constitutes a problem for a maker of writing paper who confines his brand to the drug outlet. In order to benefit from this exclusive distribution, it is essential that the druggist keep up his inventory on this social-stationery line. And it is the wholesale salesman who must attend to that important detail when he makes his rounds. But his time problem interferes seriously. To help cut the time factor for the wholesale salesman, this company has developed a pad of forms on which is pictured the company's drugstore display rack. Numbers on the picture tie in with a list of items that belong on the rack. Thus, the wholesale salesman, as he makes his drugstore rounds, can tell at a glance which items need replacement. That same plan could be used, with proper modification, in other related ways. For example, manufacturers whose men service fixtures in the retail outlet might adapt the picture plan to the forms filled out by these detail men.

3-Minute Selling to Buying Committee

Some chain buying committees report that during regular weekly meetings they may pass on more than 150 propositions—better than one every three minutes! Since this is an average figure, many propositions get only two-minute consideration, some even less. A food processor has therefore prepared a three-minute presentation of a new deal for study by the food-super buying committee. It was done on a chart similar to the chart prepared by one of the large food-super chains for the guidance of its buying committee's deliberations. The chart includes open spaces to be filled in by the manufacturer's salesman—by himself or in cooperation with the account's buyer. The salesman gives the buyer enough copies for each buying-committee member—and, when possible, the salesman even fills in on each copy the name of a buying-committee member. Clearly, merchandising programs must now be merchandised to and through the buying committee in most large chains in all fields. A three-minute chart presentation is one technique smartly based on the urgent need for putting over all of the facts in not much more than three minutes.

New Market for World's Oldest Staple

The house key may not be one of the world's oldest staples—it probably isn't. But it surely goes far back in history. And it surely would appear to be strongly resistant to new-market discovery and development. So, not because it is earth shaking in importance, but as encouragement to merchandising men contending with the development of new markets for old staples, here is a little case history. A maker of a key-duplicating machine tells the chains of an idea calculated to double brass-key sales. The idea: "Protect Your Home—Give Your Good Neighbor a Key." It's a simple idea—but really very logical. Instead of leaving the key under the doormat it makes sense for good neighbors to exchange keys. The manufacturer also points out that such a promotion could help the sale of key chains, too! Incidentally, we suspect that the suggestion "Give Your Good Neighbor a Key" will encourage shoppers to buy an extra key for many other purposes such as larger families, women at work, etc. The point here is that a strikingly new suggestion may not sell the item in volume for the featured new use—but the concept itself may stop enough traffic to make extra sales for other purposes.

Exclusive Lines in Price-torn Markets

In floor coverings, in appliances, in some soft-goods categories, several manufacturers have brought out special de luxe lines and offered them exclusively to top outlets, particularly department stores. There is little doubt that, at the time of the initial offer, this sort of merchandising program appeals to certain large retailers—especially department stores. But in practice, it is usually the case that most of the dealers who welcome this sort of merchandising program wind up putting their selling activities back of the brands and the price lines that are being actively promoted by competition. Moreover, on the selling floor, because of the low level of floor selling, the exclusive, higher-priced label gets little support from salespeople—and without the intelligent as well as the active support of the floor selling force it will just stay on the floor. As a soporific for an upset trade, as a gesture aiming for trade good will, this merchandising concept may have some merit—although the cost may be uneconomically high. But as a solution to a price-torn market, it seldom offers rich rewards.

Direct Sellers as Outlets for Private Labels

Some 3,000 direct-selling companies gross over $3 billion annually. (Some 300 direct-selling organizations account for about 80 per cent of that total volume, which suggests that these 300 organizations are giant retailers in their own right!) The direct-selling company tends to sell its own brands. (And its own brands tend to be higher priced than their national-brand twins.) For the "specifications" or "private-brand" department, the direct-selling company offers a huge, rapidly growing outlet. A large manufacturer has concluded he would rather expand his private-label volume with direct sellers than with his regular outlets. This is interesting strategy in the developing battle between manufacturer and store-controlled brands. Moreover, the direct-selling company offers market-test opportunities—for manufacturers planning to extend their private-label business—that will cause the least disturbance among regular distributors during the testing period.

In Doubt?—Try Notions Department

The notions department of the department store has been the great catchall department. Most recent example: Some notions departments are promoting tables at under $10, which also brings furniture down to the main floor! The notions department usually has a good location; excellent traffic; it enjoys a splendid impulse-buying atmosphere; it tends to be promotionally active. So there is justification, when planning department store distribution of a new item, to conclude: "When in doubt—try the notions department." Notions departments in variety chains are also exceedingly elastic. The notions department in the food outlet is also becoming a catchall. Ditto in the drug chain. It's used in all these outlets to test new items—new price lines. And it is a good "multi" department for secondary display. It may do better with special-price lines (tables under $10), special sizes, counts—where plastic dinnerware is sold in this section it tends to be low-end merchandise. The notions department in all outlets rates special merchandising planning.

Putting the Item into New Home Areas

Dinette furniture (which started out as low-end and is now smartly designed and in upper price ranges) is being merchandised for use in areas other than the kitchen. In fact, it is going into the dining room, and, designwise, the differences between so-called "dinette furniture" and dining-room furniture are shriveling. Similarly, the makers of so-called "grass rugs" have for years been trying to get their rugs used in rooms as well as on the porch—both to lengthen the season and to create a larger market. Small refrigerators are now being merchandised for the home-recreation or family room. Radio and TV are, of course, star examples of this merchandising strategy—and, interestingly, the so-called "portable TV" is actually seldom lugged around; it has become a second-room set. Shower curtains are showing a tendency, in modified form, to appear in the kitchen window and elsewhere. Bathroom scales are also coming out of the bathroom. First-aid items are now being kept in many kitchens, as well as in the bathrooms. Merchandising ingenuity has wide scope in this concept of putting the item or line into new home areas.

Mass Outlets Avoid Service Headaches

Variety chains, food chains, drug chains are clearly turning toward big-ticket lines that require servicing—appliances, TV-radio, power mowers, etc. But these outlets do not want to be involved in servicing these lines—the servicing problem is one of the main deterrents to the broad-scale merchandising of these items by these outlets. To the manufacturer, these outlets are of increasing importance as their products are bought more and more impulsively through open display. Therefore, several manufacturers have announced lately plans that relieve these outlets of any servicing headaches. One power-mower manufacturer, for example, has been making considerable progress with the variety chains because this company has its own service organization. This merchandising problem will become still more common as major outlets that want nothing to do with service show an ability to merchandise lines requiring service. As the classifications listed above move more strongly into the outlets we have mentioned, manufacturers will win a competitive lap by molding their service organization to the particular requirements of these new outlets.

Stamp Redemptions and Regular Sales

Salesmen for a manufacturer whose branded line has achieved a huge stamp-redemption volume complained that their regular retail accounts were losing volume because of this competition. The manufacturer reports: (1) A study disclosed that a big department store chain, which acts as a redemption center handling several millions in redemptions, finds absolutely no adverse effect on its regular sales of these same categories and brands; (2) retailers of this manufacturer's line, located near redemption centers, were studied and their volume compared favorably with similar retailers elsewhere; (3) cities showing largest redemptions for this brand made a good showing with comparable cities in which redemptions were at a much lower rate. The more an item is exposed to shoppers, the more it sells. The stamp catalogue gives an item brand exposure; that's beneficial. The housewife can't accumulate enough stamps soon enough, to buy all items for which the catalogue has created a desire. The result—increased volume in regular outlets. (All these facts were given the salesmen in a special bulletin.)

Getting into Wholesaler's Retail Fixtures

In several fields the wholesaler is doing a fine job of designing and installing multiline fixtures for his retail accounts. (Some drug wholesalers plan the entire store for accounts opening up in new locations.) One large drug wholesaler has been promoting a special fixture for a camera-photo department. It's 6 feet long—program includes a diagram that shows the druggist exactly what merchandise to put where in the fixture. A prominent maker of a camera accessory found no provision on that fixture for his item—he moved quickly to get in. In some instances, these wholesaler-designed fixtures are so designed as to accommodate the merchandise of manufacturers who underwrite costs—an allowance, in other words. More wholesalers in more fields will go into store fixturing. One drug trade supplier keeps close tabs on those fixtures—has a photo and specification file of them—helps his wholesalers design them. He is in!

Department Stores and De Luxe Specialties

Every so often, when a new de luxe type of big-ticket specialty line is introduced, the department store is turned to for the marketing introduction. While, from the prestige and advertising standpoints, top department stores can make a contribution in this sort of line introduction, their volume, as a rule, is disappointing. Case in point: A prestige brand of hi-fi selected (among other retailers) a group of some 30 department stores to introduce its new line. Only four turned in a successful performance! (Incidentally—the currently popular electronic organs do not owe any major part of their success to department stores.) The hi-fi maker sums up the department store failure this way: (1) Inadequate display and demonstration facilities; (2) excessive personnel turnover in the department; (3) department store buyers think of themselves exclusively as buyers—do little to win selling excitement and competency on the floor; (4) promotional emphasis was given primarily to competitively priced lines; (5) the de luxe line was lost in a sea of lower-ticket lines uniformly displayed on the floor.

The "Integrated Distributor"

The "integrated distributor" is a giant retailer who relieves his suppliers of storage, transportation, certain risks, administration details. They buy in huge quantities and perform all of the services of distributors and wholesalers. As such, they are able to buy direct—and they get discounts that recognize their total functions. The setup is common in many fields, from appliances to food and drug. But because it has developed year after year, some merchandisers have not been fully aware that, in some cases, the lion's share of their wholesale or distributor volume is not done with strictly middlemen, but with the integrated distributor who is, of course, really a *retailer*. Too often the setup of the sales force scarcely reflects this major change. Discount schedules tend to remain the same as before the integrated distributor had become a factor. Merchandisers must comprehend the full import of the rapid emergence of giant retailing as the dominant merchandising element. The new merchandising requirements of the integrated distributor involve just one example.

Old-model Disposal

The maker of a small household item—a $14.95 retailer—brought out an improved model. The old number was taken off fair trade; the new number fair-traded. The old number was then permitted to make its own market exit. Promptly, one large retailer got hold of about 1,000 of the old number—promoted them at under $10. The market was considerably demoralized; sales of the new number got off to a slow start; some trade ill will was created. When next this company brought out an improved model, it did the following: (1) Gave distributors and dealers an extra inducement (and time) to move the old model *before* the new one was announced to consumers; (2) arranged to locate all large stocks of the old model—bought them up; (3) placed these large stocks with a few strategically located giant outlets—arranged for a big promotion in each of these outlets, again in advance of announcement of new model to consumers—this event was rushed through to completion—the big stocks were disposed of quickly; (4) thus, when the new model was announced to the public, the old model had been pretty well cleaned up.

Marketing to Offices in the Home

The office in the home is becoming a new market for an amazing variety of merchandise. The take-home brief case; the multiplying number of self-employed working at home, women as well as men; longer week ends, which necessitate taking work home; and innumerable other socio-economic trends—all are conspiring to bring business into the home. Consequently, the former makeshift, make-do setup at home is now giving way to more elaborate setups. Office furniture is now being designed with a more homey touch. Typewriters have gone a long way in the décor direction. Filing equipment will follow suit. Eventually, almost every item that is part of the business office will be redesigned, repackaged—so as to serve better, decoratively and functionally, the office at home. (Even the Lazy Susan, which holds pencils, clips, etc., has benefited from this trend—some of its newer designs are captivating.) Ditto for memo pads with magnetic pencils. Ditto for scotch-tape dispensers, holders for postage stamps, etc.

Recheck the Variety Chain

The pace of change in the variety chain has been so extraordinarily rapid and broad that many manufacturers have neglected to merchandise to the new programs of these outlets. Their new giant one-stop outlets are department stores—of a new type. They offer credit and charge accounts. They are becoming a major new outlet for many big-ticket classifications—in time they will sell as much furniture as the traditional department store. They are encouraging shoppers to buy by telephone. They send salesmen into the home—something few manufacturers realize. (One variety chain sells storm windows this way.) They are going in for catalogues—Grant's has a special catalogue-order service in all of its 775 stores. They are branching out rapidly in selling from samples. Few merchandising executives have prepared programs designed to tie in with the new variety store, a department store of a new type and in a stage of vigorous dynamic growth. (In some new shopping areas, the variety chains in total are the largest outlet.) Some manufacturers who continue to cling to the traditional department store would do well to start thinking of our newest department store—the one-stop units of the variety chains—"where anything goes."

Helping Wholesalers with Order-picking Costs

The order-picking burden at the warehouse level—both the warehouse of the wholesaler and the warehouse of the chains—is becoming a matter of serious consideration by these distributors. This has suggested to some manufacturers such ideas as bringing the industry together to develop a standard form invoice, uniform standards with respect to the shipping case, better billing procedures, etc. Deals are also being re-examined from this viewpoint because deals tend to complicate still further the order-picking problem at the warehouse. Even such a matter as giving the trade a specific commitment concerning the expiration date for a deal plays a role in order-picking costs at the warehouse; such a date obviously enables the warehouse to do a better job of gauging shipments to stores. Ultimately, order picking at the warehouse will be controlled by electronic devices—electronic conveyors, electronic order-selection panel boards, electronic tabulating equipment. This will call for sensing devices (magnetic ink codes, for example) on shipping cases.

Merchandising executives would do well to check through on their contribution to the warehouse order-picking costs of distributors.

What Departments for New Items?

Departmental barriers with respect to classifications carried are breaking down in all major outlets. It becomes increasingly difficult, therefore, to predetermine in what department—or departments—a new item may ultimately wind up. Example: The various massage devices that zoomed to popularity during 1958 were stocked in as many as six different departments in the same department store, and in several departments in drug chains and variety chains. Another example: The remarkable fad for leotards resulted in this popular item being stocked, not only in the hosiery section, but in at least four other departments. Under the new looseness in department inventory practices (for which self-service and self-selection are largely responsible), it is wise not to have too-fixed ideas about where to place a new item. Different brand names, different packages, different numbers, different price lines may be advisable to lessen interdepartmental rivalries and jealousies—but the fundamental object must be to capitalize the developing store policy that permits multiple locations for the same category.

Bringing Dealers to Distributor Shows

Too many dealers claim "no time" when invited to a trade showing by a distributor or wholesaler. One manufacturer, to induce retailers to attend open-house showings by his distributors, provided his distributors with a sufficient number of an accessory (retail value, $19.95) for each attending merchant. (The retailer could actually *sell* the accessory at that price.) Now some manufacturers are planning, not merely more expensive door prizes for distribution shows, but even contests. This is a contest age—why not a contest for attendance at the showing of a distributor or wholesaler? Several drug wholesalers who occasionally bring retailers to central points are stepping up their giveaways— "samples" supplied by manufacturers (and all potential resale items) are the inducement. Special prizes for the women folk are now offered, too. All this on top of elaborate entertainment. But one manufacturer of hard goods is going in the opposite direction. He is developing a strictly business program. His distributors thus offer a real clinic, not hoopla. The giveaway is a splendid dealer manual and a summary of the clinic.

Department-store Main-floor Merchandising

The multistore department store is moving as rapidly as it can to make its operation a new type of single-floor function. This is being done not only by bringing down to the main floor limited displays of upstairs classifications, but also by squeezing onto the main floor full inventories of classifications formerly carried on other floors. This opens up new merchandising opportunities for many manufacturers. Example: Department stores traditionally have sold household rubber aids (dish drainers, table mats, bath and shower mats, etc.) either downstairs or in upstairs sections. One manufacturer decided that department stores could best meet competition of the food super and the variety chain in this classification by merchandising it on the main floor. These new competitors are, of course, single-floor retailers essentially. The manufacturer got one of the great New York department stores to test the concept in its main-floor notions department. Results were satisfactory. Now other stores are putting this line into one department or another on the main floor. Interesting note: At one time department stores worried about deserted upstairs floors if too much merchandising were offered on the main floor. Now they realize that upstairs will always get a percentage of main-floor traffic.

Overnight Distribution for New Items

A large established manufacturer selling primarily through the drug outlet had acquired or developed three new items. Problem: How to get those three new items into the 25,000 top drug stores—literally overnight. Moreover, the manufacturer wanted, not merely to have a stock in those 25,000 better drug stores, but to win effective selling display. Solution: (1) A kit was developed, containing a $6 retail assortment of the three new items; (2) 25,000 of those kits were distributed among its wholesalers; (3) each wholesaler was to give 10 kits to each of his salesmen; (4) the wholesale salesman was to select 10 of his accounts to whom he would personally hand the kits—and, since he was to offer the kits for free, he was in the nice position of making a substantial gift to some of his accounts; (5) the salesman was also given copies of a letter explaining the three new products for distribution with the gift kit; (6) the letter asked for display position—and suggested that re-orders be placed with the wholesaler. The "gift" offer obviously appealed to the wholesale salesman—and his difficult-to-win cooperation was obtained.

Finding New Mass-market Items

A large food processor, in planning a special "class" or de luxe line for distribution through selected department stores, was aiming, not only for a line that would make a modest contribution to net earnings and that would help add to the company's "quality" image, but also for an item that, it was felt, would occasionally "prove out" in the *class* line as having excellent potentials for the mass market. As we become essentially a middle-class nation, it is more true than ever that in limited-sale upper-class items, there may be found items with middle-class mass potentials. This is especially the case if and when the great middle class decides —or is sold on the belief—that the upper-class item will confer social status on those who use it. Champagne is destined for this role. It's been happening in rare cheeses. Generations ago, the grand piano became the mass symbol of social status. The mink has been through this cycle. Hi-fi is a fine example. Keen merchandisers maintain a constant watch on "class" to find an item or line that is ready for mass exploitation.

Getting into Several Rooms

Ideas for selling two (and more) of the same item for multiple rooms in homes are broadening markets in a growing number of fields. The two-car family, the multiradio-set family, the multi-TV-set family are obvious examples. Less obvious—a maker of electric clocks has a display fixture showing clocks in five different rooms in the home. Refrigerator makers are finding that about 27 per cent of families buying a new refrigerator keep their old one as a second. Special refrigerators as seconds are on the way. In much the same manner, many homes now have two or more bathroom scales—one for each bathroom. (The two- and three-bathroom home obviously creates merchandising opportunities for multiple ownership of drugs, beauty aids, etc.) The two- and three-living-room home—recreation room, den, formal living room—also multiplies ownership of the same item. The ownership of two homes is also a factor. Outdoor living has created multiple ownership of many items, including foods. Even the car has created a new market for facial tissue.

Programs for Franchised Distributors

There is clearly a trend, especially in some of the big-ticket and medium-ticket merchandise classifications, toward cutting down the number of jobbers or distributors, and franchising those selected to carry the line. These programs may develop into successful long-term distribution strategy. However, the attrition rate promises to be high—and for at least three reasons: (1) Failure to wind up with well-selected franchised distributors; (2) failure to plan specific objectives for the franchised distributors; (3) failure to police the franchised distributor so as to make certain he carries out his assigned functions. A maker of carpet sweepers, who developed a plan involving selected distribution at the jobber level, established the following objectives: (1) Jobbers should protect our suggested retail price; (2) jobbers should avoid selling **our** line to accounts that cut below our minimum; (3) jobbers should cover our retailers thoroughly; (4) jobbers should not sell outside their allotted territories; (5) jobbers should not transship.

Mail Order by Discount Chains

The discount chains have definitely turned to mail order. Manufacturers who offer special programs to discount chains (quite common now) are now including mail-order plans. The discount chains "negotiate" in their mail-order programs for (1) up to 100 per cent co-op; (2) guaranteed sales; (3) drop shipping by manufacturer direct to shopper; (4) special arrangements for floor stock of items offered by mail. (They do an amazing *floor* volume on these mail-order specials.) It is still another way for the discount chain to build its reputation for top values, and that is why this outlet likes mail-order events. Also, the discount house has too many walk-outs during its peak hours. Manufacturers who come to the discount chains with special mail-order propositions will win an attentive hearing. (Drug and variety chains are also turning to mail order, and not exclusively for Christmas.) The whole gamut of mail-order merchandising-promotion is ripe for manufacturer adaptation through regular outlets.

Merchandising via Movie Theaters

The movie theater is being used in a variety of merchandising ways. Example: A floor-covering maker, as part of a city-wide blitz, included a consumer contest run with the cooperation of seven local movie houses. The contest included lobby displays of rug samples from which consumers were invited to name the ones they preferred—entries to be completed at local dealers. Another example: A restaurant offered a free guest-admission ticket to a chain of movie houses with a regular dinner. Another example: A major appliance TV dealer arranged with his distributor for a local theater party. A theater directly across from the store is taken over for one night. The entire community is invited to join with the store in a night on the town. A complete stage show and a first-run movie are included—plus a preview of new lines. On back of each admission ticket the recipient fills in name and address and checks any appliance in which the family might be interested. These are followed up later. A 2,000-seat theater has been sold out for each of two years.

Try Visiting New Store Units

Tip: A highly successful merchandiser in the drug field reports that he makes an extended visit to at least 100 new drug-store units every year. These new store units are both chain and independent types. He also visits at least 50 new nondrug outlets stocking health and beauty aids each year. He arranges to be accompanied by a photographer. He carries a portable dictating device. Thus, both in type and pictorially, he has a continuing up-to-the-minute record of the newest in fixturing, in stock arrangements, in stock assortments, in merchandising-promotional techniques. The pace of merchandising was never so rapid as today; tomorrow it will be still more rapid. Here is an excellent way to get a practical peek into the future, because the innovations in the new stores of today will be the general practice of most stores tomorrow.

The Factory as a Test Market

For some products, factory rest rooms, factory restaurants, and other factory facilities for employees such as the employee parking area offer valid new-product testing grounds that can be used without too much disturbance of existing outlets. Example: Coca-Cola in metal cans—a development well calculated to require an exceedingly cautious approach by Coke. Coke in tins has received limited tests abroad. More recently it was tested in rest rooms and plant restaurants at the mills of U.S. Steel and Bethlehem Steel. The personnel directors of large plants and sundry other plant officials are becoming factors in new-product testing. This testing technique does not upset the trade; it is easier to control and to keep secret. (Several merchandisers use their sources of material and part supply in this way and, of course, get fine cooperation.) Market testing is demanding an increasing degree of secrecy and avoidance of irritating or upsetting regular outlets. The factory as a test market helps with both problems.

CHAPTER 28

Merchandising to the Trade:
Inventory, Co-op, Contests, Sales Training

Help Dealers Sell Credit

It is not at all unlikely that practically *all* retailing will involve one form of credit merchandising or another—anything ranging from bank-check loan plans, bank charge-account plans, credit-card plans to traditional credit procedures. In brief, all retailers have been given a new selling tool. Unfortunately, too few merchants—especially those to whom credit is somewhat new—have more than a vague idea of how to sell credit. Most merchants still use credit merely as a means of payment after the sale is closed—instead of using it as a sales closer. A large maker of major appliances has tackled this problem with a filmstrip entitled *Credit—Your Strongest Selling Tool*. It is designed to give retailers and their salespeople ideas on how to sell credit. Its basic theme is that "credit is more than a way of financing; it's a way of selling." Clearly, credit facilities for the public have outrun the smart merchandising of credit at the retail level. Here is a definite opportunity for merchandising programs by manufacturers in diverse fields.

The Pros and Cons of Guaranteed Sales

When planning any variation of guaranteed sale, bear these hazards in mind: (1) Overordering by trade; (2) selling effort of trade tends to be put back of its money investment—no money investment, little selling effort; (3) returns will arrive in deplorable condition—costs here will be extremely high; (4) returns will arrive so late in seasonal lines as to become distress inventory; (5) the trade tends to consider a guaranteed line a weak line; (6) compensation for the manufacturer's sales force becomes a problem; (7) the finance costs for the manufacturer is great—sometimes it is prohibitive when money is tight; (8) complicated agreements must be drawn up, but like all trade agreements they are difficult to enforce unless one wants to give up an account; (9) finally, once a line goes on guaranteed sale, to put it back on regular terms is extremely difficult. Some protective moves: (1) Give a guarantee on only a part of the order, 50 or 75 per cent; (2) insist on returns in factory-sealed cartons; (3) offer a special credit if no returns at all are made; (4) insist on a minimum order; (5) if the line is seasonal, get the orders in early by fixing the expiration date for orders; (6) establish a cut-off return date.

Dealer Stock-control Plans

Automatic and semiautomatic stock-control plans for dealers (which include automatic reordering) are spreading rapidly. The variety chains, incidentally, have shown a decided interest in automatic reordering programs of suppliers—and are actually pressing some suppliers to develop these programs. A plan for children's undergarments offers both a balanced inventory and automatic-reorder plan for the layette department. The basic plan was individualized for five store sizes—stores with annual layette volume of $10,000; $25,000; $65,000; $100,000; and $125,000. For each size of store, basic stocks were determined from the actual sales experience of a number of stores of that size. For each size group there is a Master Buy Plan for maintained basic stock. In addition, there is an automatic stock-control card covering style numbers, size, color, and quantity, which is filled in and deposited in a receptacle provided for reorders. A "never-out" list and an *illustrated* order blank (a fine help when salespeople make up reorders) complete the stock-control program. Of course, the supplier's salesmen must follow up closely. Automatic stock-control plans are seldom long maintained automatically!

When Opinion Tests Say "Thumbs Down"

To what extent should merchandising plans be shaped by trade and consumer *opinion?* Let's take a specific example: A leading maker of bras studied the advisability of prepackaging bras—at the time a rather new idea. Of 68 retailers questioned, only 29 approved the prepackaging concept. Among women, 58 per cent disapproved. The retailers said that prepacking would eliminate service which the store traditionally gave when selling bras; that it took too much of the sale out of the store's hands. Women objected because "we could not determine construction and quality ... can't feel the material ... would involve fitting difficulties." A psychological research organization concluded: "A bra involves a psychological defense; protects woman against anxieties caused by worries over her figure; purchase is therefore very critically made." The organization also voted against prepackaging. So trade, shopper, the psychological experts—all turned thumbs down. But the manufacturer tried prepackaging nonetheless—and on its *best-selling number.* Volume promptly shot up by 50 per cent. Today, the prepackaged bra is taking over. The ultimate test is the *purchase* test, not *opinion*—and even the former can be misleading.

Helping the Trade Fight Back

When a merchandise classification, formerly distributed primarily through one type of outlet, winds up in a variety of outlet types— the manufacturer who limits his distribution quite naturally regularly reminds the traditional outlet how he continues to stick with them. That may win good will—but it probably does little to help the traditional outlet to prevent newer outlets from leaching away its turnover. A better procedure is suggested by a large drug house in connection with vitamins—now sold house to house, by mail, through food supers, discount chains. This manufacturer, who distributes vitamins primarily through the drug outlet, offers the drugstore a complete "fight-back" event. The program includes vitamin sales-training aids for drugstore salespeople; in-store and window displays; mats and broadcast scripts; etc. A pamphlet entitled *All Vitamins Are Not Alike* strikes out vigorously at the claim of the newcomers that there is no difference in vitamins. The program also includes special fixtures to help the drug outlet sell vitamins more effectively by self-selection and self-service techniques. It also included a thirty-day free-trial vitamin offer.

A New Idea in a Trade Contest

Trade contests tend to stay in a groove. But here's a trade contest that took off in a new direction—and won the right sort of attention: Each trade ad lists a well-known retailer. The inventory setup of that dealer on the category made by the contest's sponsor is given—also unit sales, shelf price, gross sales, margin, per-facing profit. The figures are given, not only for the sponsoring brand, but also for its largest-selling competitor. (This is a case of a smaller brand fighting for shelf facing against a powerful brand.) The contestant is then asked to estimate the unit sales and profits of the sponsoring brand for a two-week period but with one change in the setup—the sponsoring brand is to be estimated on the basis of two facings instead of one. (This, of course, is the brand's objective.) The rules read: "All you do is forecast Blank's profit with 1 extra facing. You do not need to forecast figures for the other brand." There is more to the contest—but this is enough to make it clear that here is a trade contest that challenges the trade to sharpen its pencil, to do some profit figuring, and thus to absorb the net-profit story of the contest sponsor. Good thinking.

A Bonus for Low Returns or Exchanges

As part of a new plan for accepting exchanges from distributors on phonograph records, one of the large makers includes a provision under which the distributor who does not use up his total accrued-exchange credits may elect to receive up to 5 per cent in dollar credits on the balance. This bonus is described as a bonus for aggressive selling. It is a fairly new twist in an exchange offer and has a good deal to recommend it. The old plan operated by this company had varying provisions for different parts of the line. The new plan institutes—for distributors—a continuous 10 per cent exchange privilege based on the distributors' net purchase in a given period. (Distributors were given forty-five days in which to straighten out their inventories before the new program took effect.) When the cost of accepting returns or exchanges is properly reckoned, there may be merit for many manufacturers in the basic concept of a "bonus" for "good behavior."

Check Those Prepacked Trade Assortments

The prepacked assortment for the trade is, of course, a merchandising basic in many merchandise classifications. But it may be questioned whether its development has kept pace with its broadening use. In the first place, there is a tendency for the prepacked assortment to remain unchanged for too long a period. This dilutes its value because consumer habits are changing constantly. Secondly, in too many instances a single prepacked assortment is offered a trade that has become exceedingly diversified. (A manufacturer of an eye-cosmetic item offers a prepacked self-service selling unit for the drug trade, the food trade, etc. In many instances, the assortment will not be equally practical for both of these types of outlets.) Moreover, there are geographical differences in demand by style, by color, by count. More manufacturers are now making the prepacked assortment of the trade available in a wider range of put-ups. This represents a definite merchandising trend.

Ad Idea Exchange for Dealers

A maker of table and bed linens has had unusual success with what is really a retail ad-idea exchange. Through a clipping service, as well as in other ways, the company obtains clips of most of the newspaper advertising run by its accounts. It selects from these clippings the ads that appear to have the most merit—corresponds with the retail sponsors to obtain figures on results. Then it sends to its entire account list a reproduction, each month, of a number of successfully tested retail ads —together with such facts regarding the pulling power of each as it has been able to obtain. The service has had a distinct appeal. But more than merely obtaining the trade good will—it shows considerable promise of stepping up the effectiveness of the retail linage used to promote the brand. The analysis for each ad not only covers copy and art techniques —but also the number or numbers featured in each insertion. The latter information is at least as important to retailers as the former.

Paying for Shelf Space

Payments by suppliers for retail shelf space have been made for years. But now a strong trend has set in toward more insistence by large retailers on such payments, accompanied by more willingness by manufacturers to offer such payments, particularly in lieu of cooperative advertising. For manufacturers who do not have detail men calling on the retail trade, money offered for shelf space may be totally wasted. (At least co-op linage can be checked.) But larger manufacturers can see an opportunity for a decent return on funds invested in shelf space. Of course, controls are needed here too. One large food processor has developed the following controls to date: (1) Suitable bulletin instructions must be sent from chain headquarters to store manager; (2) the company's fixture must be used; (3) the specific locations in the store where the fixture is to appear are spelled out; (4) minimum inventory for each size fixture is also spelled out; (5) report forms of detail men call for detailed information on merchandise display, including out-of-stock and understock; (6) detail men will take Polaroid snaps of merchandise displays that are not up to minimum standards for use in "discussions" with chain headquarters.

A Contest to Push Higher-price Numbers

Merchandisers who are fully aware of the long-term limitations of retail salespeople nonetheless do not—and should not—take a completely defeatist attitude. Instead, they tend to fight a sort of defensive-offensive action, a delaying action. Along this line, in a category sunk deep in low-end promotional activities (mattresses), one of the big brands staged a $150,000 contest for retail salespeople. The contest offered prizes for selling mattresses starting at $79.50. (Since mattress volume continues to be done at the $39.50 level, this is really aiming pretty high.) First prize—in cash—$10,000. To qualify, the salesperson had to sell a stipulated number of units. Each time this basic requirement was sold, the salesman got a $25 bonus, plus his regular P.M. There was no limit on the number of bonuses a salesman could win; and each bonus permitted an additional entry in the big-money contest—here the salesman was asked to write in 25 words: "How I Made My Easiest Sale on (Model Name)." Promotion of the contest included a series of 10 mailings to the homes of the salesmen. A contest to win a bit more attention for the higher pricing points has merit, but don't shoot for the moon.

What Price Dealer Listing?

The merchandising program that involves listing the dealer in either national or local advertising is, of course, an old-timer. And its very antiquity has caused much of its original luster to rub off. As a consequence, retailers tend not to reach out for it as they once did. And this, in turn, means that the purchase requirements for the trade to get a listing have had to be scaled down. Another problem: Larger retailers are not overly excited by these listing propositions; their attitude usually is that they get much more from the supplier without any strings attached, and, moreover, they do not like particularly being listed along with the small fry. To alleviate both problems, manufacturers are not only lowering the purchase requirements for a listing—they are making the advertising schedule itself much more spectacular. Whereas one local ad may have formerly been the rule, the local schedule may now be two or three ads. Where one full-page magazine ad may have been the bait, the manufacturer now dangles a magazine spectacular, with the space set aside for dealer listing much more sizable. Similarly, in radio and TV the schedule has been sweetened considerably.

Getting Trade to Stock All Sizes

Never were retailers so bombarded with pleas and demands to stock all sizes as today. The very intensity of the bombardment, plus the retailer's traditional complaint that he has no more shelf room, has made the retailer increasingly resistant to stock-all-sizes pressure. One manufacturer in the drug field, whose item comes in four sizes, has had considerable success by sharing with the trade precise figures on the profit showing of each of the four sizes. Thus, the figures show that one size accounts for 30 cents of the profit dollar on the line, another for 20 cents, etc. The point is then made to the retailer that "the full Blank line dollar profit is yours only when you stock all sizes." Incidentally, in this instance there were two sizes in the regular number; two sizes in the special super number. Thus, the merchandising program was aimed to achieve a better store inventory, not merely on the different sizes, but also on the two basic numbers in the line. Especially in larger outlets, and particularly for small packaged items in these big outlets, merchandising-turnover figures, gross- and net-profit showing must now be computed and given to the trade.

Pinpointing Co-op to Hypo Sales

There is a growing trend, in connection with the cooperative advertising program, to move away from a fixed-percentage or fixed-dollar formula applied to the entire line—and to move toward a variety of formulas in order to induce the trade to push specific numbers. Example: One maker of hard-goods items offers double the percentage allowance on new items (for one full year) that is given on older items. Example: A major appliance company adds one-third to its percentage for a limited period to win support for a product improvement. Example: A soft-goods maker gives an extra percentage point on linage devoted to a super de luxe line. Example: A food producer doubles his regular co-op percentage on linage devoted to his large economy size. Every evidence makes it clear that this maneuver wins extra linage for the number or line that the manufacturer wants pushed. Indeed, sometimes the remainder of the line may be too much neglected. Another problem: The trade rather grows accustomed to the higher percentage—tends to use it as a lever to get an over-all higher percentage.

When Trade Insists on Lean Floor Inventory

In big-ticket classifications, the retailer fights fiercely for a minimum floor inventory. In major appliances, floor coverings, and furniture, retail floor stocks are primarily sample inventory. Even this sample inventory seldom displays on the floor more than a small part of the big-ticket line. This is why one major appliance manufacturer found that only 17 per cent of his retailers displayed on the floor a stove featured in a special promotion! Various plans are being developed to enable the retailer to show more of the line without adding to his inventory. An interesting plan was developed by a maker of steel kitchen cabinets, where a floor display of the full line would run into big money. This manufacturer supplies snap-on doors. Thus, with one basic model, the retailer—by merely snapping on doors in a variety of woods and colors—can show customers a major part of the line. This is one of the serious merchandising problems of the era for big-ticket merchandise; and for some lines that are not quite big ticket. (Draperies are being sold from sample racks because of this situation.) The retailer is not apt to budge unless he is liberally financed, or unless he is given a solution such as these snap-on doors (which he will probably buy only if priced below cost).

Bringing Dealers Together for Co-op

As part of the growing effort by manufacturers to plan cooperative advertising programs so as to include more retailers in more trading areas more often, ideas are being developed that encourage dealers to participate *jointly* in co-op. An interesting plan of this sort was developed by a producer of hard-surface floor coverings. He assumes that a half-page newspaper ad cost $400, and that six dealers were to join in an insertion of that size. The manufacturer and the distributor would then make eight participants in total. The cost would thus be spread equally among the eight participants; the six dealers plus the manufacturer and the distributor. If this mythical ad cost $400, the individual cost for each dealer would thus break down to $50 per insertion. The ads were prepared by the manufacturer's advertising agency, and were part of a complete retail promotion. The total allowance for each group of dealers was premised on total volume, but without an exact percentage so as to provide both flexibility and encouragement to the dealers. (A plan of this kind *could* result in a smaller dollar contribution by the manufacturer, since it obviously is not fifty-fifty.)

Help for Dealer's Good-will Program

Where the retailer has reason to make a gift of one kind or another to his customers, the manufacturer who makes the gift possible may win a competitive advantage. Example: Druggists like to make a gesture when a local mother has a new baby. Therefore, a big drug house has brought together a special gift package which contains a variety of small items (baby powder, etc.) plus a gift card and an advance mailing card. The entire unit is available to the trade for 39 cents—a substantial markdown from actual value. Thus the druggist has available a complete package for a good-will promotion. Actually, all he need do is either deliver it or mail it out. For the manufacturer, this becomes a no-cost or small-cost sampling operation—at a highly propitious time. The same idea could be used for other merchandise for weddings, engagements, graduations, vacation trips. This would be both an extension of, and a variation on, the Welcome-wagon concept.

Getting the Full Color Assortment in Outlets

Here is an item having 18 shades. Few dealers stock more than 12 shades; the majority stock only 7 to 9 shades. And the dealers stocking 12 shades are primarily smaller dealers with whom this company does the smaller part of its total volume. The big chains fight to keep down color assortments and size assortments. While they are more elastic in this respect than just a few years back, they still try to keep a tight lid on what they consider to be excessive color assortments. Solution developed by one company: (1) Liberal color exchange privileges; (2) constant checking of color movements so that inventory turnover is not slowed by sticky colors; (3) fixtures that stock colors more effectively and present them more effectively; (4) special offers that tie a slow-moving color up with a fast-moving color; (5) tests in typical stores to prove that larger color assortments mean faster turnover, better net profit—and then a constant selling of these case history facts. Results: A slow but steady increase in color assortments in large outlets—but cost factor, to date, has been excessive. However, a better expense ratio now appears in sight which suggests that these programs must be courageously backed.

Trade Inventory on Long Lines

A toy and game line involves scores of numbers. If the retailer is compelled to buy each number in minimum quantities of one dozen, either his inventory will be too large and turnover slow—or he will carry only a small part of the line. Solution: "Assorted-packed" cartons of a dozen containing four pieces of each of three numbers. The manufacturer points out to the trade—variety chains in this instance—that the plan has the following advantages: (1) Speeds up turnover; (2) lowers total inventory; (3) permits stocking counters more quickly without searching through dozens of different cartons; (4) storerooms are kept more free of open cartons that have contents exposed to dust and this also tends to lessen employee pilferage—two excellent points that make a deep impression on the trade; (5) the assortments have been planned as a result of a long-term study of actual shipments—thus are based on actual store experience; (6) the assortments are changed periodically as certain toys and games fall off in popularity and others take their place.

Contests That Offer Discounts to Salespeople

It is fairly common in some merchandise classifications for the manufacturer to make arrangements that permit salespeople to buy the item or line at discounts larger than the regular store discount for employees

—we're referring now to big-ticket items. (On small-ticket items retail salespeople tend to get "free" offers.) But in planning a contest for retail salespeople that offers the featured item or line to salespeople at discounts, it is vital to bear in mind the discount privileges now enjoyed by retail personnel; it's also necessary to bear in mind discount-house prices. (Salespeople sometimes find they can do better at a competing discount outlet than at the "special employee price" of their employer!) A large TV manufacturer overlooked these points—he tied up a consumer contest with a retail salesperson's contest; the salesperson was to be permitted to buy a TV set at a minimum discount when he sold 6 units, a larger discount when he sold 12 units, up to a free set with the sale of 24 units. The first two stages of the offer were not at all attractive to the salespeople because of discount-house pricing—and the free set for a 24-unit sale was too tough a goal for the time period involved.

Encourage Price Cutting?

Manufacturers who feature price-maintenance programs quite commonly develop merchandising programs that actually encourage price-slashing. And, of course, these price-control programs frequently include quite a remarkable degree of flexibility through such techniques as featuring an inflated list price. (A vacuum cleaner established a list price of $69.50 and a fair-trade price of $49.50.) This encourages price cutting in a sub-rosa way. But some manufacturers make it thoroughly plain that they *want* the trade to do some price slashing. A food producer urges the food super: "Advertise Blank at a price that will attract more customers to your store. Women use the price of Blank as a guide to store-wide values." (This latter point is well taken.) This suggestion simply recognizes that food supers feature price and that this brand is commonly price-featured. It sometimes makes good merchandising sense, therefore, to prod the trade to price-cut. But do it discreetly—note how the suggestion is phrased in the preceding quotation. The trade is sensitive when manufacturers suggest a margin cut!

Merchandising Statistics in Trade Advertising

One of the great areas of statistical interest among retailers involves a square (and cubic) foot of selling area. Sales per square foot, gross profit per square foot, net profit per square foot—these figures will stop the retail fraternity dead in its tracks. A top headline for this trade-copy approach read: "Can you use $6.00 profit per square foot?" (Addressed to food supers, it was a trade stopper.) The retail net-profit percentage—especially among large retailers—has been in a decline, a serious decline. Store managers are being offered incentives for net, as well as gross.

Consequently, messages in business-paper advertising based on believable operating statistics may even be avidly read by some store personnel. A fragrance house operating on a strict exclusive-franchise basis has been running an extremely persuasive trade-paper series based on operating statistics (with actual store names mentioned). Ditto for a maker of drapery hardware. The statistics must be sound, the terminology right. And if names can be used—use them; retailers love to see what other merchants are doing, statistically.

Checking Shelf Inventory

When the salesperson is selling, when the retailer is taking inventory, there is constantly the problem of determining which is the full box on the shelf. Take women's hosiery. It usually comes three pairs in a box. The average sale is from one to two pairs. Consequently, shelf stock with one or two pairs in the box is common. This adds to salesperson time costs. It also adds to inventory-taking time costs. Solution: A hosiery mill has added a removable transparent pull tape on its hosiery boxes. It's no longer necessary to open every box to check the contents. If the pull tape is on the box—the box is full. Only the untaped boxes need checking. And when the customer wants to buy three pairs—the sale is made quickly from the still-taped box. Here again we see evidence of the wisdom inherent in contemplating packaging from the standpoint of what actually takes place on the retail floor—and the particular advantage of designing packages so as to cut the time per transaction, which continues to be the grave fundamental problem of most retailers.

Tested Selling Sentences

Periodically, so-called "tested selling sentences" become popular; these are the pat phrases which presumably clinch the sale on the retail floor in personal selling. Now a maker of sterling has conducted a trade contest in which retailers have been offered prizes for "sentence sellers." The prize-winning "sentence sellers" are to be used as the basis for national advertising copy. A cosmetic producer used the same basic concept. This company had its detail men query drug chain-store managers, department store buyers, and demonstrators for tested selling sentences on its several products; then these selling sentences were used as text on point-of-sale promotional material. The idea has merit; it can be carried further—into text on packages, for example. But whether a trade contest is the ideal way to get these selling concepts from the trade is debatable; perhaps dealers with the best selling sentences may not enter the contest. Better research methodology could probably bring in better material—a contest is not research.

The Never-ending Fight to Control Co-op

Most co-op arrangements that seek to achieve better control over the investment by the retailer of the co-op dollar tend to be a step or two behind the retailer, who wants to evade or avoid these regulations (and the number of these retailers is legion). But a continuing effort must be made. Several interesting steps toward this end were taken by one manufacturer. Newspapers used must be members of the Audit Bureau of Circulation and listed in Standard Rate & Data. (The object here was to curb abuses in local shopping news publications.) Maximum amount of space eligible for reimbursement per month was cut from 600 lines to 300 lines—a check revealed that only a small number of accounts used more than 300 lines in one month. Reimbursement is to be at the rate of 50 per cent of a predetermined rate established by the manufacturer —and based by him on each newspaper's own rate card. These are not extraordinary co-op–control provisions. And, when the chips are down, there is a tendency to make exceptions. But controls must be tried.

Buying Window Space

While the window is clearly declining as a sales-making factor, it still packs a sales-making wallop. And, of course, in some categories, and in some types of stores, and in some areas (downtown, for example), the window continues to have merchandising value. A hard-goods company developed an incentive plan that "buys" windows on a "sure-return" basis. Instead of paying for the window use of its display pieces, this company pays a fixed sum for each item from its line displayed in the window. Moreover, the sum varies for the different items in the line and for the different price lines. It then arranges for a local photographer to snap store windows and, on the basis of this photo, payment is made to the dealer. This technique simply buys window display of merchandise. To win more than merely a static window, a plan of this kind should be accompanied with suggested window terms—perhaps with a window contest.

Dealer's Name on Confined Lines

Where a merchandise line is confined—or even semiconfined—there may be reason to conclude that the franchised merchant takes a degree of pride in his franchise. Otherwise, the franchise may not mean much either to the dealer or to the supplier. Following this line of reasoning, several manufacturers distributing on a confined basis have developed the idea of putting the name of the franchised dealer on his inventory of the franchised line. As a matter of fact, one manufacturer operating this way makes this name privilege part of a deal inducement to the trade. With devices now on the market, it is possible for distributors and for manufacturers who sell direct to put the dealer's name on the numbers in a confined line, especially on big-ticket merchandise, although one manufacturer using the idea successfully makes thermometers which are not a big-ticket line. The better specialty stores in particular like to have their names on merchandise moving out of their stores—ditto for some department stores. The idea is fairly new and is susceptible to much wider exploitation.

Tailor-made Mats

Retailers perpetually complain that mats supplied by manufacturers are not appropriate for their respective "images" or suitable for the local competitive situation. A maker of a franchised line of cosmetics prepares his mats in three series: (1) for the high-prestige stores, mats that are largely impression creating, institutional; (2) for the more promotional stores, mats in which sell is more in evidence; (3) for the promotional stores, mats with hard sell. Moreover, mat size is largest in the (1) group—smallest in the (2) group. A hard-goods maker offers an ad mat book that provides for extensive substitutions of copy and illustrations so the dealer can tailor his ad to local conditions. Headlines, body copy, paragraphs, illustrations—all are interchangeable. However, there must be a continuing promotion to the proper store people on the mat service —that mat book, for example, will soon languish in a pigeonhole unless it is regularly resold to the retailer and particularly to the retailer's advertising department, if any.

Outdated Dealer Floor Samples

In lines where dealers carry little, if any, stock for resale on the floor, lines in which the selling is done from floor samples, with delivery to the customer three to eight weeks later, the condition of the floor samples is obviously of considerable importance. A rug manufacturer found that too many of its dealers were not keeping their rug samples up to date. This was especially true of the bread-and-butter basics. And, in this classification, there is plus business year round when basics are smartly merchandised. This company is therefore embarked on a complete program, with the objective of getting dealers to update their floor samples. Its salesmen are now equipped to sell this program. Inasmuch as a growing number of classifications are being merchandised by dealers from floor samples—and this trend has a long way to go—other manufacturers would do well to check into the condition of dealers' floor samples. In floor-sample retailing it is true that you can't sell from an empty wagon—but you can't sell either from old models or from worn models. This rug company is telling the trade: "If your samples have been on the floor as long as two years, you're missing sales."

Salespeople's Prizes in Consumer Contests

Whether prizes offered to salespeople as a part of a consumer contest really stimulate extra selling action is a moot point, particularly when the salesperson wins automatically when a customer wins. Nonetheless, it's common procedure—and the stakes for the salesperson tend to rise. A new high in salespeople's prizes in a consumer contest included the following offers: (1) *Each week,* as customers won various prizes, salespeople whose names were signed to customer entry blanks also won prizes; (2) if a salesperson's customer won a grand prize, the salesman won 50 shares of this company's stock (worth at the market at the time about $2,500!); (3) when customers won second prize, third prize, etc., salespeople were also liberally rewarded; (4) in the event a winning consumer entry had no salesperson signature, the salesperson's awards were stepped up automatically. Actually, a separate contest for salespeople, run simultaneously with a consumer contest and based on a tangible selling contribution by the salesperson, has more merit than the lottery type.

A Contest for Trade's Children

A trade contest offering prizes to the youngsters of retailers is offbeat —and has merit. The prizes included a first prize of a $1,500 scholarship in any college or university or a $1,500 check for a family trip to Disneyland. Other angles in this food-trade contest: Every retailer who entered the contest was permitted to sponsor a youngster to whom a membership card in the Future Grocers of America was mailed. Also, 1,500 grocer winners got prizes to give the youngsters they sponsored in addition to the big first prize. These other prizes included baseball bats, dolls, record albums, etc. There have been contests for the trade's wives. Maybe, as a gag, there will be contests for the mother-in-law of the dealer. Humor can accomplish a lot in trade relations.

Why Not "Negative" Merchandising?

When a fairly staple merchandise classification has had few dynamic changes in styling, packaging, construction for a few years, it tends to be neglected by the trade. Thus, the toothbrush has been somewhat static ever since a "germ-free" brush introduced several years ago. Consequence: Toothbrushes are not getting either the space or the location they need; dentifrices (which are being changed rapidly) are doing much better in these respects. To reawaken trade interest in toothbrushes, one maker planned a trade contest offering some 1,000 prizes for merchandising suggestions to the query: "What are you doing in your store to keep toothbrush sales from becoming Lost Sheep?" Is this "negative" merchandising? And is negative merchandising poor policy? There is little negative merchandising in a program that frankly recognizes an existing situation. Taking a hush-hush posture in a situation that is commonly understood fools nobody. The damaging admission is sound merchandising—providing it is followed up with constructive action.

Winning Trade-show Traffic

While curvaceous cuties never lose their traffic-pulling appeal at trade shows, aging businessmen can absorb only so much of this biological inducement. An interesting idea, not in any way connected with that famous three-letter word beginning with s and ending with x, was conceived for a food processor at a show attended by food-chain executives. At this company's trade exhibit, a prize was offered consisting of a single share of every food-chain stock available for sale to the public. That had a nice appeal accentuated by the fact that it entitled the chain-store executive who won it to stockholders' reports from each of these chains. The food processor also installed a stock ticker and stock-market reporter at his booth—and, since businessmen have been known occasionally to dabble in stock, this too had a considerable appeal. One of the greatest and simplest ideas ever encountered at a trade show was a booth where a manufacturer gave away big juicy red apples; they were being munched all over the place.

Trade Relations for Franchised Lines

The merchandising program based on exclusive or selective trade franchises functions best when it rests on a solid base of sound trade relations. And, in turn, these sound trade relations are best achieved when the franchised outlets have some sort of continuing voice in the conduct of what is presumed to be a partnership relation between manufacturer and retailer. With this in mind, a manufacturer of major appliances who switched over to a "registered franchise" plan for "selected appliance dealers" included in the program provision for a Registered Franchise Dealer Policy Committee. The dealer members of the committee have the responsibility of reviewing any differences of opinion on franchise matters that may occur between a distributor or manufacturer's zone office and a registered franchise dealer in good standing—and of recommending a solution. Two executives from the manufacturer are on the committee—and four dealers. The franchised line is taking on new merchandising significance in this age of broad distribution, of frenzied merchandising and price slashing. Manufacturers merchandising under this setup should review their programs to give them new significance.

Capitalizing Delayed Deliveries

Retailers traditionally complain that "when a number proves hot—the factory promptly falls behind in deliveries." But, while the trade will moan and groan about delayed deliveries on good numbers, few manufacturers have ever lost accounts for this reason. (It's when the trade complains about "dogs" in the line that a manufacturer has cause for concern!) Therefore, when apologies are offered the trade for delayed deliveries on an item that has scored a great success, it's usually good policy not to be too serious about it. We like a trade ad run by a shoe company that frankly admitted: "We sure got ourselves into the dog-house last season—but we're forced to admit it with a slight touch of pride." Copy went on to explain that although they had been optimistic about the new line—they simply hadn't been optimistic enough. The headline was "We've Swapped the Dog-House for a New Factory." (Salesmen are in particular need of soft and humorous answers to trade complaints about delayed delivery on hot numbers.)

Deal Stock vs. Regular Stock

In food and drug outlets, it is increasingly common for regular stock to remain in its usual position when deal stock is put out. This is especially true with respect to staples—and innumerable deals involve staples. Some chains now have a positive rule: "Staples never move from their regular position." (Shifting merchandise around in a self-service outlet confuses the regular customer.) Facings may be cut; that's all. Consequence: Deals frequently appear adjacent to regular merchandise. Further consequence: The latter tends to go dead for the deal period. One manufacturer now makes a special allowance with major outlets to compensate them for temporarily removing regular stock from its usual position during a deal period. Others give their detail men special incentives to remove regular stock. And one food company has had discussions with chain-store management on the subject. However, it is the chain-store manager—and the stock boy—who control in this area. This is where to concentrate.

Misleading Trade Complaints

When a famous-name maker of girdles and bras offered a free $3.95 bra with the purchase of a $10.95 girdle, quite a trade controversy was aroused. (This type of deal had never been merchandised in this classification.) In the end, however, increased traffic and improved volume can prove an effective aspirin for what the trade may conceive to be a headache. In this case, trade results varied widely, not only by city, but by stores and even by departments within one store. The stores and departments that got good results ended up pleased; those that got small reaction found that the poor results automatically canceled out the problems they had contemplated. To ignore trade complaints is folly in developing merchandising programs. But to permit the possibility of trade complaints to cancel out a proposed merchandising program may represent equal folly. Few truly exciting merchandising programs have won unanimous approval within a manufacturer's own organization, even his own sales force, and unanimous trade approval is unheard of.

Controlling Expensive Trade Helps

Too often, 75 per cent of the merchandising-promotional dollar tends to wind up with trade factors that give the manufacturer 25 per cent of his volume. To achieve better control over an expensive merchandising program (in this instance, a comprehensive plan for modernizing the entire store), a greeting card company developed the following regulations: (1) The manufacturer reserves the privilege of selecting the stores to be offered the modernization service; (2) before a store is finally selected, the dealer must fill out a comprehensive questionnaire which includes details concerning the existing store layout, merchandise lines stocked, neighborhood competitors, traffic counts, calculated to scare away dealers who merely want something for nothing; (3) the manufacturer bluntly declares: "Our choice of eligible stores will naturally be influenced not only by a strong desire to remodel the store with a well-balanced layout, but also by the merchant's genuine interest in establishing a significant greeting card department." Where does your merchandising-promotional dollar wind up?

Restocking Trade after Peak Season

Special trade offers have been developed to induce retailers to restock immediately after a peak season has depleted inventory. For example, the Christmas season is a peak period for manicure implements. One company in this field therefore offers an extra 5 per cent on all orders placed early in the new year; another company, aiming for larger orders, offers 10 per cent in free goods for refill orders of $15 or more. The latter company's offer reads as follows: "Send us your wholesaler's invoice and we will send you—in free goods—10% of the value of your purchase. Send as many as you like during the 30-day period—upon receipt of each one, your refill bonus will be shipped right out to you. What's more, you have your choice of free-goods items. Jot down, at the bottom of the invoice you send in, the free instruments you desire. If no choice is indicated, we will make a selection for you." (Stock-up deals for postpeak periods must be accompanied by programs that will stimulate turnover.)

Getting Fixtures Restocked

A maker of pens distributed through wholesalers won excellent distribution for a fixture that included, not only pens, but ink cartridges and several other parts and accessories. But keeping the fixture adequately stocked proved a problem; the wholesale salesman tended to neglect checking the fixture on his regular calls. As a method of bringing the fixtures up once again to full stock, the manufacturer offered a deal involving an assortment of numbers carried on the fixture. The retailer made up his own order for a minimum of $30 retail list. Then the retailer sent a copy of his wholesaler's invoice to the factory—and got four $1 pens free. This problem of keeping fixtures properly inventoried when selling through wholesalers is troublesome—indeed, it is doubly troublesome, because the numbers that are out of stock or underinventoried are apt to be the fast-moving numbers. A deal offer that encourages the trade to restock (and which encourages the jobber's salesmen, perhaps with a special incentive, to push for the restocking order) can help to alleviate the situation.

Speeding Trade Returns

While most gripes of dealers about problems involved in merchandise returns have little justification, the trade does have a peeve when completion of the merchandise-return transaction takes "forever." A large drug house has set up a system to speed the processing of trade returns. Previously, the account had to write the nearest branch and compile lists of the returned items. Credit was granted only after the shipment was checked at another distant point. Under the new system, the company's sales representative authorizes the return, right in the customer's store. The salesman fills out a returned-goods authorization form that lists the items to be sent to the nearest branch office. Two copies of that list go into the returned-goods package, and the salesman gives the account an authorization sticker to paste on the outside of the package. When the branch office receives the package, it *immediately credits* the customer's account for the merchandise listed on the returned-goods authorization form. The entire transaction is now completed in four or five days.

How to Merchandise Stars

Merchandising programs involving personnel supplied by manufacturers for temporary retail-floor use cover a gamut of purchase requirements—and a gamut of personalities. The personalities range from baseball stars to TV-radio stars, from designers to junior Hollywood talent. When the manufacturer makes available floor talent (especially if the floor talent is a famous personality) plus expensive floor trim and display material, plus co-op, it is customary to lay down certain contributions to be made by the retailer. This may call for a specific window or windows; for specified retail advertising; for a specific location in the department; perhaps for a charge-account or monthly statement mailing; and, of course, a minimum inventory. The whole proposition is tied up in a rather formal-looking agreement. However, the experienced manufacturer looks upon the signed agreement merely as a point of departure. A thorough system for follow-through is then instituted by the manufacturer, because the larger the retailer, the more slips between the cup and the lip!

Checking Co-op Controls

Co-op advertising contracts must include controls. This is necessary, even though these controls are seldom highly effective. If nothing else, they serve as a damper on total avoidance of co-op responsibility by the retailer. Moreover, at least in the early months of a new co-op control, there is a fairly measurable degree of trade observance. It is time and the many exceptions made for favored customers—usually at the insistence of the sales department—that eventually makes most controls a mockery. But once a control clause is put into a co-op contract it tends to stay there. This adds to the innumerable trade disputes that are an integral part of co-op, and the more clauses in a contract that are, in time, ignored, the more are all of the controls weakened. A merchandising executive reports that each year this company's co-op contract is checked, clause for clause, to uncover dead-letter clauses. These are then promptly eliminated and, if possible, a new control is substituted for each one dropped. He admits this is like chasing one's tail—but it brings at least a somewhat better degree of performance by the trade.

National Campaign and the Trade

Enthusing the trade over the national advertising becomes harder each year. After all, national advertising is no longer news to the trade! Maybe this suggests a less serious approach—fewer statistics and more fun. Example: A large food advertiser has been featuring a group of cartoon characters in its national advertising. Each character has a clever name. This advertiser then planned a trade contest in which the trade was asked to identify the gallery of characters by name. Prizes were attractive—but the big pull of this contest was its good nature. It unquestionably got the trade to spend more time absorbing the details of this national advertising program than could have been accomplished with serious statistics. Incidentally, the trade, in some instances, constitutes quite a sizable *consumer* group. Example: The food trade, including all employees, their families, their friends, mounts up into the millions. Therefore, consumer-type contests for this type of trade make good sense. A similar idea was used for an electric razor—the trade was asked to identify a character used in this item's TV commercial.

Merchandising the Preselected Assortment

A manufacturer of a furnishings item reports that a deal involving a basic assortment of 12 numbers, preselected by the manufacturer, moved sluggishly. A study soon disclosed dealer resistance to the basic assortment—the assortment that pleased a dealer in the Northeast didn't please a dealer in the Southwest; the assortment one type of dealer favored, another type opposed. Yet the manufacturer wanted that minimum basic order for 12 odd numbers. Solution: The requirement for a minimum order of a dozen was retained, but the dealer was given the privilege of picking 6 out of the 12 to his own liking. Thus, the manufacturer was able to schedule production economically on at least 6 of the numbers, while the retailer was given the merchandising elasticity he wanted in order to have the assortment conform more closely to what his experience suggested was needed.

Product Family Trade Contest Prizes

When merchandise prizes are offered the trade in trade contests, too seldom is the merchandise taken from the family of the sponsoring corporation. But one of the giant drug corporations planned a trade contest in its toothbrush division in which prizes consisted of merchandise made by the corporation's other divisions—all sold through the same outlets. To avoid creating trade ill will, the merchandise won by a retailer as a prize was bought from that retailer's regular supplier and at the price the retailer would normally pay for it! Contest details follow: (1) An entry blank was enclosed in a special toothbrush deal; (2) dealer was asked to write in no more than 50 words: "I feature Blank products because...."; (3) no limit on number of entries—but each entry was to be accompanied by the printed code number cut from the shipping carton in which the deal was packed; (4) first prize was $1,000 in

merchandise of the various subsidies—a very interesting prize concept—
and 10 second prizes worth $500 in merchandise, etc.

The Tribulations of Balanced-assortment Deals

When a manufacturer has a broad and a broadly diversified distribution, is it possible to develop a single fairly substantial balanced assortment that will be properly balanced for even the majority of dealers?
Too often the so-called "balanced assortment" is really an *unbalanced*
assortment, especially for the 15 per cent of its outlets (the giant store
units) that account for over 65 per cent of the total volume. One manufacturer now has a merchandising plan on prepacked assortments involving the following procedure: (1) A single assortment was planned
for some 55 per cent of total volume; (2) its remaining accounts were
then broken down both by type (variety chain, food chain, etc.) and by
the store-size classifications of these chains; (3) specific assortments
were then planned for each type and size of outlet—*a total of some 14
assortments;* (4) the trade also had the privilege of buying a predetermined percentage of the total deal order from open stock so that
each buyer could balance stock according to his judgment.

Factory Trips vs. Round-the-world Trips

In an industry overrun with trade incentives that include vacation
trips of all types, including round-the-world trips, could the trade become
excited in an incentive that offered merely a visit to the factory? A
manufacturer of major appliances decided that a factory visit, judiciously
spiked with a bit of fun, could be made sufficiently appealing to the
trade to help achieve sales quotas. The company concluded (1) it didn't
want merely *numbers* of dealers—it wanted quality of dealers; (2)
a *better type* of dealer would respond to a factory-trip incentive; (3)
fewer wives would come and there would thus be less social pressure,
less demand for a total round of entertainment; (4) the dealers who
came to the factory would go away with a better grasp of the line, thus
able to sell it more intelligently and more enthusiastically (valuable
gains). The experience proved that vacation junkets, *when properly
analyzed,* give the manufacturer very little. Aim for fewer but better
dealers, give them fewer drinks and more facts, fewer strip-tease acts
and more stripped-down products, get them back home to their stores
sooner to sell—and results will be good.

Truckload Events for Smaller Dealers

In several big-ticket classifications, both manufacturers and distributors
are sponsoring truckload events for medium-sized and even smaller deal-

ers. This concept started as a promotion for large retailers; it has even been carried to the point of staging freight-car events in which the shopper actually goes to the railroad siding for bargains. Now it has been found that since trucks come in many sizes, all of the bargain-appeal of the truck sale can be made available to smaller retailers. A smaller truckload is contracted for by the merchant. The truck pulls up in front of his store or at another convenient location. A complete promotion accompanies the appearance of the truck. Prices are featured —this is a price promotion. But because the truck sale conveys so powerfully the appeal of low prices, experience has shown that the retailer can actually average a better margin through a truck sale than he can in his traditional everyday selling! Moreover, the retailers find that sales are made much more quickly this way—thus cutting costs while margins improve. In similar manner, it will be found that other merchandising events specially planned for giant retailers can be successfully adapted for use by medium-sized and smaller retailers.

Merchandising the Advertising via Contests

Every merchandising executive knows that the retail trade (wholesalers, too) can no longer be excited by circulation or reader-listener statistics of an advertising program. That is, merely recapitulating the statistics just fails to make a trade impression any more, even when the figures are dressed up in various ways. How *can* the trade be induced to give proper weight to the coverage of an advertising program? Solution: Run a trade contest. A large advertiser, for example, conceived a contest for retailers, wholesalers, and their employees offering substantial prizes, including as top prize a first-class round trip for two to Europe. The object of the contest was to guess how many people will see the TV spots of this advertiser. To help the trade in its guessing, the entry blank gave several clues. Thus the trade was inveigled into thinking statistically—and, from thinking statistically to becoming impressed with the resulting figures is a reasonable expectation. Certainly figures on advertising circulation that the trade arrives at itself in this way are apt to linger longer on the trade's mind and are apt to make a deeper and more persuasive impression than the usual presentation of these figures in broadsides and trade advertising.

Super Luxury Items as Trade Incentives

Several merchandising executives report unusual success with trade incentives that offered super luxury items as rewards for trade purchases or for trade turnover of inventory. Example: One manufacturer who had been offering a hi-fi set now offers one of the complicated three-channel stereo phonograph AM-FM combinations in a beautiful cabinet. Example: Custom-made furniture instead of commercial numbers. Example: Wedgwood china instead of ordinary china. Example: An electronic range instead of an ordinary electric range. This makes good sense. We are clearly entering an age in which more and more people will not only aspire to possess superluxuries—they will in time come to own these superluxuries. Consequently, previous ceilings on trade incentive awards will tend to be broken—truly, the sky will be the limit. The race for social status through the ultimate in possessions is on in full force—and smart merchandisers can capitalize on a public drive of this kind not only in trade incentives but in consumer contest awards as well —some day a consumer contest will offer selections from Tiffany's and Bergdorf Goodman. Incidentally, have you noted how both of these exclusive stores are deliberately catering to not-so-exclusive customers?

Helping Retailers with Telephone Selling

Today, retailers are again turning to the telephone as a sales-making tool. Department stores are strengthening their telephone-order boards. Thousands of independents are turning to the telephone. (A food retailer is developing a food-super operation on foods exclusively via the telephone.) The auto agency is reluctantly using telephone; ditto for some major appliance retailers. And categories that are being sold through in-home techniques by retailers—home furnishings, appliances, etc.— are hooked in with telephone selling. All this has suggested to several merchandisers that (1) scripts for use by retailers in telephone selling are in order; (2) complete programs for telephone selling are also in order—how to compile lists, when to call, etc.; (3) special allowances for the privilege of being included in telephone selling by department stores are springing up; (4) special cards with appropriate text are being furnished for display in front of the telephone-order girls; (5) contests among telephone-order girls could be a next step. (One department store reports it sold over 1,000 units of an item in one day by a mere telephone suggestion.)

Help Retailers Shoo Traffic Upstairs

As mass retailers concentrate on opening giant store units, the multi-level store stages a return engagement. (These giant store units include basement operations, too—there are more basements, today, in mass retailing than ever before; even food supers now have basement operations.) This gives mass retailers the old problem of inducing traffic to go upstairs and downstairs. Several manufacturers have lately developed specific plans to help retailers shoo traffic upstairs and downstairs.

One such plan offered by a hard-surface floor-covering manufacturer included (1) the display on the main floor of a loaned antique 1903 auto —this drew great attention; (2) an attendant, furnished by the manufacturer and stationed alongside the antique auto, giving out entry blanks to customers; (3) the customer then had to take the entry blank up (or down) to the rug department to deposit the entry slip—thus getting the traffic up- or downstairs; (4) the entry slip called for the customer's name and address and the design name of her favorite pattern in this floor-covering line; (5) drawings were then held for free rugs.

Contests for Store Ad Managers

Contests offering store ad managers prizes for outstanding ads generally are not successful. One reason: Too many retail ad managers feel they don't have even an outside chance at a prize. A second reason would be store policies in better stores that oppose these contests. (Generally, these contests pull inadequately from the very stores that provide the major volume to the contest sponsor.) Moreover, what the store may consider an effective ad—backed with proved results—may not appeal at all to the contest judges. But if a contest of this kind is to be run, here are some suggestions offered by two manufacturers: (1) Divide retailers into logical groups by annual volume; (2) offer many small area prizes so contestants will not feel they are competing with the entire nation; (3) if feasible, offer prizes to the buyers as well as the store manager—the buyer has a voice in the advertising; (4) have a rule that the ads must tie up with the national theme, must exceed a stipulated minimum size, must include certain specified units, must run during a specified time period; (5) explain clearly the basis on which ads will be judged.

Retail Policy in Demoralized Markets

When electric housewares found itself in a no-price–control market, some retailers took one or more of these steps, highly significant to any merchandiser whose line may be marketed in a demoralized market: (1) reducing lines; (2) deemphasizing products; (3) discontinuing some items; (4) carrying only best sellers; (5) dropping lines; (6) reducing selling space of electric housewares; (7) reducing displays; (8) refusing to advertise; (9) carrying no reserve stocks; (10) refusing to take repairs; (11) bargaining harder for lower costs; (12) reducing personnel service—going self-service; (13) charging $1 or more for delivery. But while many retailers threatened to take these steps, few major outlets carried out the threats. *Big retailers must be competitive;*

merchandisers can count on this fact of life. Department stores, for example, took only the more constructive of the steps listed. (Simultaneously, several manufacturers of traffic appliances curbed distribution somewhat—but the long-term wisdom of this move has yet to be proved.)

Diversified Mats for Diversified Distribution

Too many manufacturers have diversified their distribution much more broadly than they have diversified their mat services. As a consequence, retailers of different types, as well as retailers of different sizes, are being offered mats which, in too many instances, are quite unsuitable. For a line of electric clocks, this problem was tackled by determining the basic *types* of dealers (and the objectives of these dealers) merchandising electric clocks. More specifically, the mats were designed to conform with the basic store *images* that these different types of dealers were aiming to establish. Thus, there were mats for the bargain center or discount outlets at one end of the mat service; at the other end of the mat service there were mats for stores building a quality reputation. There were other mat variations in between these two extremes. While it will seldom be possible to offer a *completely* individualized mat service for all types and sizes of dealers in a broadly distributed line, neither will it be possible usually to offer a single mat concept to all dealers for a broadly distributed line. Generally speaking, mat services require more hand tailoring for variations in the dealer list than they get.

Trade Reorders on Hot Seasonal Numbers

The trade complains—and not without justification—that once a new number (especially a new style) proves "hot," the supplier has to back-order, and a good part of the season is lost. A fashion line recognized this problem in the following way: The line had been pretested in Florida, Arizona, etc. A trade ad was then run in advance of the Northern season, featuring the numbers that had sold best at these resorts. The ad then did these unusual things: (1) It gave a list of names, addresses, and telephone numbers of the line's salesmen; (2) the trade was told: "Your salesman will be happy to accept your telephone order now"; (3) orders placed within ten days were guaranteed to receive priority shipment—note this obviously important shipment promise; (4) then the trade ad also included a special order form listing the necessary details on the choice numbers—and again assuring priority shipment to coupon orders placed within ten days.

Dangers of Loading Big Chain Dealers

A deal was offered a giant retail chain involving particularly liberal cooperative advertising allowances—based on a substantial order. The offer was attractive—and the big retailer ordered liberally. The co-operative advertising (which was hardly co-op since it really did not cost the retailer a dime to run) was duly run. Merchandise movement was above normal. But the chain was left, at the end of the deal period, with a larger-than-usual inventory. As might be expected, the chain insisted on returning the inventory excess and, as might be expected, the manufacturer wound up with no possible choice other than to accept the unsold coverage. Moral: It is still possible despite IBM systems, buying committees, etc., to overload big retailers. But it isn't possible, usually, to make the overload stick and, when the inevitable return is inevitably accepted, the total cost of the transaction can be staggering. Most large retailers are not at all bashful about pressuring suppliers to accept returns even though documents have been duly signed that presumably eliminate the return privilege. Large retailers are more insistent —and less bashful—about making returns than small retailers. And the large retailer is harder to turn down.

Guaranteed-profit Plan for Dealers

Large retailers tend to operate on the premise that they know pretty well how to go about achieving a satisfactory net profit on merchandise turnover. Medium-sized and smaller dealers are more open to buying on a merchandising program that guarantees a profit. Thus, a maker of melamine dinnerware selling primarily through medium-sized and somewhat smaller department and specialty stores worked out what the manufacturer calls its "Guaranteed Results Merchandising Program." The program includes (1) a pledge of at least 150 per cent more sales dollars per square foot than the departmental average; (2) a pledge of a minimum of four stock turns a year; (3) an assurance of no mark-downs from old or unbalanced stock bought and controlled under the plan; (4) jobber checks on stock at least once every two weeks with automatic fill-in reordering to assure constant in-stock position; (5) a pledge of selected distribution; (6) a pledge of regular calls by the manufacturer's detail man and clerk-training assistance; (7) a splendid self-selection fixture; (8) model stocks planned for stores of various sizes; (9) a complete merchandising review for each dealer every four months.

Alternatives for Co-op

Both manufacturers and retailers are considering alternatives for co-op, although for completely different reasons. Retailers are not encouraging dropping co-op, but they are making more demands for payment for in-store display, position, etc. Manufacturers realize that co-op funds are largely dissipated, especially in the omnibus price ads of the food and drug outlet; they know that these ads do little selling under self-service retailing; they know that in-store display is more productive of volume. Consequently, there is something of a trend away from co-op—and toward payments for in-store display. This trend also includes more liberal budgets by the manufacturer for important fixtures. Example: On one soft-goods item the maker discontinued co-op allowances—is offering stores sales-making manikins. While buyers grumble (particularly where store accounting makes co-op important to the buyer), they tend to admit that these manikins give them far more volume than the same money invested in co-op.

Sampling the Dealer's Wife on a New Item

The dealer's wife may be the wife of a chain-store manager, of the owner of an independent store, of other store personnel. In the trade, as elsewhere, never underestimate the power of *la femme*. That's why a giant producer of domestic paper products who brought out a paper barbecue apron for women and men ran trade advertising offering a free sample, with the suggestion that the wife wear it and put it through a test. A trade contest for a new item included among the various prizes offered retailers a fairly wide selection of items for the wife of the dealer. But one group—ready-to-wear garments—languished. The explanation: The line was sold by a number of retailers in each community. The wives didn't want to be seen wearing a garment that the wives of other dealers would know had been won in a trade contest. Moreover, they didn't want to run the risk of going to a gathering and meeting several other women wearing precisely the same garment.

Co-op on Promotional Numbers

Special promotional numbers are usually closely priced—so closely as sometimes to compel a decision to refrain from giving co-op allowances on the promotional numbers. (Moreover, the manufacturer usually prefers having co-op funds concentrated on his regular numbers rather than on promotional numbers.) A home-furnishings company, making a category that is overrun with promotional numbers, decided that to continue to keep co-op funds away from the promotional numbers no longer was realistic and was causing ill will. It therefore took these steps: (1) Credits earned by the trade for co-op money could be applied to any part of the line—including promotional numbers; (2) but, on promotional numbers, the dealer is permitted to spend only up to half the co-op fund, matching the other half with his own money; (3) on the regular line, dealers may use full co-op funds. Thus the trade still has an incentive to use co-op for the numbers the manufacturer wants most to promote—but the trade also may divert some co-op money to the promotional numbers which, in this classification, are the trade's pets.

Help Dealers Stage Guessing Games

Retailers are more free than manufacturers to merchandise what are really lotteries. One reason: They are not so subject to scrutiny by the post office, which is guardian of our lottery morals. Moreover, they note the wave of sweepstake campaigns by manufacturers (which are, of course, lotteries) and conclude that today there is more latitude with respect to lottery merchandising events than ever before. Consequently, several manufacturers are now offering their dealers a succession of merchandising-promotional events which are essentially lotteries. Example: A maker of room air-conditioners suggests to its dealers that they promote a guessing game—and gives its dealers the full program. This program includes a window in which large cakes of ice are shown. Street traffic is then asked to guess when all the ice will melt. First prize is the air-conditioner—supplied on attractive terms by the distributor. Appropriate window placards have been included in the package—entry blanks, publicity releases, etc. There is obviously a lottery trend in merchandising. It will produce store traffic in volume. The sole question is: How much of this traffic will be potential *buying* traffic?

Selling Short End of Stick

A large hard-goods manufacturer, bringing out a new category, pledged it would not sell the new line directly to the giant chains. This merchandising program undoubtedly influenced many dealers to place opening orders for the new line. But, when considering this merchandising plan, note that it means shutting off big-volume outlets—giant volume is done by the giant outlets. In many merchandise categories a policy of not selling the retail giants may mean washing out up to 80 per cent of the total market. Also, any giant retailer who wants the line badly enough can always get it. The discount houses will certainly get the new line—if they want it. Successful outlets *must* be competitive. This means they must feature much the same brands as their competition. Consequently, some merchants, who bought the new line to escape competition, will wind up putting their inventory and promotional dollar back of the very brands that are widely distributed and that competition features.

Merchandising Short-season Lines

Mass retailers are disposed to take less and less gamble with inventory. As applied to strictly short-season categories, this means that they will tend to favor the supplier who reduces their inventory risks to a minimum. And, since giant retailers can offer giant volume, it may pay off for the manufacturer to assume most of the inventory burden. Example: Seeds are clearly a short-season line in most of the nation. Therefore, a famous-brand seed company offers major outlets the following proposition: (1) An ingenious display device that enables the shopper to determine, at a glance, how to plan many types of gardens; (2) that device is part of a compact merchandise-display unit; (3) the entire display was designed for minimum space—consequently, this seed company could point out to food supers that its display would provide average weekly profits per square foot exceeding those of health-beauty aids, cigarettes, etc.; (4) the seed company provides the display and the inventory; (5) the retailer pays only for seeds actually sold; (6) moreover, the seeds are paid for only at the end of the season! Clearly, this means no markdowns, no spoilage, no shrinkage, no merchandise investment.

Helping Trade with Public Relation Mats

By far the majority of mats supplied to retailers by manufacturers are concerned with specific merchandise offerings. This suggested to one of the drug supply houses that maybe it could win both wider mat usage from the druggist, plus his good will, by giving him mats that would help him to create a more desirable image in the public mind. The druggist is under considerable fire—and therefore this idea was particularly timely. The result was a series of mats such as: "Can you read your doctor's writing?" The manufacturer's products were neatly woven into some—but not all—of the retail ads. Certainly the retail trade is about as conscious of public image as are manufacturers. This is especially the case with the large chains. There is, therefore, a larger interest among retailers in image-building advertising than ever before in the history of retailing. But few retailers are in a position to get truly competent image-building advertising. Consequently, the manufacturer who supplies mats that help the retailer with his image building (and in which the manufacturer's story is skillfully but unobtrusively woven) will win wider use of his mats.

Buying Committee Check Lists

As retailers become larger, the buying function is increasingly turned over to a committee. This trend will accelerate—the individual buyer in large chains will have less authority; the buying committee will assume greater authority. Precisely how the buying committee arrives at its decisions is therefore of mounting importance to the manufacturer's merchandising executive. Here is a composite list of the factors weighed by over 70 chains at buying-committee meetings: (1) Margins; (2) consumer advertising; (3) rate of turnover; (4) advertising allowances; (5) protection against price decline; (6) easy consumer identification; (7) package, shape, weight; (8) units per shipping carton; (9) pilferage possibilities; (10) breakage possibilities; (11) easy handling; (12) price-marking spot; (13) prepaid transportation charges; (14) drop shipments to stores; (15) special allowances for carload or pool-car quantities; (16) cents off regular price; (17) multiple-quantity offers; (18) customer rebates or refunds; (19) premiums, coupons, or customer contests; (20) free-goods offers; (21) in-store demonstrations; (22) display material; (23) outserts or inserts with package; (24) trade contests.

Co-op Control for Big-ticket Line

On a big-ticket, limited-distribution line, co-op controls tend to be much more enforceable than on small-ticket, unlimited-distribution lines. But even with the former merchandising setup, the largest accounts must be handled gingerly, exceptions made. However, a reasonably reassuring degree of control over co-op expenditures can be won with this marketing picture. Having this in mind, a maker of a limited-distribution line of woven floor coverings who wanted to get more retail linage behind his regular numbers offered a limited-period co-op plan that gave the trade 3 per cent of net billings to certified dealers only on regular goods. It was specified that each advertisement must be not less than 400 lines —and then came the "cracker": layout and copy were to be submitted to the manufacturer's advertising department *in advance* for approval. This is an extraordinary control clause in cooperative advertising. It is not the sort of control clause that will be liked by the trade. But where a brand is strong, where its contribution to a department's gross and net is substantial—and where the manufacturer's sales force can be counted on reasonably to sell and back up the control clause—this approval in advance concept has considerable merit.

How Much Push Does Push Money Buy?

If a manufacturer is willing to consider the P.M. as an out-and-out allowance, that is one thing. Otherwise, it is high time that the P.M. was reevaluated. Clearly, with retail floor selling at an all-time low, the best P.M. plan can't buy the push it bought some years back. A manufacturer who analyzed his P.M. program reports there are other weaknesses to the P.M.: (1) It is difficult to control; (2) clerks know all the techniques for getting around the rules; (3) as retail organizations get larger, P.M.

systems break down between headquarters and far-flung stores; (4) store managers sometimes "grab" the P.M.; (5) clerks may be operating under a number of P.M. plans simultaneously—some competitive (a serious fault, getting worse all the time); (6) much dissension and ill will is created; (7) the little extra selling effort generated is promptly dropped once the P.M. is withdrawn, tending to make the P.M. some-what permanent, and a permanent P.M. just isn't an incentive at all; (8) some major retailers won't tolerate it; (9) those major retailers who fight for it—like some drug chains—consider it to be more of an allow-ance than compensation for clerks.

Dealer Price-lining Ignorance

While retailers worship their traditional pricing points—it is amazing how few statistics they have on turnover by price line and how little they retain mentally of these few figures. A manufacturer of shoes re-tailed in the middle price lines, as an example, found department store knowledge of shoe turnover by price line was dim. The manufacturer arranged, therefore, for an outside auditing service to check shoe price-line performance in department stores. Some 19 pricing points were studied—ranging from the $3.99 pricing point up to $19.95. This study showed that the $12.95 pricing point accounted for 21.8 per cent of department store fashion-shoe volume—a fundamental piece of factual information that was only dimly comprehended by department store merchandisers and buyers. The study also showed that the $12.95 price range for spring of two years had shown the largest percentage gain in volume. When a market is changing, mere statements to that effect will not impress the trade, which clings to notions, traditions, guess-estimates. But turnover figures by price lines can win retail attention and bring about policy changes.

Is Co-op Productive in Special Events?

A large department store on the West Coast spent $350,000 for its centennial celebration. Of that amount, 22 per cent was supplied by resources as co-op allowances. Variety, food, and drug chains regularly seek co-op arrangements for special events—and, of course, so do in-numerable independents. Question: How productive is the co-op dollar when invested in these huge, powerful, concentrated drives? Answer: On balance, these co-op dollars tend to be more productive for the manufacturer than co-op dollars spent throughout the year by the re-tailer with little or no effective control by the supplier. These special events produce giant traffic counts in the store, which means extra volume for the manufacturer. Also, because of their very size, the campaigns win unusual attention. Several merchandising executives have stated they would rather see their co-op budget go into these special events staged by giant retailers than have it disbursed in any other way. One merchandising man keeps a careful experience record of these special events, and, from this experience, has drawn up a co-op program for special events that improves performance.

Personal Selling vs. Packaging

In some departments, especially in some upstairs departments of department stores, tradition, pride, the desire to create an atmosphere that will justify higher price lines—all combine to create a certain antagonism toward packages. The complaint will be: "We aren't a supermarket or a bargain basement. And we don't want packages to take the place of our salespeople; moreover, packages just can't take the place of our salespeople." Actually, packages could and are doing a better job of selling higher price lines and big-ticket lines than the current crop of salespeople—but tradition dies hard. Therefore, a maker of girdles (a category now generally packaged for bargain-basement and main-floor selling) moved cautiously when it considered packaging for upstairs higher price lines. Here is this manufacturer's solution: (1) A brand exclusively for upstairs departments (this is a basic, of course)—in the upper price lines; (2) a beautiful package that enhanced prestige; (3) the package so designed that the girdle could be easily removed and replaced—thus automatically confirming that the salesperson was considered in the design of the package; (4) nothing on the cover but the brand name—selling information was presented *inside* the cover for discreet perusal by the salesperson. (Others could use this method to bridge the gap between package and personal selling.)

New Opportunities for Statement Enclosures

Most mass retailers—ultimately including the food outlet—will be selling on one form of credit or another. Right now, variety chains, drug chains, dry-goods chains (including J. C. Penney) have either embraced or are testing credit. There are bank-check credit plans, diners-club credit plans, bank charge-account plans. This means that still more millions of American families will be receiving each month at home a statement from one or more retailers—or from their bank. For years, the statement mailing has proved to be an excellent merchandising-promotional device utilized by manufacturers selling through department stores. Now the statement enclosure can reach a vastly larger audience. It will, of course, be made available by these other mass retailers at a price, as has been customary in the department store field for years. But in many instances, the cost is reasonable in ratio to sales impact—the statement enclosure can be a highly effective salesmaker. (Incidentally, it is entirely probable that banks will be open-minded with respect to putting enclosures into their credit-statement mailings.)

Merchandising Events for Old Customers

A rug company recently worked with an account that had been handling its line for thirty years (a long-time association as accounts go) in the development of a special merchandising event. This was not a price-promotional affair; to the contrary, it was staged as a major fashion event. A gallery of six special room vignettes was installed that coordinated other major items of room décor with the woven floor covering. A full-page newspaper ad announcing the event was run. The event was featured in the tea room. The manufacturer arranged to have a special representative on hand for three days to work with the sales staff as well as with customers. In total, both resource and retailer benefited in prestige as well as in volume. Too often, a celebration of this sort of anniversary relationship becomes simply a handout. Staged this way, it becomes a mutually profitable event that builds for the long term as well as for the short term.

Helping Dealers Balance Inventory

Unbalanced inventories at retail stem from many causes—but one of the most common causes revolves around *local* variations in demand for style, color, price line. Consequently, one approach to the problem of helping dealers to balance stock is by encouraging "swapping" among accounts. A furniture manufacturer (one of the great brands) has done this by establishing a clearinghouse type of operation. It works this way: The retailer gives the manufacturer's salesman a list of slow movers or of wanted numbers. The latter sends the list to the factory. The factory compiles all of the lists in a regularly published bulletin mailed to all its accounts. The retailer's name and address are included with each listing. The trading is then done between the dealers directly. The financial settlement is between the dealers—price is usually figured at dealer cost. The dealer buying pays for transportation. Included in the transactions, it has been found, are numbers dropped by the factory but still wanted by some dealers.

New "Spiff" Incentives

The cash "spiff" is, of course, one of the most sadly abused merchandising concepts. In major appliances, it may produce fair returns; in the drug outlet it tends to do poorly. On balance, it is suspect. A maker of phonograph record needles and record accessories has moved away from cash and turned to a "spiff" program that includes low-cut group hospitalization and medical insurance. It also includes low-cost group life insurance. And, finally, the plan offers low-cost charter travel to Europe. This producer has established a so-called "Super Bonus Club." Dealers and clerks must turn in stipulated achievements to become members of this club. Only club members are entitled to the three-pronged "spiff" program just described. The plan works this way: Bonus stamps are affixed to each item made by the sponsor. The stamp is removed when a sale is made. The stamps are saved on cards. When enough stamps are saved, application is made for the desired "spiff."

Catalogues Supplement Sample Selling

More categories are being floor-merchandised at retail through sample techniques—that is, the retailer carries only floor samples. This includes furniture, floor coverings—even some appliances. Now some retailers insist they don't want to inventory even samples of the complete line; they want to carry one each of only a few of the fastest-moving numbers! This is compelling some manufacturers to furnish retailers with catalogues showing the entire line. But these catalogues, to date, tend to be poor salesmen in print. They are too small, too uninteresting, lacking in drama. One manufacturer now has a giant-type catalogue presentation—it includes photo enlargements that are life-size; these are strongly mounted and hung from a movable wing-type fixture. There is appropriate text and the fixture is illuminated. A wholesaler provides his accounts with a gift catalogue for year-round display—it aims to sell more big-ticket gift items. Some smart merchandisers affected by sample selling are developing programs to counter the trend. These programs include better warehousing service, brilliant new floor fixtures, fast-moving assortments, smaller lines, liberal return policies.

Inventory Protection on Seasonal Lines

Distributors are much concerned about their inventory position on seasonal merchandise. A large maker of electric blankets offers the following inventory protection plan for distributors: All distributors placing what is (purposely) vaguely described as a "substantial" blanket order will receive inventory protection up to 50 per cent of blankets in stock on a fixed date so long as the stock on that date does not exceed 50 per cent of the original order. Inventory protection on seasonal merchandise, both for distributors and for retailers, is always a headache.

Most plans must be administered with a considerable degree of elasticity. Of course, where the season can be lengthened, the problem is lessened. An interesting example of lengthening a season is offered by terry cloth. It was formerly a seasonal staple. Now, by improved styling and new applications, a year-round demand has been developed for terry cloth. The application of design, new uses, new sales units and packaging, new style to limited-season items as a technique for broadening seasons is too seldom tried.

Trade Contest for Chains Only

For a line with broad distribution, a trade contest that attempts to straddle several types and many sizes of dealers automatically rules out a substantial percentage of the trade as contestants. A producer of men's cosmetics—sold through department stores, independent drug stores, some variety stores, chain drug stores, and probably through some food supers—recently planned a window contest for *chain drug stores only.* The company made much of the point that "for the first time, chain drug stores can compete in a prize category of their own." Prizes included a $1,000 top prize—and ranged down to $50. While promoting a window contest among chains of any type has questionable merit (among other reasons, because windows may be closely controlled by the chain's home office) where an adequate response may be expected from the chains in a trade contest, there is certainly merit to the thought of offering the chains, or one type of chain, its own contest.

Out-of-stock in Special Merchandisers

Counter and floor merchandisers frequently take an item or line out of its normal shelf position. This, of course, is one of the basic reasons for the fixture. But one of the disadvantages of the special location won by the fixture is that it is not apt to be in the line of routine of the stock boys. Consequently, if the fixture is not regularly serviced by the manufacturer's detail man, some of the numbers will tend to become out-of-stock more frequently than would be the case in the regular shelf location. A manufacturer of health aids who checked into this situation decided to eliminate from his fixture numbers that were carried in the fixture only in very small quantities—several of these items were stocked merely in quantities of two. The decision in this case was to stock fewer numbers in the fixture, but to have an adequate inventory of each. Studies have since been made checking out-of-stock, number by number, on the fixture and at the regular shelf location. These indicated that the fixture needed still better merchandising—and additional numbers are now being eliminated from it. Ever checked your fixtures in this way?

Co-op for Small Accounts

By far the larger percentage of the retail accounts on the books of most manufacturers do not buy enough to earn co-op allowances that are large enough for anything remotely resembling effective advertising. Generally speaking, small dealers do not use co-op. In large cities, even fair-sized dealers feel they cannot use newspaper space. This is a constant source of trade irritation. One manufacturer suggests to his smaller accounts in each city that they *pool* their co-op allowances and thus finance a substantial ad, with the names of all the cooperating stores signed to the ad. The manufacturer supplies the copy, layout, art work. What is more, the manufacturer has taken particular pains to make these ads the best his agency can turn out; he wants his smaller accounts to feel that they can thus compete with the large accounts in effective use of the co-op budget. This plan is not easily put over—it requires selling. But it has merit—and local newspapers may help in selling it. This is plus business for them.

Facts in Trade Copy

It is discouraging to note how easily controverted are so many of the "factual" presentations that appear in trade copy. Nobody is fooled—except the advertiser. Give the trade a believable fact in trade advertising—and the message will penetrate in time. Example: A small item retailing in a 39-cent size, a 59-cent size, and a 98-cent size merchandised through the drug and food outlet. In one trade ad after another, this advertiser presents striking facts concerning brand turnover, etc. —each fact impressive and each fact verified. In a typical instance, one of its trade ads reported the astonishing fact that this one small-ticket item produced "26.5 per cent of all baby toiletries sales volume" in the food super. Precise breakdown figures were then given—based, be it noted, on turnover in approximately 19,000 supermarkets. The figures included turnover in these 19,000 food supers of each of the item's three sizes—interestingly, dollar volume on the 59-cent size was more than 50 per cent larger than dollar volume on the 39-cent size and over four times the dollar volume of the 98-cent size.

Co-op for New-line Distributors

When introducing a new line through distributors—a line on which co-op advertising is indicated—the problem is to make a financial arrangement that will permit the distributor to start his co-op activities while volume on the new line is slowly building up. Otherwise, co-op support may be lacking in the initial drive. The solution for a new line of clocks marketed through distributors was a co-op arrangement under which the distributor gets a promotion fund equal to 2 per cent of total net billing for the remainder of the year. (This clock line was introduced in the spring.) Cash discounts, estimated freight allowances, and excise taxes were deducted to arrive at net billings (a practice that should be more common). Then distributors were told that, until October 1, they could use promotion money based on their *estimated* clock purchases for the remainder of 1958. The manufacturer is estimating that each distributor will take at least $10,000 worth of clocks in 1958—so each distributor is to be allowed to spend up to $200 of the manufacturer's co-op money through October 1, regardless of his clock purchases as of that date.

In-store Display vs. Co-op

Several suppliers to the food super have begun to switch from co-op ad allowances to allowances for specific display position. This could blossom into a positive trend. Reason? The food super is beginning to realize that its item price-list ads accomplish practically nothing. (One food super, for example, in a series of tests, found that its volume on items featured in this traditional way picked up less than one-half of 1 per cent during an advertised period as compared with an unadvertised period.) Both retailer and manufacturer know that the sale is made in the last couple of inches between the shopper's erratically moving hand and the shelf. Other tests prove that a good center-aisle display, or a gondola-end display, or an extra facing, or eye-level position will outsell a co-op listing ad 5 and 10 to 1. The retailer actually pockets this allowance—whereas he does spend some of the co-op money for linage. It is entirely probable, therefore, that the food super will spark a trend that will spread to other retail fields—a trend away from co-op and toward allowances for specific in-store display.

Merchandising to Dealer Service Staffs

As more items require more technical service, the dealer's service man assumes new merchandising stature. Getting closer to the service man is a specific merchandising function for these lines. One company has carried its merchandising program for service men to the point where it even provides smartly styled work clothing for them—an idea as unusual as it is sound. (Incidentally, this work clothing includes the brand symbol and is even color-keyed to correspond with the packages of parts and with store signs, featuring the service!) This same manufacturer has put together a handsome and practical kit for service men. The whole program is merchandised through distributors on a cost-covering basis. Several manufacturers have developed elaborate plans for turning service men into salesmen or sales-lead scouts while they are in the home. (The P.M. for service men is on the way.)

Out-of-stock during Peak Season?

How to cut out-of-stock during the seasonal peak? Solution: (1) A study was made for a cellophane-tape line. This study disclosed that 3 out of 10 stores would be out of stock on a fast-moving 59-cent retailer during the peak season; (2) it was decided, therefore, to concentrate on this one number—obviously, any attempt to protect the entire line against peak-season out-of-stock would be futile; (3) a dispenser is an integral part of the in-home use of this tape; (4) therefore, a specially decorated dispenser, appropriate either for the Christmas season or for year-round use, was produced; (5) this dispenser was offered to the retailer, at no charge, with a purchase of 36 of the 59-cent rolls considerably in advance of the Christmas season; (6) the merchant was told he could take home the dispenser—or sell it at a regular retail of $1.98. Out-of-stock is the mark of a successful line; no fast-moving item or line is ever out of stock. Moreover, year-round efforts to lessen out-of-stock pale on the trade. Concentrate on the peak seasons—and offer the trade an incentive.

Color Increases Trade Returns

A survey of an industry that only recently turned to color showed these developments as a direct result of color merchandising: (1) Retailers complained their inventories had become too large, that turnover rates had declined; (2) manufacturers' salesmen were bombarded with demands that returns be accepted and they, of course, bombarded their home offices; (3) various manufacturers began accepting returns, usually without a definite policy; (4) an association meeting passed a resolution (which was promptly ignored), laying down the rule that manufacturers should not accept color returns; (5) then individual manufacturers began programs designed to shrink the problem at its start; these programs included better pretesting of new colors; fewer colors; faster reporting from selected stores of actual color movement—and passing this information to the trade; specific policies governing conditions under which limited returns would be accepted. Color always increases the trade's inventory problem but, whether or not this happens, color will bring with it trade demands for return privileges.

Retailers Like Inventory-cutting Ideas

Every so often, a manufacturer comes out with a product improvement that permits the retailer to operate with a smaller inventory. Example: A bra maker developed two constructions that would fit over 90 per cent of all women. A watch bracelet that fits most watches with just a few numbers is also being merchandised. Ideas that help the trade operate with a smaller inventory tend to bring satisfactory vocal response; too often, though, the end result is not on the same level as the initial reaction. That's because these inventory-cutting ideas are not self-selling; they must be sold and promoted constantly. The broad trend of retailing is toward fighting to keep down inventories. That's why the retail giants are investing in electronic tabulators, electronic communication systems. It is also the reason automatic reorder systems developed by manufacturers for small staple items tend to be well received by the trade. (The variety chains are actively encouraging suppliers to develop automatic reorder systems.)

Check Your Window Payments

Payments for retail cooperation tend to perpetuate themselves. A clear-cut example involves payments for window space in chains. The window has been in a rapid decline for ten years as a sales-making factor. But payments for window space by manufacturers continue at an all-time high. A drug manufacturer merchandising executive who surveyed this situation recently concluded that drug-chain windows in particular were almost valueless as either sales producers or as brand promoters. It is a fearful hodgepodge of massed merchandise, with shrieking posters superimposed on the exterior of the window over the jumbled displays. Shopper time spent in front of the drug-chain window, he found, was almost nil. He concluded that, since the sale was made inside the store, it would be just common sense to take the money spent for window space and offer it for interior selling space. This company had been paying for shelf space and position but now, with its former window allotment added, it is offering the drug chains more for shelf space and position than any competitors. This is winning preferred traffic spots, best shelf height, more facings for this brand.

Consumer Contest for Dealers

Where the trade is also a big consumer—why not a consumer contest for the trade? A food processor reasoned that food trade personnel (including wives, mothers, relatives, friends) came to a sizable total. They were actual or potential consumers of most of its famous food brands.

So, instead of a typical trade contest—it planned a typical consumer contest for the trade. (Incidentally, the contest involved the whole family of products—which represents one more step toward family-of-product merchandising as differentiated from strictly item merchandising.) Trade personnel were asked to "send in your favorite recipe," using any brand in this famous family. There was an entry form featured in trade advertising (no box tops were necessary). Prizes were either cash or strictly "home items"—not items of store equipment. The contest undoubtedly appealed to women employees, to wives of store owners and workers, and, of course, to those male store employees who are amateur chefs. It's a good way to get the trade to use as well as know your merchandise—always an advantage.

Protecting Dealers on Discontinued Numbers

In hard-surface floor coverings, as in many other lines, discontinued patterns or numbers involve the retailer in markdowns. This fear leads to shallow inventories. A manufacturer of hard-surface floor coverings picked up a competitive lap with a plan under which dealers obtain a price-protection credit against future purchases of a fixed sum for every square yard of "drops" the dealer has in stock. (The retailer must buy 3 square yards for every square yard of drops.) To date, results indicate the plan has encouraged merchants to buy more evenly, and especially to maintain inventory just before market time. The long-term results of such a program are debatable—it can easily wind up as simply an extra allowance. For example, the manufacturer's salesman must check the inventory of drops among his accounts—and he is apt to be too lenient. In the absence of monthly inventory records from the trade, it is almost impossible to determine the amount of inventory tied up in drops. But there is no question that price protection on discontinued numbers has a great appeal to the trade.

Dramatizing Consumer Premium to Trade

When a giant drug producer developed a consumer premium offer based on the accumulation of a set of copperware, the merchandising executive decided to send a complete set to key buyers among the wholesale groups, chains, voluntary chains, and co-ops. The shipment was preceded by a letter explaining that the purpose was to dramatize to these buyers the appeal to the shopper of the premium offer. The package was attractively wrapped and, shortly after its arrival, it was followed by a second letter recapitulating the terms of the consumer premium program. The idea was debated at some length in this manufacturer's marketing offices because there was no desire to risk a charge of bribery. However, in the end it was decided that the package was not of sufficient value to assume the proportions of a bribe. It was also decided that the two letters, properly conceived, would eliminate any small suspicions on this score. Somewhat to the surprise of the merchandising executive, not a single complaint was received and, even more surprising, a few buyers wrote to express their thanks!

Hand-tailored Merchandising for Chains

Pigs may be pigs—but chains are not chains. Even the store units within a single chain now have wide individual variations. One merchandise manager for chain sales through variety chains remarks: "Years ago, the store units of each variety chain were pretty well standardized; even their larger units were almost identical, except for size, to their smaller units. Layouts and merchandise allocations were almost identical. Moreover, most events approved by headquarters would run through all the stores simultaneously. Today, the store units show immense variation. Also, chain management strategy calls for merchandising at the local level to the greatest practical degree; each store is not only different in layout and merchandise allocation but these differences are becoming still more marked. Consequently, even our major events are planned with many variations—and our secondary events are practically hand-tailored for each store unit." Today each store unit of the chains will (in their merchandising practices) have almost as much individuality as an independent store. Incidentally, a health-aid manufacturer pays particular attention to the older (and usually neglected) units of the drug and food chains. This is a good tip.

When Line Shows Trade a Poor Net

There are plenty of lines that—for various reasons—do not show the trade a satisfactory net profit on a margin-turnover basis. But now large retailers are realizing that some of these "loss" departments are really a vital part of total store service. The losses must be written off to service. Actually, it has been axiomatic in retailing that some categories will be merchandised at a loss, some at break-even or a bit better, some at good net profit. It is the "mix" that is important. Several manufacturers whose lines do not show up well in a typical statistical analysis have developed presentations based on what is known as the "contribution theory." This analyzes a line's performance, not exclusively with relation to turnover, markup, markdown, etc., but also with relation to its contribution to the store's over-all strategy, its contribution to other departments, its service-to-customers aspect. A soft-goods brand has furnished its salesmen with a merchandising analysis that proves the value contribution of this low-margin, price-promoted line.

Low-cost Clerk Training

Training programs for salespeople *must* be low-cost—for the good reason that they can accomplish so little! This low-cost need led a group of seven manufacturers of toiletries and related products to bring out, *jointly,* a selling manual. (This manual is distributed through wholesalers to druggists who participate in a promotion involving the products of the noncompeting manufacturers and of which the clerk manual is a part.) The manual aims to show the drug clerk how to take advantage of personal-selling opportunities to meet the self-service competition of the food outlet—although it should be pointed out that the drug outlet is also racing toward self-service. Along with the manual is a quiz contest for clerks based on the contents of the manual. Of course, distribution of such a manual through wholesalers is not efficient. Moreover, even when the manual gets into the hands of salespeople, it is apt to be poorly read, if read at all. But so long as joint participation reduces the cost for each manufacturer to a minimum, then the minimum results that may be achieved could be obtained at a reasonable cost.

On-the-job Training for Salespeople

Too much training of retail salespeople—an achievement that becomes increasingly difficult—consists of booklets and training films. The booklets are seldom read. The films leave an even more fleeting impression. But anything in the way of a sales message that stares the salesperson in the face constantly is almost bound to penetrate (maybe subliminally)! Thus, several sales features, described in a few words each, appearing on a floor or counter fixture that the salesperson can't avoid seeing, will do a better training job than some costly films. The text on a big-ticket package that is constantly seen and handled also constitutes on-the-job training. Another example: For a rug shampoo, a chart was made available listing the number of cans recommended for rugs of various sizes. The chart is hung up in the housewares section. Eventually, at least some salespeople will get to know the proper number of cans to recommend because the facts are in front of them all the time. Too much retailing training is *off* the job; try more ways involving subtle on-the-job training that also sells the shopper.

Help Retailers Figure Profit

For years, one of the great ethical drug houses has compiled an annual analysis of retail drug store profit performance. Now this same firm has developed a "profit guide" for use by its salesmen in their trade calls. The device operates like a slide rule—it includes a sliding panel that automatically shows, as it is moved, the basic operating data applicable to any store being visited. Then, again automatically, it shows in a "window" corresponding profit data for top-profit pharmacies with a similar operating basis. In this way, at a glance it spotlights store operating weaknesses that damage net profit. On the reverse side of the profit guide is a listing of store management suggestions. A somewhat similar technique was used by a maker of hard-surface floor covering— which shows how ideas jump from one merchandise category to another. Incidentally, it has been found that even executives of large chains are intrigued by these net-profit detective devices. Salesmen tend to favor them. And, if the salesman can leave one with each customer, he is particularly pleased.

Foiling Price-tag Switchers

Heard about the price-tag switcher? It's part of the shopper pilferage art. Some shoppers have become quite expert at sleight of hand with price tags. They switch low-price tags to higher-price items—fool the check-out girl in self-service outlets and even fool clerks in some service stores. Retailers get enormously upset about every facet of shopper pilferage; exaggerate it out of all proportions. But what bothers the retailer represents an opportunity for the merchandiser. In this instance, some retailers are fighting price-tag switching by double-pricing techniques. Example: A dressed doll may have the price on a pinned tag and also pasted or marked on the sole of the doll's shoe; presumably the slick shopper will overlook the latter marking. But *single* price-marking is costly to the retailer; *double* price-marking probably costs the retailer more than the actual loss traceable to price-tag switching. Some manufacturers will ship their lines with semiconcealed double marking. (Metal tags which, when removed, can't be reattached are becoming popular.)

Pulling Buyers into Showrooms

For years, simple door prizes were offered as small inducements to buyers to visit a manufacturer's showroom. Then the door prizes became more elaborate. Then the lottery idea was used—visiting buyers were given numbers, and the lucky number won a simple prize. Now the lottery prize, in one instance, is a free trip for two to Acapulco (plus 24 other big prizes). The manufacturer specifies "Nothing to write— nothing to buy—just register at any of our showrooms." Clearly, the lure for showroom visits will be stepped up. For the time being, one manufacturer reports excellent results. He insists it is all part of the broad practice of entertaining buyers, of sending Christmas gifts to buyers, of making various facilities available to buyers when they visit showrooms —including desks, free telephone, even secretarial service. It is also part of the broad trend toward magnificent showrooms. Whether the buyer who is lured into a showroom by a disguised bribe offer buys more will never be resolved. The hard facts of competition suggest that entice-ments for showroom visits will go up and up and up.

Tying Co-op to Performance

Somewhat better co-op control than is typical has been achieved by a soft-goods brand having a very broad distribution with the following plan: The co-op contract provides payment of 50 per cent to the dealer up to 12 per cent of purchases. In addition, a quarterly "promotional allowance" of 6 per cent of purchases becomes available in any calendar quarter in which total advertising by the account amounts to 6 per cent or more of net purchases. Thus, a store with net purchases of $10,000 which spent 6 per cent in advertising would receive $300 of the total $600 co-op ad cost, *plus* the "promotional allowance" of $600—*if* stipu-lated stock and display requirements (checked by the salesmen) have been fulfilled. Total allowance in this example: $900. In this instance, the manufacturer may be buying better inventory and store display than co-op advertising—the promotional allowance in this case is double the co-op allowance and requires no dealer outlay other than for movable inventory. But tying together co-op and inventory store display, under salesmen's supervision, has merit—provided the salesmen are checked.

Merchandising the Intercom

A substantial number of the newer units of the variety and other chains boast of intercom or loudspeaker systems. These are used for music, for news announcements, for announcements concerning store services, and, of course, for merchandise announcements. One variety-chain unit has a full-time announcer. By smartly selecting the merchan-dise to be plugged and by smart commercials, immediate action is won. Time and again, in this particular store unit, sell-outs have been achieved starting within a few minutes after an announcement. Some merchan-disers are, of course, making special numbers available that can be featured via intercom promotion. Others are arranging to provide the commercials which, of course, is logical. But too few merchandisers have made a careful study of the merchandising aspects of variety-chain and other intercom or public-address systems—the type of offers that pro-duce the best immediate response, the best time of the day, the most productive type of commercial. (Of course, be prepared for a rate card!)

Store-wide Big-ticket Events

Will department stores run store-wide events for big-ticket lines that could sell, during the event, to only a tiny part of the store's total traffic? Answer: It's been done. Example: Stereophonic record players have won store-wide promotions in department stores (by their newsworthiness for one reason) that included for one major brand a studio in the home-furnishings section, demonstration display in tearoom and in regular hi-fi section, signs throughout the store, windows, special department trims—all backed up with newspaper and radio advertising. Two basic techniques win this kind of support: (1) Liberal offer to store for its cooperation; (2) dramatic idea backing the event. In this instance, the dramatic idea in addition to the demonstration was registration by shoppers of the oldest phonograph in the area—to be worth $300 in a trade on a new stereo. Another example: A woven floor covering won store-wide promotions with torture tests. Both these merchandisers also developed dramatic display materials—the rug event included a demonstration of cleaning qualities, etc.

CHAPTER 29

Deals, Special Offers

Help the Trade Move Two Items

Because the retailer is so overwhelmed with special off-price deals, he shows a very natural tendency to welcome deals that enable him to move two or more items or lines rather than the single item or line made by the deal developer. Thus, the trade looked with favor on a consumer contest for a dog food in which entry rules called for the shopper to send in a label, not only from any one of this company's dog food items, *but also a label from a noncompetitive food store item.* Because of this provision, the sponsor won another advantage, namely, the company was able to offer (and win) practically store-wide promotion since *any* noncompetitive food item label was acceptable. Thus, the promotional material was planned for use in *all* food sections. This move will spark a trend toward still more extended events of this kind—a producer of one item may establish a rule in a contest, or premium event, or deal event that the shopper turn in labels from *two* noncompetitive items, as well as from the sponsoring item. Maybe the time will come when the requirement will be two labels from the sponsoring items and four labels from as many noncompetitive items. Certainly the trade will give such merchandising events more consideration than single-item events.

Deals That Create Jungle Markets

A large manufacturer recently abandoned a program that involved offering the trade substantial inducements for placing orders considerably in advance of the season. This company discovered that, as a result of this advance-of-season deal, orders were placed almost exclusively by large retailers. Of these retailers, the majority were discount chains and price-promotional outlets. This led to a true jungle-market transshipping, price promotions, no bottom to retail prices, etc. In turn, this led to a situation in which over 50 per cent of this company's volume was being done through price-cutting outlets. Moreover, each season the number of traditional dealers handling the line dropped sharply—they couldn't or wouldn't compete with the price-cutters. The manufacturer reasoned that the discount houses—notoriously tough buyers—were already strong enough to start squeezing. He reasoned that when 65 per cent of his volume came from the discounters, he would be totally at their mercy. Conclusion: It is vital to make a postdeal study to determine precisely where the deal wound up. Several merchandisers report that such studies led them to drop or revamp their deals so as to lessen the attrition they caused by creating jungle-market conditions.

When Retailers Are Not Open to Buy

A maker of fine china anticipated that his retail accounts would not be sufficiently open to buy to carry an adequate stock for the traditionally heavy summer bridal business. Clearly, the less stock carried for a peak season, the less total turnover. The company therefore offered this proposition on orders exceeding a $500 minimum: (1) The order had to be placed during a single month; (2) the retailer was permitted to pay over three months; one-third in thirty days, one-third in sixty days, one-third in ninety days from date of invoice; (3) the retailer could deduct 2 per cent cash discount from each one-third payment; (4) the retailer got an extra 10 per cent discount. It was hoped the plan would not only solve a pressing open-to-buy problem, but, in particular, would stimulate reorders that might otherwise be blocked by a poor open-to-buy situation. The program was called the "Double Bonus Restocking Plan." (The supplier who makes such liberal terms may not get the full benefit of his financial generosity; the buyer may use part of the liberal terms to unfreeze his orders on other lines. This, however, is where the manufacturer's salesman comes in.)

Offering Higher-price Lines as Free Goods

Several manufacturers report that resistance by retailers to new higher-price lines has been lessened by offering the higher-price numbers as free goods in a deal. Thus the same retailer who objects to the investment required by the new higher-price lines finds these very numbers attractive when offered for free in a deal. Moreover, when the new numbers get into his stock, they really act as samples of the new price lines and, if they move well, the retailer has positive proof that he really can move the new numbers in profitable volume. Of course, it is necessary for such a deal to be planned so that the retailer gets a practical inventory of the new number or numbers; clearly, if his stock of the new numbers is totally inadequate, the turnover will be erratic. (This same type of deal, in which the higher-priced numbers are offered as a lure, works well. Even though these numbers are not new, there is something about the offer of a higher-price line for free, as part of a deal, that the trade finds quite attractive.)

Planning Deals for Multiple Sizes

Store turnover checks have indicated that when a deal involves just one size in a multisize line, the sale of the no-deal sizes may fall off sharply during the deal period. In this connection, it is necessary to bear in mind that innumerable lines have been expanded by adding new sizes —and in these lines the merchandising man has tended to overlook the relationship between movement by sizes and deal planning. As a consequence, deals have tended to continue to involve just one or maybe two sizes, as was customary when these were the only sizes in the line. Now deals are being planned that will cover more of the total size range. In dentifrices, for example, several deals have been introduced that involve multiple sizes. For the merchandising executive this introduces new complexities—planning a deal for a number of sizes so that the deal is equally attractive for all sizes (if that is deemed desirable) calls for sharp arithmetic. But this policy is becoming increasingly necessary —and merchandising men would be wise to check back over recent deals to discover exactly what happened in one-size deals to the sizes that were not involved in the deal.

Breaking the Deal Habit

When deal merchandising becomes more of a habit than a planned procedure—it is time to reexamine the deal program. And there is no question that too many deals are more the result of habit and tradition than the result of coldly calculated planning. Example: In food, deals have nearly *tripled* since 1955. Surely the deal planning that was correct in 1955 will not be equally right in 1961 solely for this reason. Another example: In six food classifications, deals increased in a few years from 11 per cent of total merchandise moved in these categories to almost 22 per cent. Again, it is obvious that deals in these categories must be reexamined in view of this totally new competitive setup. In a few food categories, in certain areas of the country, at certain times, as much as 80 per cent of all the brands are concurrently offering a deal! In *many* food classifications 1 out of 5 retail sales are currently in deals. In some categories, deal versus deal has resulted in a stalemate, with the manufacturer taking a smaller margin. Also, experience has proved that in detergents, for example, 90 per cent of deals are bought by regular customers, 7 per cent by floaters. Only 3 per cent are bought by worthwhile new customers—and only half of these stick with the deal brand. Moral: Recheck your deals.

How Big Retailers Regard Trade Premiums

A food company offers chain-store personnel trade premiums consisting of various household items—small appliances, etc. This brand's major distribution is through the larger food-super chains. Under that kind of distributive setup, the trade premium must run quite a gauntlet. The store manager is the one to reach, but he is inclined to be cagey about overordering to get a premium. Moreover, for the premium to wind up in his home involves details and protocol that are highly complicated and even potentially explosive. In general, take-home trade premiums offered to chain-store personnel tend not to be highly productive. Most chains consider this type of premium a nuisance. This is equally true of trade premiums that involve retail supplies such as hand trucks. The latter complicates the chain's accounting and other procedures to a degree that make them downright nuisances. Take-home and supply premiums for smaller retailers have a certain attraction. But, since most manufacturers these days get the lion's share of their volume from a small percentage of giant accounts, it would appear that too many trade-premium offers are bait only for the short end of the volume stick.

The Trade Favors Cost-free Deals

It comes as no surprise that the trade prefers cost-free deals and more manufacturers now tell the trade that their deals invoke no special handling costs, etc. This is one reason retailers have tended to show marked interest in deals that offer the shopper a second package free (or at a markdown), with that second package shipped direct by the manufacturer to the customer. This type of deal involves no special pack, no price cut so far as store price marking is concerned, no special inventory costs for the trade, no special handling costs. (Incidentally, the so-called "New-Products Committee" is increasingly determined to check all of the cost factors involved in what, on the surface, appear to be attractive deals. Retailers are becoming quite convinced that they take the brunt on too many deals—a basic consideration well worth weighing when planning a deal.) Where the free-package deal compels the shopper to send to the manufacturer for a coupon which is then taken to the retailer for the free package, the retailer is obviously involved in costs—and he tends to push aside the manufacturer's argument that this sends the customer back to the store. His answer: "They'd be coming in anyhow."

Combining Cash Discounts with Free Goods

Retailers can—and do—argue interminably about the relative advantages to the trade of an extra cash discount versus free goods as part of a deal offer. That argument will never be fully resolved because among other reasons, retail merchandising concepts are not uniform among all retailers. But one way of keeping everybody in the trade reasonably happy—when planning a trade deal—is to plan a deal that combines an extra cash discount with free goods. Thus, a health-aid item offered an extra discount of $7\frac{1}{2}$ per cent plus eight free of the item on purchases running between $25 to $49.99. From $50 to $74.99, there was an extra discount of 10 per cent plus eight free of the item. (In both instances, the free item was a large economy size.) Incidentally, wouldn't a dealer be rather remiss, in an offer of this kind, not to step up his order from $45 to $50? Clearly, on an order of merely $5 more, he gets an extra $2\frac{1}{2}$ per cent on the total amount, which happens to be $5. And that, probably, was precisely the reasoning of the merchandising man who hatched out this deal. The same reasoning is behind all deals with stepped-up allowances on stepped-up orders.

Unlimited Limited-time Deals

With a trade deal involving, for example, a half-price sale, it is customary to fix a specific time limit for the event. Department stores complain that chain stores continue the deal for weeks after its fixed expiration. Of course, the department store usually returns unsold merchandise (in a cosmetic half-price sale, for instance) to keep open to buy. But the drug chain may continue to sell the half-price merchandise far beyond the specified period. Clearly, it is much easier to set a fixed time limit on deals than to enforce the time limit! And, while no deal ever fully satisfied all retail accounts, it becomes increasingly important— as a brand broadens its distribution into new outlets—to do everything possible to keep all accounts properly competitive. Violations of the time factor in deals can be extremely annoying to the trade. One manufacturer turns his detail force into a clean-up squad at the expiration of a deal to lessen this problem. Others consign deals to achieve the same end.

Advance Payment for Coupon Cashing

For a small hard-goods item, a merchandising plan was developed involving the cashing by department stores of a coupon made available by purchase of a related item in another outlet. Each coupon was worth $2 toward the purchase of a $16.95 retailer in the department store. (The coupon was a box top from a dry-grocery item bought in the food super.) To encourage department stores to cash the coupons—something to which department stores are not partial—these outlets were told that, for the period of the event, they would get, with every six orders of the hard-goods item, one free. "This," said the hard-goods maker, "pays you in advance for cashing customer's coupons—and there's no book work." (Actually, this figured out at normal markup.) It was also pointed out that the filled-in coupons could be used as live leads for other items sold under this hard-goods brand. (Actually, department stores do mighty little follow-up of coupon leads.) In any event, advance payment for coupon cashing done through deal offers may be a new approach to the basic problem of lessening the trade's opposition toward coupon cashing.

Deal Rewards for Moving Merchandise

Trade deals tend to have as their objective loading the trade. Here is a deal that rewards the trade for *moving* merchandise. Involved is a line of electric alarm clocks. The trade was told it could win a free clock (for take-home or sale as preferred) by selling six before a fixed date. The plan was explained on a card included in the pack. Another trade deal aiming in the same direction involved a metal counter display for a drug item used for babies. It was shaped like a doll cradle. Dealers were told the unit was designed for reuse in the home as a toy cradle or as a nursery planter. Presumably this would prod some dealers to move the assortment a bit faster in order to get it home—maybe the wife of a store owner or manager might do the prodding. (It is also possible that some retail people might want that doll cradle badly enough to take the merchandise out of it, put the merchandise up on ordinary display, and cart the cradle home!) A metal display for movie projector lamps was designed for after-use by the dealer as a barbecue grill. And a glass container for an artificial sweetener could be used at home as a brandy snifter.

Those Threats: "We'll throw out your line"

Retailers—large as well as small—are prompt to rage: "We'll throw out your line if you sell to so-and-so." But as manufacturers properly broaden their distribution by going after new types of outlets, the threat is seldom carried out—provided, of course, the line turns over adequately and has a strong acceptance. Actually, the very fact that an important new outlet is added may compel the older outlet to become promotionally active on the item. Example: A maker of melamine dinnerware, with distribution in large department stores, sold its brand to a huge food super. The food super was able to promote a particularly attractive offer —a 5-piece place setting for $1.98. After much gnashing of teeth, a giant department store concluded that its prestige and need for volume could not permit it to turn this market over by default to the food super. So the department store worked out a special promotion with the manufacturer—16 pieces for $5.95—and went all out promoting it. P.S. Both food super and department store did well.

Deal Fixtures for Nondeal Items

The natural tendency, when planning a fixture to hold a special deal, is to think in exclusive terms of the numbers on deal. But there are times when items from the line, retailed on a regular basis, may properly be included in the special-deal display piece. Example: A razor company offered a razor deal that included a razor, a blade dispenser, and a fishing lure, prepacked as a single unit. The display fixture was designed to carry an adequate forward stock of these deal units—but, in front of the deal display, a bin provided space for separate blade packages, shaving cream, etc., in an appealing jumble form. The entire assortment was included in the terms of the trade deal, but the only specially priced item for the shopper was the combination unit. Thus the shopper who didn't want the deal could still buy single items of his choice. And, of course, the attractiveness of the deal won both shelf position and attention that added to the volume of the nondeal merchandise. This plan appeals to the trade—regular stock need not go back into reserve during the deal promotion.

Plan Temporary Price Cuts for Top Effect

When, for reasons of overstock or late season, it is decided that a temporary price slash is advisable, should the planned off-price promotion be made available to the entire trade? Or is the better procedure to make gestures toward the rank-and-file outlets but bunch the off-price promotion with big dealers who are price-promotional minded and who have the power and the traffic to make an off-price event click? Large retailers do not show—understandably—great enthusiasm for off-price events in which all other merchants engage. This does not add to their reputation for low prices and special values, and they are as much interested in building this reputation as they are in the additional volume. Moreover, when the overstock is spread too thin, the giant outlets do not get enough to enable them to back up a giant promotion with the required inventory. A growing number of manufacturers have decided not to spread too thin merchandise that is temporarily price-slashed. Instead, they make it a major event with carefully selected (and rotated) major accounts.

Trade-deal Idea for New Item

The introductory price reduction on a new item that takes nothing from the retailer's margin is, quite naturally, the type of trade deal best calculated to win trade approval. Example: An introductory offer on a new formula for a floor wax. Under the terms of the offer, the trade was in position to offer shoppers 50 cents off on the gallon can, 15 cents off on the quart size. The trade was told: "This introductory offer costs you nothing, because you get the same discount on every can you order." The trade has become pretty expert in determining the cut in margin that it is asked to take on certain deals. The larger the retailer, the more expert the buyers, the more quickly do they spot this sort of thing. The deal that results in a smaller margin for the trade—even though volume may zoom—tends to get a cool, if not a cold, trade reception, especially from better retail accounts. And particularly from the more astute members of the New Products Committee—they are not quite so gullible as some individual buyers.

Getting Orders Far in Advance of Season

If the offer is sufficiently attractive—and that takes in a lot of territory —a sufficient number of dealers may be induced to place *noncancelable orders* sufficiently in advance of a season to enable the factory to achieve economical production. Here is what one maker of a big-ticket line offered for noncancelable in-advance-of-season (for a short-season item): (1) Carload price on original order; (2) carload price for balance of season; (3) free floor plan until a fixed date; (4) free warehousing until a fixed date or free delivery of entire order in one shipment to dealer's warehouse; (5) free demonstration display center; (6) one free model; (7) price protection through the first half of the season; (8) exchange privilege on the inventory; (9) liberal co-op allowance; and, finally (10) believe it or not, a free seven-day vacation for two at a swank Miami hotel!

Trade Margins on Combination Deals

When the premium is an accessory item—that is, an accessory to the parent item—and one that is normally sold by the trade, it is usually

wise to give the trade its usual markup on the premium. Example: A
carry case is a logical accessory for flash bulbs. The same retailers tend
to inventory both items. Therefore, when a maker of flash bulbs brought
out a combination offer that included a tote case, the trade was given an
adequate margin on the tote case as well as on the flash bulbs. The
shopper got the tote case, a $1 value, for only 25 cents by buying 24
flash bulbs at regular price. The dealer bought 2 gross of the flash bulbs
at regular cost and got six of the tote cases for 99 cents. Since the tote
case brought 25 cents at retail in the combination deal, the trade had a
gross profit on the six cases of 51 cents. Similarly, the maker of an
ironing board offered a new model priced at $18.00, with a $4.95 pad
and cover, a $22.95 value for $19.95. The shopper was offered a $3
saving—the dealer got his regular profit margin.

Picking Related Items for Deals

It is becoming something of a trend—the deal that is based on two
items: one made by the deal promoter, the second made by a non-
competitor. The purpose of this type of deal: To persuade the trade
that the deal promoter is being unselfish—he is helping the trade to sell
two items rather than merely one. How is the related item best picked
for this type of deal? A merchandiser who has developed several of these
deals sets up the following criteria: The free-riding item in the deal must
be a staple in enormous daily demand, the sort of item that the majority
of the shoppers in a store at any moment would have a need for, and
the item must be priced in an area that makes the cents-off offer
economically feasible. However, these criteria do not always apply. Thus,
a proprietary offers "50 cents for any gift your customer buys for her
sick child." The customer in this case buys the proprietary for $1.98—
mails in proof of purchase and gets a certificate worth 50 cents toward
the purchase of a child's gift bought in the drug store. As deals multiply,
the merchandising executive must develop new angles that will make the
deal more attractive to the trade. The "unselfish-twin" sale is one of
these angles.

Some Startling Statistics on Deals

One of the largest users of deals in the country, a giant maker of
detergents, reports that 90 per cent of all its deals are bought by its
regular consumers; 7 per cent are bought by "floaters"—the bargain
hunters who have no brand loyalty or brand interest; 3 per cent represents a possible addition of fairly permanent *new* users. These figures
confirm the general belief among merchandisers that off-price deals
usually make such a small lasting increase in sales as to be extremely
expensive. From this same source we learn that in some sections of the

food super, up to 90 per cent of all the items are being "dealed" at one time—for 25 to 50 per cent of all items in a food-super section to be dealed simultaneously is not extraordinary. These statistics must be weighed when deals are contemplated—naturally. But it is also necessary to try to weigh what happens when a brand does not offer deals in a category in which competition regularly offers deals. There is little question that, in at least some classifications, consumer deals are canceling each other out. But competition keeps putting pressure for deals on the merchandising executive—and this tends to make the problem one of trying to evolve deals that will give the "mostest for the leastest."

How Much for Checkstand Location?

As more types of retailers install check-outs in more types of outlets (even some shoe stores have checkstands) this top impulse-buying location becomes salable as a special position in new outlets. The time is near when 75 per cent of total retail will be going through check-outs! Merchandisers are willing—frequently—to pay for such special positions. Question: How much shall we pay for special position at the check-out? Clearly, that question will be answered differently for different merchandise categories and different types of stores. But as one indication of the value placed on it by a strong "brand," the powerful *Reader's Digest* offered an extra $3\frac{1}{2}$ cents a copy on top of the regular margin of 7 cents per copy for check-out display; that's a hefty 50 per cent extra. *Reader's Digest* was suggesting to food supers that they use the *TV Guide* fixture, which had won this location, for *Reader's Digest* too. And that, in turn, suggests that if a manufacturer can't get a solo check-out location, he may get it jointly with another supplier, particularly at a price.

Cutting Claims for Deal Bonuses

One reason for deals that involve extra discounts or rebates which are made available to the trade only when an invoice is sent to the manufacturer or wholesaler—a substantial percentage of accounts never send in the invoice. That's true even if the deal itself may have stimulated them to participate in the merchandising event. When free goods accompany the regular order—this economy is not achieved. Similarly, when the dealer must claim the rebate in other ways—for example, by filling in and giving a rebate card to the jobber's salesman—a certain percentage will neglect to do the necessary to get the rebate. However, it doesn't take the trade long to wake up in this sort of thing; right now there is a developing trade objection to deals that require the trade to mail in invoices. The druggist, for example, actually must contend with scores of this kind of deal. Moreover, competition promptly features the fact that "our deal comes prepacked; no paper work for you; no manual work; no extra cost." This appeal may sell more deals, and thus bring in more profit, than the money saved by unclaimed rebates.

What Do Display Allowances Buy?

Some trade premium offers are offered to the retailer on the basis of a specified minimum display. Typically, a food merchandising plan that enabled the shopper to get a fine picnic basket for $3 with proof of purchase also made the picnic basket available to the retailer if he put in a display of 15 cases of the product. However, this sort of tie-up arrangement can be "leaky" unless the manufacturer's detail men actually put up the display. Trade *agreements* to install displays and trade *performance* are usually two different things. This applies to special discounts offered for store display, for preferred display positions—even where accompanied by written contract. (Will a good account be dropped if the contract is not lived up to?) And it is particularly applicable with respect to large retail organizations—many chains, for example. Headquarters may propose—but the store manager disposes. And he may not have the time, or inclination, to comply with special-display agreements.

"Pick-your-free-goods" Deals

Where free merchandise is offered as part of a trade deal, the free goods are usually preselected by the manufacturer. On some occasions, though, deals are planned so that the retailer is free to select his "bonus" goods from the entire line—or from a part of the line. Example: A maker of rubber accessories made the bonus merchandise available to the retailer, on his own choice, from a preselected group of the line. The deal was explained in this way: "This deal is a real dealer's choice because you need order only what you want from our complete line and you have your choice of the bonus merchandise that suits you best. Write your own ticket. Look through your catalog—check your want pad. Make up your own $24 order, at wholesale list, of assorted rubber products. Then—from any of the profitable items pre-selected as bonus merchandise select your bonus numbers." Elasticity is too rare in most trade deals. With distribution so broad, elasticity in deals is badly needed. "Pick your own free goods" could give elasticity in deals.

Store Displays as a Resale Item

A national beer brand, as part of a promotion keyed to the theme "Holiday Time" (for the Christmas season), included a large ornamental clock for in-store display. The clock featured the words "Holiday Time" on the dial instead of numbers. The beer brand was not featured on the clock. (All of the other promotional material furnished included replicas of the clock.) It was then suggested to the store that the clock could be promoted for resale. Extra clocks were made available to the trade at $15 per dozen, individually boxed. The trade was given a suggested retail price of $2.19. Thus a manufacturer's display piece was merchandised, not only as part of the store's promotional program, but also as a resale item throwing off a satisfactory margin for the trade. A dog-food manufacturer gives the trade an appealing toy dog on the basis of one toy dog free with every 10 cases. (Shoppers can get the dog from the dog-food company for six can labels and $4.95.) Shoppers have insisted on buying the displayed dog—so perhaps this display device will also wind up as a resale item.

Made-to-order Trade Deals

It is extremely difficult to plan a deal that will appeal equally to the wide variety of dealers through which manufacturers sell these days, the wide variety of sizes of outlets, geographical locations of outlets, etc. A maker of small hardware items, for example, may have had trouble enough planning a deal with broad appeal when his sole outlet was the hardware store; today his line may be sold in big volume by food supers, by drug chains, by electrical stores, by auto accessory stores, by marinas. One answer is the make-it-up-yourself deal. Within prescribed limits, this type of trade deal permits the trade to make up a deal order that will best satisfy individual requirements. One manufacturer calls this kind of deal a "special custom assortment" deal. He asks the trade to buy 144 of this item "in any combination of dozen units." The trade then gets 3 free in every dozen.

Deals That Aim for Reorders

In the final analysis, the majority of deals aim simply to put merchandise *into* trade inventory. Moving the deal merchandise out of trade channels and into consumption is, actually, involved in only a minor percentage of all deals. A plan to move deal merchandise off the shelves is becoming more important, however, as the trade totals up its deal costs and concludes that these costs are excessive. This plan need not involve a *complete* program for stimulating turnover of deal merchandise. Indeed, it may involve no more than a trade incentive for moving the deal inventory. Example: A workable plan was based on a reorder deal that was even more attractive than the initial deal. Thus, for a pen, a deal included a special reorder card. When the original deal stock runs low, the dealer mails in the air-mail postage-paid card to the manufacturer for an exceptionally attractive reorder deal. Obviously, this manufacturer has planned the reorder deal so as to make its attractive features prod the merchant into giving the original deal an extra push in order to move it and get the very appealing reorder.

Encouraging Advance-of-season Orders

Early-buying programs for the trade usually wind up by being based on an extra allowance for the early-bird order. Thus, an electric razor offers an extra 10 per cent on orders placed by a stipulated date, which would involve advance-of-season buying by the trade. A maker of portable electric room heaters offers a baker's-dozen deal—one heater free with each dozen when order is placed before a stipulated date. (Interestingly, the bonus heater is listed as the same as the lowest-priced model on the dealer's order.) Early-buy programs should be matched with evidence of faith on the part of the manufacturer; faith in the advance-of-season movement of the line. Thus, the razor company will start its advertising earlier than usual—and makes much of this point in its trade messages. The heater company will do the same thing; this company also offers a special floor fixture to hold the line and makes the point that getting this fixture out on the floor early will encourage early sales. Incidentally, this fixture is sold to the trade for $30 but the trade gets a second heater for free when it buys the fixture and "Sale of the free heater pays for the display and gives you a profit, too."

When a Deal Is "Money in the Bank"

Some merchandisers report that deals have lingered with the trade for months—occasionally as long as twenty months (and this happened in hard-driving outlets). Apparently, through the food super, it takes well over seven months to get rid of merely 80 per cent of deal merchandise. This is on the average, of course, because some deals move out in a matter of weeks. There are many reasons for this slowness in moving deal merchandise into the shopper's hands; one common cause is that the trade may look upon the deal as money in the bank. In brief, the deal terms may be so attractive that the deal is bought, not to accelerate turnover velocity, but to achieve a better mark-on. And, if the terms are sufficiently liberal, the dealer may feel completely warranted in tying up funds in the deal merchandise. (This is as true of wholesalers as of retailers.) Such deals benefit the trade—perhaps. But they seldom benefit the manufacturer, because they simply borrow from the future and do so at most expensive rates.

Payment Plans for Shelf Space

As payment plans for in-store shelf space become more common, they also tend to become more sophisticated, more mature. Instead of simply a flat payment covering all circumstances, shelf payment plans now differentiate between stores of different types, different sizes. Example: A cigarette company offers a food super doing a $1 million annual volume a monthly payment of approximately $5 per month for giving its brands a specific location and frontage space allotment. Markets ranging up to $2 million annually will get approximately $7 per month. Food supers reporting over $2 million annually will be paid $10 per month and more. These payments are based on total store volume—including nonfoods. Payments are made quarterly upon receipt of a notarized statement saying the market has fulfilled the terms of the space-payment contract (a highly necessary legal formality under Robinson-Patman). A drug house offers the drug outlet 75 cents per dozen for shelf display, with the minimum display fixed at one dozen per store. It also offers $2.50 per three dozen floor-stand or off-shelf displays. Another drug house offers 3 per cent on purchases for a two-week floor or mass display. It is, of course, difficult to check the store's performance. Moreover, enforcement of provisions of these contracts creates much ill will.

Turnabout Deals

For one manufacturer to include, in a deal, an item made by a second manufacturer (both known brands) is not extremely unusual. But for two noncompetitive manufacturers to come up with two separate deals using items from the two lines—that's newsworthy. The two items: baby powder and cotton swab sticks—both strong brands. For the baby powder, the deal was a free trial pack of the swabs with the purchase of a 59-cent powder retailer. For the swabs, a free trial can of powder with a 59-cent or 98-cent pack of swabs. Both manufacturers gave the deal separate advertising support. Both deals were independently merchandised through the trade. The combo package for the baby powder featured that item—the combo package for the cotton swabs featured that item. In both cases, however, the item of the cooperating brand was effectively displayed on the combo setup. Incidentally, while a deal of this type is promoted, some stores will continue to sell regular numbers of the two items at regular prices in regular volume, that is, when the merchant just doesn't want to move regular stock back to reserve.

Independents Love "Free" Items for Resale

Retailers—smaller retailers especially—fall strongly for deals that include free items for resale. Example: A color film deal that included a total of eight magazines of film in an attractive counter dispenser and (here comes the free resale merchandise) eight wallet exposure guides for free that were to be sold by the merchant at 10 cents each. The films were a $16.80 retail value—the eight exposure guides at 10 cents each constituted a small plus, but since they were free they had the same appeal to the trade as that magic word "free" continues to have for the consumer. Never underestimate the power of the word "free," in all merchandising! And never underestimate the trade appeal of additional markup, including extra mark-on that comes from a resale accessory that is free to the trade. (The free resale item may not be equally attractive to giant retailers—it complicates the accounting.)

Dealing the Deal

It is sometimes possible to plan a deal in such a way that the basic deal becomes, really, the starting point for several additional deals. It works this way for a drug house: On athletic supporters, the basic deal offering a style and size assortment came to a retail cost of $20. That was the basic deal. Then this merchandiser began dealing with the deal. The result: "Price if purchased with 4 additional dozens of assorted elastic goods—$18. Price if purchased with an additional dozen of assorted elastic goods—$19." This technique of planning a deal so that it moves, not only the deal merchandise, but also other numbers in the line is not done as often as is merited by the idea. Once the trade is in an ordering mood—what better time to plus the sale? (A variation of the same idea for small appliances has developed this way: The dealer ordered any five appliances in the line at full discount and got a $5 credit certificate good on his *next* purchase.)

The Wholesaler's Invoice

In several major merchandise classifications and several major types of retail outlets—drug classification and the drug outlet, for example— deals stating: "To receive free goods, mail in your wholesaler's invoice," have reached epidemic proportions. This is now involving dealers in so much detail as to constitute a positive headache to the trade. At the start, it was a smart idea. Today, it is being overdone. Several manufacturers have dropped this plan—one made a special check of his retailers and found enough of them definitely resentful to warrant the conclusion that "send in your wholesaler's invoice" was creating trade ill will. There are other ways of obtaining verification of proof of purchase—one manufacturer pays his wholesalers to send in duplicates of their customers' invoices involving a deal purchase which, in turn, involves a special payment to the retailer. That at least removes the burden from the retailer—and compensates the wholesaler for his costs. Another manufacturer has turned to coupons in the deal package, which the trade sends in for its extra allowance. There are other ways to get around what is becoming almost a trade curse—weigh them against any existing plan involving the wholesaler's invoice.

Reorders on Short-term Deals

Large retailers complain that suppliers expect them to take in, on one order, a deal inventory adequate for the entire period of the deal. This, complains the retailer (and the wholesaler, too), places an unfair burden on the retailer. It also tends to make the retail buyer cautious. The consequence often is that, if the deal is a success, the deal inventory has been moved before the deal period has expired. One large food-super merchandising executive insists that deal merchandise should be offered on the basis of at least two orders. This makes some sense. But bear in mind that when the trade buyer knows he can reorder a deal, his initial order may be too low. Thus his total deal turnover may be just as limited by inventory shortages as when caution compels him to hold back on a one-order basis. The merchandiser must determine which is the lesser of the two evils. Assuming effective personal selling by the supplier and adequate follow-through (both pretty large assumptions), a two-order policy on deals offered big outlets will usually work better than the one-order policy.

Merchandising Plan for Free Item

In a number of merchandise classifications, when a free item is offered as part of a deal, it is frequently possible to develop a merchandising plan for the free item that will make it more than merely additional mark-on for the retailer. Example: A maker of electric wall clocks developed a program for the rapidly growing spring gift season that included two newspaper ads providing free listing for each dealer placing an order for 12 or more assorted clocks of his own choice. Also included in the tie-in merchandising package were in-store banners, circulars, and a display that accommodated 8 clocks. Then, to top it off, each dealer got a free wall clock—retail value $6.50. With this free clock, the dealer was given a number of ideas for effectively merchandising it—the ideas ranging from sales-incentive suggestions for the store's salespeople to its use as a giveaway to stimulate store traffic. This whole concept of using free items in a deal as a springboard for specific retail floor events has broad application and is too seldom used. It makes the free-deal offer more attractive to the merchant—and more productive as a turn-over stimulator on the retail floor.

The Shelf-stock—Deal-stock Problem

Prepacked deals clearly offer advantages to the trade—but they also raise problems for the trade. The most common problem stems from the obvious fact that regular shelf stock may go dead while the deal is being displayed. Also, deals tend to unbalance regular inventory. Indeed, the IBM systems of large chains frequently indicate a serious slow-down of inventory turn on total inventory of a brand during a deal period, due to sluggish action of regular stock. One solution to this problem developed by a drug house includes a prepacked floor-stand deal that provides unused space in the fixture. The retailer can then fill that space with regular stock of that brand. This unfilled space in the floor fixture may equal about 20 per cent of the total fixture inventory in this instance. Now there is no doubt that some dealers will not take shelf stock off the shelf and put it in the fixture. Other dealers may even put competing brands or nonrelated merchandise in the empty space in the fixture. But enough dealers will merchandise the fixture efficiently to justify the inventiveness of the idea. Moreover, that empty space on the fixture makes a good talking point to the trade—whether used or not.

Free-item Handling Charges

With the retail (and wholesale) trade so acutely aware of handling costs—merchandisers are developing plans involving payments to cover these costs in connection with special events. This is not at all new—where a merchandising plan has involved banding, for example, it has been customary to compensate the trade for the costs. But now this practice is reaching out more broadly. Example: A coffee roaster decided to break into one of our major cities which had no shortage of powerful coffee brands and at a time when coffee was in a very soft market. The company mailed out almost 2 million coupons in the limited area—each coupon good for one free 1-pound can with each 1-pound can bought. Not only was the food outlet paid for handling costs on the coupon—in addition, *the retailer was given 7 cents for each free can of coffee handled* to cover the handling costs on this free item. This, of course, ties in with the increasingly close analysis that larger retailers are giving to their total costs on deals.

Renting Floor Space for Full Line

Payments for space given to fixtures promise to become fairly common —the cigarette companies opened up wide this type of allowance. Now a major appliance company is offering retailers a $2 per month rental payment per appliance displayed on the retail floor—provided the dealer displays the full line. In major appliances, the number of dealers carrying more than a few numbers is a tiny percentage of the total. One major appliance manufacturer, checking the failure of a promotion on a range, found that less than 12 per cent of its accounts had the featured model on the floor. As lines become larger, inducing the dealer to stock and display even one sample from each number in the line becomes increasingly difficult. A variety of plans have been developed to cope with this problem, including particularly liberal terms on floor samples. Now it would appear as though liberal terms are to be plussed with floor-space rental offers. The floor-space rental offer may be made in lieu of co-op advertising, since display on the retail floor is worth more than the typical co-op ad.

Maybe the Trade Will Say "Yes"

There is a constant temptation to turn down certain merchandising plans "—because the trade will never agree to go along with it." Giant retailers do have policies. And proposals may be turned down "because it's against our policy." But the observer regularly notes that large retailers will accept a program that goes contrary both to tradition and practice. Example: Large department stores, it might be concluded, would not approve a free-trial event on a cookware line, especially for promotion to the charge-account list. Yet one of the largest department stores in the country sent out a *special* circular (not a charge-account statement enclosure, be it noted) to its charge-account list, offering a set of aluminum cookware on a free-trial basis. The offer included for free a $5.25 value fry pan (offered whether or not the customer kept the set after the free trial). The entire program is foreign to department store tradition. Yet it was accepted. Time and again, we hear what department stores will do and won't do in tying up with a manufacturer's merchandising event—ditto for food chains, variety chains, drug chains, discount chains. But our observation is that retail policies and traditions are broken daily when the manufacturer's merchandising program is sufficiently attractive.

CHAPTER **30**

Point of Sale:
Fixturing, Display: Demonstration,
Self-service, Self-selection

Lost—Store Display Competitive Status

Many manufacturers are getting *less* store display of their line in 1961 than they got in 1955, although they may be getting the same shelf area in 1961 as in 1955. And that's exactly why they have lost a lap in display competitive status. A large health-aids manufacturer explains it this way: "We were pretty smug about our display status in our outlets. But then we developed a new formula for measuring the current display impact we were winning in our outlets. This formula took in such new measurements as the increase in the number of competing brands over the last five years, the increase in number of competing sizes and price lines, the increase in the total store area of the stores in which we sell plus the larger variety of merchandise classifications carried by these stores. The last point, we considered to be of vital importance because everything in a store competes for the shopper's dollar—the larger the store and the larger the variety of merchandise, the stronger the competition for the shopper's dollar. On the basis of this measurement we concluded that our total visual display impact in our outlets had shriveled without our knowing it." Try this measuring rod on your store display status.

Lease Fixtures to Trade?

Fixture merchandising plans must frequently be developed that will liquidate at least part of the fixturing cost. These programs usually involve sale of the fixture to the trade, generally in connection with a prefixed minimum order. Will the next step involve merchandising costly fixtures on a leased or rental basis? Several fixture manufacturers selling directly to retailers are trying lease-rental plans. The rental of trucks, etc. has won wide adherence among retailers. The advantages to the retailer of renting fixtures would include not having capital tied up, tax advantages, smaller insurance costs. Advantages to the manufacturer would include (1) a persuasive story to the trade; (2) more elasticity in planning for the fixture itself—present cost ceilings might be lifted; (3) more of the cost might be recovered; (4) more elasticity in planning the required merchandise assortment. (Manufacturers are tending to do more financing for the retailer; this might be one facet of this trend.)

Half-steps to Self-selection

Too many self-selection, self-service merchandising programs by manufacturers take one mincing step at a time. But these programs cannot work effectively unless they are fully rounded, complete. Thus, a self-selection package without an appropriate fixture may seriously brake the performance of the package. Or, if prepricing is indicated but omitted—again a self-selection road block is thrown up. A large manufacturer of a soft-goods fashion line (some 600 items when styles, colors, and sizes are totaled up) determined to go to market with a *complete* self-selection program—at one fell swoop. His program included (1) a brilliantly planned self-selection package; (2) preticketing for price; (3) brilliant self-selection fixtures which included, at the top, full color photographic reproductions of selected numbers—and these photos could be changed periodically; (4) a basic stock for that inventory; (5) a simplified, near-automatic reorder system; (6) a dual packaging concept to stimulate multiple sales. The program was launched *as a whole*— and has been a significant success in a category in which even packaging is quite new.

Open Up the Fixture to Related Items

A check in a variety of retail outlets discloses a number of unused floor fixtures—supplied by manufacturers—originally sold to the trade as a complete section, or center, or shop. But these fixtures did not constitute a complete section or classification. The explanation is simple: The manufacturer does not cover the entire classification with his line and his fixture is limited to his own line. Consequently, the trade found that part of a classification was on the fixture—another part in the regular section. And for sound reasons of retail merchandising, the trade did not use these fixtures. A solution to this problem by a company merchandising a hair-care-center fixture was to leave open one entire side of this four-sided fixture. On this one side, the retailer could feature items of hair care not made by this manufacturer. What is more, the company supplying the fixture even listed the items that might be placed on this open side in order to make it in fact a complete hair-care center. The bitter competition for fixture space will compel other plans of this kind which give the retailer what he requires for sound retail merchandising instead of being planned primarily from the manufacturer's side of the fence. (A floor stand for a drug line includes open space for several related but noncompetitive items.)

Pay Retailers for Demonstration Models?

Over 65 per cent of the retailers of a major appliance line did not stock a single unit of a special model range that was being featured in current advertising. So regular stock is a problem. Getting retailers to stock *demonstration* models, which present an ultimate disposal problem, is an even greater problem. Solution: An offer of $50 to put in a demonstration model of a new washer! Other companies offer extraordinary terms on demonstration models—some offer both allowances and special terms. Many offer free demonstration models. But while signed contracts accompany these arrangements, the common experience is that the demonstration model too seldom is put through its demonstration paces. (Maybe electric current should be paid for? But—has the dealer enough energy to press the button?) Conclusion: Don't conclude that paying retailers to install demonstration models will solve the demonstration problem; it's only a small beginning. The next step must be to give the trade very simple demonstration techniques. And maybe "mystery shoppers" to check demonstrations would provide a further incentive.

Test Those Multiple Displays

While retailers have been quite willing to give many brands display in multiple locations, neither retailers nor manufacturers have done much to test the actual sales performance of these secondary locations. There are a lot of opinions but few facts. In particular, retailers want to know whether the secondary location draws volume primarily from the main display—or whether it wins primarily *additional* volume. A health-aids merchandiser put its secondary displays to an actual test and is able to report in trade advertising that "locations will increase Blank sales 500 per cent." The store audit offers an excellent method for obtaining a true case-history record of the contribution made to total store volume by multiple displays of a line. And with such case histories, multiple displays are more easily won. However, despite the general retail belief that for certain products and brands the multiple display is justified, the retailer is even more convinced that he hasn't shelf space. Store audits of multiple displays can do two things: (1) Show how space has been found for multiple displays by successful retail organizations; (2) present persuasive figures proving that the multiple displays actually do provide plus volume.

Dramatizing a Fixture's Tiny Space

Retailers are all—every one—convinced that in-store space is at a premium. They are always "pushing out the walls." While this is largely folklore (any retailer can find waste space in his store when he is so minded), it still is a fact that whatever the retailer firmly believes, the merchandising man is wise to include in his planning. One merchandiser of a small item wanted to convince the trade that his small fixture really required a tiny amount of space. To put this over, he ran a trade ad captioned: "Boost your sales of Blank's with only this much counter space." Then, underneath the caption was a block of white space with measurements showing that it was $1\frac{3}{4}$ inches deep plus $4\frac{1}{4}$ inches high. Text in the white space read: "This is all the counter space you need to display 12 units of Blank's." That small block of white space was mighty persuasive proof that here was a fixture for which the merchant would have little trouble finding a spot, even in a store in which the walls are —presumably—bulging. (Another fixture was presented to the trade as requiring no more space than a dollar bill!)

Restudy Fixture's Reserve Section

Self-selling floor- and counter-merchandise fixtures are seldom as well planned in the space for reserve stock as in the space for the forward stock—although the end result is bound to be unbalanced forward stocks, shortages of best-selling numbers. A maker of men's underwear has developed a floor fixture that gives forward display to 36 dozen garments —and which holds still another 36 dozen in easy-to-get-at reserve compartments. This is keen merchandising. Generally speaking, the selling-stock sections of merchandise fixtures are now well planned for self-service and self-selection. The next step is to plan the reserve-stock sections equally well. And bear in mind that an automatic reorder system, or a semiautomatic reorder system, is becoming, in some classifications, an integral part of the merchandise fixture. Inasmuch as sales-people and stock clerks tend to be closer to the fixture than buyers and merchandise managers, one manufacturer arranged a reserve-compart-ment and reserve-stock study among the lower ranks. Result: Hasty changes in his fixture. Try exposing your fixture to this kind of check.

Is Your Line in the Wrong Section?

Through tradition, carelessness, space limitations, or downright cussed-ness, retailers will sometimes insist on putting a line in a section where it cannot perform properly. Example: A reducing-biscuit line found that some food outlets were putting the line in the specialty section, the delicacy section, the diet section—sections, incidentally, that do not have particularly high traffic counts. Tests have shown that the line does better in the cracker section and that it belongs nowhere else. The com-pany is therefore pointing out to the trade, through its salesmen and through trade advertising, that sales go up 20 to 30 per cent when the line is displayed in the cracker section; that the line is advertised as a cracker on its TV programs (a good point). Case histories giving specific turnover figures are helpful in solving this problem. Where space limita-tion in the desired department is the cause, it is up to the supplier to prove with figures that his line will earn its keep. Plans that lessen space requirements will also help.

Elevated Fixtures Capture Air Space

In the self-selection and self-service outlet, with its vast open display of merchandise, the cube is taking the place of the square as the basis of selling-floor area measurement. We are coming into an era of three-dimensional retailing; even the common types of self-service fixtures are adding extra tiers, extending higher into the air. Both to capture more air space and to relieve the monotony of acres of merchandise put out in strictly uniform display, retailers are looking with favor on high-up fix-tures supplied by manufacturers. The variety chains have favored these overhead fixtures for some time; now both these outlets and the food super and the drug chain are looking up into the air. (Another reason for these fixtures is to balance out the terrific square-foot costs of new-store construction.) Makers of razor blades, cellophane tape, and headache tablets are among those capitalizing this trend in retail thought with air-space fixtures. These fixtures rise high above the counter. They usually are so designed as to permit the salesperson to see through from the rear of the fixture—although this becomes less necessary as floor attendants operate from out in the aisle.

The Strolling Demonstrator

The strolling demonstrator, parading through the aisles (or in store restaurants, rest rooms, etc.), far from the sponsoring department, has been traditional in department stores. But the strolling demonstrator has been limited—in department stores, primarily to fashion merchandise, and particularly ready-to-wear. A major appliance producer was able to persuade a group of department stores to permit models to stroll through the store (very likely for a consideration) carrying meat sandwich signs during the appearance at each store of a kitchen planning consultant. There are more strolling demonstrators in more department stores plugging more merchandise classifications than ever before—and still more are on the way. (This is one answer of the upstairs departments to the great emphasis department stores are putting on the main floor.) Also interesting is the appearance of strolling demonstrators in a few chain-store units—variety, drug, food. The floating demonstrator will become more common in these outlets, too—these outlets are strongly inclined toward multiple locations, and the roving demonstrator is a form of multiple location.

Capitalizing Consumer Folklore

In many lines, consumers have formed their own testing techniques. Some of these tests are merely folklore; some may have a sound basis. But the big point is that innumerable shoppers firmly believe in these simple tests. Many merchandisers are making capital of these tests. Case in point: In men's shoes, men habitually flex a new shoe to *test* its flexibility. Shoe salesmen also flex a shoe—in order to *prove* its flexibility. One shoe brand therefore made some of its numbers particularly flexible —and then built a complete campaign around this factor of flexibility. Whether extreme flexibility adds to foot comfort may be debatable; but it isn't debatable that a test of unusual flexibility is unusually effective in selling men's shoes—children's shoes, too. So search for tests, valid or otherwise, that users have come to swear by; then, starting with the design of the item itself, make merchandising capital of these consumer tests. Give the trade whatever is needed to make the test—and keep the test simple, very simple.

Display and Self-service Fixture

Small hardware items are being merchandised self-service with amazing rapidity. Panel display fixtures are commonly used in merchandising these lines. But these panel fixtures have tended either merely to show samples or to function as self-service units. Now a maker of bathroom accessories has combined *both* functions—this display panel features both self-service items and one permanently attached accessory of each number for nonstop selling. Combining the two functions in this way has several merchandising advantages; principal advantage is that there is always at least one of each item on open display so that—so far as display is concerned—there is no out-of-sight problem. An empty section on a self-service fixture cannot sell—under self-service and self-selection, the unseen tends to be unsold. Keeping the fixture constantly stocked is therefore a constant problem. While this concept doesn't solve the problem of *out-of-stock* it does lessen the problem of *out-of-sight.*

Selling from Freight Car

Perhaps the appliance industry pioneered selling from freight cars or from trailer trucks in parking lots, etc. Now this concept of selling from freight cars has been successfully applied to household paper products by a wholesale distributor. This distributor has ordered some 65 carloads of a leading brand of household paper products. The distributor, in turn, prevailed upon nine food supers to buy full carloads—and also sold them on the unique idea of getting shoppers to come to the freight yard and put items directly into their own cars. Shoppers have certain symbols that spell bargain; buying from a freight car or trailer truck is that sort of symbol. Incidentally, the use of huge trucks as traveling exhibits, traveling demonstration centers, is growing in popularity. Example: An auto tire producer travels a truck showing its tires. The truck is parked at gas stations—promotional material is set up —local ads are run over dealer's name inviting public to come see.

Sixteen Sizes for One Fixture?

Do 16 sizes for just one fixture sound extreme? It didn't strike a maker of electric clocks that way. His reasoning: (1) Electric clocks are sold in many types of outlets; (2) in each outlet type, there are stores ranging from giants to tiny, with clock departments similarly variable in size. Some may want or be able to display only three clocks. Others may display up to 40 clocks. Therefore, a major fixture developed for the line is actually available in 16 sizes, although the design remains basically the same. Moreover, still mindful of the enormous variations in trade requirements for fixtures, this manufacturer has developed a unique service—a display consulting service. This service offers dealers—for free—display designs, display fixtures, custom tailored to individual requirements. Dealers who want the custom service must fill in a questionnaire and also supply snapshots of the store area where the display would be used. In this era where unseen is unsold—extra effort to make a line persuasively seen in the store will justify the investment.

Outposts for Bulky Big-ticket Items

The multiple-location merchandising concept is generally looked upon as having application only with respect to small-ticket items, and perhaps only staples. But one of the big rug makers has developed a special fixture for its rugs which it merchandises as a *second* carpet department or section. Certainly there seems no limit with respect to what people will buy on impulse; even rugs are susceptible to impulse buying. (Always bear in mind that there are varying degrees of impulse.) Moreover, a rug outpost may remind some shoppers in one part of the store that they ought to get up to the regular rug department (as they had perhaps planned to do before leaving home). In any event, there is little doubt that the multiple-location concept is destined to spread considerably beyond the staple, fast-turn merchandise classifications for which it is now employed. One-stop outlets, impulse shopping, the time limitations of the shopper—all these and other factors make certain that outposts for bulky big-ticket merchandise are on the way. (In Sears stores, power mowers may be displayed at a dozen locations.) Special fixtures for these outpost locations are a must.

Shopper-conducted Demonstrations

Too often, salespeople will not conduct demonstrations—or will stage them indifferently. Consequently, some manufacturers are now developing plans that permit shoppers to conduct their own demonstrations. (And when shoppers do this, if the salesperson watches out of the corner of his eye, he gets some on-the-job training.) Examples: (1) A device for a TV set that permits street traffic to demonstrate its remote controls by pressing buttons attached to outside of window; (2) a vacuum cleaner has a shopper-conducted demonstrator called the "push-button market place"; (3) a mechanical "bedding selector" permits shoppers to lie down on a mattress and note how it distributes the weight at 17 points; (4) a portable radio-antenna maker has a counter unit that includes an ingenious self-demonstrating device; (5) an electric iron maker suggests to its dealers that they allow the shopper to try a "scratch test" herself; (6) for dust-spraying equipment, a chart with push-buttons enables shoppers to plug selector leads into 97 holes—a bulb lights up near the illustrated item which has been automatically selected.

Display Spectaculars Break Store Rules

For point-of-purchase materials, retailers don't agree on what they will use or what they won't use. Indeed, in many large retail organizations, policies may differ by departments! But every experience proves that a display piece that promises great promotional *excitement* can crash through store policies. Best current example is the so-called "display spectacular." Food supers with presumably rigid rules and extreme space limitations have used such spectaculars furnished by suppliers as (1) a 10- by 5-foot display unit featuring six cakes lighted in sequence with a flash motor; (2) an 11-foot wire tower filled with a display of 4,800 packages of a food item; (3) a 22-foot fire engine (2 feet wide) constructed of case wraps for household paper (available for a 40-case display); (4) a huge bright yellow outdoor umbrella. The display spectacular, conceived with an almost complete *disregard* of store rules, has been used by every type of major outlet (including department stores) that would never use such displays!

Dangers of "Take-one" Displays

A maker of a mass-consumed item offered a premium through a point-of-sale display. The premium involved a billfold at less than half price. Attached to the display piece was a pad. The pad contained mail-in order blanks for the premium. The shopper was to take one blank—fill it in and mail it to the manufacturer. Thus the retailer was freed from handling charges, which, of course, he likes. But in a number of stores that pad of order blanks disappeared in short order— children, in particular, yanked off entire pads (just because they are children). In most instances, there were no more order blanks long before the deal merchandise had been moved. This is one of the ever-present dangers of "take-one" offers attached to an exposed display. Whether the take-one offer involves a mail-in blank or a sample of an item—the chances are that in many, if not most, stores, the display will be stark naked long before it should be. Take two looks at take-one displays—they work better in theory than they do in actual practice.

The Drop in Package-reading Time

Every merchandising executive knows that the competition for shopper reading time for the store-displayed package has zoomed even faster than the competition for reading time for media ads. Reasons: (1) Enormous over-all increase in packages for every merchandise category; (2) total trend toward vastly increased amount of packaged merchandise out on open display; (3) more competitors in every merchandise classification; (4) the use of the package to carry an ever-wider variety of merchandising messages—premium offers, off-price events, cross-couponing, etc. And, of course, the entire situation is made still more acute by the increasing rapidity with which the shopper buys—less shopping time per purchase means still less reading time per package. Several merchandising executives, as a consequence, are planning to give package copy the same expert copy ability given to the highest-priced TV commercials; to abbreviate copy in telegraphic style; to improve copy layouts for legibility; to place prime copy message so it can be seen from any angle; to use overlays, script, arrows, other devices to focus attention.

Finding Space for Fixtures

Too many fixtures are competing for the same space. It will usually be easier to win display space if overlooked space is aimed at. Where to find overlooked space for fixtures? Right here: (1) Counter merchandisers on stilts to straddle other counter merchandisers. (2) Display units which can be hung from other manufacturer's floor fixtures—particularly the sides of floor dump baskets. (Use adhesive backs on display cartons. These satellite fixtures are getting more of a play.) (3) Merchandisers for wall shelving designed for viewing from the side rather than from the front (both sides). These will fit the space normally taken by the product, but cause it to stand out. (4) Over gondola fixtures. (5) Over aisle fixtures (chandelier type). (6) Fixtures which will attach to doors and poles. (7) Fixtures which attach near the base of glass display cabinets and extend out into the aisle. (8) Fixtures which attach to the underside of shelving—occupy the air space between shelving.

Put a Price on That Fixture

Where a fixture stocks a sizable inventory—which means that the fixture is sizable and therefore costly—it is, of course, customary to plan the package so that the merchandise investment by the dealer will underwrite the cost of the fixture. Then the fixture itself is listed as being free. But a maker of greeting cards—a field in which the trade is on the receiving end of lavish fixture offers—decided that better results would be obtained if the trade felt it was taking in the fixture itself, even though the investment might be a small one. Therefore, when this company brought out a new rack costing $40 that would stock a $240 inventory, the rack was included with the inventory, *but at an extra cost of $10*. It was put this way: "The rack is included at a discount price of only $10, making the total for both rack and stock $250." As fixtures supplied by manufacturers become more elaborate, and therefore more costly, policies for merchandising the fixture itself need review. In too many instances, fixtures are being given to the trade gratis—fixtures that could be merchandised to produce enough to cover at least part of the fixture cost, even in fields where dealers are bombarded with fixture offers.

Stock Boys Are Not Artists

Stock boys are not artists—neither are rank-and-file salespeople. Example: A new dog food was given a package design that gave major space to the picture of a dachshund. That dachshund was stretched over *three* packages—its head and back on one package, the middle of its body on a second package, the rear end on the third package. Presumably the food-super stock boy would put up those three packages in proper sequence—which would unquestionably make a really eye-catching display that would steal the shelf in the dog-food section. But stock boys just don't work that way—if 1 per cent (even though specially paid) were to set up the packages in proper sequence, that would be remarkable. And, even if stock boys did set it up in proper sequence, the chances are that the three packages would not all face directly front —so the effect would be marred. Moreover, once the shopper removed one package—the effect would again be marred. And, if the manufacturer's own detail men set up the display in the morning—what would it look like by noon on a busy day? The ideal package, from this standpoint, is the package that sells from *any angle*—any other approach in package design involves the risk of decelerated shelf selling.

Fixtures for the Small Fry

With family shopping making new peaks each year, manufacturers are turning to fixtures that will appeal particularly to the small fry. Example: A maker of children's shoes reports a unique success with a fixture called the "Lollipop Tree." It held a number of lollipops and put both mother and child into a good mood. Retailers will show a strong preference for fixtures that appeal to children—among other reasons so as to have something in the department that will keep the little savages *undestructively* occupied! Damage and loss on the retail floor mounts automatically as juvenile traffic increases. Consequently, a lollipop tree which gives the youngsters a lollipop to suck and thus occupies their energy and thoughts for at least a time is welcomed by retailers. To date, few fixtures have been designed specifically for youngsters. Here, therefore, is a phase of fixturing that still offers plenty of opportunity for exploitation and not solely by makers of children's merchandise either.

Incentives for Consumer Demonstrations

Years ago a vacuum cleaner first offered a giveaway of small value to women who visited stores to witness a demonstration. Since then, the value of the incentives offered to prospects attending a demonstration has climbed and climbed. Now one manufacturer enables his retailers, not only to offer an attractive giveaway, but also arranges matters so that each woman getting the giveaway becomes eligible for a drawing each week by the dealer, with the winner of the drawing getting free the item that is being demonstrated. Yet where the dealer stages the demonstration (even when he may get an allowance for a temporary demonstrator), the demonstration is too often poorly staged. Frequently, the dealer is totally unequipped to put on the demonstration. One manufacturer who checked during a demonstration drive found that practically the only worthwhile demonstrations were given by factory-provided demonstrators. Conclusion: The shopper incentive to witness a demonstration may not be nearly so important as a total demonstration program that may reach fewer shoppers but will give each one a more persuasive demonstration.

Itinerant Display Headaches

An itinerant window display for a high-priced stereo set has been welcomed by top retailers. Reason: The eight-panel display gave detailed facts on this new line which had the trade as bewildered as the shopper. Reports one dealer: "It tells window shoppers more than our salesmen know! It thus saves floor selling *time,* and pinch-hits for our salesmen." (It would do an even better job as a robot salesman on the floor!) In practice, there are itinerant-display headaches: (1) The dealer bangs it up quite a bit in putting it up, taking it down; (2) he doesn't pack it well—it may arrive at the next stop in deplorable condition, even though a special container is provided; (3) he doesn't pay much attention to time schedules—it may "get lost" in his shipping department; (4) some vital parts may never be shipped; (5) he may send it by the wrong transportation, to the wrong address, at the wrong time. The manufacturer must take care, through his own people or through a service organization, of every itinerant-display detail. Otherwise—expect the worst!

Perpendicular Floor Merchandising

One of the great canned-soup producers has been trying for years— and with some success—to convince the food super that its line should be displayed vertically rather than horizontally. Now the food chain and some drug chains are beginning to think in terms of perpendicular merchandising for other categories. One large food-super chain reports: "We have found perpendicular merchandising more productive than horizontal. Our volume in fast-moving items has increased; and the slow-moving items have jumped as much as 43 per cent over a year's time. We used to put deodorants on the bottom shelf. Now after striping up and down, deodorants have become one of our best items in regard to profit. Striping vertically provides more adequate exposure for higher profit items." This offers suggestions to merchandisers—including planning certain fixtures for the food supers that employ vertical principles. This trend could bring about vast changes in the whole concept of facings in the food super.

When Salespeople Depend on Commissions

Look at the rug department. The salespeople get a large part of their income from commissions. They take customers in order. If the customer is interested in a small purchase, the salesman wants to "get back in line" quickly; he almost runs away at the first chance. If the customer makes a large purchase, the salesman still wants to get back in line—and he won't fuss, for example, with a small scatter rug after having sold a $1,000 wall-to-wall installation. On these small-ticket items P.M. can seldom be sufficiently attractive. Solution: One manufacturer has turned to robot selling via ingenious fixturing and other special displays. His plan also includes special allowances to buy special location, special display, special tie-ups with related big-ticket items, etc. Finally, he has run trade advertising complimenting store buyers on doing a good job. It's been very effective.

Retailers Worry about Fixture Pilferage

Retailers talk loud and long about shopper pilferage. Actually, retailers don't know what percentage of stock shrinkage comes from shopper pilferage, from employee pilferage (which is the higher of the two), from combinations of shopper-employee pilferage, from poor accounting, from poor internal communications, from organizational gaps between receiving-marking operations and the selling floor. (Out of every $20 of stock shortage the shopper is seldom responsible for more than $1!) But—retailers *do* fret about shopper pilferage and they turn down certain self-selection fixtures because "we'll be stolen blind." One answer: A maker of combs provides a fixture in one form for open display and self-service, in another for pilfer-proof closed display. The retailer thus has a choice. Several fixtures offer a sound-making attachment—a bell tinkles when the fixture is touched. This seems to give dealers assurance. Another manufacturer conducts store tests, keeps precise records, is able to prove statistically that the pilferage rate rises minutely, while volume goes up sharply.

Shortcomings of Gravity-fed Fixtures

The gravity-fed fixture is quite popular. It encourages self-selection; it keeps the merchandise on attractive display; it lessens spoilage; it tends to get out faster the inventory that is older. A drug trade supplier, however, found that failure to arrange the fixture to enable the clerk to check the inventory too often meant that both clerk and shopper discover *simultaneously* that the gravity-fed fixture has no more gravity! It has run out of merchandise! Another problem: In some instances, the package was not designed with a gravity-type fixture in mind; consequently, sometimes the package does not show up well. This is a pick-up-and-replace-it shopping age. But it is not usually easy to replace an examined item that has been lifted out of a gravity-fed fixture. Retailers complain about pilferage. If the fixture is placed behind other merchandise it stops selling; unreachable is unsold in the gravity-fed fixture. Design can correct some of those weaknesses.

Plussing Store "Demo" out on Street

For a line of electric housewares, a complete in-store demonstration plan was plussed by arranging to supply the store with a man in a "gingerbread suit" to parade up and down in front of the store for a full week. The demonstration featured gingerbread; there were cutouts of gingerbread men in the window and in the housewares department; thus the tie-up was logical. It was not accidental that the best seller during the event was the roaster used to bake gingerbread cookies. This may suggest to other manufacturers the employment of modern versions of the sandwich man to march around shopping centers. Shopping centers are stepping up their promotional activities as competition between centers increases and ideas such as this will be welcome. A soft-goods merchandising executive has been compiling a record of joint promotional events staged by shopping centers for use in planning merchandising-promotional programs for his line. This line is usually stocked by a number of the stores in most shopping centers, which makes tie-ups for the line in joint shopping center events entirely logical. Have you studied the potentials for winning merchandising emphasis for your line in shopping center joint events?

Planning Short-season Fixtures

Merchandise fixtures are now in the age of specialization—they are being planned more and more for specific and for special merchandising occasions. Thus, there are now special fixtures in certain lines for specific holiday events. To merchandise these fixtures economically, novel ideas are being used. A lamp fixture for a short season was designed for a three-week sell-out, and the merchandise assorted accordingly. The items were prepacked and the packages price-marked. The fixture could be set up completely in a few minutes—all stocked. And the fixture's cost was carefully calculated so that it would be in sound ratio to a three-week turnover. A series of tests enabled this manufacturer to show figures indicating a splendid three-week movement and suggesting that the fixture actually produced during the limited period three times the average sales of other staple items per linear foot of floor space and six times the profit. A second manufacturer who provided a fixture for Father's Day (for razors) so designed the stand that it could be converted into after-occasion use. The problem here, of course, is to make the conversion easy—and to persuade the retailer to make the conversion—neither is easily accomplished.

Who Makes the Display Decision?

Offering the trade contest awards for displays—window or interior displays—promptly raises a question that too often is ignored, to wit: Who in the retail store makes the decision to install a display? In some instances it may be the display manager—where there is one. But more often it may be a store manager, a merchandising manager, a department manager, or even a field supervisor. Display contests (window or interior) have been losing their effectiveness because some giant retailers tend to view them somewhat dimly; nonetheless, in every trade there is almost always at least one display contest running at all times. Consequently, one manufacturer reports that he is now supplementing his display prizes, which were formerly offered exclusively to the display manager, with prizes for the several other store people, including the store manager. (This line is sold primarily through the drug chain.) Basically, the decision to put on a display is a *merchandising* decision, not a display decision—and prizes should be awarded accordingly.

The Self-selection Mobile Cart

Three great retail merchandising developments are combining to make the self-selection mobile cart a highly acceptable fixture for a number of merchandising classifications. The three are self-selection; multiple locations for a brand or item; constant shifting of locations for items. When women's gloves were made elastic so that one size would fit all hands, they became a logical item for a self-selection cart that would be mobile. A glove manufacturer who designed such a cart now has this one-size glove department on the main floor of close to 100 major department stores.

It is interesting to note that these self-selection carts on wheels are appearing also in variety chains, drug chains, and even in food chains. They are being neatly designed. They usually are made part of an assortment purchase. They usually come with an automatic or semiautomatic reorder plan. They really constitute a new type of outpost section. And several now on the planning board will be somewhat larger than the early models (which were the same size as the food-super cart from which they were adapted) and will include several items rather than just one.

New Lure for Winning Windows

A maker of portable radio and TV sets offered an "outdoor" window display setup that included some 10 items appealing to the fisherman. The items ranged from hip boots to landing net to bait bucket. Total retail value of the equipment—$65. The window theme was logical, since it tied up the great outdoors with the portable radio and TV sets. And fishing and the outdoors obviously are well related. The retailer was to put the full display in his window and then, presumably, when the display had served its purpose, he would put the fishing paraphernalia to its proper use. Window-display items that may later be used by the dealer will likely appeal to some merchants—smaller merchants in particular. (And in some cases, Mrs. Dealer will save the items for later use as gifts!) The idea's appeal to large chains, department stores, and other giant outlets is dubious.

Fixturing for High-margin Numbers

A new concept in fixturing involves the premise that it is possible, in this self-service, self-selection age to stimulate the movement of the higher-margin numbers in a line by smart fixturing. Thus, a maker of light bulbs (a line that runs from low-margin standard numbers to high-margin special numbers) is offering the food super and other outlets a fixture designed to give *major emphasis* to the high-margin numbers. The low-margin numbers in this fixture are jumble-displayed way down at ankle position in the fixture. The high-margin numbers get not only the major part of the fixture, but also the most desirable eye-level position. Moreover, showing the low-margin numbers in jumble display automatically makes the packaged high-margin numbers look that much better by comparison. In general, it is being proved that smart fixturing can lead the hands of the shopper to the higher-margin numbers, and fixturing can turn this trick more effectively than can most retail salespeople. Check your fixtures, then, for merchandising emphasis on numbers that give all concerned the best margin.

Fixtures for the Bulkiest Items

The makers of room-size rugs are showing the way to all producers of bulky big-ticket lines in brilliant fixturing for self-service, self-selection retailing. Example: One large rug maker now has a fixture that displays no less than 36 rugs each 9 by 12 feet. (Remember how these rugs used to be stacked on the store floor and how a porter would shift them for customer inspection?) The weight of these 36 rugs is considerable; this is a true bulky item. Yet the fixture requires a minimum space and is so smartly engineered that even a woman shopper can flip one rug after another *by herself* for self-inspection. The engineer's talents must be brought in to design fixtures for the bulkiest items, with the merchandising man setting down the requirements which include minimum space; minimum maintenance; use either by retail salesman or shopper; design for both self-service and self-selection; design also for the impulse shopper (*all* merchandise, including big-ticket lines, is subject to an amazing amount of impulse buying); design to permit automatic demonstrations where indicated; design also for on-the-job training of the retail salesperson.

Add a Demonstrable Feature

Whether an ice-cube compartment is the *major* feature of the refrigerator is surely debatable, but clearly an ice-cube gadget that presumably lessens the ice-cube problem can be a major factor in making the sale. Similarly, whether an oven door that lifts off is really a major factor in the use of an electric range could be debated, but it certainly offers opportunity for a quick, easy, and dramatic demonstration. Improved features for a product are, of course, important. But perhaps more important is a new feature that lends itself to exciting demonstration. (A scratch-proof bottom for an electric iron *may* qualify as a major plus—in any event it was made the basis of a dramatic test.) Sound cynical? The merchandising man who isn't yet a cynic ultimately will be! Merchandising isn't exclusively a matter of sound logic; illogic plays a big role in merchandising. A *demonstrable* new feature—like a hearing aid powered by the sun (not necessarily a better hearing aid) or the electric wrist watch—is sound merchandising.

Extending the Life of Special Event Displays

There's a constant temptation to develop ideas that will lengthen the life of a special event or seasonal display. Example: A cigarette display for Father's Day, which had a cutout of King Pop on top. Dealers were offered an Uncle Sam hat to replace King Pop's crown after Father's Day—and thus make the display timely for July 4 promotions. Where displays are serviced by the manufacturer's own representatives, these ideas have some merit. But when the retailer himself (store managers, clerks) must make the change—chances are that too often it won't be done. If the change is sent along with the original display, it won't be on tap even if the inclination to use it exists—which isn't too often. If the change is sent along later, its chances of arriving at precisely the right moment are slim. And if it does arrive at exactly the right moment, it still may not be used—either because the merchant is a bit tired of seeing the display or more likely, another manufacturer's or wholesaler's man has been around in the meantime with something that appeals to him.

More Sell on Bulky-item Fixtures

More big-ticket items are moving into the areas of preselection, self-selection—even self-service. In consequence, fixtures for bulky items are coming into general use. But too many of these fixtures simply put out these bulky items in attractive and space-saving display. That means that too much of the sale must still be made by uninformed salespeople. Typical is a floor fixture showing up to half a dozen large-size fans. There is nary a word of product feature in the display—and no invitation for a do-it-yourself demonstration. Price is kept secret. On the other hand, an air-conditioner supplied its trade with a floor fixture which, through illustration and text, summarized the product's major features. The customer could give himself a demonstration—presell. (A camera fixture permits self-demonstration of major features. An electric clock fixture permits a self-demonstration of a lighted dial feature.) Incidentally, when the salesperson's eye wanders to the display often enough, he is bound to absorb some of this information—this is on-the-job training for salespeople, perhaps the only effective program for training salespeople.

Two Counts against Floor Displays

Retailers cannot use 10 per cent of the floor displays offered, solely because of space limitations. But a merchandiser who studied this situation reports that a single-size floor display is offered all outlets. Even the chains find this objectionable—a chain's various store units may run from a few thousand square feet to 50,000 or 100,000 square feet. Most chains have A, B, and C store units graded by size—but few floor merchandisers are planned for the space and volume situation of the individual store units of a chain. (This same reasoning applies to most point-of-purchase materials offered to chains as well as to independents.) In addition, if the merchandise in the prepacked floor stand is not prepriced, it is obviously necessary for the chain's warehouse (or the individual store) to go through the considerable manual labor involved in opening the fixture, perhaps taking out the merchandise, pricing it, putting it back into the fixture, closing up the fixture for shipment to the individual stores.

Show Retailers the Way Home

Too few manufacturers whose lines are, or will be, or should be winning plus volume through in-home selling by their retailers do more than merely encourage the trade to ring doorbells. As a consequence, retailers must learn the difficult art (and it's mighty difficult) of in-home selling through expensive experience. However, in the floor-covering field, several manufacturers have developed complete in-home selling equipment, including sample kits for their dealers. A maker of woven floor coverings supplies a demonstration-sample kit that is excellently done. Several manufacturers have worked out complete in-home sales talks, demonstrations, plans for helping the trade recruit personnel, ideas for special incentive plans for regular personnel. Shown how to advertise for leads, in-home selling will continue to expand. The better equipped the dealer, the more profitable will be his results, and the more in-home selling he will do.

Invite Competition to Share Your Fixture?

A maker of bras has deliberately planned a self-selection fixture to provide space for competitive packages (the fixture is adjustable so that it can hold any manufacturer's carton). Several cigarette companies supply and merchandise fixtures in the food super for *all* brands. Another company in a sundry line has worked out specific arrangements with a competitor for mutual use of their fixtures. To pose the question: "Should competition get space on our fixture?" is to think theoretically. In practice, retailers tend to use fixtures as they see fit—and they do not usually see eye to eye with the manufacturer in this respect! Contracts don't change this situation. What manufacturer will remove a fixture "for cause"? Moreover, in many instances, retailers will not use a fixture at all if it attempts to compel them to turn the section over to one brand, particularly when the retailer's volume may be split pretty evenly among several competing brands. Sound merchandising accepts existing situations—and molds itself accordingly.

Self-service vs. Brand Displays

Several manufacturers who developed ambitious plans designed to induce the *self-service* retailer to display their merchandise *by brand* report poor success. Actually, few manufacturers achieve even a small success with this merchandising concept—except the most powerful. Reason? The whole trend of self-service retailing is to display merchandise by *type* —not by brand. That's generally true in food, drugs, hard and soft goods. The explanation is simple: The shopper shops for *items*. If it's a type of cereal, she wants to see all of that type in one spot. Ditto if it's a small appliance or drugs. In self-service shopping the shopper must be shown merchandise if selection is to be simplified. The brand merchandiser would love to see a huge mass effect secured by having his entire line displayed in just one section. But the essence of self-service display is easy selection. And compelling a self-service shopper to cover three times the distance to make her selection because of brand displays instead of classification displays is usually not the road to more volume for the retailer. The few exceptions tend to be the most powerful brands.

Secondary Uses for Displays

To induce the trade to look more favorably on displays, several manufacturers are now planning their display pieces so that the trade can use them at a later date (after the promotion) for other promotional purposes. Example: The candle is a popular prop as a Christmas display. Therefore, a food processor reasoned: "If we include a battery-equipped candle in our display for use in a November promotion—we could suggest to the retailer that the candle could then be used in any desirable way by the retailer during his Christmas promotions." This is really applying to display pieces the same concept used in so-called "reuse packages," that is, packages with a secondary use after the contents have been consumed. It is also part of the whole concept of making display material less selfish —of enabling the trade to use displays more broadly than solely for the supplier's brand. Actually, the display piece may not be used commonly for its secondary purposes, but the mere fact that it has been designed to this end may make it more appealing to the trade.

The Barnacle-type Fixture

A small barnacle-type fixture that can be attached by the retailer to another and larger fixture is assuming something of a vogue—especially when the object is to win multiple locations for an impulse item. Example: A razor-blade self-service display rack that can be clamped to gum and cigarette racks. (The blade packages are mounted on large self-service cards to discourage pilferage.) While the suppliers of the larger fixtures may not applaud the idea, the retailer is favorably disposed toward it. For years, retailers have taken all kinds of liberties with manufacturer-supplied fixtures. This barnacle-type fixture merely recognizes the practicalities of the existing situation at the point of purchase. As the concept of more multiple locations for an item becomes more widely accepted by mass retailers, the barnacle-type fixture will also gain in popularity. Another example: A maker of flavored drinking straws provides a display rack to be slipped over the edge of milk cabinets.

Tricked Up Demos for Higher-price Lines

As the special features in the upper-end numbers of a line tend, more and more, to be hidden—more showmanship is needed to persuade shoppers that they should step up. This is one reason, of course, for super de luxe packaging, for the extensive use of gold trimming. (Diamonds on watches constitute another example.) Another approach is exemplified in the merchandising program of a mattress manufacturer. Here is a line that is fiercely price-promoted. Stepping up the shopper to the higher-priced numbers is extremely difficult; one of the large manufacturers has tried special P.M.s for salespeople based on sales of the upper-end numbers. This smaller manufacturer has developed a rather weird-looking contraption in which the shopper sits. It includes some 30 plastic tubes containing a liquid. When the shopper sits down the liquid is displaced through the tubes—and, by consulting a chart, the salesman is able to show the customer the type of mattress best suited for the customer's particular requirements. This is really a case of "measuring" the customer for a mattress—in a sitting position and quite dramatically. While it has its limitations, the concept does spotlight the role that tricked-up demonstrations can play in moving higher-priced numbers.

Pricing Fixtures in Deals

Many trade deals involve putting a price on what might be termed run-of-the-mill promotional material, that is, mats, ordinary counter cards, radio scripts, etc. This price is usually purely fictitious—and the fiction is as obvious to the retail trade or the wholesaler as it is to the manufacturer. This is especially the case when the retail trade is practically submerged by a flood of freely offered, unasked-for, promotional material. It may impress somebody in the manufacturer's home office to put a price on this sort of promotional material—but whether it makes the slightest impression on the retail trade is quite another matter. Indeed, where the pricing of the promotional material is too blatantly fictitious the trade becomes suspicious of the merits of the entire deal. This may be true also of prices put on somewhat more elaborate fixtures. Example: A simple pegboard fixture, priced at $14.95 and offered free in a deal. Pegboards are common today, retailers therefore know what they cost—and any successful merchant will know that, in quantity, this fixture would not cost over $4.95. Who is being fooled?

Put Demonstrations Up to Engineers

Three-channel stereo lends itself to rather spectacular demonstrations. It is necessary only to arrange a demonstration model so that first music from one channel comes in, then music from two channels, then music from all three channels. The final results are startling! But the problem was to engineer a demonstration model that could be put through these paces. The problem was put up to the engineering department, which came through with a model that could be demonstrated by the customer himself simply by pressing buttons on a special switch. On the switch appears the suggestion: "Demonstrate it yourself," plus very simple directions. In similar fashion, it seemed quite impossible to the merchandising department to conceive a dishwasher model that would demonstrate to the shopper its precise method of functioning. But a plastic demonstrator was developed by the engineering department, with the result that trade advertising for this brand now says: "For the first time you can show how a dishwasher works." The merchandising man is not expected to be a technician—give technical problems to the technician.

Finding Underworked Display Spots

The intense battle for in-store space for manufacturers' fixtures is compelling a search for overlooked and underworked spots, which, clearly, are becoming fewer. A maker of flashlight batteries discovered a somewhat neglected spot—the shelving *upright*. Only an inch or so wide, these uprights can take a fixture several times wider without unduly hiding merchandise on the shelf itself. For these batteries, therefore, a dispenser was devised displaying a dozen or more batteries stacked vertically. It does not require the retailer to displace another fixture—it requires no new space. (This is not a totally new idea—except perhaps for batteries.) Similarly, for a yeast item, the food super was given a shelf extender so designed that it fitted neatly into unused shelf-edge space and in such a way that it actually did not extend beyond the shelf line. Of course, the problem is not merely to find unused or neglected display space, but to find such space where the fixtured merchandise will be seen by adequate traffic. It's becoming more difficult to find these overlooked display areas, but they still exist. A drug merchandising executive arranged to have photos taken of drug outlet shelving, gondolas, etc.—and studied them with a magnifying glass for neglected or underworked display spots. (Fixtures that "go up in the air," are becoming popular for this reason.)

Up-in-the-air Jumble Displays

The jumble or hash display, particularly when it is merchandised through a fixture supplied by the manufacturer, tends to be either a floor-level display—or involves a floor fixture. Actually, the jumble display got its start decades ago in the old general store where odds and ends were thrown into a pail and the pail set down on the floor. Somehow, putting a jumble display down on the floor seemed still further to get over the "bargain" appeal. But now several manufacturers are supplying the variety chain in particular with jumble merchandise-display fixtures that are designed for use *over* the counter—up in the air. There is, of course, a broad trend in the variety outlet, the drug outlet and also in the food outlet toward "upper-space" merchandising—and this has created an opportunity to get the jumble display off the floor (where it really cannot perform at full effectiveness) and push it up in the air, where more and more displays are winding up.

Fixture Cooperation with Nonrivals

On some occasions, noncompetitive manufacturers share a single fixture —either through deliberate planning or because the retailer decides that is how he wants it. (In one industry two *competitors* deliberately work together in sharing their fixtures!) Perhaps the time is appropriate for noncompeting lines sold through similar outlets to get together in designing fixtures so as to benefit all of the cooperators as well as the retailer. Consider the battle for floor fixtures in the food super. Hundreds of manufacturers selling this outlet offer floor fixtures; only a few can or will be used. If too many were used, the food super's floor would be a confusing wilderness because of the different sizes, colors, different merchandising themes. Some day, a group of noncompetitive but perhaps related manufacturers will get together, decide on a common merchandising event (which is not uncommon), then go on from there and plan individual fixtures for each that will be tied together in design, in shape, in size, in thematic development. This would bring such a promotion into the status of a major event—and the big outlets are not nearly so swamped with major merchandising events as they are with minor programs.

Designing Fixtures by Store-size Groupings

In most large retail organizations, store units are grouped into a few broad size ranges. Thus, a food chain, a drug chain, or a variety chain may group its store units roughly into four or five size categories. This practice is leading some manufacturers to plan their fixtures so as to fit in with the merchandising requirements of each of the store-size categories. For example, a gift-wrap producer offers chains a line of floor fixtures "custom-sized for every type outlet." Thus, to the food outlet, it offers no less than five sizes: (1) For large food supers doing over $2,000,000; (2) for food supers in the $1,500,000 to $2,000,000 volume range; (3) for food supers doing from $750,000 to $1,500,000; (4) for superettes doing from $500,000 to $750,000; (5) for stores doing under $500,000. The retail value of the largest fixture is $560—the smallest is $75. In another field, a manufacturer has designed a short-season fixture (for a three-week season) in a variety of sizes for various types and sizes of stores. The object here was to be able to say to practically all types and sizes of outlets that they could get a fixture that would sell out in three weeks. This is the big trend in today's merchandising of fixtures—merchandise in conformance with the store-size grouping policies of the larger outlets.

Trade Ads as Retail Displays

Every so often a manufacturer smartly uses trade-paper space in a way that permits the trade advertisement to double in brass as an in-store display piece. Example: A maker of nursing bottles ran a special color insert in trade papers that was so laid out as to permit the use of its lower part as a shelf strip. The retailer simply tore off on the dotted line, tucked in at the indicated fold point, and, presto, he had a competent shelf-strip display piece. As merchandisers move increasingly toward the spectacular use of trade-paper space, employing not only multipage inserts and special folds but also full color and heavy paper stock—the setup becomes just about perfect to plan the trade ad for an in-store display function as well as a regular trade-paper message. Display material made available in this way has the merit of permitting timing it so as to arrive precisely when the store can best use it. (Incidentally, it has been found effective with chain-store managers as well as with independent store owners.) This technique in no way takes the place of regular distribution of in-store promotional material—it serves, however, as a valuable secondary distribution technique.

Shipping Containers as Shelf Displays

The shipping container that can be used as a shelf display is clearly the next great merchandising development. Retail costs involved in opening the shipping case, price-marking the contents, getting the merchandise up and on to the retail floor, putting it on the shelves—all are too high. In some instances, these handling costs consume up to one-third of the trade's total margin! Not only will the shipping container be so planned that it can be used for shelf display, but its size will have to be planned to this same end; in many instances, shelf stock does not require the full contents of a full shipping case. (This will accelerate the trend toward smaller sizes in shipping cases and toward multiple sizes.) It should be noted, however, that this trend toward shipping containers as merchandise self-displayers will not be confined to shipping containers made of board. For

example, eggs are now carton-packed in a metal basket so designed that
the metal basket itself can be put on the food-super shelf; the egg cartons
aren't handled at all. Moreover, this whole concept will be applied in
other outlets.

Special Trucks for Truckload Promotions

As more dealers stage merchandising events built around the actual
sale of merchandise from a truck parked in front of the store, in a parking
lot, even in front of a retail warehouse, several manufacturers have concluded that the trucks used are not properly designed for their new roles.
Consequently, these manufacturers are now thinking in terms of trucks
that will not only carry an economical pay load—but will also function better as a mobile retail store. This means a small aisle left open in the truck
for the shopper, better lighting, effective fixturing. There is plenty of pre-
cedence for this plan—for years trailers have been designed for special
consumer sale events. But these trailers have seldom been used in the
current wave of truck merchandising events. It is now being reasoned that
a truck or trailer specially designed for retail selling and offered to the
retailer as still another inducement for buying truckloads and staging
truckload promotions will have a strong appeal. These truckload events
now include such ideas as a free ride for children on a Shetland pony!

Parking-lot Trailer Demonstrations

In shopping centers, the parking lot has become a new retail location
—several hundred millions in merchandise will be sold out in the open
in parking lots this year. Both total volume and total variety of merchandise involved are growing rapidly. Along the same vein, the huge trailer
truck is being developed into a rather new form of parking-lot demonstration—and particularly as a device for acquainting shoppers with the manufacturer's *full line,* which is so seldom stocked by enough retailers. Even
a food super has used a trailer truck in shopping center parking lots to get
over certain basic facts to shoppers. And, of course, one of the great auto
companies has developed a huge program centered around a trailer-truck
display in shopping center parking lots. Incidentally, this auto company's
studies showed that some shopping center parking lots are traversed by
over 200,000 people each week. This is traffic, big traffic—and wherever
there is traffic, there is a merchandising opportunity.

CHAPTER 31

Merchandising to the Consumer: Contests, Premiums, Coupons, Sampling, Special Offers

Making the Product Part of the Premium

Here is a premium and a deal idea that has unique advantages, the most appealing of which is the fact that the sponsoring item becomes an integral part of the premium in actual use. This is how it works. The sponsoring item comes in a glass jar. The premium is a so-called "Party-lite," consisting of a 6-foot pole, a brass torch holder, and a metal cap with wick. It is designed to burn kerosene—and the container for the kerosene is the empty jar of the sponsoring item! Thus, the sponsoring item is an integral part of the premium—and the housewife has regular reminders of the sponsoring item each time she uses the premium. This is a big idea because too often, in fact, most often, when the premium is used it fails entirely to remind the housewife of the sponsoring item. This particular premium, incidentally, is available with a label and $2.50—which brings out the point that the broad rise in price lining in regular merchandise is being matched by a rise in the price lining of premiums. It's logical!

Bring the User Back to the Store

In several fields it has been almost traditional to stage a "clinic" at selected retail outlets at which the featured item is "serviced." It has been done for cameras and for electric shavers. More recently, a maker of hearing aids has taken the plan a step further by not limiting the service to its own brand but rather offering free hearing-aid repairs on all makes. Clearly, this opens the way for the sale of a new hearing aid, not only to customers of this brand who have old models, but to people who are not happy with the competing brand they own. (This is fairly common among users of hearing aids.) Several makers of fountain pens have used the same idea. Here, too, there is considerable dissatisfaction among fountain-pen owners and the idea therefore has logical application. The concept is not limited to items of a mechanical nature, however. For example, it could be used for rugs, where the cleaning problem could be made the basis of a clinic. Generally, these clinics can be made self-liquidating on the basis of the sale of the service, of parts, of related items. But, more important, they can furnish leads for new sales. And, of course, the retailer likes the traffic produced by the clinic, appreciates the prestige of the event, too.

Selling the Guarantee

As more competing merchandise looks alike and, under open-display conditions, shoppers find it increasingly difficult to make a decision between brands—a selling plus is needed to make the item stand out from its rivals at the point of sale. A vacuum-bottle brand moved in this direction by taking a guarantee which it has actually offered for fifty years and merchandising it as though it were a new feature. The label on the bottle has been redesigned so as to give the guarantee a great deal more prominence; the guarantee is featured on a display card. There is still magic in the word "guarantee"—and, merchandised in new ways at the point of sale, it can be brought back to life as a sales clincher. There is a vast degree of confusion and uncertainty in the public's mind about competing merchandise. And when the shopper sees competing brands lined up one alongside the other and all looking so much alike, the buying decision tends to be delayed. Taking the buried guarantee and giving it merchandising emphasis makes sense under these circumstances.

Offer a Choice of Premiums

Retailers have, of course, for years promoted premium catalogues which offer the shopper a choice from a variety of premiums. Manufacturers, however, in their premium promotions have tended to stake the entire event on the offer of a single premium item. Several great mutual savings banks in New York have discovered that offering prospective depositors a choice between several premiums steps up returns to their new-depositor campaigns. One giant savings bank offered prospective depositors a choice between six premiums ranging from a Detecto Scale to a Cory Percolator to an Anchor Hocking ovenware set. One mutual savings bank opened a fantastic 150,000 new accounts in a six-week period with a five-item-choice premium promotion. Interestingly, a bank executive reports they have never guessed correctly the order of popularity of the various items offered—which suggests that when a manufacturer offers just a single premium he is taking something of a gamble with fickle public taste.

A Fighting Free Offer

Several programs have appeared lately involving what might properly be called a "fighting free offer." A typical example involves a food company that offers to refund the price of a rival frozen dinner. In this merchandising-promotional event, the processor suggests that the shopper buy either two of its frozen dinners—or one of its frozen dinners and one made by any competitor. Under either circumstance, the shopper gets one frozen dinner free. Interestingly, in one of these "fighting-free-offer" events, it was found that by far the majority of the shoppers did *not* buy a competing brand! Apparently, the shopper's reaction was that this manufacturer must be mighty positive his brand is superior, so "Why should I gamble with another brand?" Of course, the idea won't work too well unless the sponsoring item is so superior that in a single use the large majority of customers will promptly appreciate its virtues. Also, it is important in this sort of event to make certain that the trade doesn't use it as an ideal opportunity to move the competing lines—especially if they have been sticky. But the free offer's virtues may tend to balance out its weaknesses—give it some thought.

Price Offers on Related Items

It has been fairly common in the food field to make a price offer on a related item rather than on the sponsor's item. Example: A cake flour offers 8 cents off on a pound of butter. (In this instance, the offer was featured in national advertising and the coupon worth 8 cents on a pound of butter was packed in the cake-flour carton.) Obviously, the offer was not only attractive to the shopper—women love to save pennies on staple food items—but it had the additional benefit of winning the support of the great dairy industry, which faces increasing competition from margarine. There is little doubt that offering the 8-cent discount on butter, rather than on the cake flour, makes the deal more attractive to housewives—particularly in this instance, because the offer was part of a butter-cake promotion and extra butter was necessary. But, in addition, the dairy industry could be expected to help promote the offer. It is interesting to note that this kind of offer has seldom been used outside the food industry—although it clearly has application in other merchandise categories. So long as two or more items have a related use—and surely this is by no means confined to food—making a price offer on the related item or items can be effectively merchandised.

Free Trial for New Big-ticket Models

When a striking improvement in a long-established big-ticket line that has seen few truly major changes for many years comes along—shopper resistance stemming from habit of thought can become a merchandising problem. In such a situation the new model does not always enjoy the instantaneous acceptance that is usually expected when a major improvement is announced. To the contrary, there may be resistance initially. A large maker of mattresses, when planning the introduction of a mattress that would not include the usual buttons or tufts, concluded that this improvement might—at the start—raise some doubts in the shopper's mind, especially since this was to be a $79.50 retailer in a $39.50 price-promotional market. Therefore, a thirty-day free-trial offer was made that was legally permissible. Also, the mattress was given a particularly strong ten-year guarantee. While the free trial is subject to abuse—it is the old story here as elsewhere—if the merchandise movement engendered by free trial is adequate, it will compensate for the abuse.

Getting One Foot in the Door

Merchandising strategy sometimes calls for simply trying to get one foot in the door—as contrasted with crashing through the door. Example: One of the great oil refineries developed a new peak-performance gas. Customary procedure, over the years, when introducing a new gasoline has been to fight for a complete switch by the auto owner. But in this instance, the idea was developed of asking the customer to buy one tankful of the new gas every 1,000 miles "to restore peak engine performance." This is smart merchandising—the kind of smart merchandising that leads to smart advertising. Clearly, this kind of suggestion carries with it an implicit and highly convincing evidence of faith in the product. The customer just naturally will conclude: "They wouldn't suggest such an idea if they didn't really believe this new gas would promptly show better performance." And, as will tend to happen when merchandising tries to get just one foot in the door, it is more than likely that the very moderateness of the suggestion (and, conversely, its very audacity) will open wide the door to the full sale.

Merchandising a New Related Item

When an improved and perhaps de luxe number is brought out as an *additional* purchase, not a *substitute for* the regular number, it is common merchandising practice to program so that the new item rides to market on the coattail of the established number. But there is always the problem of convincing the shopper that she needs *both* numbers—the regular *and* the new special—otherwise, the new number simply takes volume away from the old. Solution: A deal was developed for a regular and a special number in a line of adhesive bandages. The regular number had a retail of 69 cents; the newer number a retail of 43 cents. The shopper had shown a tendency to buy one or the other; too seldom did she buy *both*, especially at one time. The deal offered the newer 43-cent retailer in a combination wrapup with the regular 69-cent number. Thus it was hoped shoppers would come to understand that they needed both. Incidentally, a 1-cent price was put on the 43-cent item. The reasoning: (1) With so many hundreds of free offers, the 1-cent price becomes more dramatic and stands out in a chorus of free offers; (2) the 70-cent price for the combination would be a good retail pricing point. This technique for sampling an addition to the line accustoms shoppers to think in terms of needing both the old and the new number.

Update Merchandising for Sophisticated Shoppers

Advertisers have long made the mistake of writing advertising down to a so-called "twelve-year-old mind." Merchandisers, too, have tended to underestimate the IQ of their public. The consequence: So many contests, so many deals, so many giveaways, so many trade-in plans, and so many other facets of merchandising are still keyed to the same mental image of the shopper that merchandisers have had for years. A large soft-goods house that concluded it had overstayed its traditional concept of the rather moronic shopper established the following program: (1) A sharp upgrading of its styling; (2) several substantial jumps in price lining; (3) advertising to sell fashion, not price; (4) deemphasize traditional January White Sale; (5) drop its annual consumer contest; (6) trade up its merchandising as well as its line. Too much merchandising appeals to economic illiterates and to the lowest income groups. But the great market for most merchandise classifications consists of people with incomes large enough to make *discretionary* purchases. The majority of those shoppers who control this nation's discretionary-buying purse strings are intelligent, increasingly sophisticated in buying keenness as well as in taste. It's time to stop merchandising *down*—try merchandising *up!*

Pay Retailers for Big Sampling?

Retailers are now being paid for handling coupons, for extra work involved in certain deals—will they soon be paid when a manufacturer samples to the home on a huge scale? This may be in the cards. Why? Because the retailer complains that a giant sampling campaign delivering samples into most homes in his trading area *cuts into his sale* of the item for the period of the sampling program. When a door-to-door sampling of 1 million 2-ounce jars of instant coffee was planned in a western area, a big retailer covering that area complained that "this will mean a half million dollars worth of instant coffee that will not be sold off our retail shelves." Of course, the manufacturer will rebut that, in time, this will be bread cast upon the water for the retailer—but all the retailer can see is that immediate loss of $500,000 in sales. He also argues that he won't do more instant coffee volume in total; that the sampling will simply switch shoppers from one brand to another. Conclusion: Either sample (via coupons, etc.) in a way that will conclude a sale in the store or begin thinking in terms of compensating the retailer for losses stemming from large-scale door-to-door sampling.

Can Premiums Substitute for Discounts?

A maker of small radio sets offered—in spring—a $2.50 (retail value) flower-seed set for 25 cents to purchasers of its receiving set. The offer was merchandised through the retail trade. Question: In a category overrun with off-list promotions, can premiums function as price stabilizers? Or can premiums substitute for price slashes? Answer: Probably not. Every experience of retailers selling a price-slashed category has been that even generous trade-in offers are not as effective usually as huge slices off list. It's important for merchandisers to remember that our public has become conditioned—by autos, appliances, discount houses—to shopping for low prices. It's become a sport as well as an art. We are no longer in a one-price marketing setup with, of course, some notable exceptions. Where list price is more of a fiction than a fact, and where the category has conditioned the public to shop for low, low prices—the premium can seldom compete with king-sized slashes off list. Moreover, large retailers want to feature low prices, not premium offers. In many instances, these retailers will throw in the premium for free but if the premium costs them money, they won't like it.

The Bounce-back Premium

The bounce-back premium is simply a merchandise item selected with an eye to persuade the shopper who gets it to order a related item. Thus, a manufacturer offering a barbecue chef's knife as a premium accompanied the premium with promotional material offering matching knives at the same price. This is not a particularly new practice, but currently it is enjoying a degree of popularity. Of course, the bounce-back involves more labels —otherwise one is in the premium business, not in the business of moving his own merchandise. Where a line has a fast repeat, the bounce-back premium has a good deal to recommend it. Its particular virtue is that it encourages the shopper to buy the line or the item often enough to become more firmly wedded to it and, since so many premium plans fail to get the product sampled often or long enough, this is a considerable advantage. In other words, when the premium program can be planned so that it induces the shopper to buy again and again, the percentage of temporary users will be cut and the percentage of the more permanent users increased. And this is important; too much merchandising money is spent achieving a single switch by the shopper.

Is the Guarantee Outmoded?

The guarantee has been around for a long time. Moreover, all responsible merchants really guarantee everything they sell. Does this mean that there is little merchandising benefit accruing to a guarantee? No it doesn't. The guarantee continues to be a great merchandising force. However, the simple phrase "It's guaranteed" is quite ineffective. Currently, the guarantee gains in effectiveness as a merchandising device when it is given exploitable features. The lifetime guarantee (not at all new, but very effective) has been adapted for foam rubber used in mattresses. A five-year guarantee on certain major appliances has been productive. (Now a refrigerator is offering a ten-year warranty.) A gold bond guarantee is being featured. A guarantee on a particular feature remains merchandisingly effective—a famous-brand glassware line continues to exploit: "A new glass if the rim ever chips." There is a vast degree of public uncertainty about merchandise. This suggests a guarantee. Self-service shopping also puts more dependence on the guarantee. But give the guarantee a unique exploitable feature—and then exploit it uniquely. Example: A trade contest built around naming a trade character featured in the guarantee.

Include Radio-TV in Contest Prizes

It is, of course, quite customary to include prizes for dealers and salespeople (for jobbers and their salesmen, too) in consumer contests. Now another factor in the complete merchandising-advertising contest program is being brought into the consumer contest—the radio-TV announcer, star, or disk jockey. In a specific case, a maker of hard-surface floor coverings planned a consumer contest over a number of radio stations involving spots on disk-jockey programs. The consumer had to visit the retail store for the contest entry blank—send it in to the disk jockey. The sponsor then offered special prizes to the disk jockeys getting the largest number of entry blanks. The disk jockey in particular is, of course, on the receiving end of many types of offers. Involving him in contest awards is something of a new wrinkle, however—and awards for announcers and other performing artists are even more unusual. This, of course, is part of the new thinking that attempts to win more cooperation from every factor involved in the consumer contest chain.

Overdone Premium Offers

A merchandising executive reports that in his future premium events he will stay away from the most commonly offered items. According to his study, the 10 most frequently used premiums are silverware, stainless steel, glass utensils, cutlery, aluminumware, appliances, plastic utensils, pens and pencils, picnic-barbecue supplies, china utensils. He points out that the potential market for these items is shriveled, not only by the frequency of use for premiums, but also because most of these items are also being fiercely price-promoted by large retailers. He has decided to concentrate on premiums selected from the broad line made by his company and to pick only those which are related in use to the sponsoring item. Moreover, his new program calls for premiums that will appeal to somewhat higher-income groups, to the more stable elements in our "shopulation." His reasoning here is that too many premium offers are geared down to segments of shoppers that show the least brand loyalty. It is clearly true that too many premium offers tend to shoot strictly for big numbers, rather than for the *more desirable customer*. Start your premium planning with a clear picture of the customers you want most to reach.

Two Sampling Ideas for New Items

Two great brands in health aids developed quite different sampling plans when each introduced a new product. Number one, a maker of one of the great dental-cream brands, brought out a new shampoo. A sample bottle was attached to the large size of the dental-cream package, and offered free. Number two, a great aspirin brand, had brought out a nasal spray. A coupon pad accompanied a counter box containing large-size bottles of the aspirin. When the shopper bought the aspirin, she tore off a coupon which offered a free 59-cent size of the nasal spray. The shopper was to fill in the coupon with name and address, attach the empty package from a 100-aspirin bottle, mail it in. Plan number two may have been slightly more simple in setting up with the trade. Against that must be balanced the extra effort to which shoppers were put. Plan number one had the advantage of combining sampling a new item with what is really a valuable special free item attached to a huge-selling dentifrice brand. The dentifrice undoubtedly benefited from the free offer, and the shampoo rode in neatly on the tail of the dentifrice.

Merchandising Miniatures as a Joint Venture

The miniature model of a growing variety of items (starting with such consumer durables as autos and certain appliances and since spreading even into a few soft goods) is now being merchandised into the home in a way that (1) makes this a self-liquidating venture that may even throw off a small profit; (2) gets the item with the brand name on it into the home in the highly desirable role of reminder; (3) permits special promotions at low cost that win additional repetitions of the sales message. Example: A carpet sweeper offers a miniature model at $2 as a premium with a breakfast cereal (two box tops). Joint advertising was run by the two advertisers—and joint promotions in the different retail outlets were also staged. This is an interesting development of the joint merchandising event sponsored by noncompetitors, and much more practical than some of the silly tie-ups such as air-conditioners and summer suits.

Coupons in Multistore-list Ads

Department stores (other types of retailers, too) are doing a mounting mail-order volume. This suggests the wisdom for a supplier, in local advertising (especially on Sunday), to include a coupon in the local advertising to be returned to the store by the mail shopper. But where a manufacturer has several outlets in an area, and where these several outlets are listed in one ad, can a coupon be practically used? A rug mill saw no great merchandising problem in this situation. One of its local ads, for example, listed six local department stores. Copy suggested: "Order Blank rugs from your favorite store." This was followed by the store listing. Then a coupon was featured. The shopper simply filled in the store name and after that filled in the coupon as would normally be done. Incidentally, coupon text also included provision for typical store regulations: no charge within delivery area, except c.o.d.s beyond delivery area, rugs shipped express, collect. The coupon also included spaces for charge number, c.o.d., check, money order.

Contests in Industry

Since so many manufacturers sell both to industry and to the general public, it is inevitable that ideas used in the latter field will be adapted for use in industrial selling. Example: A maker of tape sells both to industry and to the public. For its industrial market the company wanted to find new uses. It therefore developed a contest for factory employees of its industrial customers—a novel idea. Moreover, the contest was planned in complete imitation of a typical consumer contest; even the contest ads in the industrial press aped typical consumer contest ads in layout, copy, types of prizes offered. The contest was open to all personnel of manufacturing plants. Entries were to describe a new nonelectrical usage for industrial tapes or dispensing equipment that had actually been put to use in the entrant's plant during the contest period. It is not unlikely that some new consumer uses will emerge from this industrial contest—employees of factories develop intriguing at-home uses for parts and materials with which they work at the factory.

Dressing Up the Coupon

It is estimated that over *10 billion* coupons were distributed to shoppers in 1960. This includes distribution through all channels from media to packages. The average redemption value per coupon was about 10 cents —giving these 10 billion coupons a face value of a fantastic 1 billion dollars. Coupons not only read as deadly as stock certificates—they also *look* as dull and deadly. The heavy hand of the lawyer is all too evident in the coupon. Now, however, a few merchandisers are beginning to think of the coupon as susceptible to visual selling, over and above the terms of the offer. As a consequence, a toiletries house, staging a merchandising event involving a pad of coupons placed in its floor fixture, printed the coupons in *full color*. This, however, is just a small step forward. Years ago, in the days of unrestricted "blue-sky" promotion of securities, the promoters dolled up these securities so that they looked more impressive than the securities making up the Dow-Jones averages. It is high time that the coupon was dressed up—starting with the text and proceeding to paper stock, to form and format, to illustration, to color. The coupon may have to be a legal document—but there is no reason why it must *look* like one.

Merchandising Two-size Deals

With the number of sizes in so many lines constantly growing, it becomes necessary to develop merchandising plans that will induce the shopper to buy more than one size at a time. Thus, new combo deals are being developed that not only include several sizes in the combination package—but give the shopper a logical reason for wanting the several sizes. Example: A hair preparation brought out a combination package containing one large and one medium tube—at a price savings, of course. This hair preparation is used primarily by men. Men travel quite a bit, both for business and for pleasure. This merchandising combo event was therefore premised on the idea that the small tube constituted an ideal size for travel purposes, the large tube an ideal size for home use. In this way, the price lure of the combo offer is plussed by adding to the price factor a specific reason for buying a second size. As the effectiveness of the price lure is watered down by its too-common exploitation, it will be increasingly necessary to merchandise the combo offer involving two or more sizes in such a way as to give the shopper logical reasons for wanting the several sizes in addition to the price savings.

Brand Name Display in Homes

A maker of facial tissues has brought out a de luxe package with its brand name printed on a transparent film overwrap. The housewife may strip this off the gold-and-white dispensing carton, which then has no "commercial taint"; presumably the housewife will not display it in her home otherwise. Do women really object to brand-name display in the home? For over a century the piano makers found this no problem. In most instances this consumer objection is more fancied than real. (Major appliances find little objection to name plates, ditto for television, radio, phonograph sets.) Also it can sometimes be negated, where it does exist, by exceptionally attractive containers like the cosmetic-type bottles developed for vitamins. (Several food packages have been redesigned for table display.) Moreover, there are some brand names that confer social status; these are proudly displayed in the home. On reuse containers, the brand name may be somewhat objectionable, but even here there are exceptions.

Special Tie-ups with Giant Retailers

A definite trend is developing among manufacturers involving special merchandising programs planned in cooperation with giant retail organizations that do *not* stock the manufacturer's line. Example: A $100,000 teen-ager cooking contest was merchandised jointly by a maker of major appliances and one of the giant food-super chains. (The food-super chain does not, and did not, stock major appliances.) The two organizations split the total contest awards. The contest was heavily promoted by the food chain—and finalists were selected from each of the chain's 25 operating areas. This concept involving a joint merchandising-promotional event by a manufacturer and by an outlet that does not stock his category has been used primarily, to date, through the food outlet—obviously because of its enormous daily traffic. And, in this instance, the tie-up was logical, since this was a cooking contest and thus involved food. It is probable, however, that the concept will be extended to other major outlets—the drug and variety chains, for example.

Localizing National Contests

It's not difficult to get dealers to match prizes in a national consumer contest. All that the merchandising man needs to do is offer to foot the bill for retailers who match locally the consumer prizes offered by the manufacturer! In a national dog-food contest, the dealer mentioned by a winner could give the winner, in addition to the national prize, a $500 local prize, presumably from his own pocket, but underwritten by the manufacturer. When the retailer offers prizes, as in this instance, the national contest is given a highly desirable local impact. Assuming proper control regulations (as was done in this example), there is merit to the thought of offering to foot the bill when the dealer adds to the national offer. It wins more promotion in the store and in local advertising. Consumer contests usually need more localizing—they tend to be "too national." This is one route to that objective.

Coupons for Noncompetitive Categories

Outside of the food field it has not yet become common for a manufacturer to make available a consumer coupon that may be cashed in by the shopper for a noncompetitive category that may or may not be related. It warrants analysis in nonfood lines. The technique is simple. A typical example involves a famous maker of canned soup. A "soup 'n crackers" merchandising program was developed (food supers favor related-item events). Customers were told they could mail in to the food processor four soup labels (thus removing this detail from the retailer's problems). The food processor could then send the shopper a certificate good in the food outlet for 25 cents, to be applied to the purchase of "a box of your favorite crackers." Now that the drug outlet and the variety outlet in particular have copied so much from the food outlet—it is entirely probable that these outlets will be open to buy related-item coupon promotions of this kind. They work in the food outlet—there is little reason why they will not work well in certain other outlets.

Premium as Part of a Gift

Can a premium be made a gift given to family or friends? Or will most people conclude that "it will make me look mighty cheap to send a premium as a gift"? Perhaps a straddle will get around that objection—and it is a valid objection. Here's how it was done by a maker of small appliances. National advertising and in-store merchandising offered an electric iron as a Mother's Day gift. This was the gift the purchaser made to mother. Then, mother could tear off the end panel of the package and get three pairs of nylon hosiery for $1—a good value. Thus, the gift giver had the satisfaction of making a gift of something he had purchased—and the gift receiver could feel she was getting a double gift because the nylon premium was, as we've remarked, a fine value. (Undoubtedly, a number of those who bought this gift for mother would wrap up with it a $1 bill for the premium—which is subtle merchandising, indeed!) In any event, here is evidence that premium offers can get in on the huge gift market—a very interesting merchandising opportunity.

Getting Away from Banded Deals

To cut handling and other costs on a deal, one manufacturer developed this angle: The deal involved a small size tied up with a large size—the former a $1.98 retailer and the latter a $5.95 retailer. In the usual procedure, the two would have been banded together—one offered at half price perhaps or even free, and the other at regular retail. This manufacturer, however, planned his deal so that the shopper bought the $5.95 size at the retail counter—and then sent the empty carton directly to the manufacturer, who then mailed the free $1.98 size to the consumer. Under this plan, the manufacturer is saved the cost of banding, but incurs handling and postage costs. The retailer makes more of a savings—including the cost of breaking up unsold deals, taking regular stock off shelves during the deal period, which is very costly. Actually, the shopper is given an added burden—certainly it is more convenient for the shopper to pick up the free item banded to the paid-for item. Deal sales may be smaller, but so are costs. Moreover, many shoppers never send in for the free item.

The Tiffany Technique in Merchandising

When Tiffany features a $10,000 diamond necklace and a $10.95 item in the same ad—the aim may really be to sell the $10,000 ticket. But certainly the aura cast over the $10.95 item by the $10,000 necklace is not to be overlooked! Similarly, when a men's hat maker features a $250 man's hat—he is simply using the Tiffany technique. In many classifications, a top-bracket bellwether may be featured, not for volume, but to win attention for the bread-and-butter price lines. Example: A maker of TV-phonograph-radio sets built a special merchandising event around its 10 fastest-selling numbers. The promotional package, however, also included a top-price-line "golden achievement" TV set. The objects: (1) To win special window and in-store display because of the Tiffany appeal of the luxury set; (2) to gain the benefits of the glamour imparted to the regular numbers by the de luxe number; (3) to show a set that incorporates *all* of the features found *only in part* in the big-selling numbers—a very important point.

Sell Two Colors Instead of One

Sometimes the size of the sales unit can be stepped up by banding two or more colors together. It has been done for years in soft goods. Interesting example in another field: Two colors of shoe polish packed in a combination unit. There was good merchandising thinking back of this special offer. (A regular 50-cent value was offered for 39 cents in the special combination package.) The members of so many homes have both black and brown shoes; if they use shoe polish, black and brown polish is extremely logical. Note, too, that on a 25-cent retailer, the two shades were offered for 39 cents—a considerable saving. The application of color to categories not formerly color-conscious has not been matched by the development of multiple sales units consisting of several colors for these lines. Expanding the sales unit by multiple color combinations in a pre-packed unit, as in this shoe-polish instance, is the next step in multiple-unit merchandising in categories newly influenced by color.

Longer "Tails" for Consumer Contests

There is every indication that consumer contests are being given longer "tails" in the way of prizes that offer some reward to hundreds instead of merely scores. While the dramatic big first prize remains important, there are now so many contests with a huge first prize that, almost automatically, it becomes necessary to extend the tail. Obviously, hundreds or even several thousand small prizes convince more people that "everybody has a chance to win"; thus the longer tail pulls in more amateur contestants, as differentiated from the professional and the semiprofessional contestant. Several contests have been run with the theme "Everybody Wins." A soft-drink contest offered almost every entrant a certificate redeemable for a dollar in any merchandise at retail outlets. A razor contest also offered every qualified contestant a $1 prize. Many more women tend to enter a contest when a small prize is broadly available. Retailers know that women will "walk a mile" to save a few pennies (and squander dollars on the way).

Related Premiums for Big-ticket Lines

A recent study suggests that close to 75 per cent of premiums offered in premium merchandising events bear no relationship—in fact or even in fancy—to the sponsor's merchandise. One consequence is that when the shopper weighs the unrelated premium in her mind she is not giving any thought to the merchandise the premium is presumed to promote. This is especially true with respect to big-ticket lines. The trend toward the related premium is unmistakable—and it will continue strongly because it constitutes logical merchandising. Some good examples of related premiums in big-ticket lines: (1) A vacuum cleaner (famous brand name) offered with the sale of a rug retailing in the $400 range; (2) a maker of vacuum cleaners offered a kit containing chemicals for removing spots and stains on rugs. One problem: The shopper who has no need for the premium. For instance, the rug buyer may have at home all of the vacuum cleaners she needs. Solution: Offering the shopper a choice of several premiums—or enabling the merchant to give a cash rebate.

Cross-couponing to "Hypo" Sales

Cross-couponing, a fairly venerable merchandising device, is currently undergoing something of a renaissance. Thus, a food producer puts a coupon in one of his line's leaders to help stimulate volume on a fairly new item—the coupon is worth 7 cents off on the newer item. A maker of sanitary napkins puts a coupon in every box of 12 that is good for 10 cents toward the purchase of a napkin belt. Thus, a secondary or accessory item is stimulated by closer association with the parent item. Cross-couponing has been used to introduce a new size, to induce the shopper to buy a giant size, to get the shopper to buy a wider range of colors, to sell a de luxe number as a gift item. One objective of cross-couponing is to make it work while the customer is making the initial purchase, instead of hoping she will find the coupon in the package when she gets home and cash it in on the next shopping trip. This calls for strong copy and layout on the package featuring the coupon, special display material, and, usually, strong national advertising featuring the offer.

Plussing Free Trial at Home

Currently, several lines are being merchandised with an at-home free trial that includes a secondary free offer. Example: The offer of four sheets and pillow cases as an inducement to give a washer-dryer a fourteen-day home trial. (At end of fourteen days, if the appliance is not wanted, it is taken back—housewife keeps the linen.) Little question that these extra inducements to permit a free at-home trial will be stepped up —it may even become part of a contest or a form of lottery. (Since purchase is not compulsory the latter may be permissible.) The free trial at home has merit, but its weaknesses must be tested. The offer tends to appeal to an irresponsible fringe of shoppers; returns may be high. Costs, consequently, may be out of line. Dealers too often do not follow up adequately. Poor demonstration, poor installation, poor service may kill a potential sale that could have been saved if the buyer had made a commitment. The trial period may not be long enough to overcome doubts. (Remember, during the free-trial period there may be second-thought reasons for not buying!)

Special Attention for Men

A confectioner has brought out a special box of chocolates for men— calls it the "Sports Fan." A toiletries house, which had brought out a gift set for expectant mothers, later brought out a gift set for the neglected expectant father, smartly called it "Gentleman-in-waiting Gift Set." There is sound merchandising logic in this concept—"Pop" gets gifts as well as "Mom"; and not only on Father's Day. (Americans love to do a lot of good-natured ribbing; merchandise get-ups that appeal to rib tickling are popular.) Special aprons for men have become commonplace. So has special cooking paraphernalia—recipes, too. Food supers now put out special tables aimed at men (men constitute about 30 per cent of food-super traffic). Variety chains have more male traffic, so do department stores. The whole area of merchandising exploitation to men has yet to be adequately developed. (Greeting cards are increasingly designed for male selection and there's been talk about redesigning some food packages for greater male appeal.)

The Golden Touch in Merchandising

When a famous-brand soap was put out in a gold wrapper, it started what may very well turn out to be the *golden* era in merchandising. Examples: A vacuum bottle announces a "golden" guarantee which appears on a gold guarantee label affixed to each bottle, and an automatic coffee maker has gold trim. Example: A cosmetic line announces that its 1958 Christmas cosmetics have the "golden touch"—they're prewrapped in gold. Examples: A cigarette carton uses a gold tear tape. A bathroom scale has been designed that makes liberal use of simulated gold. A baby biscuit is wrapped in gold foil and a plastic bandage includes a do-it-yourself gold imprinter. There is a "gold crest" line of men's toiletries. And several counter fixtures are trimmed in gold. There has been a "Win Your Weight in Gold" consumer contest. A limited-edition fashion line was featured in gold displays. Gold is the symbol of luxury, of social status. Its merchandising uses will continue to multiply.

Consumer Contest to Create Store Traffic

A $60,000 two-page full-color magazine ad was used to announce a huge consumer contest—but without giving any details of what the shopper had to do to compete for the prizes. Two basic objectives were involved. The contest was a sweepstakes and this type of contest verges on the *verboten* lottery. (By not giving details in the publication ad, the post office was prevented from taking action.) Readers were told they would find the contest rules on the contest sponsor's packages—that, of course, will create store traffic and more actual sales. No doubt, this will cut down on the total number of contestants—the more road blocks put in the path of entering, the fewer entrants. But the type of contestant attracted may be of a higher order, so the fewer numbers may be balanced out by the higher quality. Incidentally, this sweepstakes contest involved

drawings on four dates. To maintain interest through all four dates contestants were told that non-winning entries would be saved and added
to the entries for the next drawing. The sweepstakes concept is sweeping
consumer contests—and other ideas will be developed to keep it from
lottery condemnation.

Trade-mark as a Premium

Getting the trade-mark or trade character into the home in a fairly
permanent way (other than on the regular package or on the item itself)
has obvious advantages. It has been done successfully via a premium offer
that involved a miniature replica of an unusual trade-mark—"20 Mule
Team" products. (The premium consisted of a miniature model plastic
kit of the 20-mule team, three wagons, a crew.) Many years ago, the
then-famous Fisk tire boy was merchandised in the home in various forms.
In more recent years, the Campbell Kids have been brought into the home
in a variety of ways. Here, again, we see the merits, when planning a
premium, of trying to tie the premium as closely as possible to the item or
line it is intended to promote. Among other benefits, when this type of
premium is featured in the advertising, the ad budget is not being diverted
to an item that is totally foreign to the merchandise the ad budget was
established to push. (A successful merchandiser predicts that the trade
character is destined for a reincarnation—his point is that in TV, in store
display, etc., the trade character can play a vastly more important role
than was possible years ago when the trade character dominated advertising.)

Free Coupons to Credit Accounts

The charge-account list and, even more broadly, the various retail-
credit-program lists have been commonly used by manufacturers in merchandising events involving statement enclosures. Now that these lists
of credit buyers, in the innumerable forms of credit currently offered by
retailers, are jumping at a phenomenal rate, merchandisers are examining
the list of credit customers to see how the traditional statement stuffer or
other mailing to these lists can be made more effective. One idea—sending to the lists a rather formal type of free coupon. A cosmetics company
arranged to do this with some of the top department stores. The mailing
included a completely personalized and beautiful booklet on this line of
cosmetics—and the booklet carried its own fragrance. In addition, the
mailing included a handsome card entitling the charge-account customer
to a free jar ($3.50 retailer) of cosmetic cream with any purchase made
at this brand's cosmetic section in the sponsoring store. Now that variety
chains, drug chains, and innumerable specialty stores have charge-account
and other credit services, merchandising these lists rates new thinking.

Planning for Rental Merchandising

Home owners turn over homes more rapidly—in Los Angeles, the tenure of home ownership is down to five years! Faster home turnover— more rentals of appliances, furniture, etc. As a method of selling new models, the rental plan has its weaknesses. It lures in too many poor credit and moral risks, especially the latter. The total costs are extremely high; almost always higher than the retailer (or distributor) anticipates. Disposal of the returns adds to the used-model problem. The percentage of final sales to rentals is too low, which, of course, makes total costs jump. So don't make rental plan too liberal; for an air-conditioner a big retailer insisted on a twelve-month lease at $7.50 a month with three months rental paid in advance. To speed up purchase, offer such inducements as applying full rental amount to purchase price within six months—only 75 per cent thereafter. Develop a complete follow-up plan; remember that rentals are merely leads for new-unit sales, and leads are not converted into sales without intensive follow-up.

Full Money-back Offer Gets Wider Use

The full money-back offer—under which the shopper mails back to the manufacturer a coupon or package identifying symbol for a full refund— is now getting new uses. It started out really as a technique for introducing a *new* product. And, generally, it was confined to just one item. Then some deals of this kind were involved in which the sponsor's item plus a related item that he did not make were offered—the former for free, the latter at regular retail. But now the idea is being applied to items that are not new—and to a multiple group of items all made by the sponsor. Example: A food processor offered three of its established items on a consumer-refund basis. The theme was "Buy All Three—Get a Dollar Free." (The three items retailed at approximately $1.) Thus the retailer was told he was being given an opportunity to sell a larger sales unit. The shopper was told to mail in one label from each product in order to qualify for the dollar refund. (The experience to date is that these mail-in-label-and-get-refund offers appeal to the shopper—but that the number who actually mail in labels for the refund is not large.) As a consequence, this type of offer may ultimately lose its appeal. As the shopper becomes aware that she seldom mails in the labels, she will be less swayed by this type of offer.

Merchandising the "Custom Exclusive"

In a wide variety of merchandise classifications—ranging from fashion merchandise to appliances, from glassware to furniture—manufacturers are beginning to merchandise what is sometimes called the "custom exclusive." This is a specially designed, sometimes specially constructed, and always specially priced line. This trend is sparked by at least two great developments: the urgent need for a line that will not be "price-footballed" and that will provide adequate margins; and the increasing receptivity of the public and the trade for traded-up lines—lines that are traded up in appearance, in quality, and, of course, in price. As part of the custom-exclusive trend, some manufacturers are offering the shopper a limited number of optional specifications; this is why the term "custom exclusive" came to be coined, although it is applied also to lines that do not provide optional specifications. We are clearly coming into an era of enormously accelerated acceptance by the public of better and more exclusive merchandise. Merchandisers are therefore giving more and more thought to the top of the line. Here is opportunity for more volume, for a better net profit for manufacturer and trade—especially when the top of the line is given controlled distribution.

Narrow Down Teen-age Appeals

Merchandising events planned for teen-agers tend to bog down somewhat in the years embraced by the term. A teen-ager can apparently be a young miss ranging from sixteen to twenty-five—yet obviously the sixteen-year-old is hardly to be classed with the twenty-five-year-old. One manufacturer who has planned several teen-age sewing contests has found it advisable to narrow down the range of years. He has also broken down his teen-age contest into several age brackets—subteen, teen, and senior. (Incidentally, by establishing the subteen range, this manufacturer was able to appeal to girls under sixteen.) The teen-ager tends to get younger with each generation. The whole practice of merchandising to the teen-ager tends to extreme looseness when too large an age span is bridged. There is very much of a question whether even a twenty-one-year-old miss considers herself a teen-ager. Clearly, many nineteen-year-olds and twenty-year-olds do not conduct themselves as traditional teen-agers—many are married at this age. There is an opportunity for some merchandisers to develop a new age bracket and a term for it—the age bracket nineteen to twenty-one, inclusive.

Horning in on Fashion Shows

The fashion show continues to be a "merchandising staple"; and not only in department stores. Innumerable specialty stores stage fashion shows—so do some of the variety chains. How can nonfashion merchandise latch onto the coattails of the fashion show? One of the great typewriter companies arranged a tie-up. It suggested to department stores that they stage special fashion shows for secretaries. It brought out its type-writers in seven new colors. There was a degree of color correlation be-tween the fashions shown and the typewriter colors. The typewriters were, of course, displayed along with the fashions in the store auditorium. A special window display was obtained. Announcements were mailed by the store to secretaries in nearby office buildings. A special mailing list was obtained of those who attended. As more merchandise "goes fashion," and certainly this is the broad trend, there is somewhat more reason to tie in with the traditional fashion show. And, since retailers desperately seek new ideas to freshen up their fashion shows, they tend to be receptive to programs such as this.

Consumer Contest for a Deal

The retail trade (wholesalers, too) are constantly in a dither about consumer deals—and not without cause. Consequently, the more im-pressive is the story the manufacturer can muster about what he is doing to move the deal off the shelves, the less the trade's groaning. One idea: A deal for a bath soap offered two bars at a saving of 6 cents. In the special deal pack there was an entry blank for a whopping big consumer contest based on the theme "Win Your Weight in Gold." The entry blanks could be obtained *only* by purchasing the deal. The contest was heavily promoted in national advertising. Clearly, the trade had reason to believe that this deal would move out quickly. It's vital for merchandisers to bear in mind that the trade is swamped with deal offers. Pushing a deal with a consumer contest—and having the deal of such a nature that the trade is involved in little extra cost (this consumer contest involved the trade in no extra cost at all)—adds up to an attractive merchandising event.

Sliding-scale Price for Premiums

Premiums are usually offered at one price. To encourage the shopper to buy more items in the family of products, a well-known drug item de-veloped the following sliding scale on its premium offer: For a flap or wrapper from any item, a doll was offered for $2.95. If proof of purchase was sent in showing the purchase of *three different items* in the line, the doll cost only $2.50. Incidentally, the doll was a replica of a nurse—tying up nicely with the drug item. Interestingly, a dealer contest was built around the premium doll. Dealers were invited to send in a photo of the doll displayed in their first-aid department. A large assortment of small prizes was offered for the most attractive displays. But the basic mer-chandising point here is planning a premium program so it sells more than one item in the line. As lines get longer, this becomes still more desirable.

Sampling for a Higher Conversion Rate

To introduce a new product, some merchandisers plan special sample-size packages which are merchandised at regular margins. For example, an antacid tablet, normally retailed at 24 for 49 cents and 100 for $1.49, brought out a 10-tablet package to retail at 25 cents. At the other extreme in sampling new products is the offer of a full rebate on the initial purchase. The customer returns a label and either gets a full refund of the purchase price direct from the producer or gets a coupon which entitles her to a second unit free when presented at the dealer. Merchandisers may find more merit in the full rebate on initial purchase. Figures indicate that a better conversion rate to regular use is obtained with the full size. (A twist to the full-rebate idea was developed by a maker of toilet tissue. Customers who mailed in the top strip from a two-pack of this item were entitled to a coupon good at the store for another two rolls. In this way, the full-rebate concept is being used to step up the unit of sale and thus get the longer use that helps step up the conversion rate.)

Faults of "Attach-them" Premiums

A premium user who experienced poor results with a premium attached to the outside of the regular package reports that the shopping public, and particularly children, are ingenious in their ability to detach the premium from the package; this tends to deface the regular package and may even make it unsalable. The retailer's handling costs rise; these "attach-them" packages are awkward for stock clerks to handle and may even require twice the normal time to remove from the shipping case and to put out on shelves. They upset shelf space allocations. Store personnel help themselves to the premium. As the premium offer runs its course, the store may be compelled to fill out its forward stock with nonpremium packages, necessitating a display half premium and half nonpremium. All this does not imply that the trade will not accept *any* attach-them premium event. It *does* mean that these very valid objections of the trade must be anticipated if such a premium promotion is to prove acceptable.

The (Buying) Battle of the Sexes

Merchandising men are finding that traditional concepts of the customer (*by sex*) are rapidly becoming outmoded in more and more merchandise lines. This applies not only to more buying by men and teen-agers (including teen-age boys)—it applies also to the purchase by women of merchandise classifications not normally associated with feminine purchasing. Take auto tires—this has been considered *strictly* a purchase by men. Yet a very successful leased-department operation has been built by a company that is selling auto tires in *department stores*—both downtown and in their branches. (Department store traffic is predominantly women.) From 50 to 80 per cent of this company's tire volume in its department store locations is done directly with women! Here was a totally neglected opportunity—neglected because "everybody knows that women don't buy auto tires." Millions of men diaper babies—but the infants' classification has yet to cater to men effectively. But the A&P has advertised food directly to men.

The "Clinic" as a Hypodermic

Perhaps the fountain-pen makers started it some years ago—the "clinic" to which owners of pens brought in the sponsor's brand for adjustment, repair, cleaning. The idea was then taken up by the electric razor brands —and with good results. It has been used, of course, for cameras. More recently, it has been used by a maker of pressure cookers. This pressure-cooker clinic was staged as a test in a department store. Ostensibly, the object was service to present owners. But the announcement ads also offered two specials. Sales were so excellent that the store's merchandise manager requested a return engagement and the "cooker clinic" was later put on the road. The clinic concept has still broader application— certainly as merchandise becomes more mechanical, the service aspects make the service clinic logical. But the sales-making potential should not be overlooked—and the development of a sales-clinching program (in this instance based on the offer of two specials) should not be neglected. The clinic can be made a sales hypodermic when properly merchandised.

"I Like Blank's Because"

Hundreds—yes hundreds—of consumer contests have been run with the very simple entry requirement to state in 25 or 50 words or less: "I like Blank's because." There is reason to believe that the public must be surfeited with this overplayed contest theme. How to refreshen this worn-out consumer contest theme was demonstrated by a large tea merchandiser. This company listed six product-benefit statements for its tea. It then asked women to pick the one out of the six that best represented their reason for preferring this brand. Then they were to complete, in 25 words or less, the reason for their selection. Not only did this add a fillip to a played-out contest theme, it also got the public to concentrate on the six major virtues of this tea brand. This same objective involving getting the trade or the public to remember the major virtues of a brand has been aimed at by a number of advertisers in various ways—for example, a P.M. plan for retail salesmen involved a telephone call during which the salesman (of rugs, in this instance) was to enumerate the five major features of this rug line. One more thought: Why not tie up the contest prizes with the promoted item? Example: A contest based on naming salads offered 1,000 salad bowls as prizes.

Perfume as a Merchandising Stimulant

It now appears as though perfume is to get a whirl as a merchandising stimulant. Indeed, a department store gave the perfume tie-up a fillip by developing a plan entirely on its own, involving lingerie and perfume. With every $3 purchase of sleepwear, the customer received a perfume gift *flacon* free. Moreover, this big department store also sold perfume in its lingerie department—and displayed lingerie in its first-floor perfume department (showing again how departmental boundaries are breaking down). In both departments, shoppers were invited to fill out entry blanks for a $500 perfume prize. A maker of bras offered a known brand of perfume (a $2.50 retail value) with each sale of two bras—an interesting example of stepping up the unit of sale in a classification in which the multiple-unit sale has not been strong.

When Premiums Go on Resale

When the premium can easily be separated from the line it is intended to promote and when the premium is a perfectly good resale item on its own, it may wind up in regular inventory. Example: A maker of kitchen-laundry accessories staged a special drive on a laundry basket. As a premium, the manufacturer offered a companion item—a wash basin. The dealer got six wash basins free with each order of six baskets. Then he received a promotion kit that included display cards, banners, etc., which the retailer was to use in promoting the free offer. The promotion was backed with consumer advertising. But it was too simple a matter for the dealer to price the "free" wash basins, put them in regular inventory, and move them at a good profit. After all, the dealer would earn a much better profit that way—even if he did not move any additional baskets over his regular turnover. (The number of shoppers aware of the premium offer would be few.) To prevent this from happening, premiums are sometimes clearly marked as such, or the premium is firmly attached to the featured item.

Couponing through Two Retail Types

Can department stores and food supers be brought together in a coupon merchandising event—and the enormous traffic of both major outlets thus won? It's been attempted. Shoppers buying a specific wash-and-wear item in a local department store were given a coupon. They were told they could exchange that coupon for a free package of a well-known detergent at any one of 300 selected food outlets in the area. The co-operating food outlet then gave the shopper another coupon, presumably offering a $106 savings at the department store. The savings were itemized as a $2 savings on a branded slip, $100 savings on a branded washer-dryer combination, $2 savings on a branded work uniform, $2 savings on a pair of pants. The event was featured by the department store—presumably with co-op. Another simpler example: a carpet sweeper and a detergent teamed up. Box top from detergent bought in food super was good for $2 toward purchase of $16.95 carpet sweeper in department store. (Department store got an extra sweeper with every six to compensate for price reduction.)

Putting Over Product Improvement

You've improved your product. The new feature has good selling potential. How can you put over the new feature in a self-service, self-selection outlet—especially if the item is a low-ticket item bought in a fraction of a second? Solution: A maker of paper towels improved his item. This brand of paper towels is completely packed—consequently, the new softness imparted to the paper (which is the big new feature) could not be tested by the shopper. Is it possible, though, to convince the shopper that she can test softness without actually feeling the product? Sounds impossible, doesn't it? But, in this instance, the problem was solved in a fascinating way. The package for the new item stressed the magic word "new." But then, in prominent display and in large type, appeared this message: "Squeeze This Package. Feel the Difference. Feel Its New Softness." Whether many shoppers could actually feel the difference by simply squeezing the package could be debated—but never underestimate the power of suggestion. Tell the shopper that a product has a new softness, ask the shopper to feel the package, and a certain number will agree that the new item is indeed softer! *That* is merchandising!

No-premium Premium Offers

When a woman buys a set of eight beverage glasses, it is probable that she has completed only part of that particular purchase—she may still need a tray or other device for use in carrying the filled glasses among guests. A famous brand of glassware therefore designed a handy and attractive brass-finished carrier—quite unique and thoroughly practical. It was packed together with a set of eight glasses—and the combination was smartly priced at $5. A good selling name was devised—"Caddy Beverage Sets." That tray is really a premium to the extent that it was purchased in huge quantities by the glass producer and was offered, in the combination package, at a combination price that made it an obvious value. Yet in no way was this offer featured as a premium offer and that was smart, because the combination package gained in dignity, in prestige, in social status by not permitting the tray to be classed as a premium. There are times when it is merchandisingly wise not to label certain things too plainly! (A giant maker of towels has developed similar special packs that combine towels and holders.)

Start-a-set Merchandising

Years ago, a maker of pearl necklaces introduced the concept of buying the necklace one pearl at a time. For years, makers of sterling and of fine china have been pushing the start-a-set concept by promoting the sale of the first spoon or plate. Now, to show how ideas roam from one market to another, a maker of luggage has applied the same concept to his line. The reasoning: Luggage is designed in sets. It is frequently bought as a set; the matched set is big in luggage. Once the first number is sold, therefore, the urge for a matched set almost automatically assures purchase of additional sizes and types. So one of the big makers of luggage applied the start-a-set concept to this merchandise classification. The manufacturer took the overnight case—one of the big sellers and a low-price unit—and offered a regular $19.95 retailer in national advertising for $16.95. The event was clearly labeled a "Start-a-set Sale." Coordinated styling is bringing still other categories into the start-a-set concept.

Merchandising Larger Sizes and De Luxe Numbers

Several consumer contests have been planned that provide extra prizes when the winner has submitted a box top from a giant size. Special P.M. plans have been developed, offering salespeople extra compensation for the sale of larger sizes. When the two procedures are tied together—both special contest offers and a special P.M. on large sizes (or de luxe numbers)—the turnover of the higher-ticket numbers usually responds satisfactorily. As more and more manufacturers turn to larger sizes, higher-priced numbers—there will be a distinct need for increased merchandising emphasis on these bigger-ticket items in the line. In addition to contests and P.M.s, there will also develop special payment plans for the display of the larger size and de luxe numbers. Moreover, manufacturers will find it wise to compile case histories delineating the net-profit performance of their giant sizes, de luxe numbers. To date, the retailer has been given too little factual proof of the net-profit performance of these numbers in the line. And, as the retailer's inventory problem becomes increasingly complicated by longer lines, he will demand more proof of performance.

Close-outs as Premiums

Close-outs are increasingly offered to noncompetitors for a premium merchandising event. Example: A shave-cream close-out offered as a consumer combination deal by a razor company (both top brand names). Another example: A cosmetic close-out was offered as a consumer combination deal by the maker of a toilet-accessory item (also two well-known brands). Generally, the company offering the close-out simply makes it available at a particularly attractive price to the merchandiser who wants to use it as a premium. The other company then develops the deal, promotes it to the trade, advertises it. The company offering the close-out may figure that it is closing out a number on a minimum cost basis; it is getting considerable advertising-promotional drive at no cost; it is "sampling" its item, and more particularly its brand name, on the coattails of another great name. How does the trade react when it still has a stock of the close-out in regular inventory? The trade tends to accept these situations as part of the merchandising facts of life.

Sampling via Full Margins

The "sampler" idea, consistently exploited by one of the famous candy brands, is a technique for sampling a line to the public on a regular-sale, full-margin basis. It has been used for cosmetics, for several food lines. Most recently, it has been exploited for cigars; called the "Selector," a box of six sizes is offered. The sampler procedure has been used for regular numbers; it has been used, also, in connection with miniature models (in fragrances). Essentially, it seeks to sample a line without the usual costs of sampling, although at times the manufacturer may take less than his usual margin, may put special value into the sampler or selector package. The sample-assortment package appeals to the gift market—and, for this reason, particularly attractive packaging is sometimes indicated. Also, inserts in these special packages are commonly used to sell the entire line, or to get certain information from those who buy or get the package. The sampler concept has not exhausted its potential; as lines tend to become longer, it will see further use.

Tying Nonfoods into Food Promotions

Both in the food outlet, where nonfoods are taking over, and in nonfood outlets, where food inventory is growing (variety chains, drug chains, discount chains), opportunities are multiplying for nonfood items to horn in on food merchandising events. Take the cookout promotion—now a traditional summer event in the food outlet. Could a maker of electric light bulbs tie in to this event? Well—it's been done, and successfully.

This is how. The maker of light bulbs selected his so-called "bug-lite" numbers. These were put into a special jumble bin with selected regular bulbs. Then the bulb maker developed the theme "Patio Party." It was suggested to the food outlet that, under the theme, the food super stage an event bringing together the proper foods, plus such nonfoods as paper plates, plus the bulbs. The special floor-bin fixture for the bulbs was so designed that it could be placed at several strategic spots in addition to the regular location. More nonfood merchandisers will develop events of this kind which can logically enable a nonfood to spearhead a food promotion.

Make a Game of It

A fascinating diversity of items are picking up extra volume—including some staples—by promoting the use of the item in crafts, games, fun. Even paper clips are in this act. (One of the first was probably the humble wood matchstick which was followed by toothpicks.) More recent example: Shredded coconut was merchandised as "The Fun Dessert of a Thousand Faces." The idea was to fill hot-drink paper cups with cake mix, bake, fold out cup handles for ears, use raisins for eyes, draw eyebrows and nose and mouth with crayons. Housewives use these ideas at parties to amuse children. They're used in lower grades in schools, especially in play school. In several merchandise lines, formerly wasted remnants have been developed into merchandising projects via the promotion of crafts—leather is one example. "Make a game of it" with the word "game" (broadened to include crafts) offers a worthwhile merchandising project. One food manufacturer maintains close connections with several large makers of games—looking upon this venture as a new type of related-products merchandising.

Merchandising the Consumer Contest

There is a general trend toward merchandising events that enables the promoter to say to the trade, in effect: "Look how unselfishly we help you sell something else in addition to our own item." In line with this consumer contests are now being planned that involve the same principle. Example: A consumer contest for a dog food requires the contestant to send in not only a label from the dog food but also a label from a noncompetitive grocery product. This consumer contest presents two additional interesting angles. Instead of being based on the tiresome "I like Blank's because . . . ," this contest asks the contestant to explain in 25 words or less why "Mrs. Blank is my good neighbor." The second interesting angle is that bonus prizes are offered if the contestant sends in three different labels from the dog-food lines. Clearly, the public is showing an increasing degree of ennui with respect to consumer contests. New themes and new merchandising concepts are vitally needed. The public is also becoming much more sophisticated with respect to consumer contests; it has heard about the professional contestant and about rigged awards. Merely stepping up the prize awards will not be sufficient as a consequence.

Double-your-money-back Offer on a Premium

On occasion, the public's notions concerning the value of a premium and the value appraisal of the manufacturer making the premium offer have tended to show a gap. Apparently, this has happened often enough to have suggested to one merchandiser the idea of offering a double-your-money-back guarantee in connection with a premium promotion. The guarantee reads: "If you are not fully satisfied with the Cold-or-Hot Bucket, as represented here, just return it with a note requesting double your money back." (The premium was available for $1 and a tea box top.) The higher the price paid by the public for the premium, the more reason there may be for a guarantee of one kind or another that ensures full satisfaction with the premium. Proof that other merchandisers are debating the public's acceptance of claimed values in premiums is indicated by the fact that at least one other advertiser began to feature a double-your-money-back offer for his premium. Other practices designed to achieve the same end will also emerge.

A Step-up Ahead for Referral Slips

Practically all large retailers now have giant one-stop, multidepartment outlets which are department stores in fact, if not in name. A universal problem in all these one-stop outlets is to get the shopper to visit more departments; most shoppers cover less than 20 per cent of a store per visit. This suggests the use of the referral slip—the slip given to the customer by a salesperson in one department for referral to another department. Off and on, the referral slip has been used by department stores for years. Now there is evidence that the referral slip is on an upswing. A maker of foundation garments which are sold in department store basements developed a referral-slip program. Customers were invited to register in the basement department for a free bra and girdle which were given daily; there was no obligation to buy. Referral slips were handed out by all basement salespeople. The salesperson with the greatest total of slips handed in by customers won a prize—a total of 10 prizes was offered salespeople. Displays featured the giveaway; these displays were spotted throughout the basement. This is a fairly typical plan—it is cited here not for its uniqueness but simply to point up the usual steps taken to get salespeople to send shoppers to another department.

The Super-colossal Gift

Gift merchandise priced up in the stratosphere has a particular appeal for men—and, in this age of credit selling, even lean billfolds may be tempted. Thus, a maker of women's jewel cases brought out a super-colossal number that "only a man would buy." (It even included a few mechanical gadgets with more appeal to men than to women!) Of course, men buy the majority of women's jewel cases—so the super souped-up model appealed to the proper market. But the merchandiser of gift lines tends to forget or overlook the obvious fact that a man setting out to buy a gift can be the world's most spendthrifty shopper. Logic can—and frequently does—go out of the window on this sort of occasion. Consequently, there is an opportunity in many gift lines bought in part by men for one or several numbers priced way up. They will move in profitable volume, particularly since they will carry a juicy margin. They will also add glamour to the remainder of the line. By the way—women, too, when buying gifts can lose some of their traditional shopping caution. The most expensive men's watches, for example, are bought largely by women.

More Trade Appeal in Consumer Contests

The development of slants that give more trade appeal to consumer contests goes on apace. Example: A consumer contest for a bleach permits the food outlet whose name is listed on the winning entry blank to give an extra $2,500 prize to the first-place winner; thus the dealer may promote the contest locally very much as though it were his own. Along similar lines for men's toiletries, a consumer contest offered the trade "full-scale publicity support if the winner comes from your store." This publicity support included press releases, providing all photos, arranging interviews with newspapers and TV-radio stations. This bow to the trade in consumer contests will become more common—and more elaborate. It will involve not only cash offers that the dealer may then extend in turn to his customers—it will also involve services with an appeal to the trade. Very likely, a manufacturer will soon be offering to the trade, under these circumstances, the services for a full month of a competent public relations expert.

The Logical Accessory as a Premium

A portable TV set out in the great outdoors is great—except that the sun can dim the picture. It was logical, therefore, for a TV-set manufacturer to offer, as a free premium, a "sunbonnet" with a portable, designed for summer outdoor use. Similarly, a special soap-saving dish was a logical premium for a soap. The premium that functions as a logical accessory or part to the parent item offers a definite reason for buying the parent item and in no way detracts, in the advertising, from the parent item. (One of the grave merchandising faults in so much premium advertising is that the premium tends to get more space than the parent item.) It makes a logical sales unit—there is no such thing as a logical sales unit in innumerable premium offers. It can be used by the retailer to close the sale because it adds to the usability of the parent item. It's harder to find a logical accessory or part for premium merchandising—but when such a premium is found, the premium program is apt to be considerably more productive.

Consumer Deals Can Be Too Attractive

Can a consumer deal be too attractive? Answer: "Yes," if the deal objective is really to sample the item. Example: A decaffeinated coffee offered a one-free-with-one offer. It helped achieve initial distribution for a new brand. It went over big with the public. But it was such an outstanding bargain that it was bought by too many consumers who were not, and would not be, logical prospects for decaffeinated coffee. Result: After the deal was off, sales dropped so drastically as to make it evident that this sampling program had been uneconomical. Consumer deals must make an appeal to the logical prospect, who will repeat purchases in sufficient numbers. Otherwise, it is simply another sampling program gone haywire. Solution: In this case, the advertiser was able to "prove out" with a deal consisting of a 10-cent-off label on the outside of the container plus a 10-cent coupon in the jar. This appealed to the trade—secured the required listings. It appealed to enough logical prospects to ensure a trial. And that coupon in the jar carried built-in insurance of repeat purchase. These repeat purchases pulled through regular stock as deal stock ran out—a merchandising necessity.

Child Appeal for Big-ticket Items

Is there any logical reason for child appeal in merchandising a big-ticket line such as major appliances? Maybe logic doesn't enter here, but a good deal of merchandising is successful, really, because it is illogical! A top brand of major appliances decided to use the child appeal as a technique for building store traffic during the Christmas season, a period of the year in which major appliances do not enjoy much of a sales lift. The idea hit upon included a 36-inch polar bear—a toy bear as large as most of the children for whom it was conceived. (There was also a 16-inch cub.) The bears, the trade was told, would build Christmas traffic if used as a give-away premium, and as displays in the window and inside the store. Father Bear and Baby Bear were featured as a $37.50 retail value; the set came neatly packaged in a single carton. The bears were made available to the trade on a low-cost basis. First-season results made it evident that in this instance the child appeal could be made a powerful appeal for a big-ticket item. This was true even though the child was not usually present when the sale was made. The idea might not work equally well at other times of the year, but during the Christmas season the polar bear set obviously had a strong appeal to parents.

Cosmetic Approach for Noncosmetics

The cosmetic industry has had a vast experience developing subtle approaches to capture feminine interest. There is now evidence that other industries, noncosmetic industries—are beginning to take a leaf out of the how-to-appeal-to-women book of experience of the cosmetic producers. Example: An aerosol spray was developed by a major shoe polish adver-tiser for the care of the upper materials used in women's shoes. The cos-metic approach was employed. The spray was scented. The package was given "beauty treatment"; it resembles a cosmetic package. The theme developed is "The Beauty Conditioner for Exquisite Footwear." Store posters, all other promotional material, and the advertising also take off from the cosmetic approach. Another example—is from the food field. (Since there are fashions in food, the cosmetic approach here is entirely logical.) This example involves a cat food—and the package was given a true high-style treatment typical of a high-fashion cosmetic. The cos-metic approach offers merchandising opportunities in a variety of noncos-metic lines—indeed, some current auto designs, particularly on the interior, begin to touch on what might be called the "vanity-table approach."

Showing Shoppers How It Is Made

Staging actual production of an item in a retail store is not unusual. But using the event to introduce a new item—and accompanying the event with a merchandising idea—constitute something new. A new type of plastic housewares (of which there are many) was introduced through a giant department store. A 15,000 pound molding machine capable of producing a 5-ounce unbreakable plastic mixing bowl was installed in the store. Shoppers could buy the $1 bowls as they popped out for 19 cents. A goal of 20,000 sales was set—and achieved. Co-op advertising was run. A contest for purchasers was included. The event was timed to be part of a big general housewares promotion in a store having one of the largest housewares departments in the country—traffic was thus excellent. (Thus, "showing 'em how it is made" was in this instance broadened to function as a device for sampling a new item and winning unique attention from a heavy traffic flow.)

Shopper Contests by Department Stores

Generally speaking, department stores are not keen for shopper contests. Few department stores will run a customer contest—except when it is part of a particularly complete promotion for a major brand in a major merchandise classification. But under these circumstances, shopper contests involving a minimum of customer effort are acceptable. Two major floor-covering brands which met the specifications just listed were successful in running customer contests in many department stores, including some high-prestige stores. One contest invited shoppers to guess what would be the most wanted colors. The other contest asked shoppers to guess how long it takes a craftsman to perform one of the hand operations in the production of a rug. These contests can usually be successful only as part of a complete promotion, because the contest is seldom featured in any part of the store other than the one department involved. Therefore traffic must be created in the department in order to ensure enough contestants—and that traffic can be created only by complete promotions.

Testing Premiums for Customer Value

Several recent studies have too vividly proved that too many premiums are not worth the price charged to the public. Implicit in the premium offer is the assumption that the public will get a better value this way than by buying the same item over the counter. But these studies show that too many premiums are not bargains at all—in some instances they cost the public *more* than would be paid at regular retail. Two large users of premiums have, as a consequence, made the following arrangements: (1) Every premium is now checked with trade buyers—that is, buyers in large wholesale and retail establishments; (2) every premium is now "shopped" by professional shoppers—these pros visit stores, buy similar items, report on value comparison; (3) a panel of housewives has been set up by one of these manufacturers, and an existing panel used by the other—every premium that has run the first two gauntlets must now get an O.K. for the value from the panel. (The merchandising executive who buys premiums is seldom able to buy *expertly* anything from a spoon to china to brushes or combs. The highest-paid buyers with retail organizations aren't that good. Therefore, testing premiums for customer value is now in process of becoming regular procedure.)

Antiques in Merchandising

Starting several years ago, a real fad developed for using the old-time apothecary jar as a container for a multitude of items, including candy. Now one of the glass makers is offering a large 1854 antique show globe free to druggists. (Remember when these were displayed in every drug store window?) It's available to druggists with specified orders of RX vials. Antiques were never more popular—especially antiques dating from the nineteenth century; women's fashions have, of course, prodded this trend. The entire home-furnishings industry has reacted to this trend—colonial furniture, for example, was never more popular. More retailers are running promotions during which floor help is dressed in century-old costumes. One merchandiser tells us he recently completed a study of the stores in Old Williamsburg—and has several ideas for antique reproductions as premiums. The antique has an enormous appeal to women—and whatever has a potent appeal to women becomes grist for the merchandiser's mill. (A leading producer of greeting cards has a clamoring waiting list for a display of antique cards.)

The Merchandising Power of Flowers

Years ago, a leading soft-drink manufacturer offered a handsome book of flower arrangements. Requests ran up into the millions! Recently a fragrance house offered the following proposition to department stores: We (the fragrance house) will arrange for a lecture at a local hall on flower arrangements. You (the department store) will give the free tickets to your customers. The customer will get a free ticket, however, only when she makes a purchase of any one of the 12 items in this fragrance line. The department store was to supply coordinated interior and window displays as well as run agreed-upon cooperative advertising, which included both merchandise and announcement-type copy. The stores were also asked to feature at the toiletries counters books on floral arrangements and a wicker basket of flowers, plus a special aisle table. Department stores found this merchandising proposal attractive. Orchids continue a good promotion. Ditto for flower seeds as a premium. With suburban living, flowers have greater appeal than ever. And new techniques make it possible to ship plants as premiums.

Science Fiction and Youngsters

Science and more especially science fiction deeply absorb youngsters. For the merchandising executive whose line is consumed by youngsters, or whose purchase may be influenced by youngsters, this suggests keeping in close touch with science fiction. One merchandising executive tells us he reads a number of science fiction publications—to keep up with the scientific wonders of the future predicted in these fantastic publications (which have such a remarkable record for coming into being). When he sees a trend in a specific direction (currently the ocean deeps and the deep interior of the earth are attracting science fiction attention) he begins to think in terms of a premium that will fit in with these scientific fancies. (We suspect that some of the premium manufacturers also do this very thing!) When a food processor developed a "Name the Space Ship" contest it found it had an exceptionally successful merchandising event—and at a low cost, by the way. (Low-cost premiums and contest prizes can be one of the virtues of capitalizing science fiction.)

CHAPTER 32

Merchandising Strategy

Merchandise to the Motivators

The remarkable success of the foreign car has led to some fascinating new merchandising concepts in other fields. They go like this. We have a growing *minority voice* in marketing. These are the people who dare to be different, who gain status by being different not by conforming—they were the ones who first bought foreign cars. It is estimated that we have actually some 30 million people who are not completely enchanted by canned prescriptions for everything they wear, use, or consume. This is a big market by itself. What these 30 million buy today—over 100 million will buy tomorrow. They are the "motivators." Moreover, they are an *articulate* minority—they more than make up in conversation, in persuasive powers, in leadership, what they lack in numbers. They are the pace setters, the style makers, the people others follow, talk about, or seek to emulate. They really *sell* what they like—certainly they sold the foreign cars in the early years because these cars then were not advertised. So—merchandise to the motivators and your merchandising will percolate down to the masses.

Merchandising a Thin Ad Budget

When an advertising budget is too small to blanket the country, and when it is small in comparison with industry leaders—what role can merchandising thinking play in making every ad dollar work overtime? Solution for a packaged-food item: Divide the country into A, B, and C markets, premised both on sales potential and on the status of this brand in each major market. Concentrate on the advertising for at least a year in the A markets. Pool the remaining ad dollars formerly allotted to the five markets in the B classification—spend all the pooled dollars in just one of the five markets for six months, then in a second market for six months. Also offer an attractive deal in the B markets not receiving any advertising. Offer especially lavish deals in all C markets, the giveaway in each C market to be larger than that of competition. Continue in these C markets with one deal after another—put reliance on the deals to move the item in lieu of advertising. (At the end of a full year, this plan is to be reviewed and changes made in status of each market, in total advertising budget, etc.) Incidentally, the markets to receive the bulk of the advertising are presently this brand's best market—in other words, put your ad dollars in your best markets where they will work best.

Line Events vs. Item Events

For years, both advertising and merchandising policy was shaped by the conviction that "shoppers buy *items* not *lines.*" Now a trend is shaping up involving line promotions, on the premise that many shoppers *do* buy the line or could be induced to do so by proper planning. As a consequence, we are beginning to see contests and premium offers that cover either the major part of a line or even the total line. One of the large food companies, for example, has run a successful sweepstake contest that encourages shoppers to mail in coupons that accompanied this producer's various detergents, its soap, its margarine, and several other products. The program applied both to national products in the line and sectional products. In such a program, the weak brands in no way drag down the strong brands, but the latter definitely help the former. Moreover, it is being discovered that trade support is more easily obtained with big line promotions behind which the manufacturer can put much more than he could possibly put back of a single item. Another point: Line merchandising events pave the way for new products as they come along because with a line event the family name comes into prominence and the family name thus acts as a stronger marketing introduction for new items.

Prepare for More Retail Telephone Selling

One of our largest department stores accounts for a fantastic 15 per cent of its total volume via the telephone. Many department stores trace 8 to 10 per cent of total volume to the telephone. Innumerable specialty stores find telephone volume accounts for 7 to 18 per cent of total volume. Now AT&T, through its local companies, has embarked on an enormous program to step up telephone selling by retailers. This program includes new telephone-order boards, systems for telephone selling, training of personnel. A particular drive will be made by the local telephone companies on downtown stores where traffic problems encourage customers to shop by telephone. Downtown stores are using newspaper advertising, radio and TV, direct mail to charge-account lists, to encourage telephone orders. All this suggests to manufacturers the development of *complete* retail plans that will tie in with the current upsurge in telephone selling. The telephone, in a few years, will be producing as much as 20 per cent of total retail volume in classifications that right now are little affected by telephone selling. Manufacturers give retailers complete plans for in-home selling—now is the time for similar telephone plans.

Drop Shipping to Stabilize a Market

A maker of small electrics has experimented with a drop-shipping plan on one fast-moving number to achieve price stability. The plan was started on a single item—an item with good turnover velocity. This item is not shipped to distributors for stock. Instead, it is shipped to selected retailers directly from the factory. However, billing is through the distributor, who gets a satisfactory margin on the drop shipments. Suggested retail prices are fixed for the item—varied to suit local market requirements. The item is drop shipped only to stores that agree to carry this manufacturer's full line—and who agree to observe the manufacturer's objectives. Profit margins for the retailer will be larger than they get on "price-footballed" items. Distributors and retailers have been told that, if the plan works well, it will be gradually extended to other items in the line. This move by a major producer spotlights two thoughts: the need for daring thinking in a demoralized market; and the small trend toward drop shipping to the retailer, with sometimes a consignment plan also involved.

No-merger Mergers

The emergence of corporate giants in fields where bigness had not formerly been common is compelling the smaller manufacturers to pool forces in unique merchandising ways. Example: The total furniture industry is now in a ferment caused by the growth of huge organizations with national selling and distributing facilities in an industry that has been traditionally sectional and even local. To meet this competition, as well as for other reasons, a maker of a lounge-chair specialty line and a maker of upholstered furniture (the two lines are related but not competitive) have entered into a selling association. This is a no-merger merger. Under this plan, the lounge-chair producer, who has an efficient distribution, sales, and advertising setup, puts this setup at the service of the maker of the upholstered furniture, who is better organized in design and production than in sales. This is just one variation of the no-merger merger concept; others have been developed and more will be coming along.

The Fighting Brand Becomes More Important

The so-called "fighting brand"—a second line—has been common merchandising practice for many years in many lines. Currently, several merchandisers report that they are reviewing their fighting-brand programs in light of new marketing developments. The new developments affecting the marketing of secondary brands include the competition of the retailer's controlled brand; the broader distribution of the manufacturer's brands through a spreading variety of outlets; changes in price lining by the manufacturer—especially when the manufacturer trades up; a small trend toward selective distribution on a franchised basis; markets troubled by price promotions. Of all these situations, it is the development of the giant retailer's controlled brand that is most seriously compelling a reappraisal of the manufacturer's fighting brands—including the manufacturer who makes his regular brands, his fighting brands, and controlled brands for the retailer and the wholesaler. In some instances, this reappraisal of the fighting brand has disclosed that it is no longer sufficiently well muscled to put up a strong enough fight. It tends now to need better packaging, more competitive pricing, new distribution concepts. How long since your fighting brands were completely reviewed?

The Long-line Problem

Obviously, the broad trend is for most lines to become longer. On the retail front, the manufacturer's longer-line trend is being blocked by a broadening retail tendency to cut back on inventory, especially in big-ticket classifications. In some home-furnishings lines this trend among retailers has not only made selling from floor samples common practice (with the customer waiting three to six weeks for delivery) but in many instances the retailer makes little investment in the samples and is loath to give floor space to the full sample line. This is compelling some manufacturers to turn to special consumer exhibits at which the public may see the full line under the most appealing circumstances. Several makers of TV-radio lines have opened exhibit stores of this kind. Manufacturers of home furnishings are working more closely with big home builders in decorating model homes to achieve somewhat the same end. Display rooms of the great public utilities are being used for the same purpose. In several resort areas, manufacturers have opened full-line exhibits for the public. The exhibit store could be a first step toward actual retailing by some makers of long big-ticket lines.

A Return to Franchised Consignment?

Many years ago, electric light bulbs were distributed primarily through a franchised distributor-consignment plan. This left *legal* ownership of the merchandise in the hands of the manufacturer until it was sold to the retailer and permitted certain merchandising policies that otherwise would be of dubious legal validity. From the merchandising standpoint, the plan permitted a degree of merchandising control otherwise almost impossible to obtain. Oddly, legalities made it wise to drop these plans in most instances. Today, the plan is being revived—after all, laws do change and so do techniques for getting around them. A large maker of major appliances has successfully tested a franchised-distributor consignment plan. A large maker of electric razors has taken the same step; under these plans, incidentally, the wholesaler or wholesale distributor acts really as an agent of the manufacturer. The objects are to get away from murderous price slashing; to obtain better control over the total marketing process. Unquestionably, there is currently a broad interest in a return to franchised consignment plans—if the initial users are successful, others will follow.

Cleaning Up Old Models

A small appliance maker has developed a premium program specifically for the purpose of taking old models off the regular market. This company works through distributors. Recently, it permitted its retailers to return to distributors, for credits, older models in the line, premised on the purchase of currently advertised models. Instead of making these older models available to a few major stores for a price promotion, this manufacturer notified its distributors that those who approved could sign contracts appointing them as soliciting agents for the sale of this merchandise for premium use. Then the distributors were given a complete program showing them, step by step, how to sell the older models to the premium market. The distributors were, of course, compensated for the premium sales. Moreover, the plan kept the older models out of the regular retail channels—funneled them where they would create the least market disturbance. In particular, the plan eliminated the great problem involved when retailers price-promote older models without indicating that they are old models.

New Twist for Related-item Events

Line events—as differentiated from *item* events—are becoming more frequent. As part of this trend, note that several manufacturers of long lines apparently have discovered that they can stage a related-item event *from within their own lines*. Related-item events involving items supplied by noncompeting producers are common. Thus, a processor of cheese and a baker of crackers will combine in a joint event. But now, as manufacturers diversify and as their lines broaden, it is being discovered that it is not always necessary to go outside the family for a related-item program. Thus, one of the big food companies staged a highly successful related-item event that involved *three* of its own products. This company's line is so diversified that it would be possible to develop a related-item program involving as many as a half dozen items, all taken from within the family. In some giant corporations, oddly, it is the corporate structure—the organizational blueprint—that actually makes it *easier* for one department to stage a related-item program with an *outside* company than with a next-door department within the corporation! The growing need for more cooperation within the company will compel organizational changes encouraging related-item events that are largely confined to the family.

Bucking Seasons

Would you think that Christmas cards would be sold—*in volume*—a day or two *after* Christmas? Don't guess—a greeting card company reports that a half-price sale event staged for immediately after Christmas had actually resulted in more cards being sold on December 26 than on a peak selling day before Christmas! A distributor for major appliances reports that October is usually a sticky month for most appliances since dealers are in a light sales period between midfall and Christmas. He tried a "talk-turkey" merchandising event. It worked this way: A dressed-turkey certificate goes to each dealer making a stipulated purchase. The dealer then offers the certificate with customer purchases. In addition, with a stipulated purchase of multiple units by the dealer, the trade got a free live turkey for store display. Billboards featuring the event were offered to dealers at a price—and special mats and window displays were also made available. The turkey was offered in addition to regular discounts from list prices.

Plugging Retailer's Controlled Brands

Manufacturers obviously must recognize the retailer's controlled brands as a fact of life. Thinking along this line, several merchandising executives have planned merchandising-promotional events which feature the manufacturer's brands and then also feature a specific retailer's own controlled brands in noncompetitive related categories. Naturally, the retailer is inclined to view with favor cooperation of this kind, since his own brands are thus given the sort of extra push that the retailer himself would like to give them. Example: A baker of a bread brand will give the food outlet a promotion which involves featuring the bread brand plus the food outlet's own brand of butter. The concept is by no means limited to food—it will be used in time through the drug outlet, the soft goods outlet, etc. Its premise is simple. The retailer wants to push his own brands. Let's help him to push one or more of his own brands where they do not compete with our own line, and thus ride into his cooperation on the tail of his own brand program. Good reasoning.

A Public Bow for Your Trade

A small airline whose name was largely unknown to the vitally important travel agent catapulted into the good will of the travel agent with a single ad suggested by a merchandising executive. This ad told the public, for the first time, about the varied services of the travel agent. (Thousands of reprints were requested by travel agents and hung up in their offices!) Similarly, a cosmetic house selling primarily through the beauty shop ran a campaign featuring the services of the professional beautician. A large ethical drug house has periodically run campaigns featuring the services of the drug outlet. A large food processor has yet to pay tribute to the remarkable growth of the food super—and the hardware dealer (who traditionally spends an hour looking for a wanted screw) has yet to be extolled by a manufacturer. A public bow for one's trade is usually smart merchandising—try it sometime. It is especially apropos when used by a manufacturer who distributes through a single type of outlet—and it is doubly effective when tied up with a store promotion.

Making Joint Merchandising Pay Off

When air-conditioners and men's shirts, woven floor coverings and paints join hands in a complete marketing program, results are doubtful. Problems: (1) The two or more lines have a dubious relationship; (2) they sell through different outlets, in different departments; (3) the respective sales forces cannot mesh selling efforts as anticipated; (4) costs cannot be equally apportioned; (5) the retail trade finds the programs complicated; (6) the programs win more publicity than sales. A good example of joint merchandising: A cereal maker included in his packages a coupon worth 8 cents toward purchase of a 3-pound shortening can. Then a recipe was developed that involved the cereal and the shortening. The offer was featured on both packages. And the event was featured on two broadcast programs. (Two great names in furniture and TV receivers got together on a special line. Very logical.) These joint events are tricky, but worth trying for. As still more retailers diversify by category, these joint events will become still more common.

Unclaimed Trade Bonuses

Deals are not uncommonly planned so as to discourage the trade from claiming its bonus or rebate or to capitalize the trade's habit of frequently failing to claim the rebate. This is especially true of deals which compel the retailer to return wholesaler invoices for bonus goods or cash rebates. It is generally known that a substantial percentage of retailers never turn in these wholesaler invoices. A drug wholesaler reports that druggists in metropolitan New York fail to return 4 out of 10 wholesaler invoices entitling them to rebates and/or bonus goods. If the object is to achieve the highest percentage of unclaimed, then the wholesaler invoice clause is the choice. But, if the manufacturer reasons that the dealer who collects his bonus may be more likely to give the item a somewhat stronger push and thus move it, then special steps should be taken to induce the retailer to get his bonus or rebate. (Is the deal planned merely to load the trade or to increase velocity of turnover?) A drug wholesaler indicates what might be done in this direction: On all deals going through his establishment involving "send in wholesaler's invoice," he *automatically* sends the original invoice to the manufacturer. A duplicate goes to the druggist.

Getting Away from Item Merchandising

Many years ago, the then-large manufacturers tended to feature the family of products, as it was then called. In recent years, the philosophy has been "The shopper buys items; not lines." This has concentrated merchandising on items rather than the line. But most recently there has been evidence—probably because so many competing manufacturers all have long lines and all have identical items—of a return toward merchandising the line. This may not involve any drop in item promotion; the line promotion may be a plus. But there is clear evidence that merchandising thinking is once again turning to the family of products or the full line. Consequently, we find that one of the largest food processors has developed a seal which will be employed to hold an umbrella over its vast family. It will appear on its packages, will be featured in institutional advertising, etc. One of the largest drug houses has a full-line campaign based on a giant sweepstake event. This manufacturer reports: "A line campaign enables us to book our accounts and promotions weeks and even months in advance. It makes a deeper impression on the trade and consumer."

Beware Store-wide Selling Events

Various stores agitate for store-wide selling events from suppliers—concepts that can be used not merely for a brand or a category but store-wide. For a limited number of major suppliers, this appeal is worth heeding. But fewer than 5 per cent (if that many) of suppliers are big enough to win a hearing for (and provide the required finances and materials for) store-wide selling events. One medium-sized food producer reports he found this out to his loss. He had been told that the food supers aren't interested in a small shelf strip or display card. So he developed a store-wide event—but promptly found out that food supers already get 5 times as many store-wide events from giant suppliers as they can use. This manufacturer has since gone back to related-product promotions involving exclusively his own section. This doesn't mean that a medium-sized manufacturer may not be able to win a store-wide event in the chains and in department stores, particularly if store-wide is reduced to a floor or a section. (A pajama manufacturer won multidepartmental promotion in department stores with a pajama-party event.) But the chances are against success; moreover, smaller suppliers can easily become lost in major promotional events.

Trends That Compel Related Merchandising

Four current shopper trends that vitally affect merchandising are fewer shopping trips per week; less time per shopping trip; more shopping as a family group; shopping increasingly concentrated into fewer hours per week. All four factors—especially the time element—are compelling stores of all types to correlate all lines (from food to high fashion) in so far as is practically feasible. This need is accentuated by the enormous increase in the size of store units—less shopping time and more time required to walk around giant stores could make a bad combination. There is, consequently, more shifting around of sections in more types of outlets than ever before, more use of special outposts or multiple locations, more bringing together of merchandise that in one way or another is related. Departmental rigidities are giving way to elasticity. This, in turn, suggests to manufacturers new assortments for these cor-related displays, new fixtures with each designed for a specific location —even new packaging that enables the shopper to correlate purchases more quickly.

Filling Seasonal Sales Valleys

While an occasional retailer may, through an extraordinary price offer, move power mowers in January, there is little to suggest that the season for *mass* buying of power mowers can be appreciably lengthened. Ditto for electric fans. And perhaps ditto for air-conditioners. The makers of blankets (including electric blankets) have not been hugely successful in extending the season. Under these circumstances, the trade resists even the most alluring out-of-season offers. Of course, seasonal sales valleys for many lines have been filled in. But there are some categories that simply defy major change in the seasonal pattern—unless the product, itself, is changed in a way that makes this feasible. (The addition of heat to the air-conditioner has so far failed to make any great changes in this respect. An electric blanket that cools in the summer might enjoy better results.) When the seasonal pattern is quite immovable it is less costly and results are better assured when a new line is developed or bought that has a contraseasonal pattern.

Moving Reconditioned Trade-ins

To bring order out of trade-in chaos, to enable the trade actually to throw off a profit on trade-ins, and to use the trade-in to help sell new numbers—these were the goals set by a large maker of power mowers. Under the trade-in program, mowers are reconditioned under factory control through authorized service stations. Only this factory's brand is included in the program. Flat hourly rates are set for labor, parts, etc. The dealer is given a reconditioning estimate. When estimate is approved—the mower is reconditioned and dealer is invoiced. When reconditioned mower is returned to dealer for resale, it carries a sixty-day authorized service warranty, that lists all work performed, all parts used. Copies go to buyer, service station, factory—serial number of mower is included. The customer deals with the service station if trouble develops. (This plan enables the dealer to say that this mower has a high trade-in value—it also enables the dealer to make a profit on the trade-in with no service responsibilities.)

Bringing Competing Stores Together

On a big-ticket prestige item—can competing dealers (competing department stores and specialty stores) be brought together in a simultaneous merchandising event? It's been done. The event was planned as a strictly *local* promotion—in other words, it did not lean exclusively on national advertising. The local program was a powerful one, including newspaper ads, TV, and radio. Each store was given several exclusive numbers. Each store was listed in the advertising. The advertising was smartly conceived; it added prestige to all of the stores. Each store was given an individualized in-store setup, plus individual window ideas. Special P.M.s for salespeople were set up. Each store was given a special follow-up plan to prospects who came in, but who delayed a buying decision. The line, itself, had a news value—it could be featured as something new. Result: In Baltimore, 11 stores—including top department and specialty stores—signed up. It immediately showed such good results that a twelfth store then asked to join in.

Pepping Up January

Most retailers are positive that the shopper is broke in January. And they are not far from wrong. The January tax date has made matters worse. But January White Sales continue to flourish. And major retailers draw traffic with other special events. Consequently, more manufacturers now plan special January promotions. Example: The electric clock-radio is a great Christmas seller; presumably it should hardly move in January. But a famous brand planned a January limited offer that included a special low list price on a special number made for the occasion. The trade was told "no reorders." Another example: A maker of aluminum housewares brought out a group of January specials carrying substantial price reductions. Another example: An electric blanket promotion tying in with January White Sale. Whether it is wise to "spit into the wind" can be argued, perhaps the extra effort added to the peak season drive can be argued, perhaps the extra effort added to the peak season drive would pay off better. But, where it is decided to pep up January, the word "sale" must be prominent in planning.

The Pre-Christmas Special

Christmas shopping tends to be concentrated in just ten shopping days—perhaps 60 to 70 per cent of total Christmas purchases by shoppers are made during these last ten days. Practically no *major* change in this great national habit has ever been made. But an occasional manufacturer can sometimes induce the public to buy Christmas gifts as early as the first several weeks in November—with a sufficiently attractive offer. Example: A luggage maker offered a regular $17.95 train case for $14.95—a $3 saving. The train case is a popular Christmas gift. Powerful advertising featured the offer, which very sensibly was limited to November 1 to November 29 only. (The line is fair-traded; prices are well maintained on this brand in a category overrun with price-cutting.) With proper adjustments for the distributing trade, the pre-Christmas special has a powerful lure for the trade—obviously because retailers are even more anxious than manufacturers to extend the Christmas season.

Eliminating Trade-ins?

The spread of the discount-house concept (which includes no-trade-in policy) is making the trade-in plan somewhat less popular. When a traditional trade-in program is dropped, a merchandising program must be developed to keep the trade happy. Here is what was done on an electric razor line when the trade-in was eliminated. Suggested retail price was dropped—one number from $32.50 to $24.95. For each of the models involved that dealers had in stock, they could buy up to an equal quantity from the factory at a special price. Dealers were permitted, for a limited time, to turn in trade-in shavers and buy two new models on a basis that gave them a credit of $2.75 on the trade-in. Approximately ten weeks were given the trade to adjust inventory. When trade-ins run riot, as they did on electric razors, retail list is a fiction. Thus, price schedules must be radically readjusted when trade-ins are dropped and the trade's inventory problem smartly handled.

New Form of Related Merchandising

Several years ago, related-item merchandising by manufacturers had gone to ridiculous extremes. Now, however, a somewhat new concept of related-item merchandising is coming into vogue. Example: A great name in bread and a great name in baby foods join forces to produce—*and merchandise*—a bread for youngsters. Another example in a widely removed field—a maker of women's skirts and a maker of women's sweaters designed "match mates"—orders may be placed with either one of the two manufacturers and will be *shipped together*. The two companies remain completely independent—but produce, merchandise, and sell as a single entity. Another example: A maker of paper bags and a maker of boxes have combined their styling to come up with coordinated bags and boxes for retailers. This plan brings together two strong names and is another technique for meeting full-line competition.

Semantics as a Merchandising Factor

When the shopping public has become completely conditioned to certain terminology, perhaps an opportunity exists for the merchandising man to score a scoop, not only by changing the sales unit, but also by changing the semantics. Example: For years it has been customary to merchandise social stationery by a sheet count—24 sheets and envelopes, etc. A promotion was tried by an exclusive Fifth Avenue merchant offering "Paper by the Pound at a Price." Actually, the paper was boxed in a handsome gift box, 190 sheets to the box or pound. But here was an exclusive shop featuring bulk quantities and 1-pound terminology in a field where the package and the sheet-envelope count have taken over. In the food field, several items are now merchandising pounds instead of dozens, or vice-versa. Clearly, a change of pace—semantically—can be the basis of provocative merchandising planning.

Main Street Moves to Wall Street

With some 12 million investors in corporate securities, it is obvious that Main Street has moved to Wall Street. Oddly, comparatively little has been done by merchandising executives to woo the stockholder, to win his loyalty to the merchandise made by the company in which he has invested. The annual report is not the province of the merchandising executive, and it does little to capture the shopping loyalty of the investor. Some special Christmas merchandise deals for stockholders are clearly within the domain of the merchandising executive; more of these special packs, specially priced for the stockholder, will come along in the near future. One merchandising executive reports that his company's big list of stockholders is now being circularized each time a new product is brought out; the same is done when a special consumer deal is announced. Another promotes its regular consumer contest thoroughly to its stockholder list. Within a few years, we will have 20 million investors. They will constitute better than 40 per cent of all family units —and much better than 60 to 70 per cent of all families with a substantial discretionary buying power. It is time for the merchandising executive to acquire a big stake in the investing public.

Riding-the-coattail Merchandising

When a famous-brand detergent conceived the idea of tying up a number of manufacturers of automatic washers in an arrangement under which each purchaser of a washer got a supply of the detergent, ride-the-coattail merchandising went into high gear. Now a new oven cleaner is using exactly the same concept; it hopes to ride into the home each time a range is installed. (This is an interesting demonstration showing how ideas used in one field can be used in another field.) The maker of a new scouring pad who arranged to have it packaged with a detergent is employing the same principle. Here we see the idea being applied in the small-item field, where many applications could be found. Maybe pickaback is a newer term—if so, think in terms of pickaback merchandising. It offers interesting potentials for sampling an item under circumstances that almost guarantee its use. Moreover, the sampled item benefits from the prestige of the brand whose coattail it rides.

Working with New-store Openings

A large company selling through the food chain recently checked its total costs involved in "cooperation" with new-store openings of food supers. This outlet is, of course, opening and renovating store units at a remarkable pace. The manufacturer found that his total costs had jumped fantastically. Just one item, namely, sending representatives to help stock and open a new unit, had involved a larger total cost by itself in 1959 than all new-store costs had involved in 1957! Looking ahead toward 1961 and 1962, this food company concluded that if a halt was not called, these costs would get completely out of hand. Moreover, too many of the things the manufacturer was doing for the new-store openings did not make a *direct* contribution to the *movement* of this line in the store. The decision was made, therefore, to draw up a complete promotional program for new-store openings *that would actively promote the line* during the opening ceremonies. Thus, not only was this form of cooperation organized, but also emphasis was put where it belonged—on *increasing the velocity of turnover of the brand*. Check your costs of cooperation at new-store openings; then check *how* these funds are spent.

Don't Overstay a Merchandising Concept

A manufacturer will design and market a product for a specific purpose. The public will find that specific purpose appealing. But when the public *buys* the item its ultimate use may be far removed from that original specific purpose. Example: The portable TV. It was made portable because, presumably, portability would appeal to the shopper. And it did. But then it was discovered that the portable TV, more often than otherwise, found a permanent niche in the home and stayed there. Further study showed that about 50 per cent of people who purchased a portable were using it as their sole receiver; another 45 per cent used it as a second set permanently located in bedroom, kitchen, etc. Not 5 per cent were ever moved! Consequently, one maker of TV sets continues to include a grip for transportability in its new sets, but he redesigned his portable line for home décor and he no longer calls them portable.

Merchandising Community Events

Large retailers and large manufacturers are establishing units in a multiplying list of communities. Both retailers and manufacturers are keenly aware of their local community responsibilities. Why not get together, then, to achieve joint goals of civic responsibilities? In one city, the manager of the branch plant and the manager of a large chain-store unit sponsored such an event. (Interestingly, in this instance, the retailer did not stock the category turned out by the manufacturer!) This was a week-long event. Principal traffic pull: The opportunity for local people to see, attractively displayed in this store, everything made by a major local industry including some future dream models. The retailer offered special values in several regular lines. The manufacturer offered several specials from its line, put in the store on consignment, since the items were not normally inventoried. Special bargain lists were distributed by the retailer to all of the manufacturer's 3,000 employees. Results: For the manufacturer—excellent sales. For both—local good will.

Sidetracked Staples during Peak Seasons

During peak seasons, retailers shrink space for fast-moving staples, also moving them to secondary locations. The claim is made that the resulting drop in volume and profit on these staples is barely balanced out by the volume and profit on the seasonally featured items. That's a tough bill of goods to sell the retail trade, however. Dentifrices, for example, are given a back seat during the Christmas season. Instead of "bawling out" the trade, or fighting for the whole hog, a great dentifrice simply suggests: "Take advantage of holiday traffic to sell more dental cream,"—and the trade is told that dental-cream volume will jump if the category is properly displayed during the peak period. The message concludes: "So—while you feature those Yule-Tide specials—it's also good business to display Blank Dental Cream where it's easy for your customers to buy it." Staples are now fighting back against Orphan Annie treatment during peak seasons. However, more than a message is needed—special deals, special displays, special put-ups are indicated. (Nursing bottles and nipples were put up in an attractive gift assortment to give them seasonal gift appeal.)

An Extra Season at Full Margin

In a number of categories, retail promotion tends to be concentrated on one or two major annual off-price events. Example: The August and January off-price promotions on white goods. A bold attempt to reverse this tradition was made by a large towel mill. A promotion was planned for fall and leading up to the Christmas season; fall is an off-season for towels. The promotion featured fashion, not price. A color spread was run in one of the great national magazines—and some 200 participating stores were listed. A complete promotional kit was made available to the participating stores. The numbers selected involved an appealing dyed-to-match line that correlated towels with bath mats, window and shower curtains. A smart theme was developed—an integral part of any major retail merchandising event. It was pointed out to the stores that regular margins would be obtained—and that the extra volume generated would thus not only be profitable, but would not be at the expense of the January promotion.

Timing Trade-up Programs

Timing is of great importance in launching a broad-scale program of trading up. That's why a soft-goods maker planned a trade-up program to begin in late October. His reasoning: The program would hit its stride just as the Christmas season hit its stride. (Christmas is, of course, the greatest trade-up season of the year.) Thus, by late November, when the power of the October drive might begin to taper off, Christmas would give it a second blast-off. A maker of electric household gadgets timed the introduction of a higher-priced line for Mother's Day, with the same reasoning in mind. A maker of lingerie also used the pre-Christmas season for a drive in a group of department stores that normally did not merchandise lingerie in his lofty price lines. His program included elevator cards, signs in fitting rooms, cards on the dining-room tables, fashion training meetings, lapel pins for salespeople, windows, and co-op. But principally he counted on the enormous Christmas demand for higher-priced lingerie to give his drive second breath.

Events Must Be Planned Further Ahead

The larger retail organizations become, the longer the time interval required to consider, approve, and then ready for the "firing gun" in each store unit a major merchandising event. (A giant food processor, for its major events, now allows a minimum of eight weeks' lead time for putting these events through the big food chains.) For decades, department stores worked on a 30-day, 60-day, 90-day time lead—varying by type of event. Now, with their developing branch organizations, the 30-day event is becoming a rarity, and the 120-day event is springing up. The lead time on major promotions is now nearer eight weeks in the larger food-super chains. Ditto for the drug chains. Variety chains tend to require even more lead time. Successful independents recognize that this is the Achilles heel of their big-time competition. Therefore aggressive independents (and the smaller chains) fight to shave days off their required lead time. But as giant retailers take over increasing slices of total retail volume, merchandising men will be compelled to plan their events still farther ahead.

Countering the Shelf-volume Ratio Plan

The concept of allocating shelf space in direct ratio to a brand's sale is swell—for the large manufacturer. What can the smaller manufacturer do to counter it? What kind of merchandising thinking can help him to win the shelf space he needs? One medium-sized manufacturer argues that reducing the space accorded the major brand does not really cut its volume. There is no exact ratio between a brand's volume and the shelf space that will work most efficiently for the retailer. A number-three or number-four brand, given the space it requires, will not cut into the volume of the major brand but will produce, in combination with the big brand, a larger total volume than if the lesser brand were shelf-starved or frozen out. Increasing the space for the lesser brand, instead of decreasing it, will greatly increase volume for the lesser brand. These merchandising arguments have some validity. In any event, they indicate that merchandising reasoning can make out a case for almost any aimed-for merchandising objective.

Picking the Number to Lead the Line

As lines become longer, the problem of selecting the number or numbers to serve as merchandising leaders for the line becomes more difficult to solve. In particular, there is constant debate over whether the line leader should be the proved volume leader or whether it should be selected on some other basis. A large tire maker reasoned that there is a vast value similarity between most competing brands of tires, number for number. Exclusive features are few. The big-volume members are not those with the most exclusive features; quite the contrary. But if a tire maker is to stand out from the welter of competition, he must feature something that competition does not have, or to which competition is giving only secondary play. Therefore, this company's advertising program is concentrated on those few numbers that are real standouts, that have true exclusive features. It finds that advertising featuring these exclusives sends the most traffic into its retail accounts (a vital consideration when so many millions merely ask for a tire). Only a minor percentage walking into tire outlets buy the featured number—but the traffic is created and the brand name gets a better play at the point of sale. Good merchandising reasoning!

Fighting Imports with Facts

Various types of retailers are turning to imports to achieve a bigger initial mark-on. Clearly, initial mark-on continues to blind the eyes of the retail merchandiser to maintained markup. It also tends to blind the retail merchandiser to turnover. One of the top brands in Christmas bulbs was faced with increasing competition from imports. Instead of haranguing the trade with generalities, this manufacturer staged a series of tests. These tests were not rigged—equal display was given to the domestic brand and to the imports. Moreover, the domestic brand was priced considerably higher than the imports. Yet, in these tests, the domestic brand outsold imports by 25 per cent in units. Moreover, the domestic brand turned in dollar profits from 77 to 124 per cent greater than the imports. In similar fashion, a maker of small leather goods compiled figures on the total performance of imports versus this presold domestic line. The figures proved conclusively that the high-margin imports were low net-profit performers. More and more retailers are turning to imports in misguided efforts to get away from price competition. But profits come from turnover and maintained mark-on, and imports seldom stand up under a statistical study.

Year-round Merchandising for Seasonal Lines

The seasons are breaking down—due to air-conditioning, faster and more travel, new concepts of living indoors and outdoors, gift giving, etc. This is paving the way for new concepts in seasonal merchandising in classifications traditionally hemmed in by seasonal limitations. Example: A maker of bedspreads is engaged in a long-term program to convince department stores and other outlets that this line can be profitably merchandised year-round. Instead of simply preaching year-round doctrine, this manufacturer has the following program: (1) Retailers are to be given month-by-month thematic promotions—each tied to a season or a seasonal event; (2) these promotions are worked out in full details; (3) several consultant-demonstrators are being traveled from store to store to aid in putting the events over and to be available to shoppers for advice; (4) exciting merchandising events have been planned—including a plan for helping shoppers to coordinate bedspreads with basic décor. This sort of program cannot work an overnight miracle, but it holds promise for at least lengthening the season.

Merchandising Anniversary Events

The anniversary event too often is simply institutional. But it becomes more than merely a pleasant celebration when it is given keen merchandising planning. Example: A line of rubber kitchen items saw its twenty-fifth anniversary looming ahead. It selected its seven fastest-moving numbers. These were given, in addition to their regular label, a special "Twenty-fifth Anniversary Sale" label. They were packed in shipping cartons clearly identified as special anniversary-sale merchandise. The retail price on each of the seven items was cut substantially. Example: A $2.49 regular retail was priced for the event at $2.18. (The retailer, however, got his full profit margin.) The event was limited to two months. Anniversary sale promotional material was packed in the shipping carton. It will be noted that, to get in on the event, the trade had to order specially. This, of course, is good merchandising sense. Concentrating on the seven best sellers was also excellent merchandising judgment. And assuring the trade of regular margins wrapped up the entire proposition neatly.

Handling Merchandising Rumors

Rumors—damaging rumors—abound in the market place. How should they be handled? Never assume that if you say nothing about it the rumor will soon die away. Competition will spread it assiduously. Don't expect that a retraction in the trade press will help considerably; retractions get less space than the rumor and they are poorly read. They *perpetrate* rumors. Don't conclude that if your salesmen are told not to discuss it they'll keep mum. They won't. Indeed they *can't* because, when the trade brings it up, they've simply got to discuss it. Don't assume that if management of competition is gentlemanly, their sales forces will be equally honorable. Moreover, wholesalers, if so minded, will spread the rumor. So will retail organizations, including salespeople who, oddly, have an elephant-like memory when it comes to rumors, expecially unfounded rumors! It may tend to die away, but it will periodically revive. Best policy usually is to meet the rumor head on, as an appliance company did when it ran full-page ads denying it intended to open factory-owned retail outlets.

Merchandising for Specification Brands

A food chain developed a program for its controlled brands under which the private-brand labels could be traded in for housewares, appliances, etc.—all described in a special catalogue. That program not only underscores the determination of all chains to develop their own brands, it also stimulated an idea by a manufacturer's merchandising executive in charge of private-brand (specification) business. He concluded that the time is coming when he will be expected to provide programs that will help the large retailers to move more of their controlled-brand inventory more profitably. He further concluded that the store-controlled brand is climbing out of the category of simple specification production and into the category of merchandising-promotional thinking by the manufacturer and he has reorganized his department accordingly. Thus, the private-brand departments of manufacturers will compete on still more fronts with the national-brand departments. This will be a whole new area of merchandising.

Related-item Events Edge into Nonfoods

The related-product merchandising event started in food and has received its greatest exploitation in food. But food is by no means the only broad merchandise category susceptible to related-product promotion;

innumerable nonfood items are related to each other in use. Some day, related-item promotion will multiply in the nonfood classifications. A step in this direction was taken when a proprietary drug item and a food item joined forces in a related-item event. The two items were found to be related in that each presumably aided in fighting the common cold —the food item because it provided vitamins and the proprietary because it provided relief from cold symptoms. This related-item event included a full-color spread by the two advertisers in a national weekly, bin merchandisers, price cards. The application of the related-item event to nonfoods becomes doubly logical as the food store moves so strongly into nonfoods—and as the nonfood store moves so strongly into food. Retail inventories are becoming scrambled, and this encourages related-item events that can be classed as mix-match related-item events.

Merchandising-plant Birthdays Locally

A large manufacturer with a plant located in a city of over 100,000 planned a month-long promotion celebrating the plant's fifth birthday. Details included a contest among the factory's employees, offering prizes for cards to be given to friends, relatives, neighbors. The employee with the most cards winding up at local dealers won top prize. Each friend visiting a local dealer on behalf of an employee received a free gift. Special prices and credit terms on items made at the local plant were offered to employees. Each employee won a badge with a legend about the anniversary and denoting the fact that he is an employee of the plant. Employees completing five years with the plant during the celebration were given five-year service pins. Local dealers were given adequate inventories, special displays. Special advertising was run locally. With giant manufacturers geographically diversified and with local manufacturers economically important in their own areas, these plant birthday celebrations can win real volume.

Retail Advisory Boards

Every so often, a manufacturer announces a retail advisory board. The majority of these boards have folded up. Why? Largely because retailers come to the sessions unprepared; tend to vent their petty grievances; become annoyed when their suggestions are not acted upon. Some delicate areas are inevitably invaded. Retailers not invited to meetings may be offended; this is one reason for the rotating-membership principle. At times, it has enabled the retailers to "gang up" on the manufacturer; this is not a mythical danger. However, a detergent manufacturer claims big contributions from an advisory board consisting of top executives of food chains. Another technique involves a poll, taken by a great uni-

versity, of retailers handling a camera line. Dealers who replied were
assured anonymity. A letter from the camera company president asked
dealers to be blunt and honest. This may be a better technique for opening channels of free communication with the trade—a major problem
these days.

Enclosures as an Index to Retail Sales

Most manufacturers have a difficult time pinpointing the precise pace
of turnover of their line at retail. The wider the marketing gap between
manufacturer and retailer, the more difficult the job. And even where the
manufacturer's own people call on the retailer, it is not safe to go by
what the retailer reports. (If the call is made on a rainy day, he just
isn't selling a blessed thing!) One maker of household electrics finds
that the guarantee card he encloses with each item in his line furnishes
a remarkably accurate index to actual purchases by the public. When
the number of guarantee cards for one month, for example, makes an
all-time high—so has retail volume; and that's positive. Another manufacturer who runs a small limerick contest through an enclosure in one
of his packages has also found that the number of contestants rises and
falls in a mathematically exact ratio to retail turnover. The tip here for
merchandising men is to check into devices similar to the guarantee card
or package enclosures or to offer a free gift that may prove an accurate
index to merchandise movement at retail.

Index to Part 2

HF
5415.
W39

Weiss
    Merchandising for
tomorrow.

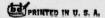